LOGISTICS AND TRANSPORTATION SECURITY

A Strategic, Tactical, and Operational Guide to Resilience

Praise for Logistics and Transportation Security

Prof. Burns's thoughtful analysis of transportation security in this book suggests that risk tolerance is a decision based on numerous factors and does not depend on linear policy analysis. As security professionals, we should maintain that larger "big picture" view while simultaneously diving deep into the assessment and management of risk.

Captain Brian Penoyer
US Coast Guard, Sector Commander and Captain of the Port
US Coast Guard Sector Houston-Galveston, TX

Timely and relevant, *Logistics and Transportation Security* is a comprehensive and thought-provoking assessment of the expanding and ever-changing hazards and threats to global supply chains and the transportation industry as a whole. Professor Maria Burns proffers concrete analysis and cogent recommendations to achieve increased security resilience in an increasingly complex threat environment. I heartily recommend Burns's work—it is a very worthwhile read and will serve as a significant resource for leaders in the logistics and transportation industries and for security professionals throughout our nation.

Kevin Clement
Texas Office of Homeland Security

Prof. Burns has captured the essence of transportation security, one of today's most pressing concerns. As the rate of globalization and world trade increases, security and supply chain resilience are at the core of one's global transportation network. This is a timely and well-written contribution to the industry.

John A. Moseley
Senior Director, Trade Development at Port of Houston Authority

In her new book, Prof. Burns covers one of the most important subjects of the twenty-first century: security, as related to transportation and logistics systems analyzing topics such as global transportation, regulatory framework, infrastructure, hazardous materials, supply chain, risk assessment and analysis, global collaboration, technology, and innovation. Prof. Burns further covers another extremely important subject, the human factor, in connection with strategic, tactical, and operating processes and the future of transportation and supply chain networks. I strongly believe that this book should be in the hands of all transportation-related employees and managers.

Capt. George M. Pontikos
Vice President Port Operations, Odfjell USA (Houston) Inc.

Influenced by geopolitics, the importance of maritime security of the supply chain is ever-increasing, though it was always an integral part of commercial shipping. Prof. Burns has shed new light on this complex and evolving field where security of the supply chain is being targeted as a geopolitical tool, breaking it down to the elements. This outstanding contribution by Maria is an essential read in understanding the various strategic and tactical objectives for every supply chain professional involved in the maritime segment.

Capt. Anuj Chopra
FNI ExC, VP Americas, RightShip

Prof. Burns has taken a comprehensive look at the global transportation system and identified the strengths and vulnerabilities of its security to human life, the environment, and the global economy. She further presents suggestions for ensuring that the importance of security, both physical and cyber, is fully understood so that stakeholders can take prudent action to ensure the viability and continuity of our transportation system.

Carleen Lyden-Kluss
Cofounder/Executive Director,
North American Marine Environment Protection Association (NAMEPA)

Prof. Burns has authored a clear and concise book detailing the issues of security in today's post-911 era. An invaluable read for those working within the transport and security industries.

Steven Neuendorff
Head of Americas, Hansa Heavy Lift Americas, Inc.

Prof. Burns does an outstanding job in presenting the critical importance of ports in the supply chain and the need for security, in a global market that moves 80% of its goods via sea transport, while increasingly depends on digital, high-tech platforms. She discusses the most common forms of attack, actors involved, and procedural gaps and offers a set of new approaches to risk management. Twelve critical issues are identified as the foundations of security and Professor Burns masterfully explains their complex interaction for security resilience and sustainability, including the collaborative relationship between the state and the private sector that must take place to ensure competitiveness, and their symbiosis with security at both the national and international levels.

Jorge Durán
Chief of the Secretariat Inter-American Committee on Ports (CIP)
Organization of American States, Washington, DC

LOGISTICS AND TRANSPORTATION SECURITY

A Strategic, Tactical, and Operational Guide to Resilience

Maria G. Burns

CRC Press
Taylor & Francis Group
Boca Raton London New York

CRC Press is an imprint of the
Taylor & Francis Group, an **informa** business

CRC Press
Taylor & Francis Group
6000 Broken Sound Parkway NW, Suite 300
Boca Raton, FL 33487-2742

© 2015 by Taylor & Francis Group, LLC
CRC Press is an imprint of Taylor & Francis Group, an Informa business

No claim to original U.S. Government works

Printed on acid-free paper
Version Date: 20160122

International Standard Book Number-13: 978-1-4822-5307-8 (Hardback)

Visit the Taylor & Francis Web site at
http://www.taylorandfrancis.com

and the CRC Press Web site at
http://www.crcpress.com

Dedicated to my beloved husband, Leonard T. Burns and family;

In loving memory of the fallen heroes and patriots who dedicated their lives to defending, serving, and protecting our country.

To the DHS, DOD, DPS, and DOT officers;
To our Veterans;
To our warriors and patriots at the furthest frontiers and most distant battlefields;
To the braves who tirelessly, night and day, fight for our freedom.

Contents

Forewords   xix

Preface   xxv

Acknowledgments   xxxv

Author   xxxix

Chapter 1   **Introduction**   1

1.1   Relationship between Transportation and Logistics   1

1.2   The Content Structure of the Book   2

1.3   Security vs. Safety: Definitions and Maslow's Hierarchy of Needs   6

    1.3.1   Defining Security   6

       1.3.1.1   Safety vs. Security   7

1.4   Security Economics: Econometric Modeling and Analysis   8

1.5   Formulas for Risk Assessment, Risk Mitigation, and Incident Investigation   14

    1.5.1   Formula #1: Security Risk Assessment   14

    1.5.2   Formula #2: Security Risk Assessment with Risk Indicates   14

    1.5.3   Formula #3: Single Loss Expectancy Formula   14

    1.5.4   Formula #4: Total Loss Expectancy Formula   15

    1.5.5   Formula #5: Risk Assessment Formula for the Structural Integrity of Assets   15

    1.5.6   Formula #6: Assessment of the Security-Related Expenditures   16

    1.5.7   Formula #7: The Security Threat Probability Model While Target Is in Motion   16

    1.5.8   Formula #8: Commodity Demand   17

    1.5.9   Formulas #9 and #10: Value at Risk   17

    1.5.10   Formula #11: Attack Types and Scenario Parameters   18

       1.5.10.1   Incident Investigation and Spatial Autocorrelation Models   19

    1.5.11   Formula #12: Spatial Autocorrelation: Moran's I (Spatial Statistics) Works   19

		1.5.12	Formula #13: *Security Threat Indicator of Spatial Correlation* Model for Risk Assessment and Incident Mitigation	20
		1.5.13	Formula #14: Structural Resilience	21
		1.5.14	Formula #15: Distance, Time, and Resilience	21
			1.5.14.1 Criminal Profiling of the Security Offenders	21
			1.5.14.2 The Econometrics of Risk Tolerance	22
		1.5.15	Formulas #16, #17, and #18: The Levels of Risk Tolerance	23
	1.6		The History of Logistics and Transportation Security	25
	1.7		Supply Chain Security: An Overview	26
		1.7.1	Supply Chain Disruptions	27
		1.7.2	The History of Logistics: An Overview	28
		1.7.3	Logistics through the Millennia	29
		1.7.4	Medieval Explorers, the First Settlers, and the Origins of Modern America	33
		1.7.5	Christopher Columbus's Voyages: A Logistics Achievement	33
		1.7.6	Jamestown: The Early Settlers to the New World	34
		1.7.7	Railroads	35
		1.7.8	The Industrial Revolution	36
		1.7.9	Railroads in America	36
		1.7.10	The *Liberty* Ships in World War II: Building Warships Faster than the Enemy Could Sink Them	38
	1.8		Conclusions	42
	References			42
Chapter 2			**The Many Faces of Security**	45
	2.1		Introduction	45
		2.1.1	The Many Faces of Security	47
	2.2		The Original Supply Chain Security Theorem	47
		2.2.1	Crime Opportunity Theory	47
		2.2.2	Lifestyle Exposure or Victimization Theory	48
		2.2.3	Crime Pattern Theory	48
		2.2.4	The Original Supply Chain Security Theorem II: The Interconnectivity between National Security and Commercial Security	52
	2.3		Terrorism: Networks and Affiliations	55
		2.3.1	Piracy vs. Terrorism	55
		2.3.2	Defining Terrorism	55
		2.3.3	Terrorism, Global Trade, and Transport	63
		2.3.4	The Categories of Terrorism	64

2.3.5 Logistics Security Threats and Terrorism 69

2.3.6 State Sponsors of Terrorism and Disruption of Commerce 69

2.4 Piracy and Maritime Security 70

2.4.1 Defining Piracy 70

2.4.2 Armed Robbery and Piracy 72

2.4.3 US DHS Maritime Domain Awareness 73

2.5 Piracy Financing Terrorism: Growing Threats 74

2.6 Air Security Threats 74

2.7 Human Trafficking and Illegitimate Traveling/Immigration 76

2.7.1 Federal Immigration and Nationality Act Section 8 USC1324(a)(1)(A)(iv)(b)(iii) 76

2.7.2 Organized Immigration Crime 77

2.7.3 The Free-Ride Effect 77

2.8 Drug Trafficking: Socioeconomic Impacts 78

2.9 Cyber Security Threats 80

2.10 Biothreat: Health and Environmental Security 80

2.10.1 Health Security 82

2.10.2 Environmental Security 83

2.10.3 Environmental Security and Impact to Human Health 83

2.11 Bioterrorism: Food Security 84

Interview and Case Study 87

References 87

Chapter 3 Global Security and Regulatory Framework 91

3.1 Introduction 91

3.1.1 A Brief Historic Overview of Security Regulations 92

3.2 Global Security Regulations 95

3.2.1 The "League of Nations" (1920–1946) 96

3.2.2 United Nations Security Council 96

3.2.3 United Nations Office on Drugs and Crime 97

3.2.3.1 Maritime Crime 97

3.2.3.2 Piracy 97

3.2.4 Maritime Security: The International Ship and Port Facility Security Code by the International Maritime Organization (UN Instrument) 98

3.2.5 UN Counter-Terrorism Implementation Task Force 98

3.2.6 North Atlantic Treaty Organization 99

3.2.7 World Customs Organization 99

3.2.8 Global CCP by UNODC and WCO 100

3.2.9   AEO Program by the WCO "Framework of Standards
         to Secure and Facilitate Global Trade"   101

3.2.10   Global Initiative to Combat Nuclear Terrorism
         (Initiated by the United States and Russia)   102

3.3   Security in the United States   103

3.3.1   Transportation Security Acts   103

         3.3.1.1   The National Security Act of 1947, USA   103

         3.3.1.2   Maritime Transportation Security Act of 2002   104

         3.3.1.3   Security and Accountability for Every Port Act
                    of 2006 by DHS   105

3.3.2   US Security: Department of Homeland Security and Its
         Agencies   105

         3.3.2.1   US Department of Homeland Security   105

         3.3.2.2   Transportation Security Administration
                    (DHS Agency)   106

         3.3.2.3   US Customs and Border Protection
                    (DHS Agency)   107

         3.3.2.4   Federal Emergency Management Services
                    (DHS Agency)   107

3.3.3   US Security: Federal Programs and Initiatives   108

         3.3.3.1   Inbound Travelers' Security Initiatives   108

         3.3.3.2   Cargo Security Initiatives   110

3.4   Maritime Security Regulations in the United States   114

3.4.1   The Secure Freight Initiative by DHS (Safe Port
         Act Element)   115

3.4.2   Free and Secure Trade Program by CBP   115

3.4.3   The Megaports Initiative, NNSA by the US DOE   116

3.4.4   CBP Collaboration with the US Food and Drug
         Administration to Prevent Bioterrorism and Agroterrorism 116

         3.4.4.1   US Emergency Response Systems   117

         3.4.4.2   Private Sector Initiatives   118

Interview and Case Study   121

References   121

Chapter 4   Critical Infrastructure Security: Resilience in Action   127

4.1   Introduction   127

4.2   CI Security   127

4.2.1   The Nation's CIKR   130

         4.2.1.1   Level 1: Lower Level: Existence Sector   135

         4.2.1.2   Level 2: Middle Level: Relatedness Sector   135

         4.2.1.3   Level 3: Upper Level: Growth Needs   135

	4.3	Physical Assets and Key Asset Protection	137
		4.3.1	Vulnerability of Physical Assets	138
		4.3.2	Physical Assets' Evaluation	139
	4.4	Trade and Transport Documentation	140
		4.4.1	Electronic (Paperless) Trade	140
		4.4.2	Contract of Carriage	141
		4.4.3	Bills of Lading	142
	4.5	E-Commerce Transforming Transportation	142
	4.6	Cyber Security	144
	4.7	Resilience in Action: BC/DR	146
		4.7.1	Disaster Recovery Plan	147
		4.7.2	The DRP Stages	147
	References	148

Chapter 5   **Classifying Security Threats through the Nine Hazardous Materials (HazMat or Dangerous Goods) Categories   151**

	5.1	Introduction	151
	5.2	Hazardous Materials (HazMat): An Overview	152
		5.2.1	HazMat Statistics	153
		5.2.2	Hazard Classification: Physical, Health, and Environmental Threats	154
		5.2.3	HazMat Incidents	155
			5.2.3.1	Mens Rea: Criminal Act or Incident	156
	5.3	HazMat Classifications	156
		5.3.1	Global and National Regulatory Framework	156
			5.3.1.1	Global HazMat Regulations	156
			5.3.1.2	US HazMat-Related Departments, Agencies, and Regulations	156
		5.3.2	OSHA'S Hazard Communication Standard (HCS HazCom)	157
		5.3.3	UN Committee of Experts on Transport of Dangerous Goods	158
		5.3.4	UN Packing Groups: Types I, II, III	160
		5.3.5	The Nine Classes of HazMat	160
		5.3.6	United Nations (UN) Identification Numbers	167
		5.3.7	North American (NA) Identification Numbers or DOT Numbers	167
		5.3.8	UN Markings of Containers	167
		5.3.9	The International Maritime Dangerous Goods (IMDG) Code	168
		5.3.10	The Dangerous Goods List, IMDG Code	168
		5.3.11	HazMat Identification System	174

	5.3.12	Shipping Documentation	174
	5.3.13	Identifying HazMat Leakage	175
	5.3.14	HazMat in the Maritime Industry	175
5.4		HazMat Security and Health Impact	176
	5.4.1	HazMat Chemicals and Health Hazards	176
	5.4.2	Radiation and Health Hazards	178
	5.4.3	CBRN: Chemical, Biological, Radiological, or Nuclear Release	180
	5.4.4	Chemical Hazards	181
	5.4.5	Biological Hazards	181
	5.4.6	Radiological Dispersal Devices (RDDs)	181
	5.4.7	Toxic Industrial Chemicals (TICs)	182
	References		183

Chapter 6	**Supply Chain Security: Mind the Gap!**		**187**
6.1		Introduction	187
6.2		Mind the Gap: The Impact of Security on Trade Flow, Trade Routes, and the Economy	187
	6.2.1	Supply Chain Disruptions and Potential Security Gaps	187
	6.2.2	The Swiss Cheese Model for Security	189
	6.2.3	The Security Threat Domino Effect	190
	6.2.4	The Pareto Principle	191
6.3		Logistics Networks: Strengthening our Supply Chains	192
6.4		Setting the Security Standards through Quality Implementation	199
	6.4.1	Bridging the Security Gaps	199
	6.4.2	"5S"	200
	6.4.3	"Kaizen" 改善	201
	6.4.4	"Lean and Agile"	202
	6.4.5	"Kanban"	202
	6.4.6	"Six Sigma"	202
	6.4.7	"TQM"	202
	6.4.8	"Deming's 14 Points on Quality Management"	203
	6.4.9	"DMAIC"	204
	6.4.10	The "4D" Methodology	205
6.5		Conclusions	205
	Interviews and Case Studies		205
	References		205

Chapter 7   Public and Private Partnerships   207

    7.1   Introduction   207

    7.2   Models of Public and Private Partnerships   209

    7.3   Threat Prevention, Mitigation, and Response   210

    7.4   Secur... abilities Impacting Logistics, Trade, and
           ...rks   216

           ...   Vulnerabilities   217

                                                                               228

                           ...ies   229

                                                                               229

           ...   d Innovation   231

           ...   and Accessibility: A Two-Edged Sword   231

           ...   f Transportation Security Technologies   232

           ...   ...ogies as "Force Multipliers"   234

                                                                               234

           ...   ...lakes Us Vulnerable   234

           ...   ...cial and Law Enforcement Tools   236

           ...   ...(Back Engineering)   240

           ...   ...isory System, USA DHS   240

           ...   ...Access Area-Denial" Threats   241

           ...   ...stics and Supply Chain Industries   242

           ...   ...: Satellite and   242

           ...   ...n Satellite System and Satellite
                  ...ologies   242

                                                                               243

                                                                               244

           ...   ...chnology   248

           ...   ...Air": Smartphones with HazMat Detectors   249

                   8.3.1.6   Transportation Worker Identification Credential
                              Card and Readers by the TSA   250

           8.3.2   Reconnaissance/Recognition Systems: Biometrics Facial
                    Recognition and Biometrics Technologies (2D and 3D)   251

                    8.3.2.1   Facial Recognition and Biometrics
                               Technologies (2D and 3D)   251

                    8.3.2.2   Iris and Retinal Scanning (Ocular-Based
                               Recognition)   251

| | | 8.3.2.3 | Facial Recognition: 2D and 3D Biometric Technologies | 252 |

8.3.2.3   Facial Recognition: 2D and 3D Biometric Technologies   252

8.3.2.4   Crowdsourcing and Facial Recognition   254

8.3.3   Cargo-Tracking and -Monitoring Systems (Sea, Land, Air)   255

8.3.3.1   Radio-Frequency Identification   255

8.3.3.2   Mechanical Seals   257

8.3.3.3   Electronic Seals   258

8.3.3.4   Real-Time Locating Systems Technologies   258

8.3.3.5   Smart Container Technologies (United States)   258

8.3.4   Non-Intrusive Inspections   260

8.3.4.1   Cargo Scanning or Non-Intrusive Inspection   260

8.3.4.2   In-Motion Scanning Technologies   260

8.3.4.3   Special Nuclear Material Detection   260

8.3.4.4   Neutron Radiation Detectors   261

8.3.4.5   Radiation Portal Monitors   262

8.3.4.6   Gamma-Ray Radiography for Nuclear Threats: Gamma and Neutron Radiation Detectors   262

8.3.4.7   Muon Tomography   262

8.3.4.8   X-Ray Radiography: Backscatter X-Rays   263

8.3.4.9   Biosurveillance   263

8.3.4.10   Thermal Imaging   263

8.3.5   Aviation Security Technologies   264

8.3.5.1   Credential Authentication Technology   264

8.3.5.2   Advanced Imaging Technology   266

8.3.5.3   Bottled Liquid Scanners   266

8.3.5.4   Explosive-Detection System   266

8.3.5.5   ETD   267

8.3.5.6   Paperless Boarding Pass   267

8.3.5.7   TIP: Security Training Software   267

8.3.6   Maritime Technologies   267

8.3.6.1   Technologies in Ships' Panic Rooms (Citadels or Safe Rooms)   268

8.3.6.2   Armed Security Guards   269

8.3.6.3   Active Denial System (Nonlethal)   269

8.3.6.4   Optical Laser Distractor (Dazzler; Antipiracy Laser Device) (Nonlethal)   270

	8.3.6.5	Boat Trap (Net) (Nonlethal)	271
	8.3.6.6	Long-Range Acoustic Device (Nonlethal)	271
8.4	Conclusion		271
References			271

Chapter 9   Security Risk Analysis   275

9.1	Identifying Security Vulnerabilities		275
	9.1.1	Security in a "High-Risk, High-Reward" Industry	275
	9.1.2	Security Risk Analysis and Its Components	276
		9.1.2.1 Risk Management	277
		9.1.2.2 Risk Assessment	279
	9.1.3	Risk Communication	282
		9.1.3.1 The Key Principles of Risk Communication	282
	9.1.4	Risk Analysis: Challenges and Opportunities	283
	9.1.5	Risk Matrices	285
	9.1.6	ISO 31000:2009 for Risk Management	285
9.2	Incident Reporting and Risk Management Software		286
	9.2.1	MSRAM	286
		9.2.1.1 Timeline of MSRAM	288
	9.2.2	DRMM	290
9.3	Conclusion		291
Appendix: If I Were a Terrorist and You Were a Port …			293
Interview and Case Study			303
References			303

Chapter 10   Combating Security Threats: The Human Factor   305

10.1	Introduction		305
10.2	Stress versus Distress Mode: The Human Body and Critical Body Functions		306
	10.2.1	Stressors	307
	10.2.2	Perceived Threat, Stress, and Distress	307
	10.2.3	Stress and Preparedness	307
	10.2.4	Distress and Lack of Preparedness	307
	10.2.5	The Impact of Distress or High Stress Levels	308
	10.2.6	Distress and Permanent DNA Methylation	309
10.3	Security, Human Mentality, and the Culture Factor		309
	10.3.1	Classification of Security Culture	310
	10.3.2	Motivating Security Employees	311

10.3.3 Maslow's Hierarchy of Needs   311

10.3.4 Improved Security through Corporate Quality   313

10.4 Preparedness: The Utility of Training, Drills, Simulations,
      and Scenarios   313

10.4.1 Large-Scale Training: Time and Resource Management   313

10.4.2 Building Muscle Memory through Training and Drills   314

10.4.3 Complacency: Atrophy of Mental and Muscle Memory   315

References   316

Chapter 11   Strategic, Tactical, and Operating Process   317

11.1 Crisis Management   317

11.1.1 Crisis Management Definition   317

11.1.2 Classifying Crisis   318

11.1.3 Crisis Management Timeline Model   318

11.2 The Three Levels of War: Strategies, Operations, and Tactics   320

11.3 Situational Awareness: Survival Tactics and Techniques   323

11.3.1 Survival Techniques and Inaccurate Situational Awareness   325

Interviews and Case Studies   334

References   334

Chapter 12   The Future of Global Transportation and Supply
              Chain Networks   337

12.1 Introduction   337

12.1.1 Forecasting the Global Economy and Trade Patterns   337

12.1.1.1 The BRICS Countries: Brazil, Russia, India,
          China, and South Africa   337

12.1.1.2 The MINT Countries: Mexico, Indonesia,
          Nigeria, and Turkey   339

12.1.1.3 The Energy Crisis and Transportation
          Challenges and Opportunities   340

12.2 Proactive Security Measures in a Cost- and Time-Saving Framework 341

12.3 The Benefits of Proactive Security Management   343

12.3.1 The Element of Time   343

12.3.2 The Element of Cost   344

12.4 Behavioral Aspects of Proactive Management   345

12.5 Case Studies on Proactive Corporate Cultures   347

12.6 Conclusions   355

Interviews and Case Studies   357

References   357

Index   359

Forewords

FOREWORD #1

Captain Brian Penoyer
US Coast Guard,
Sector Commander and Captain of the Port
US Coast Guard Sector Houston-Galveston, TX

Professor Burns's thoughtful analysis of transportation security in this book suggests that risk tolerance is a decision based on numerous factors and does not depend on linear policy analysis. As security professionals, we should maintain that larger *big picture* view while simultaneously diving deep into the assessment and management of risk.

Safety and security are, by their nature, statements about risk. We instinctively know there are no certainties in life, that we live in a probabilistic universe. One regularly hears people from every walk of life asking how safe or crime-ridden a neighborhood is, how safe the roads are during a snow storm, or how safe air flight or cruise ships are. Everyone knows there are degrees of safety or security, a range. We are asking how likely it is that we'll be hurt or robbed, and whether the theft or injury will be minor or life-threatening. Each of us makes decisions, personal and professional, based on our gut sense of the risks involved.

But that common-sense approach hides some pretty murky human nature. In my experience, each person has a very different tolerance for risk. Further, it seems people discount the risk posed by threats that are distant in future, that are seemingly random chance, or that they feel they have a greater degree of control over. Each of us will accept much more risk while driving our cars than we would while at the mercy of an airplane pilot. All risk tolerance, like politics, is local.

As maritime transportation security professionals, we can't lose sight of that fact. The precision analysis of threat vectors must, of course, drive our work. We must allocate our scarce preventative security resources and security measures toward those vulnerabilities that create the greatest risk. And our security response capabilities must be directed toward effectively intercepting threats once they are in motion and sized to manage the consequences of successful attacks or breaches in security.

Throughout my career in the US Coast Guard, I've found the basic equations of risk really define my work, because as a coast guardsman my job has always been to manage risk on behalf of the US public. Fortunately, in doing so, I work alongside safety, security, and environmental risk managers throughout the public and private sector. First, our collective job was to think critically about the threat vectors that can produce injuries, deaths, damage, disruption, and environmental disaster—not just in summary but also in specific failure modes and accident chains. As a marine investigator, my view of risk was forever changed by the work of Dr. James Reason and his thoroughly transformative works on accident causation, the error chain, and the progression of industrial accident events. In my experience, any risk manager worthy of the title is an investigator at heart—a serious student of accident, crime, and attack scenarios both historical and theoretical.

Second, having defined this universe of threats, risk managers project forward the likely consequences should the threat materialize. And while there are perhaps as many models for assessing consequence as there are risk managers, the fundamentals always resolve down to people's lives, the economy, the environment that sustains them both, symbolic psychological impact, and its cousin: organizational reputation. The consequences are most easily quantified in close, direct proximity to an accident or attack, but the cascading and indirect ripple effect is often much more difficult to quantify and even to understand. We do, in fact, live in a hyperconnected world in which a simple failure in a complex network can have unanticipated and far-reaching effect. As a coast guardsman, it's been my experience that hyperfocus on precision counting of consequences is a common failure among risk managers; the margin of error around our estimates multiplies the farther we cascade out our analysis. For this reason, I've found the best risk managers tend to keep their estimates simple, focused on orders-of-magnitude and instinctual priorities. To otherwise risks both paralysis-by-analysis and false confidence in our results.

Third, having separated the risk-producing threats into critical, important, and acceptable categories by consequence, risk managers then turn to estimating the probability these events will occur. For the busy and statistics-heavy world of accident analysis, reviewing accident rates and history is common, but for infrequent or intentional events (so-called *black swan* accidents or terrorist attacks), this type of analysis is impossible. Thus, we turn to the factors—vulnerabilities—that make it likely such an event will occur. For accidents, this is simply the number and severity of unsafe conditions latent within the transportation system at all levels. The more prevalent, and the more significant, the higher the probability that Dr. Reason's alignment will occur. For terrorism, it is both the intelligence assessment of threat and the security vulnerability to the specific mode of attack. Where there are those who clearly wish to attack us and who have the ability to do so, the vulnerability of the system becomes the best metric of whether an attack—once launched—will succeed in producing the consequences we are trying to avoid.

Having completed our analysis, we must offset the probabilities against the severity of consequence. Risk, fundamentally, is the product of consequence times the probability of occurrence, and our individual risk is defined by the amount of time we spend exposed to that risk. With the high-consequence/high-probability threats separated from the low-consequence/low-probability threats, risk managers can focus their work. Within the Coast Guard, we organize ourselves around both preventing and responding to every threat vector in the maritime: sometimes the most effective way to manage a risk is by reducing its probability of occurring… by reducing exposure to that risk, or by reducing the safety and security vulnerabilities in the system. Sometimes the most effective way to manage a risk is by reducing its consequences, either by spreading them out or by readying ourselves to limit the damage and quickly recover. But regardless which is most effective, risk managers always incorporate both prevention and response measures in their best work.

As a final note, I've observed throughout my career a great deal of confusion across the public and private sector on the fundamental business transaction that all risk managers are making. Often times, risk managers are categorized as *compliance officers* or regulators—implying a bureaucratic oversight. As risk managers, we have stakeholders and shareholders who demand a business result from us, just as any corporate shareholder would demand of the CEO. That business result is not counted financially, but rather is counted in terms of faith and confidence in that risks are managed properly to the shareholder's tolerance level. Fundamentally, our shareholders require from us proof of effective and sufficient risk management.

Thus, we collect this evidence of risk management from our customers, who in turn receive from us the freedom to operate without the constraints we can impose upon them. Our customers want to drive the best bargain they can—the least evidence of risk management for the most freedom to operate—because both risk management and providing evidence of same require time. And time is money. As risk managers, we also seek the best deal we can get—the best and most thorough evidence of risk management for the least release from constraint. This risk manager's transaction is, in my view, the natural complement to the supply-and-demand financial transaction, which always accompanies it. And just as there are thousands of different business models within the financial transaction of the market, there are thousands of different business models for risk managers within the evidence market.

As you read and think deeply about safety, security, and environmental risk in intermodal transportation, I encourage you to keep the fundamental model of risk foremost in your mind. Keep the question of risk tolerance close behind it, and ask yourself which risk-management business model might work best in each situation and why. By doing so, you will have placed yourself in the foremost ranks of risk managers.

FOREWORD #2

Kevin Clement
Texas Office of Homeland Security

Timely and relevant, *Logistics and Transportation Security: A Strategic, Tactical, and Operational Guide to Resilience* is a comprehensive and thought-provoking assessment of the expanding and ever-changing hazards and threats to global supply chains and the transportation industry as a whole. Professor Maria Burns, Director of the University of Houston's Center for Logistics and Transportation Policy, proffers concrete analysis and cogent recommendations to achieve increased security resilience in an increasingly complex threat environment. I heartily recommend Burns's work—it is a very worthwhile read and will serve as a significant resource for leaders in the logistics and transportation industries and for security professionals throughout our nation.

The security and resilience of logistics and transportations security are clearly a national security issue. Technological advances in shipping, communications, computerization, and modeling in the logistics and transportation industry have provided consumers with an ever-expanding flow of various resources and goods from around the globe. Yet, the expansion and advances in global logistical systems have, at times, made us more vulnerable and susceptible to technological hazards, terrorists, and other human-caused threats. A potential disruption of critical supply chains for significant or selected periods of time can have a pronounced negative effect on our economy, its critical infrastructure, and ultimately our national security.

The author provides a holistic approach to the security challenges faced by private sector and government entities across a variety of natural and technological hazards and human-caused threats. She adeptly leads the discussion with theory before transitioning to incisive analyses, backed by concise assessments of selected case studies. This affords the reader a more in-depth and practical understanding of the internal and external vulnerabilities involved. In turn, the work provides a series of logical and well-supported recommendations to mitigate security concerns, promote resilience, and reinforce the integrity of supply chains.

The benefits of private–public partnership are clearly identified. As global supply chains are beset with complex and multidimensional threat scenarios, it becomes increasingly apparent that effective solutions require the joint efforts of industry and government.

In this vein, the author's points are most relevant to government officials. To be truly effective partners in public–private security and resilience initiatives, government officials must do more than simply exchange business cards over coffee. Leaders from both government and industry should focus their efforts on identifying and resolving operational issues. This may be accomplished by (but is not restricted to) joint planning; developing, testing, and exercising standardized protocols; prioritizing available resources; participating in standardized training; and establishing an ongoing exercise program to improve logistics and transportation security and increase supply chain resilience.

Logistics and Transportation Security: A Strategic, Tactical, and Operational Guide to Resilience inspires discussion of the threat and environmental complexities faced by both government and industry. It provides insights to the future of logistics and the application of innovative technology, and forecasted changes in transportation security. This work highlights key operational issues and proffers recommendations to address them. Maria Burns has authored a guide to increased resilience in logistics and transportation. May our leaders take note and advance the process.

FOREWORD #3

Leonard Burns
Energy Projects Development Division
Member of International Association of Classification Societies (IACS)

My name is Leonard Burns, and in adherence to the obligation of full disclosure and with great pleasure, I make known up front the fact that Professor Maria Burns, the author of this book, is also my loving wife. A topic as broad as global supply chain and logistics security requires experience and the determination to conduct extensive research encompassing the numerous security threats that can potentially affect modern trade and transport. In fact, the lists of relevant security areas that need to be painstakingly researched and discussed seem unending: the globalization of economies, complexity of business issues, resiliency, critical infrastructure, hazardous material cargoes, criminal activity (i.e. piracy, hijackings, theft, and others), international and national regulations, political risks, public–private sector coalitions, new technologies (for both enabling global supply chain/logistics operations and mitigating risks), and the lists go on and on. As is typical of my wife's personality, and her laser-focused concentration abilities, the exhilaration of the challenge of writing an all-encompassing security book became too great for her not to accept.

Building robust, secure supply chains is a component vital to my professional background: I am a degreed structural engineer, and a manager in the Offshore Energy Division of a leading Class Society, Member of the International Association of Classification Societies (IACS). As noted on the IACS website, member class societies are, "Dedicated to safe ships and clean seas. IACS makes a unique contribution to maritime safety and regulation through technical support, compliance verification and research and development. More than 90% of the world's cargo carrying tonnage is covered by the classification design, construction and through-life compliance Rules and standards set by the twelve Member Societies of IACS." I am proud of our corporate mission and objectives, which perfectly align with the IACS mission.

Security is a vital component of classification societies, which are established to provide classification and statutory services and assistance to the maritime and energy industry; and regulatory bodies regarding maritime and energy safety and pollution prevention. Classification societies are unique in that they are entirely independent, self-regulating, externally audited, organizations. A classification society has no commercial interests related to ship design, ship building, ship ownership, ship operation, ship management, ship maintenance or repairs, insurance, or even chartering. Also, in establishing its rules, each classification society is free to draw upon the advice and review of members of the industry and academia who are considered to have relevant knowledge or experience.

While the objectives of IACS members are safe ships and clean seas, the resulting relationship to building secure, safe, and environmentally friendly global supply chains is obvious. The ocean-going transport of goods is a critical element of every global supply chain/logistics network. It is estimated that the members of IACS collectively class over 90% of all commercial tonnage involved in international trade worldwide. When one industry activity, in this case shipping, is involved in 90% of international trade worldwide, anything that threatens the security of that industry threatens the operation and efficiencies of global supply chains and logistics networks. Global trade and transport of goods would not exist without the maritime component made possible by the modern shipping industry. Accompanying maritime trade is an abundance of both natural and man-made risks and threats. These risks and threats frequently manifest themselves into events of substantial misfortunes and adversities with consequences of such significance that global supply chain destinations around the world may be impacted.

This book is impressive in the level of detail that Maria explores these maritime risks and threats, probing the dangers, in tandem with mitigation measures, of man-made security risks. For example, piracy and armed robbery at sea—particularly off the Somali coast of east Africa—remain top maritime security concerns. The area impacted by Somali piracy remains enormous at approximately 2.5 million square miles. Other serious threats to maritime security and thus global supply chains and logistics include trafficking of illicit narcotics, illegal weaponry, and undocumented human cargo. As analyzed and discussed by Maria, unless these activities are acknowledged as serious problems and subsequent action taken to mitigate them, they threaten to increase in magnitude in parallel with the increase in modern shipping supporting ever-expanding global supply chains. The book also discusses with equal thoroughness several strategies to increase the robustness of logistics networks in order to counter natural disaster threats as well.

The readers will understand through this book that transportation and logistics networks form the underpinning of global world trade and in many cases the national security of countries. Global supply chains face a mind-boggling array of potential threats and disruptions, from both man-made attacks and natural origins. Maria has authored a rigorously researched study that positions the reader to understand how dangerous a place the world can be to the security and integrity of vulnerable global supply chains, and subsequently to the economy and national security of countries worldwide.

The modern global supply chain is an efficient unified unbroken flow of goods from around the world, utilizing all cargo transport modalities. Few scientific or technical disciplines are as deeply reliant upon or so directly impacted by world trade as global supply chain logistics. The world is a small place as far as the global economy is concerned. Terrorist attacks against strategic logistically important ports, airports, or other bottleneck hubs can result in serious consequences for global supply chains that impact the delivery of goods and materials in destinations across the globe. This is where Maria's book differs from the existing pool of logistics security books. This book is not a prescriptive *how-to* manual targeting a narrow or specific application of transportation and logistics security. Instead, this book begins with a discussion of the differences between *Safety vs. Security* then advances rapidly through a developmental learning curve encompassing a wide spectrum of global threats including terrorism, piracy, and regulatory mandates, in addition to a discussion of current technology applications and the latest threat to logistics security, that of *cyber-attack*. Cyber-attack is the latest front in the logistics security battle. A computer virus infection that cripples the communications and control of a single global supply chain operation has the potential to cost billions of dollars and cause severe chain disruptions, throughout the entire supply chain, regions, or even nations.

Maria stepped up to the task of authoring this book with a background of professional experience that made her well suited to the task. For years she has been shaping her professional career based on the objective of building a bridge between the maritime, transportation and logistics, and energy industries. Her perspective on these industries is truly global. She is a certified lead auditor for security, safety, and the environment, and she obtained her advanced education in London and Brussels. She is multilingual with a foundation of work experience obtained through positions of increasing responsibility in Europe and America. Currently performing as the director of the Center of Logistics and Transportation Policy at the University of Houston, Houston, TX, she is uniquely positioned to share her professional experience and knowledge in support of the transportation and logistics industry.

I am supremely grateful and proud of being the husband of this consummate professional; I am also proud that, in my opinion, this book will serve as a valued reference for transportation and logistics professionals long into the future. As long as threats to the global supply chain exist and forward-looking solutions to transportation and logistics security continue to be crucial for maintaining the integrity of global supply chains, the information discussed by Maria in this book will be relevant and worthwhile.

Preface

This book grew out of my professional experience in the transportation industry, and the numerous security threats, near-misses, or incidents that occurred within my professional career, or within members of our supply chain, and the industry as a whole. My vision for this security book was to combine industry and federal practices with real-life examples, statistics, and trends. The increasingly alarming security threats that the industry and governments experience over the past few years (Chapter 1) have considerably changed the security patterns around the world, making the threats multidimensional (Chapter 2).

In the aftermath of the 9/11 terrorist attacks in the United States, compulsory security measures have been implemented at a global and national level. As the logistics and transport industries are critical components of the global economy and production, their capabilities and significance make them vulnerable targets of security threats. In a world increasingly exposed to threats of terrorism, cyber-security, piracy, and the trafficking of humans and narcotics, it is imperative to ensure an efficient global flow of goods and passengers without compromising security.

This book was written with the purpose of raising awareness as to the alarming security incidents that increase (a) in terms of statistical significance; (b) as to the offenders' ability to produce, access, and use advanced (sometimes home-made) technologies, weapons, and ammunition; and (c) in the rapidly growing networking, recruiting, and spreading patterns (Chapter 2).

In writing the book, I tried to offer a broader vision of the security risks that may threaten nations and industries alike and explain why the entities that may impact our industrial security could also be directly or indirectly affiliated with major national security threats.

My aim was to create an all-compassing, out-of-the-box work that serves as a security guide to trade, transport, and supply chain professionals and students of security, transportation, and political science. Its contents cover the national and international security goals, and deal with the latest concerns of the US Department of Homeland Security, i.e., in "strengthening the security and resilience of critical infrastructures." At the same time, the book has an international appeal, as the very same goals are perfectly aligned with the agendas of the United Nations (UN) and the North Atlantic Treaty Organization (NATO) for Security and Defense policies, and the security strategies of most sovereign nations around the world (Chapter 3). Once companies and industry segments have strengthened their internal processes, they can achieve resilience.

Chapter 4 focuses on the critical infrastructure sectors, explains how these are classified in 16 sectors by the US Department of Homeland Security, and compares the classification with other global nations. Furthermore, Chapter 4 verifies the prerequisites for resilience, as the ability to rapidly recover from an attack, and moves one step beyond, i.e. sustainability, which is hereby defined as the ability to achieve continuity, with minimum or no disruptions, regardless of the level of attack.

Chapter 5 focuses on the means used to attack: frequently, a security threat may be disguised as cargo or become associated with the commodities manufactured, carried and distributed. This chapter aims to classify the security treats through the 9 Hazardous Materials (Dangerous Goods) Categories.

Chapter 6 aims to bridge any procedural gaps due to the fact that industry-specific sets of rules have been designed to separately mitigate the security risks at sea, land, and air transportation. Modern supply chains are highly integrated and therefore should be addressed in a holistic manner as opposed to a segmented approach. Based on this observation, Chapter 6 includes suggestions for a harmonized approach in the sea, land, and air transportation systems.

Chapter 7 explores a risk management, risk assessment approach, offering a set of tools and approaches. Another critical element that is being addressed in Chapter 8 is the role of the public and private sectors in security investment and availability of resources. This chapter examines the benefits of a synergy between the public and private sectors, and uses a number of case studies to illustrate the increasing collaboration and benefits that result from this synergy.

Chapter 9 demonstrates a plethora of security technological innovations used throughout different stages of transportation, throughout the supply chain. It covers technologies used to scan cargoes and identify criminals, but also prevent, mitigate, and actually fight security offenders.

Chapter 10 duly focuses on the human factor, the fight or flight response, and evaluates how building muscle memory helps in combating security threats.

Chapter 11 further explores the significance of situational awareness and demonstrates a company's strategic, tactical, and operating process.

Chapter 12 investigates the past and present trends to forecast the future of global transportation and supply chain networks. It offers valuable recommendations and conclusions, and entertains thought-provoking concepts that when analyzed could lead to a sequential security publication.

**

The book's primary purpose is to serve as a strategic, tactical, and operational manual of practical and tangible usefulness within logistics and transport security. Since security is a complex and wide subject, with infinite areas for analysis, the book's primary purpose can be achieved by including the following elements:

1. Focusing on the priorities of the US Department of Homeland Security, i.e., in "strengthening the security and resilience of critical infrastructures"
2. Promoting connectedness within the logistics- and transportation-related industries

3. Bridging the public–private sector for optimum mitigation of threat and optimum utilization of resources
4. Comparing diverse industrial security components, i.e., sea, land, air, warehousing, pipelines, offshore platforms, etc.

Its secondary purposes include

1. Testing the effectiveness and efficiency of security strategies, tactics, tools, and resources at a national and global level
2. Identifying and foreseeing the security manager's future challenges and opportunities, and help develop a proactive, multilevel strategy
3. Providing guidance to governments, logistics, and transportation organizations for a better understanding of the latest security developments
4. Critically evaluating the new regulatory framework, pinpointing the industry's implementation readiness, and subsequently identifying potential problematic areas
5. Enhancing the role of a modern security manager to also encompass the latest technological developments, regulations, economy, innovation, commercial, and government case studies

This powerful sourcebook motivates readers to enhance their forward thinking and strategic thinking skills while offering empirical insight on global security practices. What sets it apart from similar works on the market is the diligent analysis of global security legislation and practices at a government/regulatory, commercial, technological, operational, financial, and sociopolitical level.

In this book, I attempted to offer a well-rounded perspective of the multiple faces of security, with the purpose of raising public awareness, and support security professionals both at the public and private sectors.

This all-encompassing approach that is offered herewith aims to assist transportation professionals, federal and state officers, risk managers, and students in evaluating and appreciating the benefits of proactive security measures, and help them identify and resolve the ongoing security challenges with a holistic view and a deeper understanding.

For organization purposes, this multitude of security risks, networks, theories, regulations, and technology-based activities has been categorized in a coherent arrangement and under four pillars: (1) situational awareness; (2) technologies; (3) partnerships; and (4) regulations. These four pillars have been sectioned into the 12 book chapters, with the common objective of achieving security resilience and sustainability, as illustrated herewith in Figures 0.1 and 0.2.

A SECURITY TALE FOR OUR YOUNG READERS

Once upon a time, a vibrant financial and commercial center was launched in a wealthy and powerful region. It was soon established as a global commercial capital that controlled key financial and trade activities and subsequently global trade routes. Each and every company established in this city enjoyed successful trade and transport activities, which entailed pertinent security risks.

There were conglomerates and Forbes 500 Companies who controlled large industry segments and most of the supply chain activities, such as financial, banking, and stock market activities; offshore oil and gas drilling; refineries; manufacturing; information

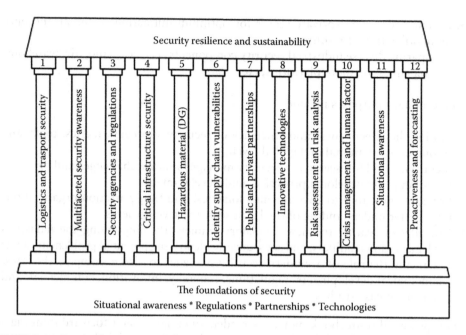

The foundations of security
Situational awareness * Regulations * Partnerships * Technologies

FIGURE 0.1   Book chapters and the pillars of security. (From the author.)

technology; trade and transport activities; and much more. The larger companies' security risks and vulnerabilities derived of their financial and commercial success, as their activities drew global attention and eventually the attention of security offenders. Most companies had a proactive security strategy; however, their proactive stance was mostly based on historical and current security events, rather than forthcoming threats based on future trends in new criminal alliances, new technologies, and potential political crises.

These large and complex supply chain(s) also consisted of small and medium enterprises (SMEs), which despite their size were adequately successful and productive companies that supported and depended upon the activities of these conglomerates. The vulnerabilities and risks of such smaller companies derived out of limited resources, budget restrictions, and inability for adequate security measures. Financial and/or time restrictions would tempt some of these companies to be fast, but not adequately thorough, and in some occasions to take regulatory or procedural shortcuts. Due to their limited resources, some companies would focus on low-cost services. Some of these companies would even hire persons that could potentially impose security threats. These were the times where the market deeply appreciated low cost, and this cost-effective recruitment solution made everyone in the supply chain happy. Unfortunately, a certain percentage of these recruits would prove to impose security threats to the entire supply chain.

Regardless of its size, every company within the supply chain entailed diverse commercial activities, which included multiple *critical infrastructure* segments, and therefore imposed a certain amount of risk. While all of these companies willingly formed a commercially and financially robust supply chain, they were a little more cautious in forming a security alliance, as most companies were cautious with their competition and felt more comfortable in mitigating their security risks as a corporate entity rather than as a public–private consortium of security partners.

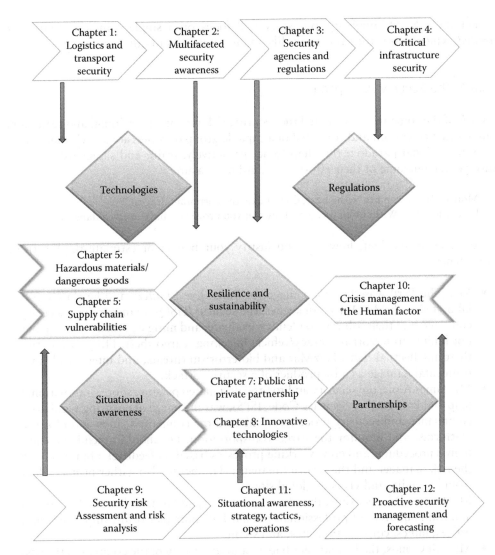

FIGURE 0.2 Book chapters and the key components of security. (From the author.)

In each and every company of our city, all corporate employees and executives in the city shared an air of success, talent, and unlimited potential for accomplishments, and all were dedicated to serving their company from their own professional standpoint.

Most companies shared three distinctive perceptions of security, contradictory by nature: each perception had merit and substance, yet these three perceptions needed to come to an agreement:

- Team A: the security perception
- Team B: the commercial perception
- Team C: the financial and resource management perception

For the sake of simplicity, our story will focus on a single company, *Bulls' Eye Limited*, which shares the same views like many companies in our city.

Team A: The Security Perception

Team A of the company represented the security, risk managers, training, and regulatory compliance perception, and consisted of a capable group of professionals who shared the same professional paradox: they had to act proactively, train, and safeguard the company, yet the outcome of their efforts was hard to measure:

Motto: "If you can't take the heat, don't tickle the corporate dragon."*
Inner thoughts: Without an incident, how can you prove you have averted danger?

Without an incident, how can you justify your budget or estimate the return on investment?

- Mr. John Peril was the risk manager of *Bulls' Eye Limited*, and he closely collaborated with Ms. April Safekeeper, the security/HSQE manager. The security component of their job was to identify, evaluate, and mitigate risks, including but not limited to terrorism, piracy/vehicle hijacking, cargo theft, IT/cyber security theft, intellectual theft, HazMat and bioterrorism threats, and intentional environmental damage as a by-product of a security attack.
- Mr. James Aloft, the security auditor and designated person ashore (International Ship and Port Facility Security Code, ISPS), was in charge of ensuring regulatory compliance and security procedures onboard the company's ships and offshore platforms, and monitor the cargo transportation. He should amend the company's procedures and crew working processes based on feedback obtained from the risk manager and the security manager. He should also gather primary data from his audits and visits to global sites.
- Ms. Lonnie Ranger-Ahoy, the training manager, had to travel around the world and train hundreds of professionals onboard offshore platforms, ships, factories, offices, mines, construction sites, and so on.
- Mr. Bill Clouds, the IT manager had a panoramic view of the company's threats, but was also familiar with the commercial pressures and financial restrictions of the company.

This group of professionals could see firsthand all the corporate security vulnerabilities and threats. Their greatest challenge was to require sufficient resources, especially time and money:

Time: they needed training, reporting, and familiarization time from crew members (at the expense of production time).
Money: they needed training, travelling, security technology, and recruitment funds.

To proactively obtain time and money for the company's security strategy, they would have to prove that an imminent, unforeseen security risk was very likely to occur in the

---

* Based on Scott Fahlman's quote.

future. Even more challenging, to justify their annual budget, they would have to prove that a physical security threat was averted.

Team A's proactive strategy would be based on three main categories:

a. *Evaluating historical security incident records of the company and similar companies in the industry.* Unfortunately, company personnel did not report security incidents or suspicious activities, as their promotion and employment retention were based on tangible performance, focused on productivity and commercial success. Similarly, companies within their supply chain did not report their minor security incidents and near-misses for commercial reasons. The only historical data available to Team A were the headline news. They did not have firsthand data, and this limited the team's ability to justify needs and funds for preventive action.

b. *Evaluating company's readiness based on security training and drill performance.* The company records showed that the overall drill and training performance was impeccable. Team A' had heard rumors that other companies' drills within the industry were shortened or skipped, due to commercial pressures and time restrictions. However, no such thing was ever reported for their personnel, and they were certain that such incidents would never happen to their company.

c. *Forecasting future security trends based on the latest security incidents, political and socioeconomic trends, global alliances, and trade agreements among countries, but also global competition and animosities.* Team A' would have to compare innovative technologies and best practices implemented by similar companies, with the innovative technologies and best practices used in each segment of security. However, the team's budget allowance was rather limited. With little or no objective evidence they had obtained from items (a) and (b) above, they could not possibly justify a security budget increase. After all, averting a major security threat cannot be easily proven: Unmaterialized profits or unmaterialized damages or losses cannot be easily verified.

Based on the above conclusions, Team A' decided not to *push* the envelope and accept their time, budget, and commercial limitations. Hence, they established a conservative security prevention and investment strategy and adopted a low-risk, low-budget option. At the same time, they were aware of the alarming global security statistics, and this kept them up at night.

Team B: The Commercial Perception

Motto: "It's all about high-risk, high profit, right? Well, I'll choose the high profit!"

Team B represented the *commercial and operations* professionals who were in charge of negotiating and materializing trade and transport agreements. Their goal was to safely, securely, timely, and economically transport commodities around the world. However, the industry and/or their clients had taken for granted the safety and security aspects; hence, their commercial success was focused on cost-effective and timely transportation. To satisfy their customers, they would have to trade and travel through war zones or piracy- or terrorist-prone areas. Occasionally they would have to collaborate with questionable partners or subcontractors, exposing the company's physical, financial, or IT vulnerabilities. To retain a good client, sometimes they would have to take commercial shortcuts that would save them time and resources.

They appreciated the viewpoint of Team A, but their commercial pressures were tremendous: high risk, low budget activities would ensure their operational continuity. Meanwhile, they were aware of the alarming global security statistics, and this kept them up at night.

Team C: The Financial and Resource Management Perception

> Motto: There is no blessing like a prudent, profitable investment.
> Inner thoughts: "If their risk is intangible and unmeasurable, why would they need tangible and measurable funds?"

Team C represented the *financial and resource management (procurement)* professionals who were in charge of the company's accounts, investments, and budget monitoring and controlling.

Their goal was to keep the company's profit and loss accounts profitable; the balance sheet balanced; and the *cash flow* flowing.

Sincerely, it made no sense to sacrifice the company's tangible and measurable funds for some intangible, unmeasurable risk that may never occur. In reality, they appreciated the viewpoint of Team A, but their goal was to keep the company thriving and afloat: in their view, the commercial department of Team B' helped them generate corporate revenue, whereas Team A' required high investment amounts to ensure security, i.e., to retain the status quo. This didn't make accounting sense. Yet, their insurance policy required the company to *exercise due diligence*, and it made perfect sense that proactive security measures equal due diligence. These thoughts kept them up at night.

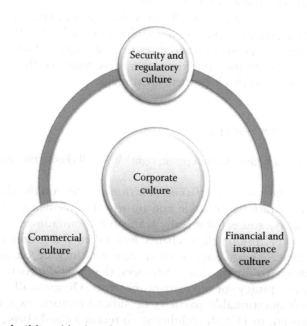

FIGURE 0.3   The building blocks of corporate culture. (From the author.)

And then, a security attack was attempted onboard the company's offshore platform. *Such an incident was a statistical exception*: nothing of the kind had ever occurred before.

Team A', the *Risk* experts said, "We knew it! It was just a matter of time!"

Team B', the *Commercial* experts said, "This incident may cost our reputation and clients' loyalty!"

Team C', the *Financial* experts said, "This is a measurable loss that will affect our corporate accounts!"

This story had a happy end, as the company's emergency response team successfully collaborated with the federal authorities. The security offenders were captured, and the media demonstrated the company's success story as a paradigm of cohesion and efficiency.

This was a day where the company's three teams perceived threat from a common viewpoint. They could now share a common security culture. Valuable lessons were learnt, and the company flourished for decades to come.

Needless to say, they all lived happily ever after!

Acknowledgments

Authoring this security book required diligent efforts in demonstrating the achievements, challenges, and opportunities of the private and public sectors in mitigating security incidents. Security threats are literally present in every component of the global supply chain. The aim of this book was to present the multiple facets of security and consider incidents where these could be demonstrated concurrently. Such presentation could only be achieved by showcasing real-life examples from industry leaders from federal, state, industrial, and world organization sectors.

I would like to express my immense gratitude to the distinguished individuals and organizations who have offered their invaluable support and contribution.

I would like to thank my husband Leonard T. Burns, with deepest love, respect, and appreciation. Thank you for the foreword you contributed for this book. Your wisdom and loving companionship are dear to me. Also, I would like to give my thanks to our parents Lawrence and Frances, George and Athanasia, and extended family, with all my love. Thank you to Wayne Mulkey, our navy hero, and his wife Ingrid.

A very special thanks goes to my publishers, CRC Press/Auerbach/Chapman & Hall/Productivity Press, Taylor & Francis Group, an Informa Business, with their most efficient team:

To Jennifer Abbott, Senior Editor, and Jennifer Stair, Project Editor, I wish to express my deepest appreciation and gratefulness for the most productive support and feedback. Thank you for everything. To Stephanie Morkert, Project Coordinator, Editorial Project Development, I appreciate her creative intervention in making this book attractive, on top of useful.

Thank you to Adel Rosario and Amor Nanas, the entire editorial team, the illustrators, graphic designers, and book cover designers. Your contribution has been tremendous.

It is a great honor to host Captain Brian Penoyer, Port Captain of *US Coast Guard* Sector Houston-Galveston; Officer Kevin Clement, Texas Homeland Security; and Leonard T. Burns, for your willingness to contribute a foreword for this book. Thank you for making this book possible with your professionalism, leadership, and integrity.

My lifelong appreciation and gratitude go to the US Department of Homeland Security, the US Coast Guard, the National Maritime Center, and the Texas Department of Public Safety.

Thank you to the University of Houston, its leaders, researchers, and colleagues. My profound appreciation goes to the Dean of UH College of Technology, Dr. Bill Fitzgibbon, and also our college leaders, colleagues, faculty, and staff. All the great things that you do make a difference. GO COOGS!

***

It is an honor to host in this book the distinguished federal agents, corporations, associations, and their most capable *corporate ambassadors* who greatly enhanced this book with primary data, images, and interviews, all of which are duly referenced. I hereby wish to thank each and every professional who generously shared information on their corporate achievements and contributed to this publication.

In particular, I would like to thank the following distinguished professionals for their contribution:

1. Captain Brian Penoyer, Port Captain of *US Coast Guard* Sector Houston-Galveston. Captain Penoyer serves as the Officer in Charge of Marine Inspections, Captain of the Port, Federal Maritime Security Coordinator, Search and Rescue Mission Coordinator, and Federal On-Scene Coordinator

2. Leonard T. Burns. Energy Projects Development Division. Member of the International Association of Classification Societies (IACS)

3. Kevin Clement CEM®, TEM®, MCP. Strategic Planner, Texas Homeland Security, Texas Department of Public Safety

4. Michael G. Dinning. Director of Multimodal Programs and Partnerships; VOLPE, the National Systems Center, Department of Transportation

5. Commander Mark Bottiglieri. USCG; Supervisory Marine Inspector, *US Coast Guard* Sector Houston-Galveston

6. Captain George Tate. MASTER at Marine Spill Response Corporation and USCG Aux. Flotilla Commander of Flotilla 6-3, District 8CR

7. Paul Fuhs. Port Demolitions Expert, Lobbyist, and President of the Board of Directors of the Marine Exchange of Alaska. Thanks for sharing your thought-provoking research titled "If I Were a Terrorist and You Were a Port"

8. John W. Pickering. P.E., MBA | President, P|N|D, PND Engineers, Inc.

9. Officer Thaddeus M. Bielecki. Assistant Master, Dredge Potter; US Army Corps of Engineers

10. Capt. Anuj Chopra. Vice President—Americas; Rightship Pty Ltd.

11. Carleen Lyden-Kluss, Cofounder and Executive Director; NAMEPA North American Marine Environment Protection Association

12. Stephen R. Merryman. Aerospace Engineer. We hope to reinvent the aerospace security practices, as most of this book's security logistics and supply chain security vulnerabilities can be applied in aerospace

13. Capt. George Pontikos. Vice President, Port Operations, Odfjell USA

14. Thomas Damsgaard. Vice President of Spliethoff Americas Inc. and Houston Maritime Arbitrators Association

15. Bobby Butler. VP and Chief Compliance Officer Universal Weather & Aviation, Inc.

16. John A. Moseley. Senior Director, Trade Development; Port of Houston Authority; Member: SIOR and NAIOP

17. Timothy Simpson. Director of Marketing; A.P. Moller—Maersk Group of Companies

18. Morten Andersen. Director of Category Management; A.P. Moller—Maersk Group of Companies

19. Steven Neuendorff. Head of Americas, Hansa Heavy Lift Americas, Inc.

20. Paul Broussard. President, Broussard Logistics

21. Hirini Reedy. TOA Inc. Energy Efficiency & Conservation Authority, EECA, Maori Alliances & Indigenous Energy Networks, New Zealand

22. Lindsey Barnes. MLIS; Senior Archivist/Digital Projects Manager; National World War II Museum; New Orleans, Louisiana, USA
23. Jorge Durán. Chief of the Secretariat, Inter-Americana Committee on Ports Security; the Organization of American States (OAS)
24. Port of Antwerp Authority, Belgium

Please accept my sincere thanks for your invaluable support.

Prof. Maria Burns

Author

**Professor Maria G. Burns** is the director for the Center for Logistics and Transportation Policy, University of Houston. She is an honorary member of the US Coast Guard Auxiliary and an appointed member of the Private Sector Advisory Council (PSAC) as established by Texas Government Homeland Security Code §421.042, representing the interests of the transportation sector. The council advises the governor or the governor's designee on homeland security issues relevant to the private sector. She serves as the chair in the Supply Chain Security Subcommittee of the National Academies' Transportation Research Board, Washington, DC, and the chair of Education for the Houston Maritime Museum, TX.

She has authored the books *Logistics and Transportation Security* and *Port Management & Operations*. Her PhD research (Vrije University, Brussels) pertains to seaports' economic and environmental impact assessment, while she holds an MS degree in international trade and transport from the London Metropolitan University. For her MSc thesis, she obtained a Best Dissertation Award by Taylor & Francis Publishers and an academic starred distinction.

She parlays two decades in the maritime industry, initially as an operator and shipbroker in global ship-owning firms, and later as a senior trainer and senior consultant for the American Bureau of Shipping. She is a certified Auditor for Maritime Security (ISPS), Safety (ISM), Quality (ISO9001), and the Environment (ISO14001). She has developed a number of maritime training manuals approved by the US Coast Guard, based on the latest regulatory, commercial, and technological trends.

She is a respected global conference speaker and an active member of the Society of Naval Architects and Marine Engineers (SNAME), the Texas Harbor Safety Committee & Education Subcommittee, the International Association of Maritime Economists (IAME), and the Houston Maritime Arbitrators' Association.

Her ongoing transportation research is enhanced with the disciplines of economics, political science, history, and archaeology.

Author

CHAPTER 1

Introduction

Transportation is the center of the world. It is the glue of our daily lives. When it goes well, we don't see it. When it goes wrong, it negatively colors our day, makes us feel angry and impotent, curtails our possibilities.

Robin Chase

1.1 RELATIONSHIP BETWEEN TRANSPORTATION AND LOGISTICS

Transportation may be broadly defined as the flow of people, commodities, information, or services from a certain area to another, be it by sea, by land, by air, by pipelines, or digitally (i.e., the Internet). On the other hand, *logistics* is the management of transportation and encompasses the efficient procurement, inventory management, and data management; shipment; handling of materials; packaging and labeling; warehousing; and distribution.

Transportation consumes one-third of the overall logistics expenditure, as the carriage of passengers and commodities impact the overall logistics efficiency to a great extent. The entire supply chain heavily relies upon transportation, from raw materials extraction, to production, warehousing, and distribution to the final consumers. This is why efficient transportation can add value to the product by ensuring optimum safety, security, and delivery speed without compromising the product's quality or quantity. Therefore, security is a significant prerequisite of modern transportation operations.

While the art of logistics is as old as the first war, the first mass migration, and the first exploration voyage in the history of mankind, the term *logistics* was first mentioned in 1810 AD by Dr. William Muller during his innovative military lectures at the Gottingen University in Germany (Muller 1810). Logistics practices were widely spread by the 1960s when containerization enabled large volumes of cargoes to be moved globally.

Over the next decades, globalization, new technologies, and the creation of multinational corporations enabled more sophisticated applications of logistics. Supply chain and logistics managers could now select among multiple global partners, products, and markets, and transportation enabled them to retain economies of scale together with cost efficiency, energy efficiency, and environmental efficiency. From the commodity production side, logistics facilitated assembly lines to create competitive output and distribution processes. From a commercial side, i.e., export, import, and distribution, transportation was the catalyst that tied together a plethora of activities, companies, and markets throughout the supply chains.

Nevertheless, the rapid growth of trade, transport, and logistics presented not only great opportunities but also great challenges. Expansion and complexity of business

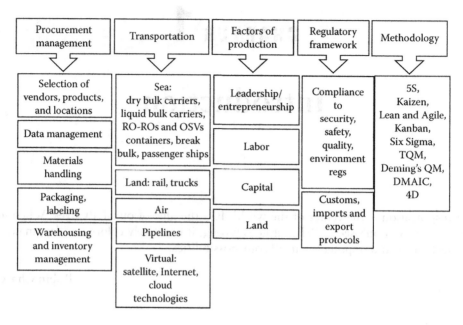

FIGURE 1.1   Logistics tools and processes throughout the supply chain.

brought about an increase in global cargoes, increase in the size of transportation vehicles, larger warehouses, and more commercial documents, which all sum up to more vulnerabilities and more opportunities for error. This is when incidents are likely to occur.

In the case of safety incidents, the damage is unintentional, as it derives from natural disasters like extreme weather, hurricanes, or even human error, negligence, and fatigue. However, security incidents pertain to intentional damage toward a specific target, within a specific supply chain, at a specific time. Security threats are therefore more serious, and potentially more harmful, as they are premeditated and directed against the most vulnerable components of a supply chain. A comparison between a safety and security incident could be a corporate computer breakdown. If this is a safety incident, the system may collapse; however, in the case of a security incident, the hackers will retrieve financial and strategic data and access bank accounts and corporate deals.

This is why industry professionals such as policy makers, law enforcement agents, or auditors consider that security plans and security risk assessments are more challenging to strategize compared to safety compliance. Security offenders will carefully examine a company's weakest links, its connections with vendors, clients, and markets, to satisfy their own goals.

Figure 1.1 provides an outline of the modern logistics processes and market components that could potentially suffer from a security attack.

1.2 THE CONTENT STRUCTURE OF THE BOOK

The intent of this book is to provide an overview of how security threats impact the integrity of the global supply chain and in many ways influence the growth of countries' economies and levels of national security. While logistics networks may be subject to safety or security threats, this study focuses on the systemic attacks motivated by either personal gain or planned destruction. The security of the global supply chain faces an intimidating array of modern-day threats. These security threats range from global terrorism and piracy on the open seas to theft from an individual container or truck in the final leg of shipment. This book is arranged to address these topics in the following structure:

- *Chapter 1* discusses the history of logistics. While the term itself has been used for only two centuries, the practice of logistics has been implemented throughout the history of mankind, both at times of war and peace. The principles of logistics were first used in warfare. Military organizers aimed to achieve sustainable resource management while troops are in motion. The lessons learned in military logistics have been successfully implemented in industrial practices, such as situational awareness; optimum performance; and lean and agile practices, usability, and the formation of strategic alliances. This chapter also explains the difference between safety and security. The ultimate goal of logistics security is to provide safe movement of goods throughout the entire supply chain in a manner that adds value to the transportation. Also, this chapter introduces several econometric formulas that use statistical and mathematical techniques to measure the security topics addressed herein.
- *Chapter 2* deals with the different faces of security that affect supply chains and pertain to both humans and cargoes. Over the past few decades, the unparalleled growth of global trade and logistics has necessitated the industry to become more complex, technology intensive, and capital intensive. As global trade and transport grows, these global networks become more vulnerable to security threats. Furthermore, as innovative technologies are used as tools to benefit the industry, when they get into the wrong hands, they can also be used as tools of destruction. Security threats seem to appear in numerous ways, expressions, and aspects, i.e., illegal transportation and trafficking of weapons and narcotics and counterfeit documents. On top of illegitimate transport of goods, security threats also impose human-related activities: containerization, the growing volume of transport, and the use of technologies have enabled illegitimate travelling, human trafficking, piracy, and terrorism.
- *Chapter 3* discusses the regulatory framework at a global and national level. It highlights the different security organizations, federal agencies, and policies and initiatives, and defines their geographical boundaries while discussing the opportunities and challenges faced in sea, land, and air transportation. Logistics necessitate regulatory compliance in areas including but not limited to safety, security, quality management, and environmental protection. Such regulations could mandate specific performance that may be achieved only with specific technologies, methods, and tools. International organizations have ratified security laws and regulations, which may or may not be harmonized with different national regulations. As a result, some security initiatives are duly covered at a global level, whereas other measures may have a limited geographic coverage.
- *Chapter 4* discusses the challenges and opportunities of critical infrastructures, factors of production, and commercial documents. *Critical infrastructure*, according to the US Department of Homeland Security (DHS), pertains to the property, tangible and intangible assets, systems, and platforms that are so fundamental to the nation that their incapacitation or damage would have a devastating impact on physical and economic security, general public health, safety, the environment, or any combination of threats. The DHS has identified 16 sectors of critical infrastructure, each of which is an instrument of a logistics activity. As such, each of these identified 16 critical infrastructure sectors requires as input all of the factors

of production, i.e., (i) leadership and entrepreneurship; (ii) labor; (iii) capital; and (iv) land. Every logistics or transportation project needs the right input, i.e., the right proportion and usage of the factors of production, in order to generate the desired output that meets the industry standards and the customers' requirements. Regarding logistics-related commercial documents, in order for the industry to stipulate what resources (factors of production = input) are needed to attain specific commercial, operational, technical, and regulatory requirements (output), the industry uses specific contracts for carriage of goods and a plethora of commercial documents. Security threats may appear both in hard-copy documents and in electronic contracts of affreightment. In fact, security threats may appear at any stage of the logistics process, throughout the supply chain, from input to output. These contracts of carriage of goods may be industry specific, carrier specific, commodity specific, and/or company specific. They may involve the multimodal or intermodal transportation of goods for door-to-door transportation or just a fragment of the trip. They may stipulate the desired performance of two or more entities concerned or may orchestrate the actions of numerous supply chain players such as the carriers, manufacturers, vendors, suppliers, importers, exporters, and so on.

- *Chapter 5* deals with hazardous materials (HazMat) or dangerous goods, which are any commodities or substances (physical, chemical, and biological agents) that may potentially cause harm to life, the environment, or property, either on its own or when in contact with other materials. Security vulnerabilities are derived not only by the increasing volume of global trade and logistics activities but also by the hazardous nature of the cargoes carried. According to the United Nations and all international and national regulations, there are nine HazMat classifications, which may become potential security threats.

- *Chapter 6* encompasses different systems, methodologies, and protocols implemented with the goal of improving logistics management to optimum levels of security and resilience. Protocols like 5S, Kaizen, Lean and Agile, Kanban, Six Sigma, total quality management, Deming's 14 points on quality management, define, measure, analyze, improve, and control (DMAIC), and 4D are demonstrated herewith as corporate tools for achieving continuous improvement that raises the industry to higher standards. These tools ensure measurable improvement of the existing system, which leads to resilience through controlled input and output, elimination of waste, elimination of error, and so on.

- *Chapter 7* explains the necessity of a public–private sector coalition. Based upon the principle that unity is power, different models and partnership arrangements are duly explained. Security threats may be detrimental at a national, state, and industry level. For this reason, the formation of robust public and private partnerships is necessary to mitigate, prevent, and recover from any security threat.

- *Chapter 8* analyzes the plethora of security technologies that are already in place and introduce upcoming technological advances related to logistics security. These logistics security technologies are intended to tackle all types of security threats in any transportation mode (sea, land, air, pipelines, or cyber) and throughout all stages, i.e., from prevention to mitigation and recovery. Innovative technologies have enabled a rapid growth in the volumes of cargo handled through real-time tracking, screening, and information exchange of transported goods or passengers; supply chain integration; and visibility of networks. Security technologies are used for the following: (i) to scan cargoes, containers, humans, and animals, i.e., x-rays and gamma rays; (ii) to identify HazMat, i.e., neutron radiation detectors and radiation portal monitors; (iii) biometric technologies, i.e., fingerprint, face, and iris scans; (iv) real-time tracking of cargoes and carriers, such as radio-frequency identification (RFID), sensors, and Global System for Mobile Communications (GSM); (v) Global Navigation Satellite Systems (GNSS), which are space-based satellite systems for real-time monitoring of carriers, i.e., the Global Positioning System for land transportation, the Automatic Identification System used on vessels, and Vessel Traffic Services used in seaports; (vi) cloud-based technologies for data storage, electronic data interchange, enterprise resource planning, systems, applications, and products in data processing for distribution and warehousing management, and so on; (vii) antipiracy technologies such as antiboarding devices, robot antipiracy boats, nonlethal slippery foam, long-range acoustic devices, and so on; (viii) information security and cyber security technologies; (ix) counterterrorism technologies versus antitechnology terrorism; and (x) security mitigation and emergency response technologies.

- *Chapter 9* focuses on risk management, which encompasses risk assessment and risk analysis tools and methodologies. While the use of technologies is fundamental to mitigate potential security threats, all transportation and logistics activities require security risk management protocols to be in place in order to predict potential system vulnerabilities. Complex supply chains and ever-expanding logistics networks lead to the increasing number of security threats and potential vulnerabilities. Risk management helps security professionals (i) to identify the need for specific technologies; (ii) to avoid overinvestment, underinvestment, or misinvestment; and (iii) to verify the return on investment for each security purchase. The US Coast Guard in collaboration with the American Bureau of Shipping has developed security threat–forecasting software, i.e., the Maritime Security Risk Analysis Model (MSRAM), and the Dynamic Risk Management Model (DRMM). These state-of-the-art tools are duly examined in this chapter, and extended applications of these technologies are proposed.

- *Chapter 10* deals with the human factor as the most critical element for mitigating security threats. During a crisis, the human brain controls our actions in terms of attitude, preparedness, and situational awareness. Most importantly, our brain controls our body. Humans tend to act in a destructive manner when in stress mode, whereas they may act in a constructive manner when in distress mode. This chapter highlights the necessity of building a proactive culture. It deals with the root cause of human error while associating the human factor with emergency response and risk assessment. Human mentality and the culture factor are also covered. Finally, the process of building muscle memory through training, drills, and simulations is duly explained.

- *Chapter 11* entails the strategic, tactical, and operating process of emergency response. It explains how crisis management can serve as a tool for mitigating security threats. Bearing in mind the limited time available to assess, prevent, or alleviate a security threat, this chapter addresses various real-life scenarios and best practices that can be used during transportation and logistics operations.

- *Chapter 12* encompasses the future of global transportation and supply chain networks. This chapter entertains the idea that logistics networks and trade agreements may be by-products of broader political alliances eventually influenced by diplomatic interests. The principles of forecasting the global economy, trade patterns, the element of cost, the energy crisis as well as the benefits of proactive security management are duly covered. As a conclusion, the future of global transport and supply chains is duly analyzed.

1.3 SECURITY VS. SAFETY: DEFINITIONS
AND MASLOW'S HIERARCHY OF NEEDS

Any society that would give up a little liberty to gain a little security will deserve neither and lose both.

Benjamin Franklin
Founding Father of the United States (1706–1790)

After the September 11, 2001 terrorist attacks, the principles of security, resilience, and systemic vulnerabilities had to be reconsidered and rediscovered within a new political, commercial, social, and technological context. The essence of security is as old as the history of mankind, and all the components of security can be recognized in all known warfare chronicles. And while security threats are a part of our modern-day reality, questions still arise as to the true meaning of security, the different forms of security, and how security is distinguished from safety.

Security is derived from the Latin word *securitas*, which means "freedom from threat or danger." During the peak of the ancient Roman civilization and the Roman Empire (27 BC–476 AD), Securitas was worshipped as the goddess of national security and protection of the *Imperium Romanum*. Security was the prerequisite to retain the unparalleled political solidity, growth, and influence referred to as *Pax Romana* (Roman peace).

1.3.1 Defining Security

Security is directly related to the national sovereignty, national state of safety and national pride. Security entails the protection of a nation, institution, or ethnic group from deliberate, illegitimate action that intents to harm national sovereignty, humans, the environment, critical infrastructure or property.

Security threats have been associated with extreme forms of national, religious or political activism. Security threat entails terrorism, piracy, genocide, human trafficking, fraud, sabotage, theft, infiltration, cyber-intelligence or other forms of espionage. It includes any and all forms of illegitimate transport of humans, animals, commodities or microorganisms that may impose political, health, environmental, socioeconomic or other hazards.

The author

As derived from the above definition, security has many faces and layers, from illegitimate trade, to hijacking, piracy and cargo pilferage, to terrorist attacks and critical infrastructure vulnerabilities. *Homeland security* encompasses all types of security described in this book. Any threat against the nation, the society, the environment, trade, transport, business, and the economy is directly or indirectly related to the national sovereignty. Hence, in the United States, the DHS is a complex yet finely attuned *cabinet department* whose mission is to secure America from a plethora of threats.

The successful implementation of security policies, programs, and law enforcement necessitates the engagement of several agencies and the coordination between the public and private sectors (Port of Hamburg 2013). To achieve its mission, the DHS operates in close collaboration with other federal departments, such as the Department of Defense, the Department of Transportation, the Department of Energy, the Department of Justice, and so on (see Chapter 3).

1.3.1.1 Safety vs. Security

For the sake of clarity, this book will distinguish the deliberate attacks from unintentional disasters by naming the former as *security threats* and the latter as *safety threats.*

- *Security threats* deal with intentional damage, such as deliberate illegitimate or criminal behavior. Security threats include terrorist attacks, piracy, identity theft, cyber security, and so on.
- *Safety threats* pertain to natural disasters (such as hurricanes, flooding, earthquakes, etc.) or unintentional human activities, such as negligence, human error, accidental damages, and so on.

Both security and safety threats have the potential to cause similar magnitudes and ranges of damages including loss of life, injuries, environmental pollution, as well as damage to tangible and intangible assets. However, due to the element of intention, security threats are subtler and potentially more damaging as the enemy may not cease identifying vulnerabilities and attacking the system until their mission is accomplished. For this reason, this book covers security attacks in the logistics and supply chains, with the perception that such attacks are not exclusively directed to the commercial or financial activities of a corporation but will directly or indirectly affect the national security for political, financial, and/or ideological reasons. Figure 1.2 demonstrates the connection

FIGURE 1.2 Correlation between security threats and economic, political, and ideological leadership. (From Burns, M., Effectiveness evaluation of the maritime security risk analysis model and the dynamic risk management model, *Washington DC TRB— Transportation Research Board of National Academies, Security Committee*, January 14–16, 2013a; Burns, M., Estimating the impact of maritime security: Financial tradeoffs between security and efficiency, *Journal of Transportation Security, Elsevier*, December, Vol. 6, Issue 4, pp. 329–338, 2013b.)

between security threats and socioeconomic, political, and ideological leadership. The figure depicts a global leader (country, company, supply chain key player), of increased economic, political, and ideological leadership. This global prominence may subsequently increase the risk of security attacks.

For this reason, this book is focused on security threats that encompass intentional deceptive acts committed for any of the following purposes:

1. *Obtaining personal gain, typically through illegitimate trade or travel, theft, or fraud.* Security threats in this category may include
    a. Compromising the integrity, confidentiality, and availability of private information (corporate or individual), such as cyber security threats, tampering trade and/or transport documents, and so on
    b. Theft (pilferage) of tangible resources, i.e., money, information, commodities, or other physical assets
    c. Sea piracy, combined with theft
    d. Illegitimate travelling, illegal immigration, illegal employment, and human trafficking
    e. Illegitimate trade, contraband, e.g., smuggling of drugs, weapons, and so on
    f. Fraud, such as providing false evidence, tampering data, and so on
2. *Causing premeditated damage, unlawful violence or threat of loss of life, injury, destruction of property, civil unrest, public intimidation, and so on.* Security threats in this category entail
    a. Activism for environmental, political, social, commercial, financial, or other motives
    b. Sabotage for political, environmental, religious, social, financial, or other motives
    c. Terrorism for political, religious, social, financial, or other motives
    d. Cybercrimes, such as gaining access to sensitive information of national significance

The differences between safety and security can be classified according to (i) the nature of the threats (Chapters 1 and 2), (ii) the potential consequences (Chapter 2), and (iii) the probability vs. consequences in a risk assessment methodology (Chapter 9). The safety vs. security threat types are highlighted in Table 1.1.

1.4 SECURITY ECONOMICS: ECONOMETRIC MODELING AND ANALYSIS

The advantage of knowing about risks is that we can change our behavior to avoid them. There are some risks we choose to take because the benefits from taking them exceed the possible costs.

Robert F. Engle III
2993 Nobel Laureate in Economics

TABLE 1.1 Safety vs. Security in Terms of Intention, Potential Targets, and Vulnerabilities

Safety	Security
A Natural disasters (unintentional)	Man-made disasters (intentional)
• Avalanche (snow slide)	
• Drought	• Exposure to drought or famine
• Earthquake	
• Extreme temperatures	• Exposure to extreme temperatures
• Cold waves	• Cold waves, snow
• Heat waves	• Heat waves
• Flood	
• Gaseous limnic eruption (CO_2 or other gas erupts from lakes and rivers)	
• Hurricane	
• Lightning	
• Storm	
• Thunder	
• Tornadoes	
• Tsunami	
• Volcanic eruption	
• Wildfire	
B Human health threats (unintentional)	Human health threats (intentional)
a. Acute vs. chronic exposure to hazardous materials	a. Acute vs. chronic exposure to hazardous materials
i. Oral	i. Oral
ii. Dermal	ii. Dermal
iii. Dust and mist inhalation	iii. Gas inhalation
iv. Gas inhalation	iv. Vapor inhalation
v. Vapor inhalation	
b. Environmental pollution (unintentional)	b. Environmental pollution (intentional)
i. Air pollution	i. Air pollution
• Primary pollutants CO_2, NO_2, SO_2, ozone, particulate matters (PM-10, PM-2.5), volatile organic compounds, etc.	ii. Surface water pollution
• Secondary pollutants HNO_3; SO_3; H_2SO_4; H_2O_2; O_3	iii. Land pollution
ii. Surface water pollution Chemical; microbiological; ground water; suspended matter; oxygen-depleting nutrients	
iii. Land pollution	
• Soil contamination Sewage waste; agricultural; mining; chemicals/HazMat; sewage leakage; acid rain: irrigation/soil salination	
• Loss of original constituents Soil erosion and desertification	
iv. Noise pollution	

(Continued)

TABLE 1.1 (CONTINUED)   Safety vs. Security in Terms of Intention, Potential Targets, and Vulnerabilities

Safety	Security

c. Human injuries and fatalities—by cause (unintentional)
  i. Accidental
  ii. Distraction
  iii. Fatigue
  iv. Human error
  v. Lack of training
  vi. Lack of familiarity
  vii. Limited situational awareness, visibility, or hearing
  viii. Negligence
	c. Human injuries (bodily, mental, or psychological) and fatalities—by cause (intentional)
	  i. Biological, medical, or other experiments
	  ii. Hostage terrorism, occupation
	  iii. Rape, sexual assault, abuse
	  iv. Shooting
	  v. Suicide (including suicide bombing)
	  vi. Torture-intentional bodily, mental, or psychological injury
	  vii. Violent act (shooting, stabbing)
	  viii. Warfare injuries: ballistic, blast, burn injuries

d. Human injuries and fatalities—by modality (unintentional) as classified by the World Health Organization • Avulsion • Blast • Burn • Crash • Epidemic • Extreme temperatures • Falling objects • Famine and/or thirst (due to extreme weather, crop failure, poverty, politics, population imbalance, and so on) • Internal bleeding • Radiation • Strain • Suffocation • Poisoning, including chemical or biological contamination • Toxic injury • Vaccine injury (WHO 2014)	**d. Human injuries and fatalities—by modality (intentional)** • Avulsion • Blast • Burn • Crash • Epidemic • Extreme temperatures • Falling objects • Famine and/or thirst (due to extreme weather, crop failure, poverty, politics, population imbalance, and so on) • Internal bleeding • Radiation • Strain • Suffocation • Poisoning, including chemical or biological contamination • Toxic injury • Vaccine injury (WHO 2014)

C   **Potential targets**

| **Potential targets**
Asset/building safety (unintentional)
Asset types include but are not limited to
  a. Assets/buildings/monuments of
    • National heritage
    • Cultural property, museums, and artifacts
    • Historical significance | **Potential targets**
Asset/building security (intentional)
Asset types include but are not limited to
  a. Assets/buildings/monuments of
    • National heritage
    • Cultural property, museums, and artifacts
    • Historical significance |

(Continued)

TABLE 1.1 (CONTINUED)   Safety vs. Security in Terms of Intention, Potential Targets, and Vulnerabilities

Safety	Security
• Religious significance; educational significance	• Religious significance; educational significance
• Charity, community significance	• Charity, community significance
• Political and judicial significance	• Political and judicial significance
b. 16 critical infrastructure assets	**b. 16 critical infrastructure assets**
• Chemical sector	• Chemical sector
• Commercial facilities	• Commercial facilities
• Communications	• Communications
• Critical manufacturing	• Critical manufacturing
• Dams	• Dams
• Defense industrial bases	• Defense industrial bases
• Emergency services	• Emergency services
• Energy	• Energy
• Financial services	• Financial services
• Food and agriculture	• Food and agriculture
• Government facilities	• Government facilities
• Healthcare and public health	• Healthcare and public health
• Information technology	• Information technology
• Nuclear reactors, materials, and waste	• Nuclear reactors, materials, and waste
• Transportation systems	• Transportation systems
• Water and wastewater systems	• Water and wastewater systems

D   **Asset/building safety threat (unintentional)**   **Asset/building security threat (intentional)**

Safety	Security
a. Corrosion	a. Electrification
b. Earthquake	b. Explosion, blast
c. Electrification	c. Fire/arson
d. Explosion, blast	d. Radiation
e. Fire	e. Toxicity
f. Flooding	f. Utility outage
g. Oxidization	g. Siege, attack
h. Radiation	h. Physical theft
i. Structural deficiencies	i. Destruction
j. Toxicity	
k. Utility outage	

E   **Machinery safety (unintentional)**   **Machinery security (intentional)**

Safety	Security
a. Breakdown	a. Arson
b. Breakage	b. Breakage, vandalism
c. End of commercial life	c. Breakdown
d. Human error	d. Intentional damage due to poor storage, exposure to extreme temperatures, etc.
e. Negligence, poor maintenance, lack of maintenance	e. Intentional overloading
f. Overloading	f. Intentional negligence, poor maintenance, lack of maintenance
g. Poor equipment quality	g. Tampering
h. Poor storage, exposure to extreme temperatures, etc.	h. Physical theft
i. Unintentional loss	i. Intellectual property; theft of technology
j. Total loss due to accident	j. Total loss, intentional destruction

(Continued)

TABLE 1.1 (CONTINUED) Safety vs. Security in Terms of Intention, Potential Targets, and Vulnerabilities

	Safety	Security
F	**Cyber systems safety (unintentional)** a. Access restrictions b. Data loss c. Connection problems d. Defective, nonworking links	**Cyber security (intentional)** a. Identity theft b. Cyber theft c. Malware • Virus (affecting performance) • Worm (damaging system) • Trojan (stealing passwords, gaining access, spying, stealing sensitive data) • Rootkit (manipulating) • Backdoor (manipulating) d. Spyware and trackware • Spying and tracking cookies e. Riskware • Monitoring, hacking, damaging

Source: The author.

Security economics: It is a discipline of economics that utilizes national, corporate and social techniques, protocols, and investment or resource management decisions concerning the financial and investment aspects of security. While security economics have been applied by conventional economists and security professionals for a number of decades, there is both a need and a potential for this discipline to be further developed and encompass the security needs of nations, corporations, and communities as a specialized discipline as opposed to mainstream economics.

Timeline for security economics: With respect to the element of time, security economics decisions are made at three stages: (i) in a proactive manner, i.e., prior to or in anticipation of a future security risk; (ii) in real time, i.e., during the security mitigation, and as a security threat is likely; and (iii) in a reactive manner, i.e., from the time that the security incident has occurred to the recovery phase.

During each and all of the three security phases, security economics influences a plethora of security-related decisions and protocols at national, corporate, and community levels:

i. Align the national, corporate, and community socioeconomic, commercial, or other goals with the security risks and pertinent financial decisions
ii. Make investment decisions related to research, technologies, regulatory compliance, social effects, and protocols to be implemented
iii. Allocate, monitor, and control the security budget(s)

Security macroeconomics: It is a division of economics that addresses the global security issues in a holistic manner, including the financial impact, investment, framework, patterns, challenges, options, and prospects of security. This discipline entails the production and testing of econometric models that demonstrate the connection among national security, innovations, and technologies used at a federal and industry level, and technologies used by terrorists, pirates, and persons involved in illegitimate activities, including disabling or deactivating technologies used. Most importantly, security macroeconomics deals with the security financing methods at a global trade and transport level, which encompasses all of the 16 critical infrastructure sections.

Finally, this economic discipline examines ways of establishing a *multiagency coalition* and a *public–private sector coalition* for financial matters, with the purpose of

    i. Achieving economies of scale
   ii. Better utilizing funds and joint resources
  iii. Better mitigating security threats by spreading the financial risk and return on investment

Security microeconomics: This discipline, on the other hand, deals with specific segments of security economics such as particular nations, regions, industries, or communities. It may focus on a specific critical infrastructure section and encompasses financial decisions, operational platforms, security risks, and patterns in a geographical, industrial, or federal segment.

This financial instrument examines security mechanisms in specific segments and evaluates the impact of security and economic tools, methods, practices, polities, and trends with the purpose of

    i. Gathering information, comparing and implementing *best practices* at a federal, industry, or geographical level
   ii. Achieving economies of scope, i.e., implementing what will serve the strategy, goals, and objectives of the particular segment
  iii. Utilizing funds and resources based on a tailor-made environment, i.e., for a specific agency, in a particular geographical location, or for a specific market
  iv. Better mitigating security threats by investing in a specific segment and focusing on specific risks

Behavioral economics of security: It is a discipline that seeks to enhance the knowledge of the conflicts among homeland security, the industries, and the attackers through behavioral testing research and experiments performed both in the clinical laboratory and through real-life examples. Interactive computer modeling systems such as the MSRAM and the DRMM (see Chapter 9) can enhance our understanding of human behavior, systemic resilience, and weak links within a nation's critical infrastructure. Furthermore, econometric models and empirical studies can lead us to reasonable conclusions of how security economics can be reinvented to serve national, supply chain, and critical infrastructure security in a more effective manner.

Behavioral security economics can help nations, industries, and communities to make the right financial security decisions by establishing behavioral patterns both internally and of the attackers. Again, there is tremendous potential for growth in this discipline and the opportunity to increase our understanding through research, econometric modeling, economic impact studies, and security impact assessments.

1.5 FORMULAS FOR RISK ASSESSMENT, RISK MITIGATION, AND INCIDENT INVESTIGATION

You ought not feel inhibited by a difficulty in making the solution precise. It may be that a part of the errors in the classical analysis is due to that attempt. As soon as one is dealing with the influence of expectations and of transitory experience, one is, in the nature of things, outside the realm of the formally exact.

Keynes, 1939. XIV: 285–321

This section deals with the econometric modeling of security. A number of formulas have been developed to assess security risk and assess the probability of a security incident.

1.5.1 Formula #1: Security Risk Assessment

Security risk can be defined as the expected consequence of an existent threat, which for a given target, attack mode, and damage type can be expressed as the estimated impact of an imminent hazard that for a specified live, critical infrastructure or other targets, attack setting, and form of destruction may be stated as

$$\text{Risk} = P \text{ (probability)} * V \text{ (vulnerability)} * D \text{ (damage)} \tag{1.1}$$

1.5.2 Formula #2: Security Risk Assessment with Risk Indicators

This original security risk assessment (SRA) method aims to assess the security risk by making use of the pertinent key risk indicators:

$$\text{SRA} = (L + I + M + I + T + S) \tag{1.2}$$

where
- L is the logistics–supply chain disruption impact.
- I is the ineffective supply chain link (machinery breakdown, insufficient funds, inability to guard the target, inability to assess most likely scenario on target).
- M is the average Maritime Security (MARSEC) level within a given time frame.
- I is the indirect impact (financial, liabilities, loss of production, delays, insurance, etc.).
- T is the target attack impact (direct) focused on potential loss of human life, asset damage, etc.
- S is the socioeconomic impact, including security resources used and social disruption.

A matrix table may be produced on a periodical basis to reflect the current costs associated and the related index values (Burns 2013a).

1.5.3 Formula #3: Single Loss Expectancy Formula

Risk assessment consists of two elements: (i) probability of occurrence, i.e., the likelihood that a hazard will affect us, and (ii) potential loss, i.e., the severity of its consequences if it does. Part of the difficulty in risk management is forecasting these elements accurately that neither of these elements can be accurately forecasted. As a result, both the public and the private sectors may overinvest, underinvest, or misinvest, whereas the human and capital resource allocation may be ineffective. Furthermore, risk assessment defines risk as the product of the harm probability categories and harm severity categories. Risks can be measured in terms of probability and impact, and in real-life scenarios, it can be very difficult to manage when faced with the scarcity of resources, especially time, in which to conduct the risk management process.

A single loss expectancy formula stipulates that

$$R_i = L_i p\,(L_i) \tag{1.3}$$

where L signifies the degree of any and all likely loss, and p represents the probability that this loss will take place. This econometric formula is implemented in each risk possibility and enables the risk manager to measure and classify the risks in line with the value of R.

1.5.4 Formula #4: Total Loss Expectancy Formula

The total loss expectancy represents the aggregate risk assessment score and is expressed as follows:

$$R_{\text{total}} = \sum_i L_i p(L_i) \tag{1.4}$$

The variables for Formula 1.4 are identical to Formula 1.3. As their titles indicate, [1.3] refers to a single loss expectancy, whereas [1.4] pertains to the aggregate (total) risk assessment. The Greek Sigma symbol is used in econometrics and math, and means "sum up."

1.5.5 Formula #5: Risk Assessment Formula for the Structural Integrity of Assets

The risk assessment formula for the structural integrity of assets applies to conduct a risk assessment of inanimate objects within the supply chain or within any and all of the 16 critical infrastructure sections.

$$R = L_v \times S_v \times S \times P \times T \times H \times EI \tag{1.5}$$

where
  R is the *risk* magnitude.
  L_v is the *location* of the asset (government facilities, offshore rigs, warehouses, etc.). In a piracy or terrorist attack incident, this entails to the structures exposed within the radius of the attack. In a natural disaster (act of God) such as a heavy wind incident, it is the radius of maximum wind, whereas during an earthquake, it is the distance from the epicenter. The value (L_v) has the element of proactive evaluation of the risk probability based on the current location and the asset's exposure.
  S_v is the *security vulnerability* of the particular asset(s) area. This could encompass situational vulnerability, i.e., in case the target is not protected by sufficient security measures, technologies, armed forces, etc.
  S is the asset's structural integrity, including
      a. *Internal structural factors* (fatigue, true structure strength)
      b. *External factors* (weather, temperature, maintenance, and age parameters)

H   is the *hazard* within the asset or in the vicinity of the asset. This includes both a security threat, such as a terrorist attack or piracy, and a natural disaster in the vicinity of HazMat that could potentially harm human life, the environment, and facilities. The nine classes of HazMat include (1) explosives; (2) gases; (3) flammable liquids and combustible liquids; (4) flammable solids, spontaneously combustible and dangerous when wet; (5) oxidizers and organic peroxides; (6) poison (toxic) and poison inhalation hazard; (7) radioactive(s); (8) corrosives; and (9) miscellaneous/general danger.

T   is the *time* factor, e.g., the longer the exposure time, the higher the risk.

EI is the *exposure intensity* factor, e.g., the greater the intensity of the attack or disaster, the higher the risk.

1.5.6 Formula #6: Assessment of the Security-Related Expenditures

Assessment of security-related expenditures

$$A = \frac{V}{D - L} \tag{1.6}$$

where

V   stands for the value of security expenditures in view of a terrorist threat and is divided by $(D - L)$.

D   reflects the terrorist attack deterrence (in terms of unmaterialized losses).

L   pertains to the losses suffered pursuant to the terrorist or piracy attack.

It is worth commenting that publicly announced security investment in a potential target can act as an attack deterrent, and the unmaterialized losses cannot be accurately estimated.

1.5.7 Formula #7: The Security Threat Probability Model While Target Is in Motion

$$S_{ij} = \frac{V_i(T)}{I \dfrac{E}{D_{ij}}} \tag{1.7}$$

This formula has been developed to evaluate the security threat probability while a target (live, commodity, or supply) is in motion, i.e., during transportation.

The values are represented as follows:

S_{ij} is the risk for a security attack.

V_i is the insured value of life, assets, and/or commodities.

T   is the average threat within the transportation area (from point a to point b) or the radius of a facility, assessed by DHS/MARSEC levels over a period of time. The target could be humans, animals, commodities, or emergency supplies, and the nature of the hazard encompasses
   – Natural disasters (safety)
   – Piracy-prone areas (e.g., Somalia)
   – Terrorism-prone areas and war zones (e.g., Iraq)

I   is the amount invested on security.

E   is the efficiency index of the supply chain (i.e., an index measuring key per-
     formance indicators for governments, facilities, and entire supply chains. This
     index includes assessment of quality, regulatory, and commercial compliance,
     no disruptions or delays).

D_{ij} is the distance between the two locations in voyage days.

1.5.8 Formula #8: Commodity Demand

An econometric model has been developed based on the energy formula developed by
Dees et al. (2003) to reflect the global and regional demand for commodities as a result
of trade agreements, the real commodity value, and the time element. The model also
reflects technological advancements connected to a smart logistics network consisting of
raw materials, services (trade and transportation, warehousing, and so on), and value-
added operations, such as manufacturing and refineries. The formula incorporates time-,
temperature-, and quality-sensitive commodities and aims to reflect the key elements that
affect the demand for a specific commodity:

$$\text{Dem}_i = \Phi\left[Y_i \frac{V_{\text{com}}}{V_i^{\text{D}}} E_i, \text{time}\right] \tag{1.8}$$

where

Dem$_i$ reflects the commodity demand.

   i is the number of units per region or nation.

   Φ is used in mathematics and statistics to reflect the cumulative distribution func-
       tion of the normal distribution.

   Y_i stands for real gross domestic product (GDP).

   V_{com} is the US dollar commodity value.

   E_i is the rate of exchange compared to the US dollar value.

   V_i^{D} is the consumer price index (CPI) index.

While the GDP deflation index was applied, the statistical results were insignificantly
affected.

1.5.9 Formulas #9 and #10: Value at Risk

Value at risk (VaR) is utilized to calculate the risk vulnerability of a specific target, a
critical infrastructure sector, a region, an industry, or an entire nation. The VaR can
be applied to any and all types of risks, including all security and supply chain risks. It
consists of a given amount of decrease in price, a standard risk assessment time frame,
and a certainty phase.

It is frequently used to estimate the possible value reduction pursuant to a security
risk during a particular time.

To calculate the likelihood of damage, it is essential to estimate the probability distribution of each likely risk, the aggregate risk correlation, as well as the damage impact
in terms of asset valuation (Willis et al. 2005).

Based on the assumptions above, the VaR is reflected as follows:

$$p^{\text{ext}} = 1 - F_{Zn}^{\text{asymp}}(-\text{VaR}) = \exp\left[-\left(1 + \tau\left(\frac{-\text{VaR} + \beta_n}{\alpha_n}\right)\right)^{\frac{1}{\tau}}\right] \tag{1.9}$$

The VaR can be calculated to reflect possible damage and value reduction:

$$\text{VaR} = -\beta_n + \frac{\alpha_n}{\tau}[1 - (-\ln(p^{\text{ext}}))^{\tau}] \tag{1.10}$$

Security threat econometrics offers the benefits of evaluating multiple damages, both for man-made and for natural disasters. Users may assess the big picture of a security incident by classifying and contrasting damage within a critical infrastructure unit and sub-entities, such as a hub port, and its warehouses, rail, port terminals, container areas, pipelines, etc.

Security assessment formulas offer users the opportunity to proactively assess potential risks and become more efficient in investment decisions, people management, and asset management processes. Most importantly, as the accuracy of the formulas is subject to the data input, the users are not restricted to a single entity of the public or private sector but could represent a security consortium from a specific region, supply chain, or specific industry.

1.5.10 Formula #11: Attack Types and Scenario Parameters

This formula is used to calculate traffic. Time series modeling plays an important role in the field of security statistics and risk assessment. The technique suggested herewith accurately validates

　　a. The hub-and-spoke interconnectivity during supply chain disruptions
　　b. The geographical and time relevance entailed in a single security target or a
　　　　series of targets

The author hereby uses the terms *security economics* and *security econometrics* to describe disciplines of high significance whose development can be useful to the industry. While a *domino effect* is the collective result generated when a single occurrence triggers a sequence of related events, *interconnectivity* in security economics is defined as the financial connection between two seemingly independent security targets.

The following formula applies a spatial economic base model (EBM) based on the spatial auto-regressive and moving average (SARMA) model to estimate the geospatial interconnectivity from an economic perspective. At a designated region (i), the spatial EBM can be described as the aggregate economic interconnectivity (E_i) generated in a number of sites or security targets (j) (Biles 2003):

$$\text{EBM}_i^* = \sum E_{ij}/E_i \tag{1.11}$$

Using the aforementioned model enables users to map aggregate spatial interconnectivity in separate targeted areas and/or the entire area afflicted with a security hazard. Interconnectivity in supply chains suggests that any disruption of production or transport in a single supply chain component will result in geospatial economic impacts throughout the supply chain.

1.5.10.1 Incident Investigation and Spatial Autocorrelation Models

Spatial autocorrelation models can be especially valuable when adopted by security investigators. In particular, during the incident investigation of man-made catastrophes, illegitimate trade and travel, and other criminal activities, the model may be used to examine the pattern of criminal behavior. Since the geospatial element is associated with the element of time, this econometric formula can be associated with the crime opportunity theory and the categorical trinity of *means, motive, and opportunity*, with focus on the timeline of events. A criminal or illegal activity can be tied in with certain persons of interest (suspects) if a timeline of their physical whereabouts can be connected with the crime scene in a specific geographical location or a cluster of locations. The map in Figure 1.3 depicts the cluster of the Boston Marathon bombings and the timeline indicated by numbers. Similar spatial clusters of events could be linked with the element of time and the suspects' opportunity.

Geospatial econometrics also assists in mapping the network formations and action patterns of illegitimate or terrorist activities, providing useful data for the security professionals and incident investigators.

1.5.11 Formula #12: Spatial Autocorrelation: Moran's I (Spatial Statistics) Works

Measures of spatial autocorrelation: Moran's I measures serve as instruments to calculate global spatial autocorrelation demonstrating single, independent areas and multiple areas concurrently (Moran 1950). Granted a range of capabilities and an affiliated attribute,

Timeline of events:
1. Boston Marathon explosions — April 15, 2013
2. MIT police officer was fatally shot — April 18, 2015, 10:30 pm
3. Carjacking a Mercedes in Cambridge area — April 18, 2015, after 10:30 pm
4. Owner of the car was released on Memorial Drive — April 18, 2015, 11:00 pm
5. Watertown shootout. Tamerlan Tsarnaev is apprehended. Dzhokhar escapes. — April 19, 2015
6. and 7. Watertown manhunt for Dzhokhar Tsarnaev — April 19, 2015

FIGURE 1.3 2013 Boston Marathon bombing. Timeline of events and the manhunt. (Timeline composed by the author, based on Wikimedia Map.)

Moran's I model can be used in security risk assessment and security mitigation as it can verify if the pattern depicted is random, dispersed, or clustered.

Moran's I index value and a Z score assess whether spatial clustering or dispersion occurs. In particular, clustering is signified when the index value is in close proximity to +1.0, whereas dispersion is signified when the index value is close to –1.0:

$$I = \frac{n}{S_0} \frac{\sum_i \sum_j w_{ij}(x_i - \overline{x})(x_j - \overline{x})}{\sum_i (x_i - \overline{x})^2}, \qquad (1.12)$$

where

n signifies observations.

x is the variable.

$\overline{x}$ is the mean of the x variable.

i, j are the locations.

w_{ij} are the elements of the weight matrix.

S_0 is the total amount of the components of the weight matrix. It equals as follows:

$$S_0 = \sum_i \sum_j w_{ij}.$$

The Moran's I measurement encompasses multiple regions, while it is more accurate in estimating extreme values.

1.5.12 Formula #13: *Security Threat Indicator of Spatial Correlation Model for Risk Assessment and Incident Mitigation*

The *security threat indicator of spatial correlation* (STISC) model demonstrates the spatial association of numerous security incident locations. The model is hereby used to match a security mapping metric with the following attributes:

a. The STISC model reflects the degree of spatial clustering of comparable security values pertinent to the observation.

b. An aggregate estimation of the STISC encompasses a larger mapping or a global indicator of spatial correlation.

The STISC formula is reflected as follows:

$$STI_i = I(A_i, A_{ij}), \qquad (1.13)$$

where

STI_i is the security threat indicator, broadly representing a security incident that may entail numerous security sub-incident elements in various geographical locations $(A_i, A_{ij},...)$.

I represents the incident.

A_{ij} is the score of incident i ensuing from indicator j.

1.5.13 Formula #14: Structural Resilience

According to security terminology, resilience is the capability of a physical structure, critical infrastructure target, or component to recover from a security threat. In physics, *proof resilience* is described as the optimum energy that may be absorbed within the elastic limitation without resulting in an irreversible damage.

The resilient value M_R is the recovery elasticity, based on the recuperation pressure under recurring or repetitive attack, and is described as

$$M_R = \frac{\sigma_{\alpha\chi}}{\varepsilon_r} \qquad (1.14)$$

where

M_R structural resilience.
$\sigma_{\alpha\chi}$ represents the stress of (repetitive) attack.
ε_r reflects the recoverable elasticity of a target.

1.5.14 Formula #15: Distance, Time, and Resilience

The following security resilience formula assumes that the security mitigation during an incident $\left(S_j^m\right)$ is directly proportional to time, both the time elapsed between the incident occurrence and the time emergency responders (E_j) arrive at the incident scene to alleviate the attack, and the elasticity of time $\left(R_j^t\right)$ reflecting the duration of the attack:

$$S_j^m = E_j R_j^t \quad \text{where } E_j > 0. \qquad (1.15)$$

A decrease in either elasticity is associated with higher response success and therefore higher resilience rates. Therefore, if responders manage to reduce the time between the incident occurrence and their emergency response, or to eliminate the distance between their basis and the incident scene, systems and communities will become more resilient.

In this section, a number of econometric formulas were used to measure and verify the security-associated risks and consequences and forecast possible threats.

1.5.14.1 Criminal Profiling of the Security Offenders

In order to support the authorities and security professionals, a five-point classification system has been established to be used in the criminal profiling process. An examination of the following security breach parameters will provide investigators with valuable information about both the security incident and the offender's personality profile.

The legal concept indicating motivation, means, and opportunity as the three aspects of a crime may suggest that an in-depth examination of a single aspect will likely highlight information on the other two aspects.

a. *Security offenders' motive*: The motive behind an act of security breach relates to a security offender's purpose, reason, and *ethical justification* of an attack. Poverty may be the motive for cargo pilferage or even piracy, whereas religious or racial hate may motivate acts of massive destruction. A proactive examination of the possible motive of targeted security offense groups (i.e., political, religious, or socioeconomic terrorism typically has different motives than piracy or cargo theft) may enable the authorities to accurately outline the background and motivational profile of persons and groups of interest. A social and psychological profile of each distinguished motivation category will help the authorities to assess the means and opportunity elements in the crime adage and identify potential targets, threat levels, and likely damages.

b. *Security offenders' means*: Refers to resource management of security offenders, i.e., the gathering, management, handling and maintenance of resources, assets. This classification is directly related with the four *factors of production*, i.e., management, labor, capital, and land. These are the four resources that an illegitimate or criminal action is based upon, from concept to execution:

   i.   The *management* element relates to the mastermind(s) that engineer(s) and coordinate(s) the security attack, generate(s) land and capital resources, and most importantly, recruit(s), coach(es), and motivate(s) *labor.*

   ii. Labor entails to the operational or *expendable* criminal members that are recruited, motivated, and frequently brainwashed by the masterminds.

   iii. Capital pertains to the financial resources and assets related to the security offenders' expense coverage, from inception to execution of security breach plans.

   iv. Finally, the land element covers (a) the geographical range of illegal activities that could entail a regional or global network mapping of illegitimate security actions and (b) the hideout or the *physical premises* of the outlaws.

c. *Security offenders' opportunity*: This component entails the element of presence and activities in a specific time and space setting, with pertinent prospects and restrictions to plan and execute a security breach.

d. *Security offenders' group size*: Ranging from lone wolves to large terrorist or crime groups, the group size of security offenders is usually directly associated with the intensity, consequences, and overall outcomes of a security threat. While examining the latest security attack statistics, typically, larger groups have easier access to resources, training, and coverage and the ability for mass recruitment with the use of social media and social networks.

e. *Security offenders' risk tolerance*: This component may be related to the criminal personality, opportunity, means, and motive. Although the level of risk is directly proportional to the benefits derived from a security attack, different types of offenders may establish different rates of risk tolerance.

In the eyes of a terrorist or religious hater, the significance and value of a security attack may justify even the loss of the offender's life. However, in the case of criminal actions with social or financial motives, such as illegal immigration or cargo theft, the risk tolerance level is significantly lower and would not justify loss of life.

1.5.14.2 The Econometrics of Risk Tolerance

This section will elaborate on the risk tolerance element and provide an econometric formula to reflect the variations of risk tolerance.

Under the assumption that there is a directly proportional correlation among risk, investment cost, and expected returns, a security threat (terrorist attack, illegitimate trade or travel, or criminal activity) will be planned only if the anticipated return exceeds the expected cost.

The following econometric formula classifies the different types of security offenders according to their tolerance to bear the cost or consequences of their attack.

An offender's cost may include

1. *Physical cost*: imprisonment, injury, or casualty during or after the attack incident.
2. *Economic cost*: financial cost related to planning, orchestrating, and carrying out the attack. In the case of a terrorist attack or piracy, this could involve the purchase or leasing of vehicles, attack weapons, ammunition, training, and so on.
3. *Emotional (or moral) cost*: In contrast with habitual and repeated criminal activities conducted by offenders of low moral, ethical, and emotional standards, certain examples of deviant behavior and criminal activity may also be products of poverty, mind control—or coercive persuasion—or even physical threat. In the case of human trafficking and illegal immigration, the offender must assess the cost of separation with family, friends, and a familiar environment. In the case of involuntary participation of criminal activities, such as in the case of child suicide bombers, the act of children being recruited by their own parents may be an act both emotionally and ethically charged yet overshadowed by political, racial, and/or religious fanaticism.

1.5.15 Formulas #16, #17, and #18: The Levels of Risk Tolerance

a. *Low risk tolerance*: At this level, security perpetrators will only be involved in a security attack if the cost of the attack is smaller than the benefits. Security officials can relatively easily avert or eliminate attacks deriving from such personality types, as the subject's *crime-motivated* or *crime-brainwashed* levels are rather low.

$$C_i < V_i \cdot R, \text{or comparable with} \quad \frac{C_i}{V_i} > R \tag{1.16}$$

where
C_i represents the cost of the attack to the perpetrator.
V_i reflects a vulnerability index, which may encompass national, political, legal, socioeconomic, physical, and critical infrastructure losses.
R is the risk of arrest, prosecution, or even death at the scene of the attack.

b. *Medium risk tolerance*: Security offenders are willing to take a risk only if their rewards will be high enough to make this illegal activity worthwhile.

$$C_i = V_i \cdot R, \text{or comparable with} \quad \frac{C_i}{V_i} = R \tag{1.17}$$

c. *High risk tolerance*: This personality type refers to individuals that would be willing to take the highest risks for a specific cause that is more significant than their own survival, social isolation, material deprivation, and so on. This category includes individuals that are incapable of caring for their own well-being, such as substance abusers; mentally incapacitated; or victims of physical, political, religious, and/or emotional abuse. Here, the subject's *crime-motivated* or *crime-brainwashed* levels are high.

$$C_i > V_i \cdot R, \text{or comparable with} \quad \frac{C_i}{V_i} < R \tag{1.18}$$

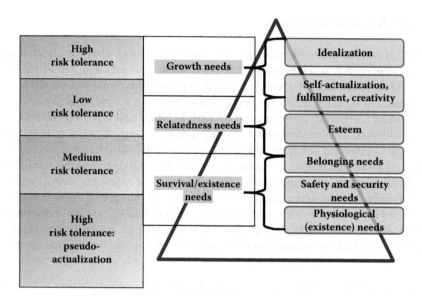

FIGURE 1.4 Combined security attacks and risk tolerance in Alderfer's Existence, Relatedness, and Growth Theory and Maslow's Pyramid of Needs. (Composed figure courtesy of the author, based on Alderfer and Maslow's theories.)

Figure 1.4 demonstrates the three levels of security offenders' risk tolerance related to the survival and growth needs as reflected in the theories of Abraham Maslow and Clayton Alderfer (Maslow 1943, 1954; Alderfer 1969, 1972; see also Chapter 10, Section 10.2).

1. *Low risk tolerance*: The greater the actualization and self-esteem levels of the individual, the lower the risk tolerance.
2. *Medium risk tolerance*: For this social group, the willingness to take risks may be associated with belonging and related needs or even with the need for survival.
3. *High risk tolerance*: In this category, subjects are willing to risk their safety-, survival-, and existence-related needs. Three subcategories are formed herewith to reflect the personality types and motives that dictate such behavior:
    a. *Type A: The survivor*. Security offenders in this category belong to the lowest level of Maslow's pyramid. They may pursue illegitimate activities under a life-threatening state, i.e., driven by depletion of resources, poverty, or social turmoil. Theft, illegal immigration, or certain cases of marine piracy may belong to this category.
    b. *Type B: The martyr*. This category of security offenders entails victims of physical, political, religious, social, or emotional abuse, such as victims of human trafficking, drug victims, suicide bombers, and so on. Interestingly enough, the subjects in this category may be victims of their own *belonging needs*, i.e., their decision to commit a crime is directly proportional to their social, political, or religious sense of acceptance. Therefore, they belong to the midlevel of Maslow's pyramid.
    c. *Type C: The pseudo-achiever*. The paradox with this subject type is that although they belong to the lowest level of Maslow's pyramid (i.e., below the survival needs), in fact, they are motivated by the illusion of self-actualization

and self-righteousness, which is found at the top tier of the pyramid. Therefore, the pseudo-achiever term refers to the mirage-like reflection of the top, i.e., the highest ideals and a noble cause, whereas in fact, they may commit the most violent and severe crimes.

1.6 THE HISTORY OF LOGISTICS AND TRANSPORTATION SECURITY

Forget logistics, you lose.

U.S. Lieutenant General Franks
7th Corps Commander, Desert Storm

Logistics in this book is considered the strategic architecture, monitoring, and controlling of the entire value chain. It entails the flow of trade and transport in a safe, secure, and time- and cost-efficient manner from the point of origin to the final point of distribution and consumption.

Logistics is defined as a military discipline associated with the procurement, maintenance, and transportation of supplies and employees and the provision of amenities and services (*The Oxford English Dictionary* 2014). From a commercial perspective, logistics is defined as the comprehensive synchronization of a sophisticated process entailing people, amenities, or materials (*New Oxford American Dictionary* 2014).

Logistics distribution may entail physical or abstract components:

a. Physical logistics distribution includes merchandise, such as raw materials, livestock, foodstuff, medicine, chemicals, and energy commodities. The strategic planning of physical commodities typically requires the combination of data exchange, safe and secure product handling, inventory management, product manufacturing, labeling and packaging, haulage, storage, and customs clearance.
b. Service logistics includes the abstract distribution of virtual commodities including information technology, quality, safety, just-in-time (JIT) schedule, and others.

To ensure efficient logistics distribution in both tangible and abstract commodities, a number of managerial functions are required:

a. *Resource management*, which requires optimum utilization of resources in order to avoid waste, benefit from economies of scale, avoid duplication of efforts, and ensure optimum output based on efficient processing of the input.
b. *Information management*, which is achieved through state-of-the-art web applications and systems.
c. *Corporate asset management*, which is required to safeguard the company's tangible and intangible assets. Tangible assets include buildings, office equipment, technologies, and transportation assets; intangible assets may include innovations, market credit, industry reputation, goodwill, networks, and so on.

The optimum performance of a supply chain is achieved through quality management and reliability of its infrastructure system from production to the final consumer distribution. Effective and efficient logistics is achieved through optimum allocation of resources, high service quality, minimum delays in production and transportation, regulatory compliance, and concurrence with the principles of *lean and agile* and JIT. Customer satisfaction is attained through the *value-for-money* principle and minimum instances of time disruptions, resource waste, or compromising of the quality (Burns 2013a).

In the era of globalization, rapid growth of global trade volume, and the development of new global markets, the industry's greatest challenge is to seek a balance between efficient logistics management and secure flow of commodities and information. Coalitions among the private and public sectors strive to achieve this balance: on one hand, a focus on fast transportation processing time may result in reduced security checks and increased security threats and incidents; on the other hand, a focus on security may impede the global flow of trade and transport, with significant repercussions in the global and national economy, job market, and standards of living.

1.7 SUPPLY CHAIN SECURITY: AN OVERVIEW

Upon the conduct of each, depends the fate of all.

Alexander III the Great

Upon the assumption that a supply chain is as strong as its weakest link, resilient supply chains are characterized by visibility, real-time monitoring, efficient resource management, and mostly risk management and contingency plans that encompass all the components of the supply chain.

To achieve optimum levels of supply chain security, a public–private alliance is required with the purpose of sustaining and/or improving the supply chain capacity, sustainability, haulage, and logistics processes at a global and regional level. This common goal brings together alliances that practice standard supply chain management techniques with the safety and security measures implemented to mitigate terrorism, piracy, and theft.

Standard supply chain security actions involve

- Background checks of all individuals involved in the supply chain network
- Cargo screening, monitoring, tracking, and verification
- Advance notice of the cargo contents from the place of origin to the place of destination
- Optimizing cargo security from storage areas, while cargo is in-transit, through its final destination, via the utilization of surveillance cameras, locks, tamper-proof seals, and other security technologies and methods
- Checking shipments upon entry
- Developing efficient security networks and security information exchange at a national and global level through the use of partnerships, technologies, and security metrics

In order to consolidate efforts toward national sovereignty, homeland security, and economic prosperity, it is necessary for nations to secure the worldwide supply chain while making certain that it operates in a safe, secure, sustainable, and commercially optimum manner.

As global nations depend upon the commodities moved by the global supply chain platform, it becomes evident that moving secure commodities is a primary goal for all nations, and all key players should join forces to ensure its resilience. The international supply chain is vibrant, intricate, and ever expanding, and is susceptible to a number of risks and perils, which include natural catastrophes, incidents, and intentional man-made attacks.

The National DHS Strategy ensures two goals:

1. To support the reliable and safeguarded flow of goods
2. To promote a proactive supply chain platform at a global level, which is prepared for and can endure increasing risks and perils and rapid recuperation from interferences (DHS 2013)

1.7.1 Supply Chain Disruptions

Throughout the past decades or so, globalization and increased global trade volumes have contributed to more complex supply chain networks, with severe implications in the fields of safety and security. These implications have affected nations, communities, markets, and industries in an adverse manner. Modern globalization practices require multiple global locations to be involved in the trade and transport activities of a single supply chain. Numerous nations collaborate to mine, drill, refine, manufacture, add value, trade, and distribute products globally. To effectively combat the several weakness points throughout this process, assertive and efficient supply chain security practices must provide wisdom, insight, and information to offset hazards.

When examining the modern complex supply chain networks, merchandise could be corrupted, tampered, degraded, or lost due to five major risk factors:

1. *Deliberate damage, as a result of low-quality materials and spares used, with the purpose of economic gain* (Hsieh 2014).
2. *Trade disruption, deviation from the original authorized markets, and the trading of merchandise in new, substitute markets.* Trade interruption occurrences including warfare, strikes, social turmoil, adverse weather, and other occasions considerably influence local and global trade and transport each year. In 2013, almost $250 billion were lost globally due to trade interruption. The so-called supply chain terrorism causes severe problems in numerous countries such as India, Colombia, the Philippines, and regions in Northern Africa and the Middle East (BSI 2014).
3. *Freight pilferage (theft).* This item alone causes the US economy a loss of $65 billion in Canada, $35 billion in the United States, and over $16 billion in Europe (BSI 2014; Hsieh 2014).
4. *Producing and manufacturing imitation products, thus creating fraudulent competitive advantages.*
5. *Cyber espionage, obtaining illicit access to critical information of governments, corporations, and individuals, with the purpose of monetary, commercial, and other gains.*

Over the previous decades, an array of incidents such as natural disasters, terrorist attacks, and criminal activities has significantly disrupted international supply chains, leading to long-term implications to companies, industries, markets, and nations. To manage potential supply chain distractions, new regulations, innovative technologies, and alternative risk management techniques are used by nations and industries alike. However, to fully benefit from these novelties, profound improvements need to be made in the following key areas (Hicks 2012):

- *Supply chain integration and visibility.* To achieve this, companies need to establish a centralized platform of monitoring and controlling. Increased visibility will enable complex supply chain networks to become more efficient and overcome problems of obsolete or diverse spare part components. Innovative information systems also contribute to establishing a harmonized network communication and eliminate tunnel vision.
- *Use geospatial criteria to select supply chain partners while retaining leaner supply chains.* The latest corporate trend includes the selection of new vendors located closer to the end market. Nevertheless, this switch creates more delays, errors, and complications as the supply chains become more intricate.
- *Increase real-time monitoring and response.* The increasing growth of global trade volume, combined with the emergence of new global players, has intensified competition. Businesses are pressed to reduce time and increase real-time monitoring and response.
- *Employee empowerment.* Most importantly, employees need to be authorized, trained, and motivated to take critical decisions and offer real-time solutions to their global supply chain partners.

1.7.2 The History of Logistics: An Overview

Logistics is a fairly recent term that refers to a millennia-old discipline: the art pertaining to the movement, coordination, and supply of humans, troops, and commodities. Logistical practices are used to serve different purposes, which are frequently overlapping. For the sake of organization, we hereby distinguish logistical functions into three key sectors, namely,

1. *Survival logistics:* these are associated with emergency response/contingency planning. Arguably, the first applications of *survival logistics* are rooted millennia back, in times where prehistoric men survived in harsh weather conditions and fought to survive during natural disasters. The first early human migrations for survival purposes were performed about 600,000 years BC by *Homo heidelbergensis,* the possible predecessor of the Neanderthals, *Homo sapiens,* and the modern humans. Prehistoric findings of *H. heidelbergensis* in Africa, Europe, and Asia prove that these were proficient toolmakers who were accustomed to killing animals like deer, horses, and elephants for food and able to protect their families and stay away from dangerous predators such as lions, tigers, and wolves.

    Modern-day survival logistics entails mass migration to avoid natural disasters, such as the major tsunamis and earthquakes in Thailand and the Indian Ocean (2004), Indonesia (2014), and others. Based on the US Geological Survey, the earthquake that resulted in the major Indian Ocean tsunami of 2004 is calculated to have discharged the energy of 23,000 Hiroshima-type atomic bombs (National Geographic 2005; USGS 2014). The ensuing tsunami impacted 12 nations within the Indian Ocean, with Indonesia enduring the greatest damage.

The United Nations and other national and local authorities had to collaborate for major survival logistics operations: In Aceh, the north province of Sumatra (Indonesia), around 131,000 persons were confirmed dead and 37,000 missing. In Sumatra, Indonesia, over 80,000 residences suffered major destruction or total loss, and emergency responders had to assist over 500,000 citizens to evacuate their homes, as well as attend the disruptions to the region's massive critical infrastructure damage and disruptions: buildings, hospitals, public amenities, infrastructure, energy and electricity, dams and bridges, and others.

Hurricane Ike was a Category 4 major hurricane (tropical cyclone) that seriously impacted the Gulf of Mexico in 2008. It cost the lives of 195 people and financial losses exceeding US $37.5 billion related to the damage of critical infrastructure and commercial and residential properties, thus becoming the most expensive natural disaster in Cuba and the third most expensive hurricane in the United States (FEMA 2008).

Such events require a coalition between the public sector (federal, state, and local authorities) and the private sector (nonprofit organizations; community groups; supply chains, including transportation and logistics companies; critical infrastructure; and emergency responders).

2. *Military logistics*: pertaining to warfare and military strategies. According to NATO Dictionary (1997), it is defined as "The science of planning and carrying out the movement and maintenance of forces." In its most comprehensive sense, those aspects of military operations which deal with:
   a. design and development, acquisition, transport, storage, distribution, maintenance, evacuation, and disposition of material;
   b. crew transport;
   c. acquisition or construction, maintenance, operation, and disposition of facilities;
   d. acquisition or furnishing of services; and
   e. medical and health service support (AAP-6).

3. *Procurement logistics*: related to supply chains, trade, and transport, whose functions contribute to the sociopolitical and economic sustainability (Burns 2014a). Procurement is a crucial supply chain function that may impact the corporate sustainability, growth, and success by helping accomplish maximum efficiency and effectiveness. The procurement process is implemented in the internal supply chain process converting the demand for a product or service into measurable deliverables capable to meet the market's needs.

   Procurement logistics entails the procedures and functions employed in the trade, transport, distribution, storage, and receipt of commodities traded between companies. In the majority of technology-, manufacture-, and transportation-based industries, procurement logistics constitute the nucleus of the corporate activities. The principal aspects of successful procurement logistics systems are centered on cost efficiency, resource management, and service optimization.

1.7.3 Logistics through the Millennia

Contrary to popular belief as to the timeline of logistics, their practices go beyond the eighteenth century AD. In fact, logistics are millennia-old practices that had to be reinvented over the history of mankind after significant technological, scientific, and sociopolitical changes.

The aim of the following section is (i) to validate the continuation of logistics prac-tices throughout the centuries, (ii) to relay the connectivity between key logistics prin-ciples practiced in different geographical locations and at different times, and (iii) to demonstrate through a concise description of significant historical events that logistics practices of past centuries may well be applied in modern commercial, military, and pro-curement situations.

The following case studies concisely demonstrate how the world's greatest military leaders exercised logistics over the past millennia.

CASE STUDY: ALEXANDER C' THE GREAT (JULY 356 BC– JUNE 323 BC): A QUEST FOR THE "ENDS OF THE WORLD AND THE GREAT OUTER SEA"

My Son, seek thee out a large kingdom equal to thyself for our kingdom of Macedonia is too small for you. *(Note: Macedonia is one of the Ancient Greek tribal states.)*

Phillip II (382–336)
Alexander's father

Alexander C' the Great is considered to be one of the greatest military logistic geniuses of all times, who has set up the standards of warfare. Determined to travel and seize the "ends of the world and the Great Outer Sea," it only took him 11 years to conquer the great empires of Asia, from Asia Minor to what is modern-day Turkey, Israel, Jordan, Lebanon, Palestine, Syria, and the mighty Persian Empire (modern-day Iran; see Burns-Kokkinaki 2004).

He managed to conquer the mighty Persian Empire, Egypt, and Asian nations, while his army was substantially outnumbered, and he was combating in unfamil-iar lands against nations defending their own country (Engels 1978).

After the death of his father, Philip II, who under the Macedonian hegemony had brought together an alliance of other Greek tribal states, Alexander the Great became the king of Macedonia. The consolidated military assets that he managed accounted to a fleet of 160 triremes (ships with three rows of oars, manned with one sailor per oar) and troops of around 38,000–41,000 soldiers and 6100 cavalry. From 332 to 323 BC, Alexander and his troops fought and marched 19.5 mi a day in order to conquer 2,180,000 mi^2 of land in Asia and Egypt, Northern Africa, as depicted in Figure 1.5.

To replenish his land and sea military forces, Alexander ensured that his land forces carried at least 10 days of supplies, and his fleet carried at least 30 days of supplies. Alexander established strategic alliances with the nations he invaded, facil-itating his troops to be continuously replenished in terms of food, shelter, and vari-ous military resources throughout their transcontinental expedition. Furthermore, numerous regions relinquished their military control and territory, whereas others eventually joined Alexander's armed forces, bringing their own military resources. Alexander developed a contingency plan, for his troops and fleet to meet at regular intervals, to ensure the storage and allocation of the new supplies gathered through their long journeys. Most importantly, Alexander had with him geographers, bota-nists, historians, and multidisciplinary scientists in order to record the particular characteristics of all the lands they conquered in terms of geography, geology, agri-culture, climate, language, culture, religion, and so on.

FIGURE 1.5 Map of the Empire and expeditions of Alexander the Great by Delamarche, 1832, "Geographicus Alexandri Magni." (From Delamarche Publishing House, 1832. Courtesy of Wikimedia Commons, available at http://commons.wiki media.org/wiki/File:1832_Delamarche_Map_of_the_Empire_of_Alexander_the _Great_-_Geographicus_-_AlexandriMagni-delamarche-1832.jpg, accessed April 4, 2015. Public Domain Map. This file has been identified as being free of known restrictions under copyright law, including all related and neighboring rights.)

CASE STUDY: GENGHIS KHAN (1162–1227 AD)

Genghis Khan was a great warrior and ruler of the Mongol Empire, who brought new forms of warfare and new military technologies and tactics. Genghis Khan is acknowledged with enhancing the Silk Road through a single rulership that over the centuries helped enhance trade and transport between Asia and Europe.

Pax Mongolica and the Great Mongol Empire were built upon mass extinction of the enemy through a well-sustainable military supply chain that led to death, starvation, disease, mass migration, and eventually extreme population decrease.

Khan with his Mongolian tribe hordes secured 5000 mi of trade routes in order to conquer 12 million mi^2 of territory in Northeast Asia, as depicted in Figure 1.6.

This military achievement would not have been possible without the military tactics, training, resources, favorable climate, and other factors:

1. *Mongolian horses: an agile transportation*
   "If my horse lives, I live, If my horses die, I die" was a popular quote among Khan's men. Khan's soldiers owned about four horses each; hence,

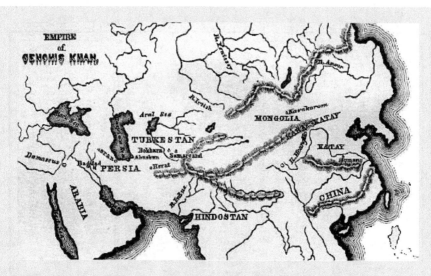

FIGURE 1.6   Empire of Genghis Khan (1162–1227 AD). (From Abbot, J., *Genghis Khan, Makers of History Series*, Harper & Brothers Publishers, New York and London, available at http://www.gutenberg.org/files/28667/28667-h/28667-h.htm, accessed November 18, 2014, 1901.)

they would switch horses multiple times a day to keep their horses free of fatigue. This enabled them to move fast with minimum delays, sometimes ride 100 mi a day, making them insuperable in the battlefield. The Mongols treasured their horses and covered them in armor to protect them from the enemy's arrows. The mobility of individual soldiers made it possible to send them on successful scouting missions, gathering intelligence about routes and searching for terrain suited to the preferred combat tactics of the Mongols.

Pederson et al. (2013) discovered a possible cause for a Mongolian tribe with their horses to conquer most of Asia: their cold and dry steppes savored 15 years of rain and moderate weather, which favored the Mongolian hordes in practicing and expanding their warfare strategies (Smith 2014).

The weather factor seems to have positively impacted Khan's expansion plans, estimating that each horse eats approximately 25–35 lb. of food per day, and therefore, each Mongol rider would need 120 lb. of food each day to feed their four horses. Under the normal weather conditions in Southeast Asia, characterized by cold and dry weather, Khan's horses would not be able to find this amount of food in order to make 100 mi a day. Therefore, under more harsh weather conditions, Khan's hordes would not be able to conquer this vast territory in Northeast Asia (Burns 2014b).

2. *Weapons, cannons, and bombs*: Though criticized for his violent military raids, Khan's army was well-equipped and self-sufficient, ensuring victory. Each Mongol soldier in Khan's heavy cavalry would carry a battle-ax, a dagger, two bows and numerous arrows, a 12-ft. lance, and a lasso.

3. *Espionage networks* were in place for numerous months prior to a strike, involved in conducting exploratory forays, mapping the enemy's territory,

infrastructure, and escape routes while evaluating the enemy's military power, defense strategies, and supply chain connectivity.

4. *Synchronized attacks* included
   a. *Ambushing*, i.e., the tactic of hiding and using the component of surprise to unexpectedly strike the opponent.
   b. *Hit and run,* which is a military tactic intended to diminish the opponent's morale by not actively seizing territorial occupation but destroying critical infrastructure targets and instantly leaving the location, thus preventing the enemy's retribution.
   c. *Fake retreat* was Genghis Khan's signature strategy and involved his troops pretending to retreat from the battlefield and subsequently return and attack toward the chasing opponents.
5. *The Yam postal system for military and political news*: This communication system much resembled numerous ancient postal systems: the Assyrian postal system of Hammurabi, dating back to 1700 BC, the ancient Persian system Chapar-Khaneh, the ancient Indian system Dagana, and the Roman *Cursus Publicus.*

Khan's postmen would ride their horses to convey messages through the warzone and the new empire. The *Yam system* courier postmen would ride 200 mi a day to ensure that there was ongoing communication through a network of relay stations to pass messages to and from the battlefront.

1.7.4 Medieval Explorers, the First Settlers, and the Origins of Modern America

While the first recorded logistics achievements pertain to warfare, the medieval expeditions to the New World are a typical example of logistics management at times of peace. The following explorers' procurement management entailed not only their food and medical and navigational supplies but also the know-how and preparedness to establish new colonies in unknown lands by using materials available locally. The art of improvising is a critical component of logistics.

1.7.5 Christopher Columbus's Voyages: A Logistics Achievement

Columbus was an Italian navigator who served as an *Admiral of the Ocean Sea* for the Spanish crown. From 1492 to 1502, he led four transatlantic voyages with the purpose of exploring and colonizing the Americas. During his first journey, Columbus headed with three vessels and 90 seafarers. Columbus was the master of the carrack vessel *Santa Maria*, Captain Vicente Yáñez Pinzon was the master of the caravel ship *Niña*, and Martin Alonzo Pinzon was the shipowner and master of the caravel ship *Pinta* (Figure 1.7). Voyage planning in the fifteenth century required not only navigation maps but also the knowledge of celestial navigation, i.e., geospatial orientation by observing the positions of the sun, moon, planets, and navigational stars visible with the naked eye. Columbus and his men also needed to estimate not only sufficient quantities of food (water, olive oil, wine, salted meat, cheese, raisins, and biscuits) but also ship supplies and other consumables such as ropes, sail cloth, etc.

FIGURE 1.7   1492: The arrival of Columbus in the Caribbean (State Archives of Florida). (From The Telegraph Blog, available at http://blogs.telegraph.co.uk/news/dominicselwood /100283798/columbus-greed-slavery-and-genocide-what-really-happened-to-the-american -indians/.)

1.7.6 Jamestown: The Early Settlers to the New World

Jamestown, Virginia was named after the British King James I. This was one of the early settlements of the British in the United States, and as such, it was dependent on resupply from the United Kingdom. In 1607, the Virginia Company of London dispatched an expedition of 104 men and 39 crewmembers to build a British settlement in the Virginia Colony (Figure 1.8). The three ships of the expedition were the *Godspeed*, the *Susan Constant*, and the *Discovery*. The journey lasted over four months, i.e., much longer than prior similar journeys (Congressional Record 1975, 1976).

The Virginia Company of London had cautioned them to settle in an area that would be protected from potential assaults by competing European settlers from Spain, France, and Holland. The early settlers selected Jamestown Island as a suitable settlement area due to its natural remoteness from the mainland and visibility of the ocean in case enemy ships would arrive. However, soon after the settlement, the island appeared to be unsuitable for colonization since its forested wetlands had contaminated water swarmed with mosquitoes. Regardless of the initial goals of the settlers to become self-sufficient while growing their own food, the harsh living conditions led to disease, famine, and death of numerous settlers. The adversities encountered over the first decades (sixteenth century) forced the settlers to either abandon the colony or become more reliant upon the supply missions. The historic *first supply* (1607), *second supply* (1608), and *third supply* (1609) were examples of constantly improved logistics processes through trial and error.

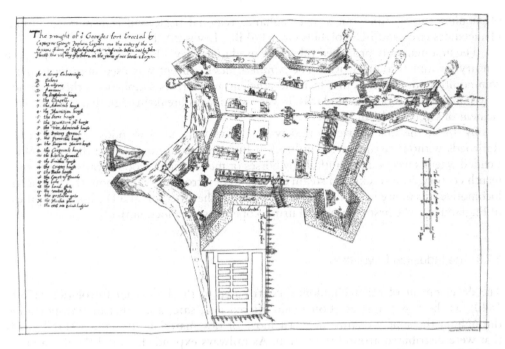

FIGURE 1.8 Jamestown settlement. (Courtesy of Wikimedia Commons, available at http://upload.wikimedia.org/wikipedia/commons/3/3f/Maine_Fort.St.George_Map .1607.jpg, accessed April 4, 2015. Public Domain Map. This file has been identified as being free of known restrictions under copyright law, including all related and neighboring rights.)

Gradually, the settlers asked from the Virginia Company of London investors to send them skilled and experienced craftsmen, farmers, masons, blacksmiths, and fishermen. Jamestown endured years of war, famine, disease, and drought. It also enjoyed years of prosperity due to agriculture and trade of tobacco, beads, iron, and copper. The first wooden fort build of Jamestown was built around a church, a general store, and a small community. Successful application of logistics, learned through trial and error, greatly contributed to the legend of Jamestown being established as the first lasting British settlement in North America and the capital of Virginia from 1616 to 1699 (Smith 1624; Dill and Tartar 1980; APVA 2014a,b; NPS 2014a,b).

1.7.7 Railroads

Rail has been historically a significant component of logistics at both times of war and peace. The advancement of the railway can actually be separated into two components: (i) the advancement of the rails and wagons and (ii) the progress of motive power and the use of energy as a means of moving the wagons.

The first known railway in history was constructed in ancient Greece: the *paved tramway* of Diolkos was a significant innovation of the seventh century BC that, according to Pliny the Elder (50 AD), extended over 5 mi through the Corinth Canal in Peloponnese. It served for transporting ships across a peninsula and thus avoided an unsafe sea passage. The purpose of this ancient rail was not only to facilitate military logistics and exchange of supplies among allies but also to enhance regional trade and transport operations (Thucydides circa 450 BC; Polybius circa 170 BC; Lewis 2001).

The first manually propelled tubs were used in medieval Europe around the fifteenth century for underground works. The *parallel-tracks* concept was used in order to move commodities out of mines in a fast and efficient manner. As simplistic as this invention may sound to our modern standards, it was a significant breakthrough that enhanced the element of safety in the industry.

By 1603, the first above-ground wagon ways were used to boost regional trade. Railroads without engines were utilized in European coal mines since the mid-1500s. Loaded wagons were pulled initially by horses or men through wooden rails. By the eighteenth century, iron tracks and steam engines were introduced, and soon, the first steam locomotive was in use in Wales, England. By 1825, the Stockton and Darlington Railway of England was the first commercial firm to operate steam locomotives.

1.7.8 The Industrial Revolution

The development of rail technologies contributed to the Industrial Revolution (1760–1840), as the new transportation mode offered fast, safe, and efficient transportation throughout the supply chains, i.e., fast move of raw materials to manufactured goods that were distributed around the region. As railways expanded, so did the demand for raw materials and railroad spare parts. Moreover, this growth of trade and transport increased the standards of living through high demand for workers. Consequently, by the mid-nineteenth century, rail transportation took over as the prevailing mode of carriage of goods and people.

1.7.9 Railroads in America

While the British inventions of steam locomotives boosted the nation's trade and transport during the eighteenth and nineteenth centuries, the US key trade players were looking for groundbreaking technologies that would help them grow out of their intrastate commercial activities, most importantly, the rapidly growing US East Coast. During the eighteenth century alone, the East Coast regions, which were closer to the European coasts, grew 10-fold in terms of population and inhabited parts of land. As their industrial, agricultural, and overall trade activities blossomed, the East Coast traders were looking for faster and safer transportation modes to expand their activities to the Wild West. To measure the growth of America, it is worth noting that the United States is a vast nation with a total area of approximately 3.8 million mi^2 or 40 times the size of England. In terms of population, in the late-seventeenth century, US inhabitants were only 1/20 of the British population; from 1820 onwards, the US population would steadily exceed the British population. The first engines and rails employed in the United States were bought from *Stephenson Works* and other British manufacturers, and this trend continued right until the Civil War broke out. The growing American traders were eager to reap the benefits of this new land transportation mode that would decrease the hauling expenses by almost two-thirds. Benjamin Franklin (1706–1790), one of the founding fathers of America, who at the time was a newspaper editor, forecasted that the political and financial superiority would soon move from England to the United States (Lemon 2001).

The Baltimore and Ohio Railroad was the first common carrier railway and the first to deliver scheduled cargo and passenger service to the general public in the United States. While Baltimore was located closer to major inland trade networks of the eighteenth century, railways seemed to be the only way of competing the other major ports of the East Coast, such as New York (NY), Boston (MA), Philadelphia (PA), and Charleston (SC).

The *Mohawk & Hudson* rail was New York State's first chartered railway established in 1826. Its initial steam motor was known as the *DeWitt Clinton* (Figure 1.9), named after the designer of the Erie Canal. While built before the Baltimore and Ohio, financing delays postponed the construction of its route for several years. Once built, its 40-mi drifting canal journey that required an entire day to complete now became a 17-mi journey that required much less than an hour's time.

The Transcontinental Railroad became available in 1869. Its development was a major technological accomplishment of the United States, whose materialization could only be completed through a rail infrastructure of rocky soil extended over 2000 mi. Prior to its operation, inland travel was possible through either land (stagecoach) or sea. The price for stagecoach transport was over $1000 and required five to six months of travel in challenging landscapes such as deserts and mountainous regions. The second option was to navigate for over 18,000 nautical miles around South America. Both these options were costly and unsafe, yet the transcontinental railroad enabled a safe, luxury voyage in only five days at a price of $150 per person for a first-class cabin. The railroad set up an advanced transcontinental transporting network that changed the clusters of settlers and determined the financial growth of the Far West by connecting the advanced eastern states with the rapidly expanding west through trade and transport that was safer, faster, and cheaper.

FIGURE 1.9   The Dewitt Clinton Railroad. (Courtesy of American Rails. Photo of the Dewitt Clinton Railroad, circa 1893. The Columbian Exposition in Chicago. Available at http://www.american-rails.com/mohawk-and-hudson-railroad.html.)

1.7.10 The *Liberty* Ships in World War II: Building Warships
         Faster than the Enemy Could Sink Them

The Liberty ship program in World War II (WWII) was an effort to mass-produce ships capable of carrying military supplies, weapons, and even troops from the United States to the war in Europe. The significance of the Liberty ship is that when production was ramped up, the impression was that the ships could be built faster than the German U-boat submarines and the surface craft could sink them.

During WWII, President Franklin D. Roosevelt envisioned the United States to be "the great arsenal of democracy" and support the Allies that would defend the United States, which was neutral at that stage of the war. The Lend-Lease bill that was enforced on March 11, 1941 was an innovative concept formulated by US President Franklin D. Roosevelt and England's prime minister, Sir Winston Churchill. According to the agreement, the United States would provide England and its Allies with war equipment by means of purchase or leasing agreement. Over the next 4 years of the war, the United States provided its Allies with war equipment of a value exceeding $50 billion.

The notorious *Liberty ships* are the 2710 vessels of *EC2-type* single design, which were built as an *emergency* construction stipulated by the US Maritime Commission in WWII. The tremendous commitment and collective work to construct Liberty ships, the fact that ships of a sturdiest construction were built in less than five years at times of war, and the reality that many of these vessels lasted for multiple decades, i.e., exceeding the initial intention for a lifespan of five years, are the reasons why these ships deserve a special place in the global history of logistics and the history of America. The average shipbuilding process was about 70 days, although *SS Robert E. Peary* was built in less than 5 days (USMM 2014).

In Figure 1.10, holding a "Deeds, Not Words" banner, these proud men showcased that it only took them 41 days to complete the ship's construction. This is quite

FIGURE 1.10 "Deeds, Not Words". Twenty-eight male Delta Shipyard company workers in New Orleans, Louisiana during WWII, building Liberty Ship's Hull Number 34 of 2,560 tons in 41days. (Courtesy of the National World War II Museum, New Orleans. *Images Gift of Earl and Elaine Buras*, 1999.)

an achievement considering that almost a century later, it takes about seven months to construct a wooden recreational boat and about one to two years to construct a modern commercial vessel.

This was a standardized, mass-produced design: each ship had five holds that could carry around 9000 MT of cargo. From a logistics perspective, the entire country became a huge Liberty factory where 250,000 parts were prefabricated. Eighteen shipyards in the United States were exclusively established and dedicated for the assembly and welding the 250-ton sections. While 200 ships were sacrificed during WWII, the remaining 2510 ships were converted into tanker ships when the war was over.

The money to build the ships was raised through war bonds. Since the ship's cost was around $2 million, any group that raised $2 million in war bonds could suggest a name for a Liberty ship (Figure 1.11).

FIGURE 1.11 The construction of a Liberty ship at Bethlehem-Fairfield Shipyards Inc., Baltimore, Maryland (USA) in March/April 1943. (Courtesy of the United States Library of Congress's Prints and Photographs division under the digital ID fsa.8e01462. Author: United States. Office of War Information. Overseas Picture Division. Washington Division; 1944. Source: WikiCommons.)

The Liberty ships were a part of this support package: based on a simple and efficient yet outdated British ship design of 1879, American men and women across the nation developed the thousands of spare parts and ship components at an unparalleled rate of construction and assembly processing time in this remarkable logistics achievement. Figure 1.12 shows Miss Eastine Cowner, a former waitress, in Kaiser shipyards in Richmond, California. Miss Cowner is putting the finishing touches in her task as a scaler in the construction of the Liberty Ship SS George Washington Carver launched on May 7, 1943. ID: HD-SN-99-02466. On top of the 13 million men that were recruited in the US army and navy, it has been recorded that a large number of woman and minorities greatly contributed to this large-scale production. In 1943, the Young Women's Christian Association approximated that 12,000 young American-Indian females decided to leave the reservation in order to be employed in defense. By 1945, around 150,000 Native Americans were exclusively involved in defense areas of manufacturing and agriculture or recruited in the military. Figure 1.13 demonstrates the US contribution in WWII.

FIGURE 1.12 Scaler Eastine Cowner, Liberty Ship construction. (From http://www .dodmedia.osd.mil/DVIC_View/Still_Details.cfm?SDAN=HDSN9902466&JPGPath =/Assets/Still/1999/DoD/HD-SN-99-02466.JPG. Author: E. F. Joseph, US Office of War Information. Source: WikiCommons.)

US Army 1939		US Navy 1939	
Recruited men	174,000	Recruited men	126,400
Army Air Corps men	26,000	Marine Corps men Coast Guard men	19,700 10,000
Airplanes	2500	Warships	760
US Army 1945		**US Navy 1945**	
Recruited men	6,000,000	Recruited men	3,400,000
Army Air Corps men	2,400,000	Marine Corps men Coast Guard men	484,000 170,000
Airplanes	80,000	Warships, Liberty ships	2500
US Army Ships		**US Navy Ships**	
Over 1000 tons	1665	Large combatants	1388
Under 1000 tons, seagoing	1225	Auxiliaries	2048
Under 1000 tons, harbor	11,154	Large landing craft	4436
		Patrol/mine craft	1792
Named/numbered vessels	14,044	Yard craft	4070
Barges	8596	Named/numbered vessels	13,734
Amphibious assault craft	88,366	Small landing craft	60,974
Total army vessels excluding pontoons	**111,006**	**Total navy vessels excluding tracked amphibious vehicles**	**74,708**
Deadweight capacity of dry cargo and passenger ships	**17.3 million tons**	**Deadweight capacity of dry cargo and passenger ships**	**8.0 million tons**

FIGURE 1.13 US contribution in WWII. (Data compiled by the author based on data from Funk, C.E. and D. Litt [eds.], *International Year Book, A Compendium of The World's Progress For The Year*, R.S. Kain and M. Harmon, [associate eds.], New York and London, Funk & Wagnalls Company, 2014; Grover, D., *U.S. Army Ships and Watercraft of World War II*, Annapolis, MD, Naval Institute Press, 1987; Army, U.S. Army Center of Military History, Army Divisions in World War II, available at http:// www.history.army.mil, 2014; History, Navy, *Naval History and Heritage Command. US Navy Personnel in World War II and WWII Pacific Battles*, available at http://www .history.navy.mil, 2014; USMM, *Liberty Ships Built by the United States Maritime Commission. American Merchant Marine at War*, available at http://www.usmm.org /libertyships.html, 2014a; USMM, *World War II. American Merchant Marine at War*, available at http://www.usmm.org/ww2.html, 2014b.)

1.8 CONCLUSIONS

A concise history of logistics and transportation was presented through the stories of this chapter in order to show how necessity and the human desire to grow better and stronger shaped logistics into its modern form. At this point, very little has been discussed on the security challenges entailed that typically halt the logistics process. Theft, illegitimate trade and transport, piracy, and terrorism are among some of the numerous security threats that attack supply chains and hinder progress, reliability, and sustainability. All of these hazards, which represent the many faces of security, will be discussed in Chapter 2.

REFERENCES

Alderfer, C.P. 1969. An empirical test of a new theory of human needs. *Organizational Behavior and Human Performance*, Volume 4, Issue 2, pp. 142–175, May.

Alderfer, C.P. 1972. *Existence, Relatedness, and Growth; Human Needs in Organizational Settings*. New York: Free Press.

APVA. 2014a. Historic Jamestown. Available at http://apva.org/rediscovery/page.php ?page_id = 30. Accessed November 18, 2014.

APVA. 2014b. Historic Jamestown. Available at http://www.virginiaplaces.org/vacities /jamestowncap.html. Accessed November 18, 2014.

Aristotle. *Economics*. Book 2, Section 135. Available at http://www.perseus.tufts.edu. Accessed November 18, 2014.

Army. 2014. U.S. Army Center of Military History. 2014. Army Divisions in World War II. Available at http://www.history.army.mil. Accessed November 18, 2014.

Biles, J.J. 2003. Using spatial econometric techniques to estimate spatial multipliers: An assessment of regional economic policy in Yucatan, Mexico. *The Review of Regional Studies*, Vol. 33, No. 2, pp. 121–141, Oklahoma State University. Available at http://journal .srsa.org/ojs/index.php/RRS/article/viewFile/63/14. Accessed November 18, 2014.

BSI. 2014. BSI Supply Chain Solutions, Global Intelligence Report. April. Available at http://www.prnewswire.com/news-releases/bsis-global-intelligence-team-reports -supply-chain-trade-interruption-exceeded-300-billion-in-2013-256690551.html.

Burns, M. 2013a. Effectiveness evaluation of the maritime security risk analysis model and the dynamic risk management model. *Washington DC: TRB—Transportation Research Board of National Academies, Security Committee*, January 14–16.

Burns, M. 2013b. Estimating the impact of maritime security: Financial tradeoffs between security and efficiency. *Journal of Transportation Security, Elsevier*, December, Volume 6, Issue 4, pp. 329–338.

Burns, M. 2014a. A Texas tale of logistics and transport in the land "where 17 railroads meet the sea." *Houston History Magazine*, University of Houston. Available at https://houstonhistorymagazine.org/wp-content/uploads/2014/11/The-History-of -Logistics-by-Maria-Burns.pdf.

Burns, M. 2014b. Maritime Heritage Rediscovered: The Legacy of Sea Transport & Logistics from Prehistory to Modern Days. Houston Maritime Museum, History Lecture. Available at https://www.youtube.com/watch?v=PwWWwJqMMwg. Accessed November 18, 2014.

Burns-Kokkinaki, M. 2004. Alexander the Great of Macedonia, Greece. The True Story. Available at http://www.asxetos.gr/articles/greece/mega-alexandros-o-makedon-i -alithini-istoria-ii.html#ixzz3J9n4JkmU. Accessed November 18, 2014.

Congressional Record. 1975. Congressional Record 1975. US Senate Index, Congressional Record 121.

Congressional Record. 1976. Congressional Record 1976. US Senate Index, Congressional Record 122.

Dees, S., Karadeloglou, P., Kaufmann, R., and Sanchez, M. 2003. *Modelling the World Oil Market Assessment of a Quarterly Econometric Model.*

DHS. 2013. National Strategy for Global Supply Chain Security. March 18. Available at http://www.dhs.gov/national-strategy-global-supply-chain-security. Accessed August 1, 2014.

Dill, A.T. and Tartar, B. 1980. The "hellish scheme" to move the Capital. *Virginia Cavalcade*, Vol. 33, No. 1, Summer, pp. 4–11, USA.

Engels, D.W. 1978. *Alexander the Great and the Logistics of the Macedonian Army.* Berkeley: University of California Press, p. 119.

FEMA. 2008. Hurricane Ike Impact Report. Available at http://www.fema.gov/pdf/hazard/hurricane/2008/ike/impact_report.pdf. Accessed October 21, 2014.

Funk, C.E. and Litt, D. (eds.). 1944. *International Year Book, a Compendium of the World's Progress for the Year.* R.S. Kain and M. Harmon (associate eds.), Funk & Wagnalls Company, New York and London.

Grover, D.H. 1987. *U.S. Army Ships and Watercraft of World War II.* Annapolis, MD: Naval Institute Press.

Hicks, H. 2012. IT Matters, Managing Supply Chain Disruptions by Henry Hicks. Available at http://www.inboundlogistics.com/cms/article/managing-supply-chain-disruptions/. Accessed October 21, 2014.

History, Navy. 2014. Naval History and Heritage Command. US Navy Personnel in World War II & WWII Pacific Battles. Available at http://www.history.navy.mil. Accessed October 21, 2014.

Hsieh, D. 2014. Pharmaceutical Supply Chain Security Best Practices. Tyco Integrated Security Published. Available at http://www.tycois.com/blogs/business-security/pharmaceutical-supply-chain-security-best-practices. Accessed October 21, 2014.

Lemon, J. 2001. McIlwraith, T.F. and Muller, E.K. editors. *North America: The Historical Geography of a Changing Continent.* J. Lemon. *Colonial America in the 18th Century.* Rowman and Littlefield Publishers.

Lewis, M.J.T. 2001. Railways in the Greek and Roman world. In Guy, A. and Rees, J. (eds.), *Early Railways. A Selection of Papers from the First International Early Railways Conference.*

Maslow, A. 1954. *Motivation and Personality.* New York: Harper. p. 236.

Maslow, A.H. 1943. A theory of human motivation. *Psychological Review* 50 (4) 370–396. Available at http://psychclassics.yorku.ca/Maslow/motivation.htm. Accessed October 21, 2014.

Moran, P.A.P. 1950. Notes on Continuous Stochastic Phenomena Biometrika 37, pp. 17–23. Institute of Statistics, Oxford University.

Muller, W. 1810. The elements of the art of war. *The Scots Magazine*, Edinburgh Literary Miscellany, January, Germany.

National Geographic. 2005. The deadliest tsunami in history? Available at http://news.nationalgeographic.com/news/2004/12/1227_041226_tsunami.html. Accessed October 21, 2014.

NATO Dictionary. 1997. Available at http://www.nato.int. Accessed April 12, 2015.

New Oxford American Dictionary. 2014. Available at http://www.oxfordreference.com. Accessed November 12, 2014.

NPS. 2014a. National Park Service, Virginia. Available at http://www.nps.gov. Accessed November 9, 2014.

NPS. 2014b. Available at http://www.nps.gov/jame/historyculture/life-of-john-smith.htm. Accessed November 9, 2014.

Pederson, N., Hessl, A.E., Baatarbileg, N., Anchukaitis, K.J., and Di Cosmo, N. 2013. Pluvials, droughts, the Mongol Empire, and Modern Mongolia. K.W. Butzer (ed.), The University of Texas at Austin, Austin, Texas, *Proceedings of the National Academy of Sciences of the United States of America*. Vol. 111, No. 12, pp. 4375–4379.

Pliny the Elder. 50 AD. The Natural History Plin. Nat. 4.5.

Polybius. circa 170 BC. Histories. 4.19.77-79 and 5.101.4. Histories of. Polybius published in Vol. III of the Loeb Classical Library edition, 1922–1927.

Port of Hamburg. 2013. CRS Report for Congress, 2004. Received through the CRS Web Order Code RL32705, Border and Transportation Security: Overview of Congressional Issues, December 17, 2004. Available at http://www.hafen-hamburg.de. Accessed May 12, 2013.

Smith, J. 1624. *The General History of Virginia, New England & the Summer Isles, Together with the True Travels, Adventures and Observations, and a Sea Grammar—* Volume 1, Chapter XII. The Arrival of the Third Supply, published 1624 (Source: Library of Congress).

Smith, R. 2014. Genghis Khan's secret weapon was rain. *National Geographic*, published March 10. Available at http://news.nationalgeographic.com/news/2014/03/140310-genghis-khan-mongols-mongolia-climate-change. Accessed September 3, 2014.

The Oxford English Dictionary. 2014. Available at http://www.oed.com. Accessed November 12, 2014.

Thucydides. Circa 450 BC. *A History of the Peloponnesian War*. 3.15.1 and 8.7–8.

United Nations. 2009. Annual Session 169 CDS 09 E rev 1—The Growing Threat of Piracy to Regional and Global Security. Lord Jopling (United Kingdom)—General Rapporteur. Available at http://www.nato-pa.int/default.asp?SHORTCUT=1770. Accessed September 3, 2014.

USCG. 2014. Tsunami and earthquake research at the USGS. USGS Coastal and Marine Geology Program. Pacific Coastal & Marine Science Center. Available at http://walrus.wr.usgs.gov/tsunami. Accessed September 3, 2014.

USMM. 2014a. *Liberty Ships Built by the United States Maritime Commission. World War II. American Merchant Marine at War*. Available at http://www.usmm.org/libertyships.html. Accessed December 3, 2014.

USMM. 2014b. United States Merchant Marine. *World War II. Merchant Marine at War*. Available at http://www.usmm.org/ww2.html. Accessed September 3, 2014. Accessed December 3, 2014.

WHO. 2014. World Health Organization. International Classification of External Causes of Injury (ICECI). Available at http://www.who.int/classifications/icd/adaptationsiceci/en/. Accessed April 10, 2015.

Willis, H.H., Morral, A.R., Kelly, T.K., and Medby, J.J. 2005. Estimating Terrorism Risk. By Rand Corporation. Available at http://www.rand.org/pubs/monographs/MG388.html. Accessed December 3, 2014.

CHAPTER 2

The Many Faces of Security

> If your enemy is secure at all points, be prepared for him.
> If he is in superior strength, evade him.
> If your opponent is temperamental, seek to irritate him.
> Pretend to be weak, that he may grow arrogant.
> If he is taking his ease, give him no rest.
> If his forces are united, separate them.
> If sovereign and subject are in accord, put division between them.
> Attack him where he is unprepared, appear where you are not expected.
>
> **Sun Tzu**
> *The Art of War*

2.1 INTRODUCTION

This chapter addresses the diverse aspects of security that impact the resiliency of supply chains. Such security threats may be motivated by financial, commercial, political, ideological, or other motives. Based upon the principle that commercial disruptions have a direct impact on the security of societies and nations, it is not uncommon for any illegitimate activities such as drug smuggling, piracy, security, and human trafficking to have a commercial, social, and national security impact.

Globalization and new technologies have enabled global supply chains to expand geographically in search of supply chain partners that will offer low-cost, high-value commodities or services. The rule is that "our supply chains are as vulnerable as our weakest links." Indeed, as global networks spread out to encompass new global players (be it investors, manufacturers, vendors, distributors, and so on), supply chains become more vulnerable to security threats.

Global supply chains and logistics need to be secure for a number of reasons; among others,

- They fuel the globalization process and help form powerful alliances with companies around the world.
- They are strongly related with national security: their systemic vulnerabilities become critical infrastructure vulnerabilities (Chapter 4) and hurt our nation, whereas their systemic integrity and compliance in security regulations support national security.

- They are the backbone of economy, generating jobs and tax money, therefore contributing to the standards of living and the nation's economic, diplomatic, and eventually military power.

Let us just consider that a major supply chain may consist of a handful of key players (i.e., major government entities, investors, conglomerates, oil majors, and manufacturers) and literally thousands of smaller players (i.e., vendors, warehouse facilities, exporters, brokers, distributors, and so on).

Whereas larger corporate entities may have risk management security systems and technologies in place, smaller companies may struggle with security compliance due to limited resources.

In a real corporate world setting, smaller companies or businesses located in less-developed regions may not have the time, finances, or knowledge of the global regulatory framework. As a result, they may not be able to follow the proper security protocols during, e.g., human- and cargo-screening processes, or when conducting in-depth background checks of their partners. In cases of cargo theft, or smuggling of illegitimate cargoes and human trafficking, it is not uncommon of internal employees to assist and support the intruder or to work on their own. Indicative examples of such cases include tampering of security technologies, falsification of records, or deviating from the standard security protocols.

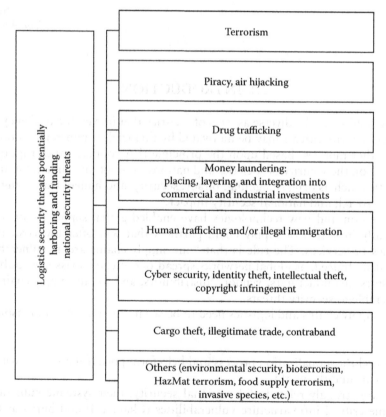

FIGURE 2.1 Logistics security threats potentially harboring—and funding—national security threats.

At a more challenging level, it is not uncommon for activists or terrorists to penetrate specific supply chains in order to become familiar with the security protocols, technologies used, and systemic vulnerabilities.

As depicted in Figure 2.1, this chapter deals with the many faces of security and associates logistics and supply chain security with threats that may spread beyond economic and commercial damage.

2.1.1 The Many Faces of Security

Human security and national security cannot be narrowed down to strictly territorial or military threats. Instead, the national security is closely aligned with the human factor, which is vulnerable due to threats of terrorism; social, cultural, and religious disputes; socioeconomic disintegration; pollution; human and drug trafficking; health threats; famine; illegitimate trade; and so on.

The *United Nations Human Development Report 1994* (UN 1994) of the United Nations Development Program (UNDP) considers that national and human security are vulnerable to seven main categories of threats, including (1) economic security, (2) food security, (3) health security, (4) environmental security, (5) personal security, (6) community security, and (7) political security.

2.2 THE ORIGINAL SUPPLY CHAIN SECURITY THEOREM

Based upon the principle that breaching security is a crime, this section commences by applying existing theories on social crimes, such as

- The crime opportunity theory (Section 2.2.1)
- The victimization theory (Section 2.2.2)
- The crime pattern theory (Section 2.2.3)

Furthermore, the original supply chain security theorem (Section 2.2.4) is introduced, which distinguishes the motives for breaching security rules into financial and ideological. Moreover, it explains how regardless of the motive, an industry-intended security attack will impose damages to national security and vice versa.

Such theories may well fit into the trade and transport industries, and their scope is to better understand the motives, reasons, and forces behind unintentional and deliberate attempts to breach security.

2.2.1 Crime Opportunity Theory

The crime opportunity theory suggests that offenders plan their criminal actions based on rational decisions, preferring targets of maximum benefits and minimum risk. This chapter investigates the different security-related crimes and depicts that this is typically the case in most crimes, from cargo theft to piracy, with the exception of terrorist attacks, where ideology and empathy seem to outweigh the risk taken.

The likelihood of a crime relies upon two elements: (1) the existence of at least one determined offender who is prepared or ready to participate in a criminal action and

(2) the environmental circumstances that will empower the offender to commit the crime. All criminal activities necessitate opportunity; however, not every opportunity is associated with crime (Hindelang et al. 1978). In the same manner, a determined offender may be the catalyst that carries out a particular criminal action, but other factors and resources are also required to be in place.

2.2.2 Lifestyle Exposure or Victimization Theory

For a crime to be conducted, three essential elements must exist: (1) a determined offender, (2) a target that will bring criminals the anticipated rewards (i.e., be it money, civil unrest, or revenge), and (3) target vulnerability. (Cohen and Felson 1979; Cohen et al. 1980). This may entail structural vulnerabilities, insufficient security controls, lack of guards or scanning technologies, or even an insufficient regulatory framework to provide for security measures.

Security threats, like any crime, need to have an inclined, determined perpetrator that will identify potential vulnerabilities within a specific time and place framework. Within a logistics and supply chain environment, vulnerabilities such as lack of monitoring or lack of defense may entail the 16 critical infrastructure sections as stipulated by the Department of Homeland Security (DHS; see Chapter 4: Table 4.2: USA: 16 Critical Infrastructure Sectors and Sector-Specific Agencies).

The crime opportunity theory suggests that a potential offender has identified a suitable and vulnerable target within a specific time and place.

Therefore, opportunity will become the constraining factor that impacts the consequence in circumstances vulnerable to criminal activities, since the offender typically has virtually limited control over the circumstances of the environment, and the conditions that allow specific crimes are usually uncommon, improbable, or avoidable.

People or groups of people may commit crimes when there is a triggering occurrence and a method by which such people can identify a vulnerable target or a victim that matches within a feasible crime pattern.

The *victimization theory* may well fit into supply chains and logistics activities, as perpetrators can examine the scheduled day-to-day procedures, which take place at diverse nodes of activity, in particular spatiotemporal activity patterns. This leads us to the crime pattern theory.

2.2.3 Crime Pattern Theory

Crime is seldom accidental; it is either intended or opportunistic. Crime can only occur when an offender's activity territory crosses a target's territory within a specific time and space, including cyberspace. Given that an industrial, national, or personal territory consists of nodal points, the crime pattern theory suggests that a security offense can only take place when the activity orbits of both meet.

Vulnerabilities may be created in places and times of limited situational awareness due to distractions. In other words, security vulnerabilities within a supply chain or a nation's critical infrastructure sections may occur due to a high flow of goods and people combined with limited monitoring. Therefore, security offenders choose to strike specific targets, at a specific time and place, when the attention span is limited (e.g., Boston Marathon bombings of 2013).

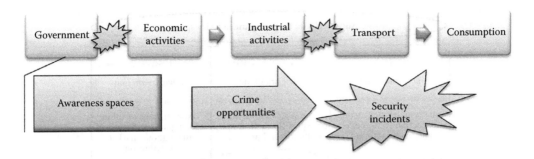

FIGURE 2.2   Mapping supply chain security threats based on the vulnerability and crime theories.

Figure 2.2 depicts a map of security threats and how the activity space is targeted based on the vulnerability and crime theories. Furthermore, Figure 2.3 shows the security vulnerabilities in a typical supply chain network.

The main principles of the vulnerability and crime theories entail

1. *Awareness space*: A boundary created by the routes to and from supply chain nodes.
2. *Personal pathway*: The route that companies or social groups take to and from usual locations of activity.
3. *Node*: A specific activity point that an industry or a group of people occupies regularly or at a predictable time, e.g., critical infrastructure sectors either serve regular large-scale activities (highways, hub ports) or follow a scheduled pattern of operations at a specific timetable, i.e., churches and offices.
4. *Critical activity area*: Identifies a location of critical significance where security incidents are likely to occur, e.g., critical infrastructure sectors.
5. *Crime generator*: An area that attracts a large amount of social or commercial activities. For example, cargo theft (pilferage) in busy ports or terrorist attacks targeting crowded areas. Crime-generating areas may eventually become crime attractors as the opportunity of criminals being unnoticed is high.
6. *Crime attractors*: A location that attracts offenders due to its recognized opportunity for crime.

Based on the crime theories and motives, this chapter is focused on security threats, which encompass intentional, deceptive acts with the purpose of *obtaining personal gain* typically through illegitimate trade or travel, theft, or fraud. Security threats in this category may include

a. Compromising the integrity, confidentiality, and availability of private information (corporate or individual), such as cyber security threat, tampering trade and/or transport documents, and so on
b. Theft (pilferage) of tangible resources, i.e., money, information, commodities, or other physical assets
c. Sea piracy, combined with theft
d. Illegitimate traveling, illegal immigration, illegal employment, and human trafficking
e. Illegitimate trade and contraband, e.g., smuggling of drugs, weapons, and so on
f. Fraud, such as providing false evidence, tampering data, and so on
g. Cybercrimes, such as gaining access to sensitive information of national significance

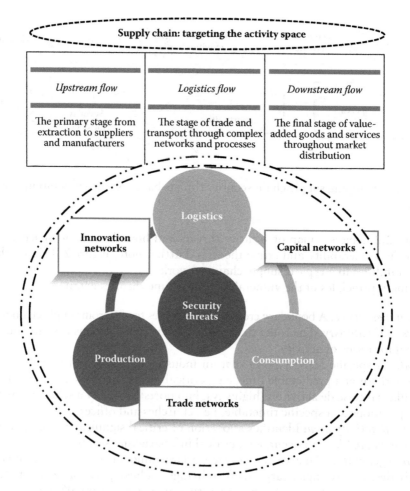

FIGURE 2.3   Global supply chain security: Vulnerabilities in activity space. (From the author.)

As illustrated in Table 2.1, the US Department of Transportation's (DOT's) Vulnerability Assessment threats are classified into four categories:

- Physical attacks
- Biological attacks
- Chemical attacks
- Cyber and command, control, and communications (C3) attacks

Among these categories, physical, biological, and chemical attacks are mostly driven by ideological motives, whereas financial motives are likely to target cyber attacks (together with piracy, theft, illegitimate trade, and travel as explained in Section 2.2.4). Table 2.1 provides a list of scenarios considered in the US DOT Vulnerability Assessment.

The global supply chain and logistics activities typically entail a plethora of key players and processes that are classified into internal and external logistics. Internal logistics is focused on improving the corporate performance, by increasing cost efficiency and

TABLE 2.1   Scenarios Considered in the US DOT Vulnerability Assessment

Attack Type	Scenarios
Physical Attacks	
• Car bomb at bridge approach • Series of small explosives on highway bridge • Single small explosive on highway bridge • Single small explosive in highway tunnel • Car bomb in highway tunnel • Series of car bombs on adjacent bridges or tunnels • Bomb(s) detonated at pipeline compressor stations • Bomb detonated at pipeline storage facility • Bomb detonated on pipeline segment • Simultaneous attacks on ports • Terrorist bombing of waterfront pavilion • Container vessel fire at marine terminal • Ramming of railroad bridge by maritime vessel	• Attack on passenger vessel in port • Shooting in rail station • Vehicle bomb adjacent to rail station • Bombing of airport transit station • Bombing of underwater transit tunnel • Bus bombing • Deliberate blocking of highway–rail grade crossing • Terrorist bombing of rail tunnel • Bomb detonated on train in rail station • Vandalism of track structure and signal system • Terrorist bombing of rail bridge • Explosive attack on multiple rail bridges • Explosive in cargo of passenger aircraft
Biological Attacks	
• Biological release in multiple subway stations • Anthrax release from freight ship	• Anthrax release in transit station • Anthrax release on passenger train
Chemical Attacks	
• Sarin release in multiple subway stations	• Physical attack on railcar carrying toxics
Cyber and C3 Attacks	
• Cyber attack on highway traffic control system • Cyber attack on pipeline control system • Attack on port power/telecommunications	• Sabotage of train control system • Tampering with rail signals • Cyber attack on train control center

Source: National Research Council, Improving Surface Transportation Security, a Research and Development Strategy, Washington, DC, National Academy Press, 1999.

regulatory compliance, while eliminating errors and duplication of efforts. Internal security threats may occur when potential criminal activities penetrate the supply chain and affect the production, manufacturing, and value-added services by theft; sabotage; cybercrime; forging of documentation; obtaining critical financial-, commercial-, or government-related information; and so on. Conversely, external logistics includes raw materials, vendor and trade activities, warehousing, and transportation. Therefore, external security threats may be caused by entities who may attack the external functions of logistics, affecting diverse geographical locations, and one or more key players of the supply chain. What internal and external security threats have in common is that they can encompass the same categories of attacks as stipulated in Table 2.1, i.e., physical, biological, chemical, and cyber and C3 attacks. Furthermore, as reflected in Figure 2.4, security vulnerabilities appear in both the internal and external logistics processes.

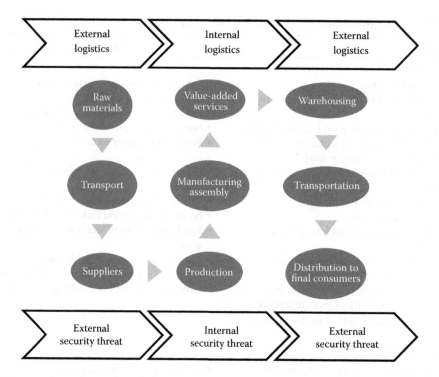

FIGURE 2.4   Security vulnerabilities in internal and external logistics' processes. (From the author.)

The following sections of this chapter demonstrate the many faces of security and show how different motives may trigger different security threats, and cause distinct impacts, at different levels.

2.2.4 The Original Supply Chain Security Theorem II: The Interconnectivity between National Security and Commercial Security

In an effort to classify and explain the reason beyond security threats, the attackers' motives can be roughly classified as either financial or ideological (political, religious, and so on).

The supply chain security theorem reflects the interconnectivity between national security and commercial security. As demonstrated in Figure 2.5, in the case of financial motives, the criminals focus on obtaining tangible benefits (i.e., money or commodities) or intangible benefits (such as commercial intelligence or financial information) and therefore are most likely to attack the industry. Their criminal acts include but are not limited to sea piracy, illegitimate trade, contraband, illegitimate travel and human trafficking, cargo theft, cyber attacks, and so on. Despite their motive, such actions affect not only the economy but also the social and national (or regional) security structures.

On the other hand, Figure 2.6 shows that when the motives are driven by ideological empathy, such as political, religious, cultural, or other social differences, the attackers are most likely to attack the government or innocent civilians. However, supply chains and critical infrastructures become their inadvertent target. As an example, the 9/11 terrorist

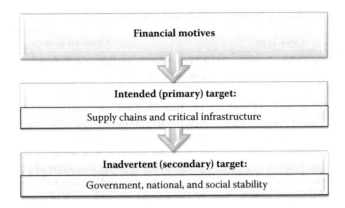

FIGURE 2.5   Security attack targets based on financial motives.

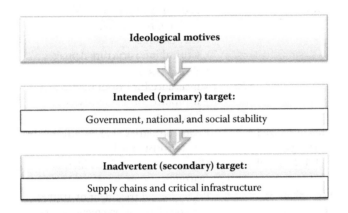

FIGURE 2.6   Security attack targets based on ideological motives.

attacks were aiming to cause loss of life, social intimidation, and political instability in the United States; however, these attacks also destroyed the World Trade Center. The latter action did not bring them financial gains but was regarded as a powerful symbol of the American economic and military supremacy.

To support this interconnectivity between national security and commercial security, it is worth considering some major terrorist attacks: although their motive was ideological, i.e., religious or political, such acts of terror seriously impacted trade and transport. The contrary is also correct: typically, financial motives dictate acts of illegitimate transport such as for

a. Humans, i.e., the use of transportation modes such as container boxes or trucks for illegitimate immigration or human trafficking
b. Cargoes, i.e., contraband and narcotics

Although the motives behind these actions are strictly financial, the vulnerabilities uncovered and exploited from such actions can be detrimental to national security. Tables 2.2 and 2.3 demonstrate major terrorist attacks where the supply chain theory can be verified.

TABLE 2.2   Socioeconomic Consequences of the 9/11 Attack

Consequences	Loss Type	Detailed Losses	
Social aspects	Loss of life	2752 fatalities, including 400 law enforcement officers	
	Increase in – Stress and anxiety – Post-traumatic stress disorder (PTSD) – Depression Decrease in – Employee health – Security – Productivity	8–10% of the New York City residents claimed signs and symptoms commensurate with PTSD and depressive disorders 40% of the nation's population encountered considerable signs of emotional stress and anxiety linked to the attacks	
Economic losses	Direct and indirect losses	Direct loss of physical assets – Federal- and state-related losses – Building restoration – City cleanup – Critical infrastructure damages	$28 billion
		Indirect losses – Insurance for loss of life – Insurance for loss of assets – Trade and transport losses	$36 billion
Economic losses	Unmaterialized earnings $11.4–14.2 billion	Reduced salaries in areas afflicted by the terrorist attack	$3.6–6.4 billion
		Victims' unmaterialized lifetime earnings	$7.8 billion
Socioeconomic losses	Psychological treatment	Psychological treatment of 10,000 persons (law enforcement agents and civilians) affected by the attack (PTSD, depression)	$4.3 billion
Total socioeconomic losses attributed to the 9/11 terrorist attack			$79.7 billion
Economic and Commercial Losses Attributed to the 9/11 Terrorist Attack			
Direct financial and asset losses	Loss of assets	Federal emergency funds (increased sea, land, aviation security, sky marshals, federal government airport and port security, aviation antiterrorist technologies, Afghanistan operations)	$40 billion
		Four commercial aircrafts	$385 million
	Insurance costs	Insurance	$40 billion
	Cleanup	Incident cleanup costs	$1.3 billion
Critical asset damages	Damages	Critical infrastructure damage	$10–13 billion
		Pentagon, asset damage	$1 billion
		World Trade Center, building damage	$3–4.5 billion
		Damaged assets	$21.8 billion
			(*Continued*)

TABLE 2.2 (CONTINUED)   Socioeconomic Consequences of the 9/11 Attack

Consequences	Loss Type	Detailed Losses	
Unmaterialized financial gains		Direct loss of employment: 83,000 Lost wages: $17 billion	$17 billion
		Aviation industry losses	$10 billion
Estimated total loss of assets		New York City, state losses (damages, jobs, taxes, loss of resources)	$95 billion

Source: Burns, M., Supply *Chain Security: A Strategy to Resilience through Policies, Partnerships, and Technologies*, DHS Supply Chain Security Workshop, April, Houston, Texas, 2014; Burns, M., *Journal of Transportation Security*, December 2013, Volume 6, Issue 4, pp. 329–338, May 31, 2013; Comptroller NYC, New York City Comptroller Report: One Year Later, The Fiscal Impact of 9/11 on New York City, available at http://comptroller.nyc.gov/legacy-url/?q=press/2002_releases/02-09-054.shtm, accessed October 6, 2014, 2002; ILO, International Labour Organization: The impact of the 2001–2002 crisis on the hotel and tourism industry, available at http://www.ilo.org, accessed October 12, 2014, 2003; Milken Institute, The impact of September 11 on U.S. metropolitan economies, available at http://www.milkeninstitute.org/pdf/National_Metro_Impact_Report.pdf, accessed October 15, 2014.

2.3 TERRORISM: NETWORKS AND AFFILIATIONS

2.3.1 Piracy vs. Terrorism

Even though global and national legislations view that both terrorism and piracy are criminal acts, there appears to be a contrast among the motives, degree of threat, and potential of damage. The author hereby distinguishes man-made security threats into piracy and terrorism based on their motive.

   a. *Piracy, whose motivator is purely financial.* Their key objective is to attain financial benefits through hijacking ships and their cargoes, and occasionally through capturing hostages, to leverage ransom payments.
   b. *Terrorism, whose motives are typically associated with prejudice, hostility, and hate crimes.* It is ignited by political, social, economic, racial, religious, or dogmatic differences and seeks to induce social turmoil and fear. According to the US Department of State, *terrorism* signifies premeditated, politically motivated violence perpetrated against noncombatant targets by subnational groups or clandestine agents (US Department of State, 22 USC Sec. 2656f). Terrorists aim to generate social turmoil, and intimidate a nation's or ethnic group's sense of pride, through loss of life, destruction of critical infrastructure, and socioeconomic stability.

2.3.2 Defining Terrorism

Acts of terrorism are defined as the "intentional acts that are committed with the aim of seriously intimidating a population, or unduly compelling a Government or international organization to perform or abstain from performing any act, or seriously destabilizing or destroying the fundamental political, constitutional, economic or social structures of a country or an international organization" (Europa 2002).

TABLE 2.3 Organized Terrorist Group Attacks (Connected Type)

Attack Date and Place	Fatalities	Injuries	Other Impacts
September 11, 2001 (New York City and Pentagon, United States)			
Attack Type	2977	6294	Commercial and Economic Impacts:
Plane hijacking	victims,	hospitalized	The national economy slowed down. Billions of dollars' financial loss, including
Terrorist Affiliations	19	10,000 PTSD	trade, transport and travel insurance, unmaterialized costs due to cancelled trade
Al-Qaeda	hijackers		and transport activities, including
Attack Motive			• Supply chain disruptions caused by closure of air, land, and sea transportation.
Religious/political fanaticism			• Supply chain deviations.
Citizenship			• Closure of businesses.
Vast majority: Saudi Arabian citizens			• Change in diplomatic relations and trade agreements.
			Economic Recovery:
			One year, i.e., much faster than economists initially anticipated.
			Resilience, Lessons Learned:
			20% of members increased business security measures.
			52% implemented more robust risk management protocols and vulnerability
			assessments.
			47% improved security at access points.
October 12, 2002 (2002 Bali bombing, Bali, Indonesia)			
Attack Type	202	240+	Commercial and Economic Impacts:
Suicide bomb, car bomb, bomb			The national economy slowed down. Billions of dollars' financial loss, including
vest; use of potassium chlorate.			trade, transport and travel insurance, unmaterialized costs due to cancelled trade
Terrorist Affiliations			and transport activities, including
Jemaah Islamiyah, a violent			• Supply chain disruptions caused by closure of air, land, and sea transportation.
Islamist group affiliated with			• Supply chain deviations.
Al-Qaeda.			• Closure of businesses.
Attack Motive			• Change in diplomatic relations and trade agreements.
Religious/political fanaticism.			• 57% reduction in tourism revenue.
			• Tourists were warned not to travel to Indonesia.

(Continued)

TABLE 2.3 (CONTINUED) Organized Terrorist Group Attacks (Connected Type)

Attack Date and Place	Fatalities	Injuries	Other Impacts
			• Bali generated over 25% of Indonesia's foreign exchange revenue, and this was reduced to 12% within a year.
			• Hotel occupancy after the attack dropped from 80% to 18%. As a result, 2.7 million tourism workers were unemployed.
			Resilience, Lessons Learned:
			• The government implemented more robust antiterrorism strategies and admitted that they had been previously overoptimistic—despite the 9/11 attacks.
			• Terrorists were arrested.
			• Financial losses and collapse of the tourism industry motivated the country to work harder and better. As a result they obtained numerous global tourism awards and managed to recover within a year from the event.
			• The nation has retained their stringent antiterrorism and security protocols.
			• Improvements in emergency response and medical response.
March 11, 2004 (Madrid, Spain)	191 + 4 suicide bombers	2050+	Commercial and Economic Impacts:
Attack Type			No financial or commercial impacts.
Mass transportation: backpack bombs in rail network			Spain's tourism and trade were not affected.
Terrorist Affiliations			Political Impacts:
Islamic extremists "inspired through the Internet" by "terrorist cells"			The attack, which occurred four days after the national elections, supported the labor party.
Drug traffickers of Moroccan origin, remotely linked to al-Qaeda cells			Resilience, Lessons Learned:
			Lone-wolf attacks vs. organized terrorist groups.
Attack Motive			• Despite the social fear and emotional impact, in lone-wolf attacks, national economic and commercial activities are less impacted, and likely to recover rapidly, especially if the terrorists are arrested or killed.
Religious fanaticism			• The least resilient attacks are the ones related to organized terrorist groups. In these cases, even the death of the terrorists is not a social relief, as these individuals represent much larger terrorist groups, which may be likely to strike again.
Citizenship			
Spanish with Moroccan origin			

(Continued)

TABLE 2.3 (CONTINUED) Organized Terrorist Group Attacks (Connected Type)

Attack Date and Place	Fatalities	Injuries	Other Impacts
October 7, 2004 (Sinai, Egypt)	34	105	
Attack Type Bombings made of TNT and other explosives, cell phones, washing machine timers, and modified gas cylinders			Commercial and Economic Impacts: • This attack occurred in luxury holiday resorts and hotel complexes in North Sinai (Tamba, Sharm, and Dahab regions that are popular among Israeli and *western* tourists). This is a region that played a crucial role in the *six-day war* or *Arab–Israeli war* of 1967.
Terrorist Affiliations Al-Qaeda and Islamic extremists: militant group Tawhid and Jihad (meaning monotheism and holy war)			• Egypt's tourism industry generates over $6.4 billion each year. It is speculated that the attackers targeted the region in order to damage the country's tourism industry. Nevertheless, after the arrest of the suspects, the economic and commercial impacts to the country were minimal.
Attack Motive Religious/political fanaticism			Resilience, Lessons Learned: • The loss of lives and injuries impacted the community. However, due to long-term security threats, India was able to recover fast.
Citizenship Egyptians and Palestinians (3 terrorists sentenced to death and 2400 were arrested)			• This suggests that preparedness and psychological familiarization with security-related disasters may help the rapid recovery from the most challenging disasters.
November 26–28, 2008 (Mumbai Attacks, India) (26/11 is India's 9/11)	164 + 10 attackers	600+ injured and numerous local and foreign hostages	
Attack Type 60-h nonstop bombings, siege, shootings, and hostage crisis; 10 militants armed with AK-47 assault rifles, rioting with grenades and bags of RDX explosives			Commercial and Economic Impacts: The national economy slowed down. Billions of dollars' financial loss, including trade, transport, and travel insurance, unmaterialized costs due to cancelled trade and transport activities, including • Supply chain disruptions caused by closure of air, land, and sea transportation. • Supply chain deviations. • Closure of businesses. • Change in diplomatic relations and trade agreements.

(Continued)

TABLE 2.3 (CONTINUED) Organized Terrorist Group Attacks (Connected Type)

Attack Date and Place	Fatalities	Injuries	Other Impacts
Terrorist Affiliations Members of Lashkar-e-Taiba, Pakistan; it is called "the next Al-Qaeda," and affiliations with Al-Qaeda are suspected Attack Motive Religious/political fanaticism Citizenship Pakistani			• The 2008 economic crisis hit India even harder. • Political resignations. • −3% of GDP and annual growth slowdown compared to previous fiscal year. • Discouraged foreign investors. • Both losses of traditional tourism and benefits from *terror tourism*. • The Mumbai economy slowed down, as the city contributes to 40% of India's foreign trade, 60% of the country's customs duty collections, $10 billion in corporate taxes, and 40% of national income taxation, as well as 20% of central excise collections. Resilience, Lessons Learned: • The loss of lives and injuries impacted the community. However, due to long-term security threats, India was able to recover faster than the United States in 9/11 or United Kingdom in 7/21. • It has been reported that despite the psychological effect, the public transportation was available an hour after the event. Offices, schools, and government buildings remained open. • This suggests that preparedness and psychological familiarization with security-related disasters may help with rapid recovery from the most challenging disasters.

(Continued)

TABLE 2.3 (CONTINUED)   Organized Terrorist Group Attacks (Connected Type)

Attack Date and Place	Fatalities	Injuries	Other Impacts
December 8, 2009 (Baghdad, Iraq)			
Attack Type	127	448	Commercial and Economic Impacts:
Five suicide car bombings in three targets: Iraq's Ministry of Finance and Ministry of Labor and a courthouse			The series of attacks in Iraq are targeted against the Iraqi government and the United States. Nevertheless, since these events are frequent in the region, the national economy and industries have become more resilient in such attacks.
Terrorist Affiliations			Resilience, Lessons Learned:
Al-Qaeda group formed by Iraqi citizens, affiliated with former Baathists based in Syria; more recent incidents followed where Pakistani extremist groups joined this terrorist consortium			• The loss of lives and injuries impacted the community. However, due to long-term security threats, Iraq was able to recover faster than other nations where similar events occur for the first time. • This suggests that preparedness and psychological familiarization with security-related disasters may help with rapid recovery from the most challenging disasters.
Attack Motive			
Attacks aimed to cause disruptions and fight the Iraqi government and US forces in the country; this terrorist attack was followed by subsequent attacks			
Citizenship			
Iraqi			

(Continued)

TABLE 2.3 (CONTINUED) Organized Terrorist Group Attacks (Connected Type)

Attack Date and Place	Fatalities	Injuries	Other Impacts
2013–2014 (ongoing attacks) (Nigeria)			
Attack Type	3400+	Numerous	Commercial and Economic Impacts:
Suicide bombings usually by women	killed in	thousands injured	The national economy slowed down. Billions of dollars' financial loss, including trade, transport, and travel insurance, unmaterialized costs due to cancelled trade and transport activities, including
Terrorist Affiliations	146+	Hundreds	• Supply chain disruptions caused by closure of air, land, and sea transportation.
Boko Haram, Islamist extremists	attacks in	kidnapped, among	• Supply chain deviations.
Attack Motive	2013	which many	• Closure of businesses.
Religious fanaticism	and	young girls	• Change in diplomatic relations and trade agreements.
Citizenship	2014		• The 2008 economic crisis hit India even harder.
Nigerian			• Political resignations.
			• –3% of GDP and annual growth slowdown compared to previous fiscal year.
			• Discouraged foreign investors.
			• Both losses of traditional tourism, and benefits from *terror tourism*.
			• The Mumbai economy slowed down, as the city contributes to 40% of India's foreign trade, 60% of the country's customs duty collections, $10 billion in corporate taxes, and 40% of national income taxation, as well as 20% of central excise collections.

(Continued)

TABLE 2.3 (CONTINUED) Organized Terrorist Group Attacks (Connected Type)

Attack Date and Place	Fatalities	Injuries	Other Impacts
			Resilience, Lessons Learned:

• The loss of lives and injuries impacted the community. However, due to long-term security threats, India was able to recover faster than the United States in 9/11 or United Kingdom in 7/21. It has been reported that despite the psychological effect, the public transportation was available an hour after the event. Offices, schools, and government buildings remained open.
• This suggests that preparedness and psychological familiarization with security-related disasters may help with rapid recovery from the most challenging disasters.

Source: Compiled by the author based on 911 Memorial, National September 11 Memorial & Museum, available at http://www.911memorial.org/faq, accessed November 1, 2014, 2014; Acharya, A., Mandal, S., and Mehta, A., *Terrorist Attacks in Mumbai: Picking Up the Pieces. A report by* International Centre for Political Violence and Terrorism Research (ICPVTR), S. Rajaratnam School for International Studies, Nanyang Technological University, Singapore, available at http://www.pvtr.org/pdf/globalanalysis/analysis%20of%20the%20november%202008%20 mumbai%20terror%20attacks.pdf, accessed November 1, 2014, 2008; GAO, Government Accountability Office. *Health Effects in the Aftermath of the World Trade Center,* available at http://www.gao.gov/new.items/d041068t.pdf, accessed November 1, 2014, 2004; LCCI, The economic effects on terrorism on London, London Chamber of Commerce and Industry, available at http://www.londonchamber.co.uk/docim ages/754.pdf, accessed November 1, 2014, 2005; Panagariya, A., *The Economic Cost of the Mumbai Tragedy,* available at http://www.forbes .com/2008/11/29/mumbai-economic-cost-oped-cx_ap_1129panagariya.html, accessed November 1, 2014, 2008; Princeton, Non-American casualties of the September 11 attacks, available at https://www.princeton.edu/~achaney/tmve/wiki100k/docs/Non-American_casualties_of _the_September_11_attacks.html, accessed November 1, 2014, 2002; Sherlock, S., *The Bali Bombing. What It Means for Indonesia,* Foreign Affairs Defense and Trade Group, Department of the Parliamentary Library, Australia, available at http://www.aph.gov.au/binaries/library /pubs/cib/2002-03/03cib04.pdf, accessed November 1, 2014, 2002.

2.3.3 Terrorism, Global Trade, and Transport

The association between terrorism and global trade became obvious during the terrorist attacks of September 11, 2001, which targeted the Twin Towers, the premises of World Trade Center. While these attacks were mankind's wake-up call as to the underlying actions, motives, and capabilities of global terrorists, such actions are not new to the world. Nitsch and Schumacher (2002, 2004) have conducted extensive research upon bilateral trade and transport patterns among over 200 nations from 1960 to 1993. Their study, which was based on econometric formulas, proves that terrorism and major acts of violence are closely associated with global trade and transport and have the power to reduce global trade by approximately 6%. It is worth noting that for most of the years of this study, globalization, e-commerce, and satellite communication were merely utilized, which suggests that in more recent attacks, a higher economic and commercial impact due to terrorism caused economic losses, such as

a. *Trade disruptions and closure.*
b. *Unmaterialized profits due to cargo.* Insurance costs connected to transporting any kind of cargo, even people, are going to increase. Because there is the danger present of something happening on an airplane or a ship that is carrying valuable supplies to the country, they become potential targets for terrorists and need to carry more insurance.

This is demonstrated in Tables 2.2 and 2.3, namely, Table 2.2 is a case study on the 9/11 terrorist attack and describes all the types of loss, from loss of life and injuries to the psychological impact at a social level, and finally the commercial and economic losses. Furthermore, Table 2.3 shows the losses pertaining to a number of global of terrorist attacks conducted by *organized terrorists* or so-called *connected groups*.

CASE STUDY: THE 9/11 TERRORIST ATTACK

As communities, trade, and transport tend to grow simultaneously, it is essential for policymakers to create robust, highly effective contingency laws capable of encompassing both the social and the economic/commercial aspects of security.

For example, the 9/11 terrorist attack targeted New York's Trade Center and planned the tragic death of 2752 innocent people, causing national and global grief and a sense of social insecurity and helplessness. While it was the deadliest terrorist disaster in US territory throughout the nation's history, the social consequences were coupled with severe economic and commercial consequences (Burns 2013). The loss of physical assets was originally estimated to amount to US$28 billion; however, indirect losses such as insurance for loss of life, business collapses, commercial- and employment-related losses, critical infrastructure damages, and other liabilities amount to an additional US$32 billion, plus the unmaterialized earnings of the deceased, or the underemployed as a result of the attacks, amount to US$11.4–14.2 billion, plus insurance and trade and transport losses, amounting to a total of US$95 billion. The breakdown is reflected in Table 2.2.

2.3.4 The Categories of Terrorism

Terrorism may be classified according to (a) the degree of connectivity among terrorists, i.e., group terrorism or individual actions, and (b) the motive of terrorists, which typically dictates their mode of attack and ferocity of actions.

1. Terrorism classifications in terms of connectivity

There are three principal categories of terrorism:

a. *Connected*: These actions belong to one or more organized terrorist groups or networks ranging from affiliations with piracy and narcotics to extremist political or ideological networks. Such organized networks typically operate under the direct control of a head terrorist team, and their action plan is executed under a specific chain of command.

Most importantly, terrorist groups offer ideology- and target-specific training as a part of their recruitment propaganda. During the interrogation of terrorists who participated in major attacks, their recruitment included training in the following areas:

　i. Ideological, religious, or political conversion

　ii. Psychological victimization, empathy, and perceived previous suffering from targeted victims

　iii. Basic and advanced combat training, including survival, weapons, and explosives training

　iv. Specialized commando training

　v. Logistics training, including use of satellite systems, software, and advanced technologies, navigation skills, etc.

Table 2.3 illustrates that the major terrorist attacks belonged to organized terrorism by *connected groups* and describes the terrorists' motives as well as facts and figures on the damage caused. Most importantly, it illustrates the lessons learned as to the terrorists' trends and the level of resilience on behalf of the afflicted populations, which is estimated by the time needed for full recovery and the ability to avert financial and commercial losses.

b. *Semiconnected*: These semi-autonomous groups may occasionally act independently yet collaborate with one or more illegal teams associated with political, religious, piracy, narcotics, human trafficking, or other affiliations. Their collaborations could be ongoing or project based.

In the instances of connected and semiconnected terrorism, the authorities have the ability to identify the group members from their communications and social media interactions. Typically, terrorist networks aim to actively recruit younger members, and these are frequent opportunities for their actions to be known to the authorities.

c. *Individual acts of terrorism*, i.e., lone-wolf terrorism. In this type of action, terrorists typically operate without immediate control of a head terrorist and need not obey to rules or a group chain of command. They act for their own reasons and ideologies, train themselves, and strategize with minimum exposure and outside communication. For this reason, they are the most difficult to trace by the authorities, as they can operate under the radar for a longer period of time without being caught. A characteristic individual act of terrorism is shown in Table 2.4, the Boston Marathon bombings of 2013, which caused the death of 3 people and the injury of 264 people.

TABLE 2.4   Terrorist Group Attacks (Individual Acts of Terrorism)

Attack Date and Place	Fatalities	Injuries	Other Damages
July 7 and 21, 2005 (London underground bombing, London, UK)			
Attack Type Suicide bombers Terrorist Affiliations None, independent group Attack Motive Religious/political fanaticism Citizenship UK citizens, Pakistani origin	52 victims + 4 suicide bombers	700	Commercial and Economic Impacts: The national economy slowed down. Billions of dollars of financial loss, including trade, transport, and travel insurance, unmaterialized costs due to cancelled trade and transport activities, including • Supply chain disruptions caused by closure of air, land, and sea transportation. • Supply chain deviations. • Closure of businesses. • Change in diplomatic relations and trade agreements. • Currency decrease. • Panic selling in London Stock Exchange. • Billions of dollars' financial loss, including trade, transport and travel insurance, unmaterialized costs due to cancelled trade and transport activities. • 300-million GBP impact on UK tourism. Economic Recovery: • One year, i.e., much faster than economists initially anticipated. Resilience, Lessons Learned: • Increased business security measures. • Robust risk management protocols and vulnerability assessments. • Improved security at access points. • Billions of dollars' financial loss, including trade, transport and travel insurance, and unmaterialized costs due to cancelled trade and transport activities. • Supply chain disruptions caused by closure of air, land, and sea transportation. • Supply chain deviations. • Closure of businesses. • Change in diplomatic relations and trade agreements. *(Continued)*

TABLE 2.4 (CONTINUED)   Terrorist Group Attacks (Individual Acts of Terrorism)

Attack Date and Place	Fatalities	Injuries	Other Damages
July 22, 2011 (Two Norway attacks)			
(a) Oslo Attack, Norway	(a) 8	(a) 209+	Commercial and Economic Impacts:
(b) Utøya Island, Norway	(b) 69	(b) 110+	None. Since the only terrorist was immediately arrested, the society, the stock
	Total 77	Total 319+	markets, or industry segments had no threat to halt their normal commercial
Attack Type			activities.
(a) Car bombs made of ammonium nitrate (AN) fertilizer and fuel oil (FO)			
(b) Semiautomatic carbine and semiautomatic pistol			
Terrorist Affiliations			
None. Neo-Nazi			
Two independent *lone-wolf* attacks by a single person (Anders Behring Breivik)			
Attack Motive			
Religious/political			
Citizenship			
Norwegian			

(Continued)

TABLE 2.4 (CONTINUED) Terrorist Group Attacks (Individual Acts of Terrorism)

Attack Date and Place	Fatalities	Injuries	Other Damages
April 15, 2014 (Boston Marathon bombings, United States)			
Attack Type	4 victims,	264+,	Commercial and Economic Impacts:
Pressure cooker bombs, shootout	1 terrorist	including	Supply chain disruptions and deviations.
Terrorist Affiliations		amputations	Economic Recovery:
Lone wolves			One year, i.e., much faster than economists initially anticipated.
Attack Motive			
Extremist Islamic beliefs			
Citizenship			
US citizens, origins from Kalmyk			
Autonomous Soviet Socialist			
Republic, North Caucasus			

Source: The author, based on DOJ, "United States vs. Dzhokhar Tsarnaev," Case 1:13-mj-02106-MBB, United States Department of Justice, April 21, 2013. Retrieved September 12, 2014, 2013.

As a conclusion, certain lessons were learnt in the comparison between organized terrorist groups and lone-wolf attacks, as reflected in Tables 2.2 and 2.3. Despite the social fear and severe emotional stress, national economic and commercial activities are less impacted in lone-wolf attacks. The stock exchange, trade, and transport activities are likely to recover rapidly especially if the terrorists are arrested or killed.

The least resilient attacks are the ones related to organized terrorist groups. In these cases, even the death of the terrorists is not a social relief, as these individuals represent much larger terrorist groups, which may be likely to strike again.

Furthermore, the examples of terrorist attacks stipulated in this section showed that nations can work toward more resilient societies and industrial segments by building more proactive security contingency plans.

2. Terrorism classifications in terms of motive

In line with the National Advisory Committee on Criminal Justice Standards and Goals, terrorism may be distinguished into six categories, according to their goal and motive, all types being equally violent and dangerous:

a. *Civil unrest and riots* may be characterized by an aggressive type of demonstration, and their motives may be political, financial, ideological, cultural, or social. While the aim of the individual or group terrorists could be the expression of their beliefs, such groups may evolve into violent manifestations and lead to loss of human life, injury, damage of property, and interference with public safety. If prolonged, civil unrest may lead to long-term social turmoil or even civil war. While a number of riots have taken place in North America, Europe, and other global regions with limited acts of violence, in other parts of the world, riots have initiated a number of violent acts leading to looting or even civil war and loss of life.

b. *Political terrorism* may be defined as a political act initiated internally, i.e., citizens of the same country, or externally, i.e., international terrorists who are opponents of the target nation's national or political beliefs. Acts of violence may be used for intimidation. This category of terrorism may be common in neighboring countries with disputes related to territory, national sovereignty, or the use of national resources. In certain parts of the world, i.e., in the Middle East, Africa, and Eastern Europe, this type of terrorism may be ongoing for a long period of time, i.e., decades, trade agreements are inevitably affected, and destruction and a climate of hostility discourage global partners to invest or include these regions in their supply chains. The region may be classified as dangerous by governments, insurance companies, and underwriters, and extra costs for *war and terrorism insurance coverage* may be needed.

c. *Ideological terrorism or nonpolitical terrorism* may initiate acts of violence by fanatics due to religious, cultural, or ideological reasons. Regardless of the motive, this type of terrorism may be extremely violent, threatening a nation's social stability, while it frequently leads to loss of life, torture, and retribution among social groups. Its acts may include but are not limited to (a) the deep belief on behalf of the attackers that their actions are justified due to religious self-righteousness, social superiority, etc.; (b) the desire to provoke public opinion, the media, or the global community; (c) the element of unexpected and often unprovoked attacks; (d) the hit-or-miss execution style of civilian groups; and (e) mass executions, public rape, amputations, and various types of torture.

Some of the most atrocious genocides in the history of mankind were committed by this type of terrorism, with literally millions of victims.

d. *Quasi-terrorism* refers to aggressive acts and techniques similar to terrorist attacks yet without the motivational background, for example, acts of mass shooting and the taking of hostages in an effort to get away. While the premeditated actions, the weapons used, the methods, and the consequences resemble terrorist attacks, these actions usually lack the motive.

e. *Small-scale political terrorism* refers to less violent acts of protest against a political regime, decision, or strategy. While the protesters' intentions may be to express their political views, such actions may be infiltrated by more radical terrorist groups or cause larger-than-intended social turmoil, violence, damages, and disruptions.

f. *State terrorism* describes any aggressive behavior started by a current political regime against another nation or political minority in order to obtain a specific objective, i.e., access to natural resources and violation of the principle of the territorial integrity, to promote border changes. Usually, this type of terrorism leads to warfare among nations with human rights abuses and civilian casualties.

All of the above manifestations of terrorism may use physical violence and psychological abuse in order to impose their views to the society and their political, religious, or ideological opponents.

2.3.5 Logistics Security Threats and Terrorism

Terrorist groups involved in an array of criminal actions to generate necessary funds, among which the most frequent and lucrative methods include but are not limited to illegitimate trade and transport, marine piracy, and even using the transportation modes for human trafficking. Private contributions are also recorded as primary generators of money for terrorists and pirates.

Many of the terrorist types included in this chapter may be using modern assault weapons of mass destruction or explosive mechanisms and HazMat substances (Crime Museum 2014). Security threats may occur at any stage and component of the supply chain, and the criminal groups' ability to penetrate high-security technologies, and be *virtually invisible* among vast volumes of global cargoes, makes them extremely dangerous, with severe impact in supply chains and the society as a whole. Most importantly, in certain occasions, low-level breaches in security can open the doors to more significant security violations, even terrorism.

2.3.6 State Sponsors of Terrorism and Disruption of Commerce

To identify a country as a state sponsor of terrorism, the Secretary of State should establish that the government of such country has consistently provided assistance for acts of global terrorism. Once a nation is designated as such, it remains a state sponsor of terrorism until the status is rescinded in line with statutory criteria. An extensive number of sanctions are enforced as a result of a state sponsor of terrorism designation, including

- A prohibition on arms-associated exports and trade.
- Regulations over exports of dual-use products necessitating a 30-day congressional alert for services or goods that might significantly improve the designated nation's military power or capacity to assist terrorism.
- Banning on monetary assistance.
- Encumbrance of various fiscal, commercial, or other restrictions (DOS 2013). In case of discontinuation of diplomatic relations among countries, this leads to trade disruption and change of the supply chain players.

2.4 PIRACY AND MARITIME SECURITY

2.4.1 Defining Piracy

Piracy is a millennia-old global phenomenon, which to date continues to disrupt supply chains through maritime piracy. The origins of the word *piracy* derive from the Greek words "pirateia" (πειρατεία), which means "attempt," and "peirates" (πειρατές), which was later adopted by the Romans and became the Latin word "peirata" (compare with expert, ex-periental, and em-pirical, which are derived from the ancient root word "peira").

Since maritime transportation covers over 80% of global logistics, and is therefore a crucial component of supply chains, it has been strongly affected by piracy incidents. Piracy ransom amounts exceed $7 billion each year, most of which are covered by the public sector and reimbursed through piracy insurance underwriters. Piracy-prone areas include the Gulf of Guinea in West Africa; the sea off the coast of Somalia in East Africa; and Asia's Malacca Straits, Singapore Straits, Indonesia, Malaysia, and South China Sea. Other areas include the Gulf of Aden in the Arabian Sea. In the Americas, piracy-prone areas include Brazil, Peru, Venezuela, and Haiti (IMO 2014). Figure 2.7 shows the annual global statistics on sea piracy incidents (1984–2013), whereas Table 2.5 shows the 2013 statistics. Global pirates are very familiar with the different ship types, their value, and the cargoes they carry; hence, they are targeting specific ship types as the value of the ship and the value of the cargo will define the ransom money they will ask from the shipowners. As shown in Figure 2.8, the pirates target chemical tankers of high quality; then bulk carriers, which transport grains, sugar, iron ore, and other valuable commodities; and finally, large crude oil carriers, which carry high-value petroleum products. In order to avert piracy attacks, shipowners invest vast amounts of money in order to deviate into longer but safer sea routes, hire armed guards onboard ships, invest their ship against piracy attack incidents, and so on. Table 2.6 shows a typical expenditure breakdown for large crude oil carriers.

The International Maritime Organization (IMO) under the United Nations (UN) umbrella aims to promote collaborative efforts among member states, supply chains, as well as global and national agencies, and departments of defense. These initiatives aim to promote awareness as to the latest incidents, patterns, and statistics in order to develop a common set of regulations, resources, and recommendations. In this respect, the IMO's role in combatting piracy and mitigating supply chain disruptions is paramount. Among others, the IMO works closely with the UN Office on Drugs and Crime (UNODC), thus demonstrating the potential affiliation between piracy and other crime segments such as narcotics.

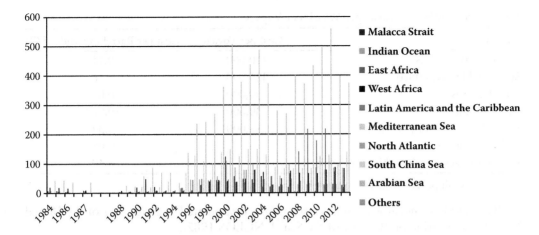

FIGURE 2.7 Annual global statistics on sea piracy incidents (1984–2013). (From IMO Annual Reports on Acts of Piracy and Armed Robbery against Ships. Reports from 1984–2013, available at http://www.imo.org, accessed December 20, 2014.)

TABLE 2.5 Global Statistics on Sea Piracy Attacks, 2013

Piracy Incidents by Continent	
Americas	18
Africa	79
Indian Subcontinent	26
Southeast Asia	128
Far East	13

Source: IMO Annual Reports on Acts of Piracy and Armed Robbery against Ships, available at http://www.imo.org, accessed December 20, 2014, 2013.

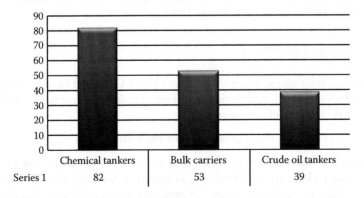

	Chemical tankers	Bulk carriers	Crude oil tankers
Series 1	82	53	39

FIGURE 2.8 Most targeted vessels during sea piracy attacks. (From IMO Annual Reports on Acts of Piracy and Armed Robbery against Ships. Reports from 1984–2013, available at http://www.imo.org, accessed December 20, 2014.)

TABLE 2.6   Antipiracy Costs per Vessel, per Voyage

Cost Type	Cost per Voyage	Cost per Barrel of Crude ($/B)
Vessel diversion costs	210,000	0.11
Additional bunkers (fuel)	326,000	0.16
Armed guards	50,000	0.03
Hull insurance	30,000	0.02
Total additional transport costs	616,000	0.32
Added capital costs		0.08
Total antipiracy costs per ship, per voyage		0.40

Note: VLCC ship, very large crude carrier.

The standard meaning of modern sea piracy is stipulated in article 101 of the United Nations Convention on the Law of the Sea (UNCLOS 1982):

Piracy consists of any of the following acts:

1. Any illegal acts of violence or detention, or any act of depredation, committed for private ends by the crew or the passengers of a private ship or a private aircraft, and directed:
   a. On the high seas, against another ship or aircraft, or against persons or property on board such ship or aircraft;
   b. Against a ship, aircraft, persons or property in a place outside the jurisdiction of any State;
2. Any act of voluntary participation in the operation of a ship or of an aircraft with knowledge of facts making it a pirate ship or aircraft;
3. Any act of inciting or of intentionally facilitating an act described in subparagraph (a) or (b).

According to the antipiracy stipulations of UNCLOS, the regulatory framework of piracy covers acts occurring on the open seas or in a location beyond the territorial jurisdiction and exclusive economic zone of a nation. For incidents that take place within a nation's territorial waters, the attack is regarded as armed robbery and is handled differently according to the international and national laws. Nevertheless, recent piracy incidents that take place both in a nation's territory waters and beyond generate the need to redefine piracy and its legal boundaries (UN 2014).

2.4.2 Armed Robbery and Piracy

Armed robbery against ships, according to the IMO's Code of Practice for the Investigation of the Crimes of Piracy and Armed Robbery against Ships (resolution A.1025 (26), annex, paragraph 2.2), is defined as follows:

Armed robbery against ships means any of the following acts:

1. Any illegal act of violence or detention or any act of depredation, or threat thereof, other than an act of piracy, committed for private ends and directed against a ship or against persons or property on board such a ship, within a State's internal waters, archipelagic waters and territorial sea;
2. Any act of inciting or of intentionally facilitating an act described above (UNCLOS 1982; IMO 2013a,b,c).

In comparison, the interpretation used by the London-based International Maritime Bureau (IMB), which is a distinct division of the International Chamber of Commerce, serves as the primary contract for reporting piracy incidents globally. IMB covers both legal categories of piracy and armed robbery widely defined as "An act of boarding or attempting to board any ship with the apparent intent to commit theft or any other crime and with the apparent intent or capability to use force in the furtherance of that act" (NATO Parliamentary Assembly 2009).

Piracy may be distinguished by occurring at port or in the open seas:

- Piracy at port is typically less dangerous, as pirates are local underemployed individuals seeking money, the ship's stores, and valuables. Although they may be armed, they are less violent than the open sea pirates, as their sole purpose is theft driven by poverty.
- In comparison, a more severe type of piracy happens amidst the open seas, executed by global piracy gangs. These organized syndicates have considerable resources, such as state-of-the-art technologies like fast-speed boats, high-caliber machine guns, and extensive training systems in place. Most importantly, they use sophisticated Automatic Identification System (AIS) and Global Positioning System (GPS), smartphones, and open-source intelligence (see Chapter 8). They have access to shipping industry intelligence in order to track the position of vessels within their region. Typically, groups of 10 or more pirates board vessels equipped with blades and assault rifles similar to the AK-47 type. Pirates are usually of young age, i.e., around 20–25 years old. Their cartel leaders train them on how to hijack ships and kidnap crew members in order to leverage ransom money, which typically reflects the value of the ship and its cargo.

2.4.3 US DHS Maritime Domain Awareness

In the United States, the National Plan to Achieve Maritime Domain Awareness (MDA) is one among the eight plans created in sustenance of the National Strategy for Maritime Security, as stipulated by National Security Presidential Directive-41/Homeland Security Presidential Directive-13.

MDA was designed by the US Coast Guard and contains two key components: (i) monitoring of maritime activities at sea and (ii) accumulating intelligence pertinent to the fleet history and navigation paths. Since 9/11, the MDA emphasis has integrated all vessel and smaller boat movements based on the acknowledgment that any illegal activity at sea can affect security. The intention is to build a database on illegitimate operations at sea from a wide array of sources and develop an intelligent database that can then be made available to interested entities, subject to categorization, according to their user-defined operating picture. The operating picture is distributed among the US agencies involved in logistics and supply chains. This powerful, measurable, interactive mapping is of high utility to the industry (DHS MDA 2012; DHS 2014).

The pirate of today, could be the terrorist of tomorrow.

The author

2.5 PIRACY FINANCING TERRORISM: GROWING THREATS

This section examines the concept of piracy funding terrorism from two distinct perspectives: first, from a legal framework, and second, from a virtual stance, i.e., based on actual piracy incidents, where their connection with terrorist networks was suggested.

The British law permits private entities such as shipowners and cargo owners to pay ransoms for the discharge of hostages and hijacked ships. Nevertheless, under the British antiterrorist legislation, it is a criminal offense to make available funds if the issuer has *reasonable cause* to believe that they could be used in order to fund terrorism. The legal definition of terrorism in such cases is not limited to acts of aggression but encompasses any acts that may impose a threat or distress to human life, the society, the environment, and property.

With regards to motive, the global and national legislations adopt the broad concept that terrorism may be driven by religious, political, or other ideological motives. In this framework, the legal system has firmly established a connection among the pirates and terrorist organizations, in which case the payment of ransoms is no longer regarded as extortion but as funding terrorism, and is legally prohibited.

On the other hand, the connection between piracy and terrorism has been verified over the past few years, where terrorist groups have proven to cultivate piracy as a means of generating funds for their acts of terror.

Somali pirates have long been suspected of connections with organized crime especially with criminal actions pertaining to weapons smuggling and human trafficking. Within this context, piracy nourishes criminal activities and seems to obtain financial advantages from illegal activities involving human trafficking, narcotics, and contraband.

This may explain why modern pirates are in possession of state-of-the-art technologies, such as fast speed boats, satellite systems, and high-caliber weapons, and why modern piracy incidents have tripled over the past few years. It may also explain the fact that piracy-prone zones around the world are clustered exclusively and precisely in the sea passages where large tanker ships carry oil from the oil well to the refinery. Due to the alarming piracy statistics over the years, their association with terrorist groups needs to be further examined.

Most importantly, a proactive stance needs to be adopted in order to prevent future affiliations based on geographic or religious commonalities. It is necessary for the global community to use diplomatic and legal instruments in order to address the motives, causes, and affiliations of pirate groups.

2.6 AIR SECURITY THREATS

Aircraft hijacking or aircraft piracy is defined as the illegitimate seizure of an airplane by a person or group, with mostly political motives, such as terrorism or political asylum, and less financial or commercial motives. Therefore, this type of piracy differentiates from maritime piracy, whose motives are mostly financial. The majority of aircraft hijackers capture the passengers as hostages typically to leverage certain political or legal requests. Less frequently, they impose financial requests, which are typically paid by the airlines and governments and rarely by the passengers themselves. Generally, before 9/11, the hijackers made negotiable demands, and once these were met, they did not impose serious threats upon human lives, the plane, or property. This was not the case in September 11, 2001, when organized terrorists used civil aviation as a weapon of mass destruction targeted toward specific locations of political significance (Pentagon) and commercial significance (World Trade Center). While in the majority of cases, the pilot is pressured to fly in line with the requests of the hijackers, in the case of the 9/11 terrorist attacks, the terrorists flew the planes themselves.

Since the post-World War II era, i.e., from 1945 to 1979, the rapid expansion of civil aviation, coupled with numerous hijackings and security incidents, has raised valid security concerns on behalf of governments, airlines, and the industry. For many decades, aviation security was considered as a national task or as a commercial obligation that could be addressed by passenger and freight airlines. However, since the 9/11 terrorist attacks, where commercial planes were used as weapons of mass destruction with thousands of victims, the United States has implemented a rather effective and stringent security framework that has essentially influenced the global air security protocols, technologies, and preventive measures. While its efficacy has been tested and verified over the last decade or so, increasing terrorist threats necessitate even more stringent aviation measures.

The industry's standards and recommended practices have been set by the International Civil Aviation Organization (ICAO), a specialized agency of the UN headquartered in Canada. ICAO codifies the guidelines and methods of global air navigation and promotes the organizing and continuing development of the industry to ensure safe and orderly growth.

Before 9/11, nations had their own distinctive legislative framework for aviation, yet this was not governed by a binding mechanism to ensure their complete and adequate application. Initiatives on behalf of the US government, the UN, the European Union, and other significant global players have made a proposition to harmonize the regulations of aviation security, under a homogenous context, to be implemented at a global level. Such initiatives resulted in the implementation of national and regional regulations setting up common guidelines and laws for civil aviation security. Table 2.7 shows a

TABLE 2.7   Timeline of Aircraft Hijacking Incidents

Year	Incident
1931	The first documented airplane hijack occurred in February of 1931 in Peru. Byron Rickards was seized and incapacitated by armed radicals while flying a Ford Tri-Motor.
1948–1977	From 1948 to 1957, 15 hijackings took place at a global level, amounting to about an incident per annum. Forty-eight incidents occurred in the next decade, i.e., from 1958 to 1967, amounting to approximately five incidents per annum. From 1968 to 1977, the yearly statistics involved 41 incidents.
	Common-strategy tactic was approved by the FAA with the purpose of teaching both pilots and flight attendants to negotiate and abide by the hijackers' requests, ensure that the airplane will land securely, and enable the security specialists to deal with the event.
2001	On September 11, 2001, 19 terrorists led by Osama bin Laden hijacked a number of planes operated by US companies, namely, American Airlines and United Airlines, and directed them right into the World Trade Center (Twin Towers, WTC), the Pentagon building, and Stonycreek Township in Pennsylvania. A total of 2996 people were killed in these three locations, thus making the hijackings the most deadly in the global history of terrorism.
	Until the 9/11 disasters, the *common-strategy* tactic was not intended to manage suicide hijackings, and therefore, the hijackers had the ability to take advantage of security system weaknesses. The new strategy pursuant to the attacks stipulates that pilots and flight attendants must obtain considerable antihijacking and self-defense training in order to ward off a terrorist attack, bombing, or hijacking scenario.

concise timeline of aircraft-hijacking incidents. It is worth noting that certain commercial aviation incidents related to aircraft disappearance are still under investigation, and the possibility of planes being hijacked cannot yet be determined.

2.7 HUMAN TRAFFICKING AND ILLEGITIMATE TRAVELING/IMMIGRATION

While supply chain and logistics security deals primarily with the cargo flow that is manufactured and distributed globally, the human factor, i.e., illegitimate traveling, is another significant parameter of logistics supply chain security vulnerabilities. For every action entailing voluntary or involuntary transportation, be it through crossing land-based borders, or being hidden in 20 or 40 TEU (twenty-foot equivalent unit) container boxes, such action not only imposes threats to human life but also place a significant strain in the system's integrity. Therefore, a brief examination of logistics vulnerabilities and trends will serve as a guide to further improve regulatory and systemic gaps.

According to the UN Convention against Transnational Organized Crime, human smuggling is defined as "the procurement, in order to obtain, directly or indirectly, a financial or other material benefit, of the illegal entry of a person into a state party of which the person is not a national." Human smuggling may also be defined as the illegal entry or actual or attempted transportation or facilitation of humans to cross international borders while violating one or more countries or state laws, either clandestinely or through fraud, such as the use of fraudulent paperwork.

When human trafficking is attempted by the use of transportation vehicles such as ships, planes, cargo trucks, or intermodal container boxes, their health and own life may be jeopardized as they are exposed in extreme temperature conditions and inadequate ventilation. From a strictly commercial perspective, such illegal activities cause severe interruptions of the cargo flow and capture government and industry resources, time, and manpower that would otherwise be used toward growth and productivity.

There are two classifications of illegal immigrants, i.e., the ones that enter a country legally, and overextend their stay, and the ones that use deception to enter a country's borders either by forging documentation or by entering a country secretly.

2.7.1 Federal Immigration and Nationality Act Section 8 USC 1324(a)(1)(A)(iv)(b)(iii)

According to Title 8 Section 1325 of the US Code, "Improper Entry by Alien," an alien is any citizen of any nation other than the United States who

- Enters or attempts to enter the United States at any time or place other than as designated by immigration officers.
- Eludes examination or inspection by immigration officers.
- Attempts to enter or obtains entry to the United States by a willfully false or misleading representation or the willful concealment of a material fact is considered as a federal crime. A similar legislation exists in other nation's legal immigration system.

In the context of logistics security, illegal transportation of humans is a manifestation of border patrol deficiencies. Again, this section will not deal with the socioeconomic aspects of illegal human traveling, which can greatly impact a nation's taxation system and economy and potentially impose security threats. Instead, it will focus on their impact on supply chain and transportation security.

2.7.2 Organized Immigration Crime

Human smuggling and human trafficking are the two principal immigration crimes in most national legal systems. In the case of human trafficking, victims are involuntarily transported, with the purpose of being physically and financially exploited while living unregistered in life-threatening conditions. On the other hand, human smuggling pertains to voluntary migration, when victims compensate to criminal cartels in order to arrange their illegal transportation. These individuals are called coyotes (Mexico) or snakeheads (China), as their skills to cross people through the borders resemble animal survival skills. Coyote's fees are approximately $20,000 per person to transport illegal immigrants from Mexico to the United States, whereas the fees of Asian *snakeheads* range from $30,000 to $70,000 in order to move people overseas, usually in container boxes. Transportation is affected by such acts, as international criminal gangs hide illegal immigrants in container boxes, or trucks, usually containing large quantities of cargoes. Sometimes, humans are hidden in cardboard boxes within vehicles or containers, whereas frequently, special constructions are made, such as secret panels or hidden packets on the ceiling or side of container boxes, to hide these people.

While the statistics of such criminal acts cannot accurately estimate the number of illegitimate humans and cargoes documented, the daily incidents of border patrol officers discovering humans hidden in cargoes are rather alarming for many reasons:

1. These criminal groups are frequently affiliated with contraband and drug cartels, in which case, their span of activities inflicts global trade and security to a wider extent. While smuggling of cargoes and humans is aimed toward high-traffic trade routes, new locations, and transportation modes, criminal networks use the industry in order to spread their activities with serious impact on transport security.
2. The illegitimate humans could impose security threats, i.e., by being involved in global acts of terrorism or criminal activities.
3. Biological or HazMat security threats could be harbored in this illegal transportation, e.g., humans afflicted with the Ebola virus, biologically contaminated foods, or invasive species could also be transported intentionally or unintentionally but always illegally.

2.7.3 The Free-Ride Effect

Due to the increasing growth of containerized cargoes, criminals seem to know well how to break the seals of container boxes and use the assets of well-established corporations for their illegal actions. Most container vessels carry more than 1000 container boxes, and national immigration and border patrol agencies do not have the resources or time to check every box in a diligent manner. The interior of these dark, 40-ft. metal boxes hides illegitimate people of different ages and ethnicities, who are willing to travel for about a month with limited oxygen and no light, in search of a better life. While such practices have been widespread since the 1990s, this illegal trade of humans and drugs seems to surge the world's greatest hub ports in literally every continent. Not only the UN but also the US DHS, the European Union, and many other nations all over the world have developed harmonized rules in order to combat this alarming threat.

Formerly, the human and drug smugglers preferred soft-top container boxes, as their canvas ceiling allowed oxygen and light while could potentially become an emergency exit. Nevertheless, illegal immigrants still die in such constructions. The snakeheads' new technique is to impose their illegal clients into traveling within enclosed spaces, such as all-locked metal containers, in order to make it harder for customs agents to identify their cargoes (USCIS 2008).

2.8 DRUG TRAFFICKING: SOCIOECONOMIC IMPACTS

The illegitimate trade and transport of narcotics certainly affects global supply chains. Many of these drugs are distributed without the knowledge or consent of the transportation entities, i.e., cargo owners, carriers, and cargo receivers. In addition, the authorities' efforts to combat such illegitimate trade lead to severe delays and obstacles into the legitimate markets, as the world customs clearance processes and regulations become more severe.

In 2013, 80,035 cases were reported to the US Sentencing Commission; among these, around one-fourth, or 22,215 cases, concerned drug trafficking, mostly powder cocaine, methamphetamine, and marijuana. Drug cartels are accountable for at least half of the illegal drugs shipped into the United States from Mexico on an annual basis.

Drug trafficking is an international unlawful trade relating to the cultivation, production, distribution, and selling of drugs that violate the national and global drug prohibition laws. Presently, based on statistics from authorities, global heroin production of 430–450 tons is shipped into the international heroin market. Also, opium from Myanmar and the Lao People's Democratic Republic produces about 50 tons, whereas the remaining 380 tons of heroin and morphine is generated entirely from Afghan opium. Although around 5 tons is used and captured in Afghanistan, the remaining 375 tons is transported globally by sea, land, and air routes streaming into and via the nations adjoining Afghanistan.

Furthermore, the Eastern Europe and northern Eurasian channels are the primary heroin corridors connecting Afghanistan to the large trading markets of Russia and Western Europe. The Balkan route crosses Iran, Pakistan, Turkey, Greece, and Bulgaria throughout Southeastern Europe to the markets of Northwestern Europe, comprising an annual market worth of over $20 billion. The northern Eurasian trade routes cross Tajikistan, Kyrgyzstan, Uzbekistan, or Turkmenistan through Kazakhstan and Russia. This market segment exceeds $13 billion each year (UNODC 2010–2014). Figures 2.9 and 2.10 show the global drug trade of heroin and cocaine, respectively.

Such actions expose the industry's vulnerability to scan, monitor, and eliminate illegitimate trade and transport. This weakness could prove to be detrimental for more serious threats. Terrorism, international criminals, suicide bombers, or dirty bombs could well be hidden in transportation modes or palletized or container boxes.

Each year, billions of container boxes travel around the world. Among these, 5%–8% are tagged as *high risk* and are thoroughly scanned or undergo physical inspection. Chapter 3 pertains to the global and regulatory framework to combat illegitimate trade and transport, whereas Chapter 4 deals with the state-of-the-art technologies used to scan cargoes, promote communications, and ensure resilience in our global supply chains.

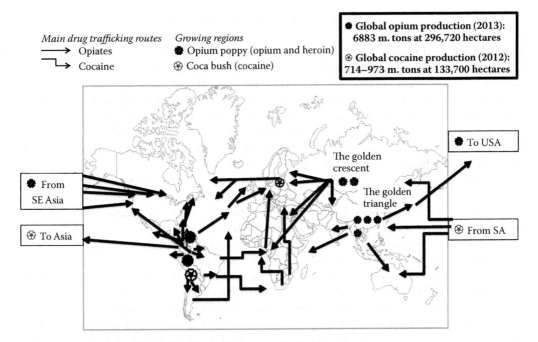

FIGURE 2.9 Global heroin flows from Asian points of origin, 2010. (Courtesy of the author, based on UNODC, 2008–2014, World Drug Reports, available at http://www.unodc.org, accessed December 12, 2014.)

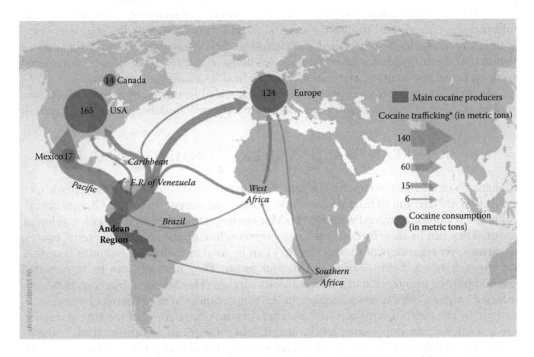

FIGURE 2.10 Main global cocaine flows, 2008. (From UNODC World Drug Reports, 2008–2014, available at http://www.unodc.org, accessed December 12, 2014.)

2.9 CYBER SECURITY THREATS

Global trade and transport companies are also affected by cybercriminals who employ increasingly more intrusive and sophisticated means in order to target particular computer networks, government entities, organizations, and individuals. Over the past years, trade and transportation businesses have experienced numerous serious hacks and breaches. In this ongoing technology battle among cyber attackers and organizations, IT departments and security professionals will have to stay on top of the new game tactics and techniques used by cyberterrorists in order to safeguard their organizations. A timeline of cyber security threats from 1998 to 2014 is depicted in Table 2.8.

Cyberterrorism is becoming an increasing threat to global logistics and supply chains. Twenty percent of security incidents pertain to cybercrimes, whereas combatting cyberterrorism costs 20% of annual US budget, amounting to about $57 billion per annum, on top of corporate investments for safeguarding their company.

Despite new regulations, systems, and software, critical cyber infrastructures such as cloud-based systems remain vulnerable to cyber attacks.

Although governments and the industry heavily invest in cyber security programs, they are involved in a never-ending battle with entities of ample determination, strategic skills, and technological expertise. Cyber security breaches may be conducted by global organized crime networks. They may be lone wolves, hired by governments or corporate entities, or even freelance professionals, occasionally used to accomplish targeted missions, whereas the identity of their employers may or may not be known. In line with the other security threats of this chapter, acts of cyberterrorism may be associated with other criminal activities, and the information obtained may be used in acts of terrorism, sea piracy, or even the use of private and confidential government and corporate information.

Cyber security is considered as a *critical infrastructure* sector of major security significance for nations and industries alike. Critical infrastructure is the resources, programs, and networks, both physical and virtual (i.e., cyber security), so fundamental to a nation that their incapacitation or damage would have a devastating impact on national security, economic security, and national public health or safety.

As such, an overview of cyber security was provided in this section, but an extensive analysis of cyber security as a critical infrastructure sector will be duly analyzed in Chapter 4.

2.10 BIOTHREAT: HEALTH AND ENVIRONMENTAL SECURITY

Biohazards or chemical weapons are hazardous materials such as toxic gases, liquids, or solids that are harmful to humans, animals, plants, and the environment. Certain chemical hazards cannot be traced without HazMat equipment, as they have no color, odor, or flavor. They can be dispersed into the environment, having the form of bacteria, toxins, or viruses, yet regardless of their form, they can be used as biological weapons transmitted through water, food, coating, virus, and so on. They not only can be transmitted intentionally or unintentionally, as hazardous cargoes (HazMat or dangerous goods) or infected cargoes, but can also circulate in the ventilation system of carriers by sea, land, and air by the form of viruses. Occasionally, they may have invaded the transportation mode itself, i.e., the ship, plane, truck, or rail, and thus spread and infect all the cargoes to be carried therein. Chapter 5 extensively analyzes the classifications, types, and characteristics of these hazardous materials, which may be commodities, biological threats, or weapons.

TABLE 2.8 Timeline of Cyber Security Threats

Year	Incident
1988	The Morris virus was one of the initially identified viruses created to destroy the global cyber security and one of the most common viruses to attack American computers. The virus cracked through systemic vulnerabilities in the UNIX system Noun 1 and cloned itself while incapacitating computers due to extremely low speed. The virus was created by Robert Tapan Morris, who was the first individual to be charged under the "US Computer Fraud and Abuse Act." At the time, he claimed that he was simply attempting to measure the size and functions of the Internet, whereas he is now an MIT professor.
2006	NASA was compelled to stop emails with attachments prior to shuttle launches to prevent the potential of hacking. International cyber criminals stole the plans for the newest US space launch vehicles.
2007	Following Estonia's disputes with Russia for disposing a war memorial, Estonian federal networks were attacked through a denial-of-service attack by unknown foreign intruders. A number of government web-based services were temporarily unavailable, and Internet banking was ceased. The episodes appeared to resemble cyber rampages instead of debilitating assaults. The Estonian government handled the event smoothly, while most of the services were recovered shortly.
	Within a series of cyber attacks aiming to gain access and exploit the Pentagon's network systems, unidentified international criminals compromised the US Secretary of Defense's unclassified e-mail account.
2008	In the United States, the electronic files of the Republican and Democratic presidential campaigns were hacked and obtained by unidentified international cyber criminals.
	In Georgia, cyber infrastructure was compromised by unidentified international criminals at about the time that the nation was in hostility with the Russian Federation.
2009	Cyber criminals assaulted Israel's web networks in the January 2009 military attack in the Gaza Strip. At least 5 million computers were involved in the cyber attack that aimed at compromising Israeli government Internet sites.
	Israeli authorities considered that the assault was executed by a criminal organization operating out of a former Soviet state on behalf of Hamas or Hezbollah.
2011	In the United States, the Deputy Secretary of Defense announced that hackers compromised the networks of a defense contractor company and stole 24,000 files from the Department of Defense.
2012	Kaspersky, a Russian organization, uncovered a global cyber attack known as *Red October* that has been functioning for the past five years. Hackers collected data by cracking through systemic weaknesses in Microsoft's Word and Excel software. The cyber attack appeared to target nations in Eastern and Western Europe, former USSR countries, and North American and Central Asian countries. The virus collected information from government embassies, research organizations, military systems, energy companies, and nuclear and other critical infrastructure sectors.
2014	Operation DeathClick, a malvertising cybercrime organization, was uncovered by Invincea while targeting a number of US Defense Contractors.
	GreatFire.org, a cyber group that keeps track of censorship by the Chinese government's nationwide firewall program, announces that China is utilizing the program as a means of a man-in-the-middle cyber attack on the Chinese clients of Apple's iCloud service. Apple confirms the attack.
	The Warsaw Stock Exchange is allegedly compromised. An advocate of ISIS claims accountability for this attack, which has resulted to the compromise and leak of 30 Mb of data.

(Continued)

TABLE 2.8 (CONTINUED)   Timeline of Cyber Security Threats

Year	Incident
	A substantial DDoS cyber attack penetrates the official website of Ukraine's election commission (cvk.gov) on the eve of Ukraine's parliamentary surveys. The pro-Russian CyberBerkut group claims responsibility for the cyber assault.
	The cyber activity of APT28 is announced. APT28 is a Russian government-sponsored espionage party targeting numerous Eastern European government authorities and security agencies, whereas cyber assaults are meant to obtain confidential political and government data.
	The unclassified network of the US President's Executive Office is violated by hackers thought to be employed by the Russian authorities.

Source: NATO Parliamentary Assembly, *The Growing Threat of Piracy to Regional and Global Security*, 023 CDS 09 E, Lord Jopling (United Kingdom) General Rapporteur, NATO 2009, available at http://www.nato-pa.int, accessed December 20, 2014, 2009; NATO, The history of cyber attacks, a timeline, available at http://www.nato.int/docu/Review/2013/Cyber/timeline/EN/index.htm, accessed December 23, 2014, 2014; US DOS, Country Reports on Terrorism, United States Department of State, Bureau of Counterterrorism, available at http://www.state.gov/documents/organization/225050.pdf, accessed November 14, 2014, 2013; US DOS, Country Reports on Terrorism, US Department of State, available at http://www.state.gov/j/ct/rls/crt/2014; Accessed November 14, 2014, 2014.

2.10.1 Health Security

The expanded definition of *security* includes not only military threats but also threats to the environment, health, and economic stability. The spread of infectious disease can be considered a security threat along with the drug trade. Safeguarding the health of the public is usually a domestic concern. However, with the onset of globalization, public health is increasingly recognized as important for foreign policy, and, conversely, foreign policy is seen as an important mechanism for protecting public health. Governments at all income levels are increasingly prepared to cooperate to prevent the emergence and spread of infectious diseases and provide public health security, which is defined as the provision and maintenance of measures aimed at preserving and protecting the health of the population. There is an inevitable linkage between public health security and bioterrorism, but foreign policy is also concerned with broader dimensions of cross-border health risks including, for example, the transmission of antimicrobial-resistant organisms, as well as health risks associated with noncommunicable diseases, environmental degradation, etc. (WHO 2014).

The Global Health Security Agenda was released on February 13, 2014 to improve the planet safe and secure from transmittable disease hazards and to gather nations throughout the world to generate new, tangible commitments and to increase global health security as a national leaders–level top priority (The White House 2014).

Health security threats entail the outbreak of infectious or zoonotic diseases:

a. *Infectious diseases* are attributable to medical conditions that can be transmitted from one human to another due to pathogenic microorganisms including bacteria, viruses, parasitic organisms, or fungal infections.
b. *Zoonotic diseases* entail contagious medical conditions of animals that may induce serious medical diseases when passed on to humans.

While shielding the public health is typically a household issue, globalization has brought to our attention the large-scale impact of a regional disease and has therefore acknowledged the importance of protecting public health through foreign policy. National health systems are in place to raise federal and public awareness as to the prevention, manifestation, and outbreak of contagious diseases. Public health security is described as the preventative actions and sustainability of systems targeted in protecting and safeguarding the inhabitants' health. Bioterrorism is closely related with public health, but international policy is engaged with broader dimensions of cross-border health hazards, including the transmission of antimicrobial immune microorganisms, in addition to health risks connected with noncommunicable illnesses, environmental deterioration, and so on (WHO 2014).

2.10.2 Environmental Security

Environmental security encompasses any deliberate, intentional, or unintentional threat to damage the environment, its flora and fauna, while impacting human health, public security, economic robustness, and to some extent, national security.

The environmental risks imposed upon countries and industries around the world are a combination of the degeneration of local environments and that of the global ecosystem. Among the most severe ecological threats relate to contaminated water, which is also transported as a product or as a consumable for the transportation industry.

2.10.3 Environmental Security and Impact to Human Health

Some of the security challenges associated with logistics and transport pertain to the biological threats transported through cargoes and humans, which impose considerable risks upon national health and the environment. Transportation practitioners are familiar with the legal, commercial, environmental, and ethical consequences associated with infected cargo. When a portion of the cargo is infected prior to transportation, the visible inspections and the random cargo sampling during industry's preloading surveys are not sufficient to monitor the damaged cargo and control the biological, health, and environmental threats it may impose.

This has been the case not only with invasive species transferred through ships' ballast water tanks but also with contaminated food cargoes, such as grains, wheat, sugar, fruits and vegetables, and so on. Such threats may be imposed by naturally contaminated cargoes or by intentional contamination.

In order to assess the extent of the potential threat, and explain the reasons that monitoring 100% of the cargoes transported is a tedious task, it is worth noting that as of 2015, around 10–12 billion metric tons (MT) of cargoes are traded globally, among which, 90% is carried by ships. According to different research projects initiated by the UN, the IMO, and other educational and private entities, it is estimated that by 2030, global trade will reach at least 20–25 billion MT of cargo. This suggests that the task of scanning, testing, and approving imported cargoes is anticipated to be increasingly challenging. Innovative technologies, industrial regulations, and protocols need to be in place in order to mitigate these biological threats to human health, the environment, and the societies.

CASE STUDY: ENVIRONMENTAL SECURITY

Interview: Captain George Tate

Master at Marine Spill Response Corporation and US Coast Guard Aux. Flotilla Commander of Flotilla 6–3, District 8CR

Security threats could potentially target, i.e., intentionally damage, our environment. Considering the actions in the past, this is not a new concept. In 1991, during the first Gulf War, Iraqi forces purposely opened the valves at the Sea Island Terminal and dumped oil from several tankers into the Persian Gulf. The oil moved southward and began to accumulate on the north coast of Saudi Arabia, endangering the fragile intertidal zones and mangrove forests and destroying wildlife habitats. The spoiled shallow coastal areas normally provided feeding grounds for birds and feeding and nursery areas for fish and shrimp. Because the plants and animals of the seafloor are the basis of the food chain, damage to the shoreline had consequences for the whole shallow-water ecosystem, including the multimillion-dollar Saudi fisheries industry. In October 2002, a French oil tanker was attacked off the coast of Yemen. One crewman was killed in the blast, which spilled tens of thousands of barrels of oil into the waters off the Yemen coast.

Targeting the fragile coastal ecosystems with toxic chemicals could result in severe consequences to local economies as a result of damage to commercial fisheries, aquaculture, and tourism. These acts could impact the supply chain as well through cleanup operations that impede passage of viable waterways that provide access to major ports. Imports and exports would be effected.

In areas where water filtration and desalination plants provide drinking and irrigation water, the effects would be even greater. This would result in a decrease in potable water and a decrease in viable food sources for the local community. The impact could impose a severe hardship on the local community and possibly the region that would be felt for years.

We do not need to be paranoid but to understand that the environment is just another avenue for security threats to affect our everyday life. The world that we live in is dynamic and ever changing. We must never let our guard down and know that there are those in the world community who will utilize all resources available to inflict harm to the human race and the world. To not acknowledge this is to be sacrificially complacent. We must be vigilant and hyperaware of the actions of these security threats in our area of operation, so we can prevent their actions from disrupting the supply chain and impacting our communities.

2.11 BIOTERRORISM: FOOD SECURITY

Food security can be defined as the proper protection of food and nutrition from damage through the admission of hazardous microorganisms; chemicals; and corrosive, radioactive, or other substances into the water, food, or storage facilities. Nutritional safety deals with the intentional or unintentional contamination of foodstuffs by natural, biological, or chemical hazards throughout the food supply chain, which extends from raw materials to processing, warehousing, distribution, and consumption. The primary hazard risks entail harmful bacteria, chemical substances, and foreign objects. Chemical risks consist of environmental pollution, hazardous food ingredients, heavy metals, different toxin types, insufficient storage, temperature, packaging, handling or warehousing conditions, chemical substances, and so on. Quality control and safety processes have the capacity to eliminate hazards throughout the food supply chain stages.

The food damage may be natural or accidental, yet it can also be intentional by people trying to jeopardize the general population health. To ensure that food security is in place, all people should continually have access to fundamental nutrition and a public food distribution process in place. Availability of suitable and nutritious food, access to food, equal distribution of food among social tiers, and a nation's purchasing power enabling citizens to be adequately nourished are all factors to be considered. Malnutrition or micronutrition (inadequate vitamins and protein) is an equally harmful facet of famine.

Famine can be a by-product of poverty, restricted food access due to natural disasters or war, or deliberate deprivation of food at times of peace:

1. *Poverty*: According to the UN Food and Agriculture Organization, between 2010 and 2012, approximately 870 million people out of the 7.1 billion people around the world (or one in eight people) suffer from famine or chronic undernourishment. The vast majority of undernourished populations live in developing counties, and around 30% of these live in Sub-Saharan Africa (FAO 2012).

2. *Restricted food access due to natural disasters*: Both natural disasters and intentional man-made actions have the capacity to disrupt or pollute the food supply chain, damage food storage or distribution amenities, and trigger disease and famine (see also health and environmental sections). Such occurrences entail natural disaster events, such as hurricanes, flooding, extreme temperatures, earthquakes, and prolonged power outages.

   Natural hazards pertain to hurricanes, tsunamis, extreme temperatures, earthquakes, volcanic eruptions, and so on. Famine is a major implication of natural events triggered by natural catastrophes, as they frequently entail not only the destruction of crops, cattle, and natural food sources but also the destruction of food storage, thus eliminating the population's capacity for nutrition.

   The recent years' hurricanes, earthquakes, and tsunamis, which have occurred in many global regions, have outlined the necessity of proactiveness and coalition between the public and private sectors in order to strategize emergency response and humanitarian aid routes.

3. *Restricted food access due to intentional contamination*: Food terrorism, or the act of deliberately contaminating or destroying an opponent's food supply chain, is a century-old strategy. The tampering and interference with a social group's food supply are among the highly successful methods of affecting a community. Although the outcome of food terrorism is typically loss of health and loss of life, its true aim is to instigate fear, political unrest, socioeconomic turmoil, and a sense of helplessness in view of an unseen enemy.

   Throughout the course of history, the act of deliberately contaminating food has been common. However, a nation's preparedness and alertness in safeguarding food from deliberate contamination are a quite recent concept. Agricultural, food manufacturing, storage, and distribution centers entail a number of systemic vulnerabilities that may provide a relatively easy target for individuals who intentionally plan to instill large-scale damage.

Over the past few decades or so, global diplomacy is experiencing significant changes due to a number of international crises, warzones, and the rise of international terrorist groups. Globalization, new technologies, and the increasing growth of trade have empowered governments and communities to mitigate threats just as much as they have empowered bioterrorist groups to seek for systemic vulnerabilities in the food supply chain industry. Within a framework of multiglobal food supply chain, an imminent threat entails the governments' difficulty to proactively identify bioterrorist risks. To date, food inspection systems are mainly focused on the infestations of terrestrial and aquatic invasive species, i.e., the threatening presence of a large quantity of microorganisms, parasites, or insects. While the national and global legal systems stipulate specific protocols as to the restrictions and inspections of foods imported, the increasing cargo volumes coupled with the limited customs authorities make it difficult to conduct scans and visual tests for the majority of imported foods.

The global population seems to be particularly vulnerable to deliberate food contamination, as most harmful substances are commercially available, and the act of bioterrorism *per se* is quite challenging to be recognized until the attack has already taken place.

Although there are regulations and protocols on emergency response and humanitarian support during emergency situations, both entailing natural disasters and man-made security threats, there is a compelling need to urgently develop guidelines on how to protect the community in case of bioterrorism and food-related hazards.

4. *Deliberate deprivation of food at times of peace*
   Stalin and Ukraine's Holodomor: The Great Hunger (1932–1933)
   Soviet Union's leader, Joseph Stalin, deliberately caused the *Great Hunger* with the purpose of eliminating Ukraine's farmers. In 1927, the former Soviet Union suffered a food shortage due to poor harvest. Stalin considered that Ukraine's farmers had not embraced his political views and therefore held them accountable for the wheat shortages in the urban markets. He instructed a large number of young urban communists to get hold of all the grain they could find in Ukraine's rural areas. As a result, millions of farmers starved, and between 7 and 9 million people died from 1932 to 1933. This is considered Ukraine's holocaust, and over the recent years, it has been confirmed historically.

5. *Restricted food access due to war*: When examining the circumstances under which war leads to famine, in the majority of cases, hunger is closely associated with restricted access to food as opposed to actual lack of food. Under this presumption, famine and humanitarian aid during warfare can be approached in two different ways:
   a. *Restoration of food supply chains*: dealing with the reasons behind starvation by examining whether the supply chain disruptions are due to natural disasters or man-made. Once this has been established, alternative supply chains can be created, and the starvation issue can be resolved.
   b. *Alternative food supplies*: providing food support in order to assist famine victims in case regular supply chains and food distribution are not recovered (ICRC 2014; Red Cross 2014).

INTERVIEW AND CASE STUDY

Tate, George, Master at Marine Spill Response Corporation and USCG Aux. Flotilla Commander of Flotilla 6–3, District 8CR, Case Study: Environmental Security.

REFERENCES

911 Memorial. 2014. National September 11 Memorial & Museum. Available at http://www.911memorial.org/faq. Accessed November 1, 2014.

Acharya, A., Mandal, S., and Mehta, A. 2008. *Terrorist Attacks in Mumbai: Picking Up the Pieces*. A report by International Centre for Political Violence and Terrorism Research (ICPVTR). S. Rajaratnam School for International Studies. Nanyang Technological University, Singapore. Available at http://www.pvtr.org/pdf/globalanalysis/analysis%20of%20the%20november%202008%20mumbai%20terror%20attacks.pdf. Accessed November 1, 2014.

Burns, M. 2013. Estimating the impact of maritime security: Financial tradeoffs between security and efficiency. *Journal of Transportation Security*, December, Volume 6, Issue 4, pp. 329–338.

Burns, M. 2014. *Supply Chain Security: A Strategy to Resilience through Policies, Partnership, and Technologies*. DHS Supply Chain Security Workshop, April, Houston, Texas.

Cohen, L.E. and Felson, M. 1979. Social change and crime rate trends: A routine activity approach. *The American Sociological Review* 44, 588–608.

Cohen, L.E., Felson, M., and Land, K.C. 1980. Property crime rates in the United States: A macrodynamic analysis, 1947–1977; with ex ante forecasts for the mid-1980s. *The American Journal of Sociology*, 86, 90–118.

Comptroller NYC. 2002. New York City Comptroller Report: One Year Later, The Fiscal Impact of 9/11 on New York City. Available at http://comptroller.nyc.gov/legacy-url/?q=press/2002_releases/02-09-054.shtm. Accessed October 6, 2014.

Crime Museum. 2014. Types of terrorism. Available at http://www.crimemuseum.org/crime-library/types-of-terrorism. Accessed October 6, 2014.

DHS. 2014. *The Complexity of Violent Extremism*. US Department of Homeland Security. October. Available at http://www.dhs.gov/topic/countering-violent-extremism. Accessed November 14, 2014.

DHS MDA. 2012. *The National Plan to Achieve Maritime Domain Awareness (MDA)*. Available at http://www.dhs.gov/national-plan-achieve-maritime-domain-awareness. Accessed November 15, 2014.

DOS. 2013. Country Reports on Terrorism 2012 Report. May 30, 2013. State Sponsors of Terrorism. US Department of State. Office of the Coordinator for Counterterrorism. Available at http://www.state.gov/j/ct/rls/crt/2012/209985.htm. Accessed November 13, 2014.

Europa. 2002. Council of the European Union. Available at http://europa.eu/legislation_summaries/justice_freedom_security/fight_against_terrorism/l33168_en.htm. Accessed January 10, 2015.

FAO. 2012. The State of Food and Agriculture. FAOSTAT Statistical Database. Available at http://faostat.fao.org. Accessed January 12, 2015.

GAO. 2004. Government Accountability Office. *Health Effects in the Aftermath of the World Trade Center*. Available at http://www.gao.gov/new.items/d041068t.pdf. Accessed November 1, 2014.

Hindelang, M.J., Gottfredson, M.R., and Garofalo, J. 1978. *Victims of Personal Crime: An Empirical Foundation for a Theory of Personal Victimization.* Ballinger Publishing Co. Florida, USA.

ICRC. 2014. International Committee of the Red Cross, Famine and war. 31-10-1991 Article, *International Review of the Red Cross*, No. 285, by Alain Mourey. Available at https://www.icrc.org/eng/resources/documents/misc/57jmbj.htm. Accessed November 3, 2014.

ILO. 2003. International Labour Organization: The impact of the 2001–2002 crisis on the hotel and tourism industry. Available at http://www.ilo.org. Accessed October 12, 2014.

IMO. 2013a. Annual Piracy Reports, 2013. International Maritime Organization. Available at http://www.imo.org/OurWork/Security/SecDocs/Documents/PiracyReports/208 _Annual_2013.pdf. Accessed November 20, 2014.

IMO. 2013b. Piracy and armed robbery against ships. International Maritime Organization. Available at http://www.imo.org/OurWork/Security/PiracyArmedRobbery/Pages /Default.aspx. Accessed November 4, 2014.

IMO. 2013c. Reports on acts of piracy and armed robbery against ships. Annual report—2013. MSC.4/Circ.208, March 1, 2013. Maritime Security. Available at http://www.imo.org/OurWork/Security/SecDocs/Pages/Maritime-Security.aspx. Accessed November 7, 2014.

IMO. 2014. *Piracy. International Maritime Organization.* Available at http://www.imo .org. Accessed November 12, 2014.

LCCI. 2005. The economic effects on terrorism on London. London Chamber of Commerce and Industry. Available at http://www.londonchamber.co.uk/docimages/754.pdf. Accessed November 1, 2014.

Milken Institute. 2014. The impact of September 11 on U.S. metropolitan economies. Available at http://www.milkeninstitute.org/pdf/National_Metro_Impact_Report.pdf. Accessed October 15, 2014.

NATO. 2014. The history of cyber attacks, a timeline. Available at http://www.nato .int/docu/Review/2013/Cyber/timeline/EN/index.htm. Accessed December 23, 2014.

NATO Parliamentary Assembly. 2009. *The Growing Threat of Piracy to Regional and Global Security.* 023 CDS 09 E, Lord Jopling (United Kingdom) General Rapporteur. NATO 2009. Available at http://www.nato-pa.int. Accessed December 20, 2014.

Nitsch, V. and Schumacher, D. 2002. Terrorism and Trade. Workshop on the Economic Consequences of Global Terrorism. DIW, Berlin, Germany.

Nitsch, V. and Schumacher, D. 2004. Terrorism and international trade: An empirical investigation. *European Journal of Political Economy* Volume 20, Issue 2, 423–433. Accessed November 4, 2014.

Panagariya, A. 2008. *The Economic Cost of the Mumbai Tragedy.* Available at http:// www.forbes.com/2008/11/29/mumbai-economic-cost-oped-cx_ap_1129panagariya .html. Accessed November 1, 2014.

Princeton. 2002. Non-American casualties of the September 11 attacks. Available at https://www.princeton.edu/~achaney/tmve/wiki100k/docs/Non-American_casual ties_of_the_September_11_attacks.html. Accessed November 1, 2014.

Sherlock, S. 2002. *The Bali Bombing. What It Means for Indonesia.* Foreign Affairs Defense and Trade Group. Department of the Parliamentary Library, Australia. Available at http://www.aph.gov.au/binaries/library/pubs/cib/2002-03/03cib04.pdf. Accessed November 1, 2014.

The White House. 2014. *Fact Sheet: Global Health Security Agenda: Getting Ahead of the Curve on Epidemic Threats.* Office of the Press Secretary, September 26. Available

at http://www.whitehouse.gov/the-press-office/2014/09/26/fact-sheet-global-health
-security-agenda-getting-ahead-curve-epidemic-th. Accessed November 14, 2014.

UN. 1994. *United Nations Human Development Report 1994*, published for the United
Nations Development Program (UNDP). New York, Oxford University Press.

UN. 2014. Central Asia. United Nations Counter-Terrorism Implementation Task Force.
Available at http://www.un.org/en/terrorism/ctitf/pdfs/centr_asia_implementing_concept
_note_eng.pdf. Accessed October 12, 2014.

UNCLOS. 1982. United Nations Convention on the Law of the Sea. Available at http://
www.un.org/depts/los/convention_agreements/texts/unclos/unclos_e.pdf.
Accessed November 21, 2014.

UNODC. 2008–2014. World Drug Reports. Available at http://www.unodc.org. Accessed
December 12, 2014.

UNODC. 2010–2014. Drug Trafficking. Annual Reports, 2010–2014. United Nations
Office on Drugs and Crime. Available at https://www.unodc.org/unodc/en/drug-traf
ficking/. Accessed November 22, 2014.

USCIS. 2008. US Citizenship and Immigration Services. Available at http://www.uscis.gov.
Accessed September 18, 2014.

US DOS. 2010. 22 USC Sec. 2656f. Available at http://www.gpo.gov/fdsys/granule/USCODE
-2010-title22/USCODE-2010-title22-chap38-sec2656f. Accessed January 12, 2014.

US DOS. 2013. Country Reports on Terrorism. US Department of State. Bureau of
Counterterrorism. Available at http://www.state.gov/documents/organization
/225050.pdf. Accessed November 14, 2014.

US DOS. 2014. Country Reports on Terrorism. US Department of State. Available at
http://www.state.gov/j/ct/rls/crt/2014. Accessed November 14, 2014.

WHO. 2014. Glossary. World Health Organization. Available at http://www.who.int
/trade/glossary/story030/en/. Accessed November 4, 2014.

CHAPTER 3

Global Security and Regulatory Framework

Within the last two years the world has witnessed devastating catastrophes of enormous scale, whereby global supply chains were disrupted, affecting businesses and livelihoods across the globe.

Allen Bruford
Deputy Director, Compliance and Facilitation Directorate, World Customs Organization

3.1 INTRODUCTION

A security regulatory framework is one of the most effective tools of global nations and industries together with security technologies, training, and security awareness.

Whereas Chapter 2 discussed the different types of security threats, and their manifestations by sea, land, and air, this chapter examines the regulations that are in place to combat such risks.

The first section of the chapter focuses on global regulations, whereas the second section analyzes regulations at a national level, specifically pertaining to the US regulations, while referring to similar security laws implemented by other nations the world over.

The purpose of this chapter is to make available to trade and transport professionals a plethora of regulations that are in place to eliminate security risks and help the industry adopt a more proactive stance. It is worth noting that these security organizations and regulations entailed herein have been designed to reflect the specific national and industrial requirements based on the existing threats, specific industrial processes and protocols, and state-of-the-art technologies. With regulations being more flexible than legal systems, they tend to be regularly amended to mitigate new security threats and processes and emerging technologies.

Although these regulations are segmented geographically, or industry-wise, they have all been designed to fit like pieces of a puzzle: different rules apply to different industries and transportation modes or cover different regional boundaries. Some rules have a global effect and are all-encompassing, whereas others are regional, state specific, or industry specific. Some security initiatives presented in this chapter have been initiated by governments, yet require the industry's collaboration, whereas others have been initiated by key industry players and require the government's support. This is why a public–private partnership is essential, as will be discussed in Chapter 7.

Transportation professionals are thereby asked to comply with this plethora of regulations and be flexible with the requirements that tend to change as cargoes are moved from one region to another. Table 3.1 shows the regulatory framework throughout the entire supply chain stages. It demonstrates how these rules may vary in sea, land, or air transport and how these security rules apply in different stages of the supply chain, i.e., from production to export and import checks, warehousing, and finally distribution to the markets.

Furthermore, Figure 3.1 demonstrates which regulations apply in different geographical and transportation segments.

3.1.1 A Brief Historic Overview of Security Regulations

The United Nations (UN) has joined with customs authorities around the world to eliminate the unlawful transport of humans, guns, and narcotic substances frequently hidden in the millions of cargo containers that are carted about the world on a daily basis.

Meanwhile, at a national level, federal and state administrators aim to promote growth, development, and the transportation of people and commodities without compromising the national security. The US Congress and the administration restructured the federal agencies in order to prevent security threats that harm both the nation and/ or trade and transport activities. Containers expedite the trafficking of humans, high volumes of narcotics, and smuggled commodities. Additionally, they are frequently utilized to facilitate the illegitimate transport of weapons, chemical substances, and money laundering, i.e., illegitimate funds earned by criminal activities. A large number of global borders and ports lack the customs and border checks required to distinguish legitimate from illegitimate trade and transport (UN 2004).

However, the model of a global organization that maintains global security, peace, and an equitable sociopolitical system is not a modern concept. It was introduced in the eighteenth century by the French philosopher, author, and innovative thinker Charles-Irénée Castel de Saint-Pierre (1658–1743).

De Saint-Pierre was among the first to discuss the potential for an international league of nations that ensure global security and self-defense. He spoke of a uniform, global legal system and a novel sociopolitical system of autonomous yet affiliated states. He also emphasized the necessity for nations to invest in critical infrastructure in order to promote and safeguard trade and transport. In his essay on perpetual peace, he describes a sociopolitical condition where security and sustainable peace are ensured at an international level. His "Project for Perpetual Peace" essay was written while he was employed as an official arbitrator for the Treaty of Utrecht.

De Saint-Pierre was a visionary thinker and a great influencer of two great European philosophers of the eighteenth century:

1. Jean-Jacques Rousseau (Geneva, 1712–1778). In his essays on "The Social Contract" (Rousseau 1762) and "Discourse on Inequality" (Rousseau 1754), Rousseau envisions a united political community that is empowered to resolve the commercial and sociopolitical security problems.
2. Immanuel Kant (Germany, 1724–1804) and his ideas on "Perpetual Peace: A Philosophical Sketch" (*Zum ewigen Frieden. Ein philosophischer Entwurf*) (Kant 1795).

TABLE 3.1 Supply Chain Security Initiatives: Regulatory Framework

Stage 1: Production →	Stage 2: Preshipment Regulations for Import and Transit →		Stage 3: Transport and Distribution →
Commodities' Production	**Regulations per Transportation Mode Segment**	**US-Driven Sea–Land–Air Security Initiatives**	**International Initiatives**
Raw materials Industry assembly Refinery	**By sea:** Global: ISPS; AIS (Automatic Identification System); Long-range Identification and Tracking US: Safe Port Act; 24-h Advanced Manifest Rule; 96-h Electronic Notice of Arrival **By air:** Global: IATA-ICAO; ADSB/GPS and next-generation avionics US: CBP Global Entry Europe: EC Regs: 831/2006 and 2320/2002	**CSI** • Targets high-risk containers coming into the United States • Cargo security screening prior to loading, i.e., at origin • Technology applications, i.e., "smart" containers **C-TPAT by US CBP** • Mitigates supply chain security risks • "Trusted" entities, database with security-cleared carriers, manufacturers, exporters and shippers **Operation Safe Commerce** • Assessment of diverse protocols, systems, and methodologies	**IMO under the UN umbrella** • **ISPS Code** amendment to **SOLAS** Convention (equivalent to US C-TPAT for ports and vessels, see left column) **WCO Framework of Standards** • Task Force on Security and Facilitation of the International Supply Chain **ISO 28000, (International Standard for Security Management).** The standard provides a structure for a comprehensive security management program. The security management system is a tool used to help implement the Facility Security Plan required under MTSA. **ISO TC8 (Technical Committee 8)** • To establish standards for data, process, and technology for marine cargo

(Continued)

TABLE 3.1 (CONTINUED) Supply Chain Security Initiatives: Regulatory Framework

Stage 1: Production	Stage 2: Preshipment Regulations for Import and Transit		Stage 3: Transport and Distribution
Commodities' Production	Regulations per Transportation Mode Segment	US-Driven Sea–Land–Air Security Initiatives	International Initiatives
	By land: GPS; RFID International Working Group on Land Transport Security Mass transit and passenger rail security programs	24-h Advance Cargo Declaration (ACD or AMR) • Proactive data gathering and security evaluation methodology to facilitate targeting SSTL project The Public Health Security and Bioterrorism Preparedness and Response Act of 2002 (or Bioterrorism Act). Stipulates new rules and protocols for registering of ownership, usage, and transportation of select agents and toxins that may impose biological hazards to humans, flora, fauna, and the environment. Security risk assessment is a critical component of this rule in order to classify individual profiles in terms of permission to use or opportunity to access these substances.	ISO Technical Committees: and ISO/TC 292 on "Security" • The ISO has established 293 committees to encompass different classifications of raw materials and industry segments, as well as set the standards for sea/land/air/pipeline transportation. As of January 1, 2015, the ISO/TC 292 Security Committee is established and will encompass all homeland security issues, security management, business continuity management, resilience and emergency management, fraud countermeasures and controls, and security services. Strategic Council on Security Technology • Launched SSTL

Security Initiatives throughout the Supply Chain:

WCO; TAPA; ISO/PAS 28000:2007 (Security); ISO/PAS 17712:2013 (High-Security Seals) C-TPAT (USA); AEO (EU); PIP (Canada); BASC (South America)

Source: The author, based on Burns, M., *Supply Chain Security: A Strategy to Resilience through Policies, Partnerships, and Technologies,* DHS Supply Chain Security Workshop, Houston, Texas, April 2014.

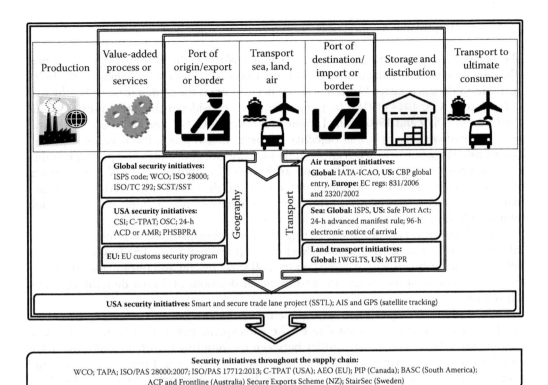

FIGURE 3.1   Security regulations in different geographic and transportation segments. (From the author, based on Burns, M., *Supply Chain Security: A Strategy to Resilience through Policies, Partnerships, and Technologies*, DHS Supply Chain Security Workshop, Houston, Texas, April 2014.)

De Saint-Pierre's works inspired the global security and peace initiatives of the nineteenth and twentieth centuries, such as the "League of Nations" (LN) and the "UN."

The regulations in this chapter are organized as follows:

- Global organizations and security regulations (Section 3.2)
- US agencies, regulations, and harmonization with other nations' rules (Section 3.3)
- Private sector initiatives (Section 3.4)

3.2 GLOBAL SECURITY REGULATIONS

Where the legal system fails, violence begins.

Hugo de Groot (1583–1645)
Dutch jurist and a towering figure in the modern legal and political theory

The perception of global peace had previously been described in the works of De Saint-Pierre, Rousseau, and Kant. In their works, they consider that singular governments are not adequate by themselves to ensure and retain global peace; instead, a league of nations is required.

3.2.1 The "League of Nations" (1920–1946)

The *League of Nations* in English, or *Société des Nations* (SDN) in French, was a pre-UN international governmental organization (IGO) established on January 10, 1920, pursuant to the Paris Peace Conference that decided upon the termination of World War I (The Great War, 1914–1918). Its predecessors are considered the international Hague Conventions (1899 and 1907). The League of Nations (LG) was the first global organization entrusted with the duty and objective to ensure global peace. Its covenant stipulates that its mission was to avert warfare and de-escalate global disputes and acts of hostility via concerted security, conciliation, and arbitration. In addition, the LN and pertinent treaties aimed to monitor and eliminate human and drug-trafficking activities, illegitimate arms trade, war prisoners, protection of indigenous populations, child and adult labor conditions, and the welfare of minorities.

The diplomatic viewpoint supporting the formation of the LN symbolized a significant change from the past century's global political practices. The league was not a self-sufficient entity; instead, it leaned on the collective insight and resources of the Great Powers to implement its resolutions and financial decisions and provide military forces when required.

After numerous distinctive achievements in the early 1920s, the league's structural weaknesses were revealed due to the subsequent political climate, which was characterized by warfare and conflict between its founding members and most influential nations of the times. In 1936, the Nazi Germany, the Empire of Japan, and a number of anticommunist nations signed the Anti-Comintern Pact. In 1937 Italy joined the pact and led to the formation of the *Rome–Berlin Axis*, a military alliance that was later to form the *Axis powers*. The league proved incapable of handling internal conflicts and the misuse of power from certain members; this inability weakened the league's influence, which led to a number of sociopolitical setbacks and losses. One of the league's initiatives was to reach a global disarmament agreement, i.e., an initiative to limit army sizes. In 1933, Adolf Hitler became the German chancellor and announced that the Nazi Germany will withdraw from the LN; this decision was followed by Japan, Italy, and other nations. The league's ineffectiveness in protecting member states against the Axis forces in the 1930s fueled the Second World War and therefore revealed that the league had failed its primary purpose, which was to ensure global security. After 26 years of operations, the league was officially disbanded in 1946 at the end of World War II. The UN substituted it, yet was based on similar basic principles, and inherited numerous agencies and organizations launched by the league.

3.2.2 United Nations Security Council

The United Nations Security Council (UNSC) was established on October 24, 1945 as part of the UN pursuant to World War II, with the mission of retaining global security and peace. Its first session was held on January 17, 1946. It is one among the six key instruments of the UN and is involved in the preservation of global peace and security. Its capabilities consist of the constitution of peacekeeping missions as a mediator, the endorsement of global sanctions, and the approval of military action by means of security council resolutions; among all UN bodies, the UNSC has the exclusive power to promulgate binding agreements to all member states.

According to the UN Charter, the security council's capabilities and responsibilities entail focusing on international security, disarmament, counterterrorism, peacebuilding, and peacekeeping. According to Chapter VI of the "Pacific Settlement of Disputes" Charter, the UN Security Council has the authority to examine disputes and suggest suitable methods of adjustment in cases that may impose a threat to international security and peace.

According to Chapter VII, the UN Security Council has a more expansive power to determine what actions are required to mitigate acts of aggression, threats, and breaches of the peace, whereas these actions may entail the use of armed forces.

The council consists of a total of 15 members, i.e.,

a. Five permanent members: the United States, China, Russian Federation, the United Kingdom, and France
b. Ten nonpermanent members: Argentina, Australia, Chad, Chile, Jordan, Lithuania, Luxembourg, Nigeria, Republic of Korea, and Rwanda

In addition, over 60 nations are considered as noncouncil member states, i.e., are UN member states yet have never been members of the security council (UNSC 2014).

3.2.3 United Nations Office on Drugs and Crime

The United Nations Office on Drugs and Crime (UNODC) is a member of the UN development group and was founded in 1997 as the Office for Drug Control and Crime Prevention. Headquartered in Vienna, Austria, UNODC comprises both the secretariat of the International Narcotics Control Board and the UNODC Terrorism Prevention Branch.

Through offering government support, research, and guidance, UNODC addresses the interrelated issues of illegitimate immigration, human trafficking, drug smuggling, piracy, terrorism, money laundering, and organized crime (UNODC 2014a).

3.2.3.1 Maritime Crime

Maritime crime consists of any unlawful action aimed toward ships or offshore structures and entails organized criminal groups involved in illegitimate trade and transport of persons, substances, and commodities. The UNODC Maritime Crime Program facilitates nations to reinforce their ability to eliminate illegitimate maritime activities.

3.2.3.2 Piracy

Since the early years of maritime piracy, the act of hijacking ships and recreational boats for the pursuit of ransom was enhanced by new piracy styles. To increase the ransom amount, pirates exercised shore-based kidnapping or took crewmembers as hostages. Over time, some piracy groups tried to hamper the hostage recuperation mission by dividing hostages into smaller groups and moving them to different shore areas.

The Counter Piracy Program was founded in 2009 as a result of global request to mitigate piracy and serve criminal justice in the Indian Ocean, Western Africa, and the Horn of Africa. It established a local piracy prosecution model, which entailed collaboration among global governments and marine powers.

- The *prisoner transfer program* entails the arrest of pirates that are subsequently brought to justice.
- The hostage support program was created to support hostages (UNODC 2014b).

3.2.4 Maritime Security: The International Ship and Port Facility Security Code by the International Maritime Organization (UN Instrument)

The International Ship and Port Facility Security (ISPS) Code is a wide-ranging set of protocols, methods, and processes seeking to increase the security of ships and port facilities. It was created pursuant to the recognized threats against ships and port facilities during the 9/11 terrorist attacks in the United States. The ISPS Code is implemented via the International Convention for the Safety of Life at Sea (SOLAS), 1974, namely, SOLAS Chapter XI-2, "Special measures to enhance maritime security." The code contains two parts, part A' being obligatory and part B' being recommendatory, i.e., offering recommendations for implementation (IMO 2013). The ISPS Code is applicable to ships on global trade routes (i.e., passenger ships, cargo ships of 500 gross tonnage (GT) and greater, and mobile offshore drilling units) and the respective port facilities assisting these ships and structures.

Essentially, the code determines that the security of ships and port facilities is a risk management activity, and in order to confirm what security measures are appropriate, a risk assessment methodology should be used for each specific situation. The objective of the code is to offer a consistent, sustainable platform for risk assessment, enabling the industry and nations to eliminate security threats by eradicating vulnerabilities in their ships and port facilities. This is accomplished by way of identifying distinct security levels and taking security measures.

The key objectives and goals of the ISPS Code are (a) to determine security threats and put into action security procedures; (b) to assign tasks and responsibilities relating to maritime security for federal governing bodies, regional administrations, ship and port industrial sectors, and so on; (c) to accumulate and exchange security-relevant information; and (d) to provide security assessment recommendations, plans, and security mitigation methods.

Due to the different types, structures, and utility purposes of the ship and port facilities, the ISPS Code does not specify measures where all ships and port facilities should adhere to. Instead, it defines a standardized, maintainable framework for risk assessment.

The shipboard and shipping company requirements relate to company security officers, ship security officers, ship security plans, and ship security equipment.

The port security requirements comprise port facility security officers, port security plans, and port facility equipment; the conformity requirements for all professionals and authorities associated with ISPS ensure (a) that security details are easily obtainable and available, (b) access monitoring and controlling, and (c) the movement of people and commodities monitoring and controlling (IMO 2013).

The ISPS Code has been enforced at an international level through the International Maritime Organization (IMO) under the umbrella of the UN.

3.2.5 UN Counter-Terrorism Implementation Task Force

The Counter-Terrorism Implementation Task Force (CTITF) was founded in 2005 and approved in 2006 by the General Assembly via the UN Global Counter-Terrorism Strategy. Its mission is to improve planning and collaboration within the UN in supporting counterterrorism endeavors. The task force is composed of 34 global entities that, due to their scope of activities, are in a position to support counterterrorism initiatives. Each individual organization contributes and operates in accordance with its mission.

Although the member states are mainly in charge of executing the global strategy, CTITF promotes the UN functions in line with member states' requirements for policy support, sharing information on strategic decisions, and providing technical assistance.

The four pillars of the strategy include (1) activities to tackle the circumstances that foster terrorist activities; (2) actions to avert and fight terrorism; (3) methods to strengthen the member states' ability to reduce and fight terrorism and to reinforce the position and purpose of the UN; and (4) activities to confirm that human rights are valued, and all are equal under the global legislation. Equality and respect for human rights are the primary foundation for the combat against terrorism.

CTITF sets up its functions with working groups and assignments related to counterterrorism in sectors where cohesiveness between UN members and key players can reinforce the mission and strategic goals (UN CTITF 2014).

3.2.6 North Atlantic Treaty Organization

The North Atlantic Treaty Organization (NATO) or the North Atlantic Alliance is an intergovernment armed force coalition established in 1949, in the aftermath of World War II, in line with the North Atlantic Treaty. NATO is a model of multinational military defense through which its member states consent to common defense as a result of an external attack. NATO consists of 28 members from the Americas and Europe and is headquartered in Brussels, Belgium. Twenty-two nations engage in NATO's Partnership for Peace plan along with 15 other nations associated with national dialogue programs. The total military investment of all NATO member states comprises more than 70% of the international overall investment (NATO 2014b).

NATO offers the opportunity to member states to take advice and decide upon security concerns through different areas and stages.

A *NATO decision* expresses a group statement and decision of all 28 member states, considering the fact that the decision-making process is obtained by consensus.

NATO Headquarters is the place where government delegations, the NATO officials, military services, and private sector stakeholders exchange data, make recommendations, and assist in the decision-making process.

NATO assumes a leading role in a wide variety of crisis-management missions and tasks, among them civil emergency operations. NATO is an advocate of security and peace at a global, multinational level. By means of its crisis-management procedures, the coalition illustrates both its determination to operate as a constructive change agent as well as its ability to fulfill the security issues during the most crucial eras throughout the modern history. NATO continues to be involved in projects and tasks that meet the whole array of crisis-management missions: at times of war and peace, it covers the entire supply chain of production, strategic planning, procurement, transportation, security monitoring, and humanitarian relief. Currently, around 55,000 armed force employees are actively involved in global NATO missions in the Mediterranean, Afghanistan, Somalia, Kosovo, or around the Horn of Africa (NATO 2014b).

3.2.7 World Customs Organization

Pursuant to the European Customs Co-operation Council established in 1948, the World Customs Organization (WCO) was established in 1994 and is globally accepted as the heart of customs experience, methods, and techniques. The WCO implemented the Framework of Standards to Protect and Expedite Global Trade in 2005. Headquartered in Brussels, Belgium, it comprises supply chain security requirements for global customs authorities such as the *Authorized Economic Operator (AEO) programs.*

The WCO is a global coalition of 169 customs administrations covering over 99% of international trade. Based in Brussels, Belgium, it supports global trade and transport by establishing and endorsing recommendations to assist customs authorities in collaborating closely to ensure fast customs clearance of limited hazard, international commodities. WCO members have created the Framework of Standards with the purpose of "Securing and Facilitating Global Trade" (SAFE). In 2006, 135 nations around the world conveyed their plan to put into practice the WCO SAFE Framework. The WCO is an IGO, i.e., an organization made up mostly by sovereign member states. It is an advocate of secure customs, trade, and transport and is focused in the advancement of supply chain security, global trade facilitation, customs administration functions, global conventions, resources, freight categorization, appraisal, origin requirements, collection of customs income, dealing with intellectual property (IP) rights, and so on. The WCO regulates the technological elements of the World Trade Organization (WTO) Contracts on Customs Valuation and Rules of Origin while preserving the global Harmonized System.

The WCO has launched the global Container Control Program (CCP), developed in partnership with the UNODC, in order to enhance synergy among the global enforcement agencies, custom administrators, trade, and transport entities. Its aim is to create reliable container checks at specific hub and nodal point areas around the world and to eliminate illegitimate transportation of people and goods (WCOOMD 2014).

3.2.8 Global CCP by UNODC and WCO

As global population grows, developed and rapidly developing economies tend to increase their annual freight volume of exports and imports. In 2012, global container port throughput exceeded 602 million 20-ft. equivalent units, resulting into an annual increase of 3.8% (UNCTAD 2013).

The global CCP was developed pursuant to a collaboration between the UNODC and the WCO, with the purpose to eliminate the trade and transport of illegitimate substances, chemicals, and other smuggled goods while enhancing the collaboration among the customs authorities, trade, and transport stakeholders (UNODC 2006, 2014a,b,c,d,e).

The volume of freight transported by sea containers has significantly increased during the past years. Over 220 million containers are being transported globally each year, and the annual increase in global freight is anticipated to increase the volume of illegitimate commodities smuggled in containers. The major threats imposed by containerized transportation are duly analyzed in Chapter 2 and include

1. Terrorism and explosives. Terrorist groups may utilize the increasing volume of containerized cargo flows, to penetrate specific states, with grave consequences. The large number of containers being shipped to and from international nodal points offers numerous possibilities to terrorists to transport and release bombs, chemicals, or weapons of mass destruction on the territory of nonterrorist, sovereign nations. Through the years, terrorist groups seem to be familiar with the new antiterrorist technologies, legislations, and processes and seem to be resourceful in their effort to attack innocent civilians. Explosives have been found not only

in shoes and undergarments of airline passengers but also in machinery and containerized cargo traveling by sea, land, or air.

2. Terrorism and radiological dispersion devices. Container boxes may also be the terrorists' preferred transportation mode for planting radiological dispersion devices (or simply dirty bombs). These devices comprise traditional explosives covered with radioactive components that disperse into particles after the explosion, and may spread throughout a critical infrastructure location, and cause (a) acute damage such as fatalities, (b) chronic health threat, and (c) environmental damage through the dispersion of radioactive particles and toxic substances.

3. Bioterrorism, biological weapons, and infectious diseases. Bioterrorism can be described as the deliberate utilization of a virus or biological substance or compound to damage human communities, flora, fauna, and the environment with the ulterior purpose of impacting the national, political, and socioeconomic status or even controlling and terrorizing a nonmilitary population. Throughout the history of mankind, the manifestation and outbreak of infectious diseases have been much more fatal than warfare. Containers could also harbor infectious diseases and other biological threats.

4. Drug smuggling is also a serious concern. According to the World Health Organization, over 230 million people globally (1 out of 20) are using drugs (WHO 2014).

5. The international CCP has accomplished impressive results, identifying cargo shipments of illegal drugs, invasive species, hazardous materials, and others. Since March 2006, CCP has seized over 36 tons of cocaine, 26 tons of marijuana, and roughly 770 tons of chemical substances. UNODC aims to maximize the results with a plan focusing on global airports in West Africa and South America (UNODC 2011).

6. Smuggling of illegitimate cargoes entails commodities that are being transported, either being mixed together with legitimate commodities or hidden in other products' packaging. According to the European Commission (2002), modern smuggling practices ensure that

   a. Illegitimate cargoes are hard to locate, as criminals hide them in vast volumes of legitimate commodities.

   b. The criminal activities are conducted by a small number of people, hence the vast majority of supply chain stakeholders is not familiar with the illicit activities and yet unintentionally facilitate this trade.

   c. Consequently, illegitimate cargoes are shielded under legitimate transactions, which may not be targeted if hidden among well-reputable brands.

   d. In case of legal complications, criminal organizations may not appear to the customs offices to claim their cargoes and therefore may avoid arrest.

   e. Typically, illegitimate cargoes and humans are hidden behind false partitions of the container structure, i.e., double walls, floors, ceilings, and so on.

3.2.9 AEO Program by the WCO "Framework of Standards to Secure and Facilitate Global Trade"

The international trade expansion combined with escalating security risks throughout the global supply chain networks have necessitated the world customs community to monitor and control the global commodities well beyond the typical process of customs functions. For this reason, the WCO composed the "Framework of Standards to Secure and Facilitate Global Trade" (SAFE). Among its key objectives, SAFE launched an "Authorized Economic Operator" initiative.

The AEO certificate is a globally accepted quality designation suggesting that the company's operations and functions within the global supply chain are secure and that their customs regulations and protocols are in conformity with the security standards. While the AEO compliance is not obligatory, it is considered as a favorable commercial choice as it provides cost-efficient expediting from customs clearance and occasionally the ability to expedite and clear the cargo dispatches via specific regulatory protocols.

For a global trade and transport entity to become an AEO, it should be "involved in the international movement of goods in whatever function that has been approved by or on behalf of a national Customs administration as complying with WCO or equivalent supply chain security standards. Authorized Economic Operators include inter alia manufacturers, importers, exporters, brokers, carriers, consolidators, intermediaries, ports, airports, terminal operators, integrated operators, warehouses and distributors" (WCO 2014).

The majority of WCO members around the world are compliant with the SAFE platform, and customs authorities are anticipated to encourage more national AEO participants.

As of 2014, the following national initiatives are in line with the AEO framework:

- United States: Customs-Trade Partnership against Terrorism (C-TPAT), where only US importers can participate (see also C-TPAT section in this chapter).
- European Union (EU): the AEO framework was established by the Taxation and Customs Union (TCU) of EU. AEO certification is open to global supply chain players, and combines security clearance with simplified customs regulations, duties, and clearance protocols. The AEO designation may be offered to companies that are set up in the EU, directly associated with customs procedures and global commerce, while are designated an Economic Operator Registration and Identification (EORI) number. Under specific conditions, non-EU corporations established outside the EU may also be eligible for AEO status as long as they can prove that they are global industry players with direct interests in EU trade and transport. Such companies may include commercial air carriers, maritime, or other transportation companies. The European Commission's (EC's) AEO data bank enables authorities, companies, and professionals to verify which global and local partners are eligible for AEO certification along with pertinent commercial information (EU TCU 2014).
- Asia Pacific: Asia Pacific Economic Cooperation (APEC 2014).
- New Zealand Customs Service: Secure Export Scheme (SES) (NZ Customs 2014).
- Singapore Customs: Secure Trade Partnership (Singapore Customs 2014).
- Taiwan: Taiwan AE Operator (UCTC 2014).

3.2.10 Global Initiative to Combat Nuclear Terrorism (Initiated by the United States and Russia)

The *Global Initiative to Combat Nuclear Terrorism* (GICNT) was established in 2006 by US President George W. Bush and Russian President Vladimir Putin. This is a global voluntary effort targeted at cultivating global synergy so as to eliminate terrorists from obtaining, carrying, or employing nuclear or radioactive substances, to prevent hostilities toward nuclear establishments, and to address emergency incidents concerning the use of radiological or nuclear materials. Eighty-five countries and four official observers collaborate in an attempt to boost capacity on a global, regional, and national level for the prevention, monitoring, and elimination of a nuclear terrorist incident.

Partner nations may work with the GICNT by supporting the Statement of Principles, which entails pre-set goals related to nuclear security. The GICNT partners may also coordinate and attend workshops, conventions, and drills to exchange best implementation practices for the Statement of Principles. Furthermore, the GICNT maintains plenary sessions to explore developments and modifications.

The Statement of Principles includes the following key objectives:

- Produce, as appropriate, and enhance data processing, management, and physical security systems for nuclear, radioactive, or other hazardous materials and substances.
- Improve security measures of private nuclear facilities.
- Strengthen the capability to scan and identify nuclear, radioactive, or hazardous materials and substances to avoid illegal trafficking in these types of substances within a synergistic framework that enhances the development and research of nationwide detection capacities, which would otherwise be interoperable.
- Ameliorate the members and participants' effectiveness to seek out, confiscate, and achieve secure control over illegitimately held nuclear or radioactive materials, compounds, or equipment utilizing them.
- Prevent the harboring of terrorists and monetary or asset resources to terrorists aiming to obtain or employ nuclear or other radioactive materials and compounds.
- Assure that national laws and regulations can efficiently and effectively provide for the execution of suitable criminals and, if appropriate, civil accountability for terrorists and individuals who assist in acts of nuclear terrorism.
- Strengthen the potential of members or participants related to incident response, elimination, and inspection in the event of terrorist assaults relating to the use of nuclear, radioactive, chemical, or hazardous materials or compounds, such as the production of technical methods to scan nuclear or other radioactive, chemical, and hazardous materials and compounds that may be related to the incident.
- Promote data exchange related to the elimination of nuclear terrorism and relevant acts while taking suitable actions in line with their national legislation and global commitment to safeguard the secrecy of any confidential data they may share.

3.3 SECURITY IN THE UNITED STATES

3.3.1 Transportation Security Acts

3.3.1.1 The National Security Act of 1947, USA

The National Security Act of 1947 dictated a considerable reorganization of the international policy and military facilities of the United States around the world. The act developed a number of establishments that US presidents found beneficial when creating and employing foreign policy, such as the National Security Council (NSC) (US DOS 1947; US Senate 1947).

The *National Security Act of 1947* was enforced with the purpose of endorsing national security by administering "for a Secretary of Defense; for a National Military Establishment; for a Department of the Army, a Department of the Navy, and a Department of the Air Force; and for the coordination of the activities of the National Military Establishment with other departments and agencies of the Government concerned with national security" (NSA 1947).

The National Security Act of 1947 was designed to greatly reorganize the US national military and intelligence agencies immediately after World War II, with the main objective to bring together the army, navy, and air force into a federated framework. Apart from the military restructure, the act enabled the foundation of the National Security Council, a critical area for synchronization of national security planning in the executive side, and the Central Intelligence Agency, which was the first intelligence agency during peacetime. The council's purpose was to inform the US president on national, international, and military strategies and policies, as well as assure synergy involving the different military and intelligence agencies.

In addition, the 1947 act also triggered long-term modifications in the military organization. The war department and navy department merged into a solitary Department of Defense, which also runs the newly established Department of the Air Force. Nevertheless, each one of the three divisions retained their own service secretaries. During 1949, the National Security Act was revised to allow the Secretary of Defense additional control over all services and secretaries. Additionally, it founded the Central Intelligence Agency (CIA), which developed as a continuation of the Second World War "Office of Strategic Services" and minor postwar intelligence agencies. The CIA functions as the most important private intelligence-accumulating agency in the US federal government (US DOS 1947; US Senate 1947).

3.3.1.2 Maritime Transportation Security Act of 2002

The primary objective of the Maritime Transportation Security Act (MTSA) of 2002 is to protect against a maritime transportation security incident, described as any occurrence that leads to (a) loss of life, (b) environmental deterioration, (c) hindrance of transport networks, or (d) economic or commercial dysfunction to a specific geographical or industrial segment.

MTSA represents an important legal component that reinforces the international and regional significance of security for the sea transport networks and ensures the security of sea trade in connection with the national ports.

Inside the maritime industry, protecting against transportation security incidents (TSIs) has become a central mandate of the US Coast Guard (USCG) since its inception.

MTSA requires a *family of plans* to be submitted at a domestic, seaport, and single ship/facility level, as this system has proven to be effective in cases of oil spills with particular focus in risk assessment, contingency planning, and emergency response.

Ships and facilities involved in the transportation and storage of hazardous materials should have particular security plans that address essential security procedures including entry controls; hazardous material communications; confined areas; hazardous materials handling; monitoring and controlling; and training, emergency drills, and incident reporting protocols.

The Area Maritime Security (AMS) plan entails the security plan of specific facilities, seaports, and designated water areas, which include recreational marinas or public berths whose individual security plans are not mandatory.

The AMS plan is produced and executed by an AMS committee with not only representatives coming from federal, state, and regional authorities but also stakeholders from public and private entities. These boards combined with the AMS plans are essential components in ensuring monitoring, proactiveness, and mitigation of any hazards that may impact the maritime infrastructure (MTSA 2014).

3.3.1.3 Security and Accountability for Every Port Act of 2006 by DHS

The "Security and Accountability For Every Port Act of 2006" or the "SAFE Port Act 2006" was ratified by the Senate and House of Representatives of the US Congress to enhance the existing maritime security legislation and develop a number of new programs.

The SAFE Port Act of 2006 stipulates the nonintrusive scanning and radiation-detection protocols of containerized freights in foreign ports before they are imported in the United States. For the DHS to achieve its goal of scanning 100% of the foreign containerized cargoes, it is imperative to secure resources including funds, advanced technology, and additional personnel.

DHS officers through the *Container Security Initiative* (CSI) utilize the existing resources available by targeting and scanning high-risk containers and conducting scarce inspections at around 60 global ports that expedite approximately 80% of sea freight containers intended for the United States.

The US DHS multileveled strategy is to enhance seaport and container security (GPO 2006a,b).

3.3.2 US Security: Department of Homeland Security and Its Agencies

3.3.2.1 US Department of Homeland Security

The Department of Homeland Security (DHS) concept was initially recommended by the US Commission on National Security in 2001. Pursuant to the 9/11 terrorist attacks, the US federal government established a security platform to defend our nation from security attacks while strengthening government, state, and regional functions to proactively organize, mitigate, and ensure resilience from homeland risks and catastrophes. A crucial component of this security strategy involved the establishment of the US DHS in 2003, merging 22 independent federal agencies toward an executive department. The DHS is responsible for safeguarding the US territory from terrorist threats, man-made disasters, and natural disasters. The DHS assumes the duties comparable to other nations' *Ministry of Internal Affairs*.

While the mission of the US Department of Defense is to train and supply military forces to prevent warfare and to safeguard the national security (US DOD 2014), the DHS supports the civilian sector to shield the US territory and its borders and extend the defense outside its borders. Its mission is to plan for, avert, and respond to national emergencies, especially terrorist threats. With over 200,000 personnel, DHS is among the largest US Cabinet departments, following the Departments of Defense and Veterans Affairs. The US Departments of Energy, Health and Human Services, and Justice also bear considerable homeland security responsibilities (DHS 2014, http://www.dhs.gov).

The DHS vision entails establishing a safe and secure nation that is resilient toward the risk of terrorism and other threats. The basis of the DHS security strategy involves three principles intended to accomplish this vision: (i) security, (ii) resilience, and (iii) customs and exchange.

The five core homeland security missions include

1. Preventing terrorism and strengthening security
2. Securing and managing our borders
3. Enforcing and complying our immigration laws and regulations
4. Safeguarding and securing cyberspace
5. Creating a strategy of resilience during and after disasters

Furthermore, the nucleus of the DHS strategy is to develop and improve the homeland security department.

3.3.2.2 Transportation Security Administration (DHS Agency)

The Transportation Security Administration (TSA) is a DHS agency in charge of the public transport security within the United States. It was developed as a section of the Aviation and Transportation Security Act ratified in 2001 by US President George W. Bush. Since its establishment in November 2001, the TSA is in charge of the national transportation security and has significantly succeeded to deal with the aviation security conditions. In 2003, the TSA was transferred from the US Department of Transportation to the DHS. TSA was intended to reinforce the security of the US transportation networks. Its mission and vision are to safeguard the country's transportation to facilitate the unimpeded mobility of people and cargoes while fighting terrorism. It implements a risk-based technique and operates directly with law enforcement, transport, and intelligence agencies and organizations in order to ensure superior, flawless transportation security.

Within the first year of its inception, TSA employed and trained more than 60,000 employees as federal air marshals, employees for air passengers' security screening, and for around 90% of all checked travel luggage for explosives. TSA further focused in identifying training and emergency response drills, as well as tackling systemic weaknesses.

The USCG being in charge of the maritime and coastal security developed a set of security recommendations, carried out initial risk assessments of US ports, and launched an all-inclusive evaluation of security vulnerabilities at 55 of these.

The Customs Service as well as the Immigration and Naturalization Service are focused on reinforcing seaport security (GAO 2003).

Despite the substantial investment in resources, training, and organized efforts; the increasing volume of trade; and the increasing threats in terms of illegitimate trade and transport, cyber security, and terrorism threats related to mass transit systems, there is still a lot to be done in order to eliminate vulnerabilities and achieve optimum security.

The Departments of Transportation and Homeland Security encounter persisting impediments related to national transportation security, which necessitate (1) the design of an all-inclusive risk management methodology to encompass all aspects and threats of transportation security; (2) the development of an efficient budget funding, monitoring, and controlling that recognizes and itemizes the transportation security monetary requirements; (3) reliable synchronization among the private and public sectors related to transportation security issues; (4) empowering human resource development through delivering satisfactory training, skillsets, and drills that will prepare them for real-life security scenarios; and (5) establishing security specifications for transportation establishments, employees, and security technologies.

While collaborating with global, national, and regional key players, the TSA ensures security for transportation critical infrastructure, including pipelines, motorways, seaports, airports, railways, buses, and all mass transportation systems. In fact, aviation security is a principal goal for the TSA, which is in charge of screening travelers and scanning baggage at over 450 national airports (TSA 2014a,b).

The TSA mandates that travelers display a valid photo ID at the security gate prior to boarding their airline flight. A legitimate photo ID may entail US or international passports, drivers' licenses and formal government photo ID, or armed service ID. Traveler identifications are contrasted with the no-fly list, a record of over 21,000 names of assumed terrorists and persons of interest that are not permitted to travel. TSA has admission to historic travel records with schedules, assets ownership and lease data, physical attributes and features, as well as background checks, arrests, and intelligence data (TSA 2014a,b).

Based on TSA statistics, the volume of passengers who have tried to carry weapons onboard air carriers in their carry-on luggage has accelerated in the past few years, i.e., from 976 in 2009 to 1813 in 2013. The volume of traveler screening also increases each year; hence, in 2013, TSA screened 638,705,790 travelers, i.e., over a million more passengers compared to 2012. This amounts to a daily screening of more than 1,700,000 passengers.

Almost five weapons are found in carry-on luggage every day, amounting to 1813 weapons found in the United States in 2013, which signifies an increase of over 16% compared to 2012. Among these weapons discovered, over 81%, i.e., 1477 weapons, were loaded. The disturbing statistics suggest that over 70% of the firearms that travelers try to carry onboard are not identified by scanning equipment (TSA Blog 2013, 2014).

3.3.2.3 US Customs and Border Protection (DHS Agency)

The US Customs and Border Protection (CBP) Agency is headquartered in Washington, DC. It is the greatest national law enforcement agency of the US DHS with over 45,600 federal agents and officials. The CBP is accountable for controlling and facilitating global trade, receiving importation fees, and implementing US policies, such as commerce, customs, and immigration laws.

CBP evolved into an established agency of the US DHS in 2003, integrating officers from the US Customs Service, the US Animal and Plant Health Inspection Service, and the US Immigration and Naturalization Service. Hence, while its principal goal is to safeguard against terrorists and enemy weapons from getting into the United States, it is additionally accountable for any illegitimate travel and/or trade (Europa 2002). This includes arresting persons trying to enter the United States unlawfully; arresting immigrants with criminal convictions; and mitigating the movement of illegitimate narcotics, nuclear or hazardous substances, and additional contraband activities. Their role is to safeguard the U.S. environment and agriculture from invasive species, biological and/or health hazards, and thus prevent or eliminate social, commercial, and financial losses. They also protect the public and private sector from cyber threats, copyright infringement but also patents and trademarks issues.

3.3.2.4 Federal Emergency Management Services (DHS Agency)

The Federal Emergency Management Agency (FEMA) is a US DHS Agency, whose concept as a disaster/emergency response initiative was envisioned back to the Congressional Act of 1803. It was developed in its current form by the Presidential Reorganization Plan No. 3 of 1978 and enforced by two executive orders in 1979. Dedicated to the American society, FEMA's mission is to support the survivors of all disasters, both safety related (natural) and security related (man-made, such as terrorist attacks). It harmonizes the federal function by being proactive, eliminating, mitigating the consequences of, addressing, and recuperating from such disasters. FEMA employs about 15,000 professionals nationwide, with their main goal being to be prepared and well trained so that they can effectively synchronize the emergency response incidents in collaboration with federal, state, and private sector professionals. If a disaster occurs, the governor of the pertinent area should declare a *state of emergency* and officially ask from the president of the United States that FEMA and the government support the emergency response operations (FEMA 2014).

3.3.3 US Security: Federal Programs and Initiatives

3.3.3.1 Inbound Travelers' Security Initiatives

3.3.3.1.1 CBP Initiatives for Inbound Travelers' Systems and Procedures

Through the Joint Terrorism Task Force and platforms including the Advance Passenger Information System (APIS), the Office of Biometric Identity Management (OBIM), and the Student and Exchange Visitor System (SEVIS), CBP screens and evaluates all travelers coming into the United States for terrorist threats.

3.3.3.1.2 Joint Terrorism Task Forces by CBP

These are America's premium antiterrorism forces comprising about 4000 members across the United States and originating out of more than 500 local and state agencies and 55 government agencies, such as the DHS, the US Military, Immigration and Customs Enforcement (ICE) officers, and the TSA among others.

These are very experienced, highly capable professionals from various law enforcement agencies and of various skillsets including investigators, SWAT specialists, examiners, multilingual interpreters, and so on.

Antiterrorist veterans gather and share confidential data, investigate suspicious activities, assemble evidence, initiate incarcerations, ensure security during specific venues, carry out specialized training, and respond to terrorist and other security hazards at a last minute alert (FBI 2014).

3.3.3.1.3 Advance Passenger Information System by CBP

The Advance Passenger Information System (APIS) is an electronic data interchange (EDI) system set up by the US CBP to acquire digital traveler and manifest data at each port of entry. Its principal end users and stakeholders include the CBP Office of Field Operations (OFO), TSA, Department of State (DoS), commercial airlines, maritime companies, domestic flight terminals, and US Ports of Entry (CBP ISF 2014).

In 1988, US Customs, in synergy with the US Immigration and Naturalization Service (INS) and commercial airlines, launched APIS as a voluntary tool that gathers and evaluates travelers' data such as name, birth date, nationality, and visa details from aviation passengers just before traveling to the United States from abroad.

During the early 1990s, the US Customs in collaboration with the authorities of Australia and New Zealand, created the Electronic Data Interchange for Administration, Commerce, and Trade (EDIFACT) concept for the preliminary setup of the Advance Passenger Information System (APIS), which is also known as the United States/Electronic Data Interchange for Administration, Commerce, and Trade (US/EDIFACT). As of May

2009, private aircraft pilots and commercial airlines must also provide the necessary information to the CBP (NBAA 2014).

Pilots of private or commercial airlines supply to the CBP the APIS data in electronic form before the aircraft's departure. Data are obtained from the personal identification available in travel records related to the passengers' boarding. The CBP seeks to monitor persons of interest, or persons that impose a threat to national security, by contrasting the passengers' data against police force warning lists, such as the Terrorist Screening Database. APIS expedites fast clearance of legitimate passengers, whereas recognizes travelers that overstay their visa arrangements, through comparing arrivals and departures (EAPIS 2014).

Application Programming Interface (API) entails a government acquiring data about passengers, crewmembers, and transit travelers prior to their planned arrival. These data are then examined against security alert databases and employed for immigration control, security, and customs applications. The primary objectives of API systems are to offer authorities advance alert of persons of interest prior to visiting the country and to expedite faster low-risk passengers (see also APIS in the US Security measures).

3.3.3.1.4 The Office of Biometric Identity Management by DHS
The Office of Biometric Identity Management (OBIM) by DHS was launched in 2013, superseding the US Visitor and Immigration Status Indicator Technology System. OBIM is a component of the National Protection and Programs Directorate and reinforces the DHS's responsibility to safeguard the United States by administering biometric identification services that assist government, state, and regional authorities to effectively recognize which individuals may be persons of interest or impose a security threat to the nation. OBIM provides the technology for gathering and retaining biometric records, offers assessment, revises its watchlist, and verifies the data accuracy and reliability (DHS OBIM 2014).

3.3.3.1.5 The Student and Exchange Visitor System by DHS
The Student and Exchange Visitor Program (SEVP) is a component of the National Security Investigations Division and serves as a bridge for federal and state authorities that may be seeking data on nonimmigrant travelers that visit the United States in order to study.

3.3.3.1.6 The US Immigration and Customs Enforcement Initiative by DHS
The US Immigration and Customs Enforcement (ICE) Initiative by DHS enforces national laws and regulations related to customs and border patrol, trade, transport, and immigration rules, all aiming to enhance homeland security and public safety. As a segment of the DHS, and US ICE, SEVP handles education, nonimmigrant students in the F and M visa categories and their family dependents. The DoS deals with exchange visitor programs, nonimmigrant exchange visitors in the J visa categorization, and their family dependents. Equally, SEVP and DoS make use of the Student and Exchange Visitor Information System (SEVIS) to monitor and control students' activities in educational institutions; exchange visitor programs; as well as F, M, and J nonimmigrants as they enter the United States to become actively involved with the US education and learning activities (DHS ICE 2014).

3.3.3.1.7 The Secure Electronic Network for Travelers Rapid Inspection Program by CBP
This program enables prescreened, reduced-risk visitors from Mexico to be admitted into the United States. Secure Electronic Network for Travelers Rapid Inspection (SENTRI)

offers fast CBP processing for pre-accepted, reduced-risk passengers. To be approved, travelers should voluntarily go through a detailed criminal record check against illegal, customs, immigration, terrorist, security, and other law enforcement charges; a 10-fingerprint law enforcement examination; and an individual appointment with a CBP officer. SENTRI was initially enforced in 1995 at the Otay Mesa, California port of entry. In addition, SENTRI Dedicated Commuter Lanes are available in Texas (El Paso, Hidalgo, Brownsville, Anzalduas, and Laredo), California (San Ysidro and Calexico), and Arizona (Nogales, San Luis, and Douglas) (SENTRI, DHS 2014).

3.3.3.1.8 The NEXUS Inspection Program by CBP

This program enables prescreened, reduced-risk visitors from Canada to be admitted into the United States. NEXUS (previously frequent traveler program and presently component of *Trusted Traveler Program*) is a synergistic program by Canada–US authorities, created to permit preapproved, limited-risk passengers to get across the Canada–US boundaries with minimum delays. NEXUS members can ensure rapid clearance and refrain from extended stay at border points of entry through the utilization of self-serve kiosks at airports and designated lanes at land crossings, or by calling border administrators when traveling by water. The system is enforced by the US CBP and the Canada Border Services Agency. A NEXUS membership card is a legitimate document to be used according to the Western Hemisphere Travel Initiative (WHTI) for all passengers using water, land, and air points of entry.

Authorized passengers are issued a photo identification, the radio frequency identification proximity (RFID) prox-card, which has to be scanned in close vicinity of an authorized reader machine and can exclusively be read from a few inches away. Card members must utilize either one among the three modes of passage, i.e., they can either demonstrate their NEXUS card to a federal officer, or obtain an iris scanning, or demonstrate a WHTI and make a declaration (DHS NEXUS 2014; DHS RFID 2014).

3.3.3.2 Cargo Security Initiatives

3.3.3.2.1 C-TPAT by CBP

The DHS *C-TPAT* initiative is affiliated with 6000 of the world's major US freight importers in an effort to monitor all shipments entering the United States. Within domestic ports, DHS has stationed sufficient radiation portal scanners capable of monitoring about 80% of all freight entering the country (DOE/NNSA 2006).

The C-TPAT is a voluntary conformity supply chain security system directed by US CBP and dedicated to enhancing the security of privately owned companies' supply networks in relation to terrorism threats. C-TPAT was introduced in November 2001 with the directing guidelines of voluntary participation, joint best practices, and execution procedures. In return for the security funds invested, C-TPAT collaborations obtain decreased examinations at the port of arrival, quick border clearance, *front-of-line* or priority examinations, minimum charges, and other benefits, with the most significant being the partners' active participation in the battle against global terrorism. As of late 2014, the system has almost 11,000 partners, whereas the importing companies exceed 4000 and account for around 54% of the US imported commodities' price.

For a company to obtain C-TPAT certification, it should demonstrate a recorded procedure for identifying and eliminating hazards in its entire global supply chain. Once the system is approved, companies are classified as low risk, which leads to quick cargo processing and less frequent customs checks.

C-TPAT members may include the following categories:

- US importers of record, i.e., the owners or purchasers of commodities
- Cross-boundary interstate freight carriers, i.e., traveling between the United States, Canada, and/or Mexico
- Mexico long-term freight carriers
- Sea, land, rail, and air carriers
- US maritime port authorities and terminal managers
- Importers and exporters (US air cargo brokers and consolidators, sea transport mediators, and nonvessel operating common carriers)
- Mexican and Canadian manufacturers, as well as selected invited global manufacturers
- Accredited/certified US customs brokers
- Third-party logistics service companies

C-TPAT Mutual Recognition Agreement (MAR) pertains to an agreement made between C-TPAT and an international program, confirming the harmonization of processes in practice and theoretic principles, leading to the mutual acknowledgement of the validation results between two programs. MARs enable reciprocal data exchange that enhances security and visibility throughout the entire supply chain network.

C-TPAT has achieved mutual recognition with these global entities:

- New Zealand Customs Service—Secure Exports Scheme (SES) Program—June 2007
- Canada Border Services Agency—Partners in Protection Program—June 2008
- Jordan Customs Department—Golden List Program—June 2007
- Japan Customs and Tariff Bureau—Authorized Economic Operator (AEO) Program—June 2009
- Korean Customs Service—AEO Program—June 2010
- EU—AEO Program—May 2012
- Taiwan—General of Customs, Taiwan Ministry of Finance's—AEO Program—November 2012
- Israel—June 2014

By means of these particular initiatives, CBP is inquiring organizations to assess and verify the reliability of their security systems and convey and validate the security procedures of their corporate associates inside their supply chain networks.

3.3.3.2.2 Importer Security Filing "10 + 2" Rule by CBP

As of 2009, the US CBP has enforced the Importer Security Filing (ISF), also referred to as 10 + 2, which for security purposes demands containerized shipments data to be conveyed to the CBP at minimum 24 h prior to the loading of freights onboard ships, with destination US ports of call (19 CFR section 149.2[b]).

In accordance with section 203 of the SAFE Port Act, 10 + 2 demands importers to make available 10 data elements to CBP:

1. Manufacturer (or supplier) name and address
2. Seller (or owner) name and address
3. Buyer (or owner) name and address

4. Ship to name and address
5. Container stuffing location
6. Consolidator (stuffer) name and address
7. Importer of record number/foreign trade zone applicant identification number
8. Consignee number(s)
9. Country of origin
10. Commodity Harmonized Tariff Schedule number to six digits

Furthermore, two data files need to be provided from the carrier:

1. Vessel stow plan
2. Container status messages

The ISF "10 + 2" system was designed to serve as a risk-management program, an element of the DHS tactic to recognize and evaluate high-sea transport cargo shipments imported to the United States. The importing party is eventually accountable for submitting the expected data elements or relying on a third-party entity, for instance, a broker, agent, or a freight forwarder, to provide the correct merchandise data (CBP ISF 102 2014).

3.3.3.2.3 The Advanced Manifest Rule/Advance Cargo Information by CBP

The Advanced Manifest Rule (AMR)/Advance Cargo Information (ACI) was implemented by US CBP in accordance with the Trade Act of 2002 and since 2005 has been fully executed in 99% of the US ports. It demands in-depth shipment information for all transportation modes and intermodal transportation to be sent to US CBP before to the cargo has arrived in the United States. A containerized shipment by maritime transportation can only be accepted in the United States if comprehensive data on the shipment's articles have been submitted online (digital format) to the US Customs no less than 24 h prior to the container being loaded onboard the vessel at the international port of origin. The requested data are utilized for prescreening suspicious containers or entities of interest, before arriving in US ports of call, and for targeting specific containers for examination at ports of entrance and departure:

- More than 21,180 CBP officers examine and inspect global travelers and shipments at more than 300 ports of entry. Approximately 1050 Marine and Air Interdiction agents avert the illegitimate entrance of individuals, guns, drugs, and contrabands by water, land, and air.
- Approximately 2500 personnel in CBP revenue placements gather more than $30 billion on an annual basis in admittance dues and taxation via the administration of commerce and tariff regulations. Most of these collections supply the US federal government the second biggest revenue.
- More than 21,370 Border Patrol Agents safeguard and patrol 1900 mi (3100 km) of national boundaries with Mexico and 5000 mi (8000 km) of national boundaries with Canada.

3.3.3.2.4 The CSI by CBP

Following the terrorist attacks of September 11, 2001, the US Customs Service commenced establishing antiterrorism systems to safeguard the US security. The CSI is one of these systems. It is directed by the DHS and its largest federal law enforcement agency, the US CBP. The CSI aims to facilitate CBP officials currently operating in 58 foreign ports and collaborating with over 25 nations to scrutinize high-risk containerized cargoes prior to their loading onboard ships intended to all US ports. Their aim is to control the containers imported in the United States (85%) by the use of

a. Intelligence info exchange, fast-tracking, and AIS
b. Prescreening of cargoes
c. Smart, tamper-evident containers
d. Detection technology (e.g., gamma rays)
e. Inspections

This initiative seeks to maximize supply chain security by increasing inspections and monitoring cargoes from global destinations to the United States. This necessitates prescreening of containerized cargoes in conjunction with fast-tracking when the shipments reach the United States. This is a significant security action, as the selected ports represent over 80% of the shipboard container freight that is hauled to the United States, and containerized cargoes are increasingly preferred targets for illegitimate transport and terrorist attacks (DOE/NNSA 2006).

The CSI serves as a significant instrument for the CBP to collaborate with its global partner ports, in an effort to target and monitor container shipments that may present a hazard at the international loading port, before the containers are boarded on ships with US destinations. As demonstrated in Table 3.2, the CSI initiative is applied to 58 global ports, which represent over 80% of scanned containerized freight shipped to the United States by water. The CSI partnering ports are located in North America, Europe, Asia, Africa, the Middle East, and Latin and Central America. Among these, 20 major ports represent significant container cargo volumes sent to the United States on an annual basis (CSI Brief 2014).

The four primary goals of CSI include

1. Prescreening and evaluation of potential high-risk containers as early in the supply chain as feasible, i.e., typically at the port of departure prior to their arrival at US ports of call.
2. Using non-intrusive inspection (NII) and passive radiation detection technologies to swiftly prescreen containers without delaying the cargo flow. NII technologies used may entail gamma-ray radiography, large-scale x-ray radiography such as dual-energy and backscatter x-rays, and passive radiation detection devices such as muon tomography, gamma spectroscopy, as well as gamma and neutron radiation detectors (see also Chapter 8).
3. Via CSI, CBP authorities collaborate with global port authorities and employ strategic intelligence and critical information to recognize and target high-risk containerized shipments, while developing efficient risk-assessment metrics.
4. Employing intelligent, tamper-evident containers.

CSI has influenced and motivated other international initiatives to enhance shipping security measures. In 2002, the WCO approved a resolution that will allow seaports in all of the 161 member states to enforce initiatives similar to the CSI. In 2004, the US DHS and the EU finalized a memorandum of agreement that mandates the enforcement of CSI in all the European member states.

TABLE 3.2   58 Global Ports Partnering with the CSI Program

Continent	Port: Country
The Americas	Canada: Montreal, Vancouver, and Halifax Brazil: Santos Argentina: Buenos Aires Honduras: Puerto Cortes Dominican Republic: Caucedo Jamaica: Kingston The Bahamas: Freeport Panama: Balboa, Colon, and Manzanillo Colombia: Cartagena
Europe	The Netherlands (Holland): Rotterdam Germany: Bremerhaven and Hamburg Belgium: Antwerp and Zeebrugge France: Le Havre and Marseille Sweden: Gothenburg Italy: La Spezia, Genoa, Naples, Gioia Tauro, and Livorno United Kingdom: Felixstowe, Liverpool, Thamesport, Tilbury, and Southampton Greece: Piraeus Spain: Algeciras, Barcelona, and Valencia Portugal: Lisbon
Asia and the Middle East	Singapore: Singapore[a] Japan: Yokohama, Tokyo, Nagoya, and Kobe China: Hong Kong, Shenzhen, and Shanghai South Korea: Busan[a] (Pusan) Malaysia: Port Klang and Tanjung Pelepas Thailand: Laem Chabang United Arab Emirates: Dubai Taiwan: Kaohsiung and Chi-Lung Sri Lanka: Colombo Oman: Port Salalah[a] Pakistan: Port Qasim Israel: Ashdod and Haifa
Africa	Egypt: Alexandria South Africa: Durban

Source: The author, based on data from DHS, CSIP, Container Security Initiative Ports, available at http://www.dhs.gov/container-security-initiative-ports, accessed December 12, 2014.

[a] "Secure Freight Initiative" Ports.

3.4 MARITIME SECURITY REGULATIONS IN THE UNITED STATES

A nation's socioeconomic strength and resilience depend upon its ability to successfully trade at an international level. More than 90% of international trade is carried by sea, and most of it entails containerized cargoes. Container shipments represent approximately 50% of US maritime imports in terms of value. Every year, almost 7 million containers transported by sea are discharged in US ports of call. Last year's containerized trade exceeded 500 million 20-foot-equivalent units (20 TEUs), and this amount is anticipated to grow significantly over the next decades.

The global community has expressed concerns about possible attempts of terrorist groups or countries of proliferation to use containers as a means of hauling nuclear or radioactive substances, equipment, or weapons. As terrorist organizations progressively seek to damage commercial and economic infrastructure to impair the growth of nations around the world, the susceptibility of the global maritime industry is being examined (DOE/NNSA 2010).

Maritime and seaport security play a crucial role in the US security, safety, and economic stability and the nation's 361 large- and medium-sized seaports. The DHS and its agencies, the USCG, the Transportation Security Agency (TSA), and US Customs and Border Protection (USCBP) are accountable for the nation's security including the maritime, coastal, and border protection (GAO 2007).

In the United States, a regulatory platform harmonizes the national security regulations with the global maritime security standards of the IMO, i.e., SOLAS and the ISPS Code. In addition, the framework stipulates the provisions of the Maritime Transportation Security Act of 2002. Namely, the Code of Federal Regulations, i.e., 33 CFR, Parts 101–107 consists of the domestic ship security policies, along with procedures applicable to international ships in US territory waters.

3.4.1 The Secure Freight Initiative by DHS (Safe Port Act Element)

The Secure Freight Initiative (SFI) is another DHS initiative and an element of the SAFE Port Act of 2006. SFI has developed a number of established technologies and tested nuclear sensor units to a number of strategic foreign ports. Before the containerized cargoes depart from these international ports for their US destination, they will undergo radiation scans by utilizing NII and radiation sensor technologies. In case of a radiation security alarm, the homeland security officers along with the local authorities will be notified (DHS SFI 2014).

Information obtained from global ports in foreign ports also involved in the SFI regarding containerized cargoes destined for the United States will be given in actual time to US Customs and Border Protection (CBP) authorities operating in international seaports and to the DHS National Targeting Center. This information will be cross-examined with additional accessible risk assessment data, such as presently requested cargo manifest applications, and these are expected to enhance the findings of risk assessment, targeting, and inspection of high-risk containerized cargoes around the world. Phase one of the SFI initiates collaborations with the United Kingdom, Pakistan, Honduras, Oman, Singapore, and South Korea with the purpose of increasing visibility as to the hazardous cargoes that may be hauled in these foreign ports (DOE/NNSA 2006).

The SFI entails two related projects:

a. The CSI (also called the International Container Security scanning project)
b. The "Second Line of Defense, Megaports Initiative" by the US Department of Energy's (DOE's) National Nuclear Security Administration (NNSA) (DOE/NNSA 2006, 2010)

3.4.2 Free and Secure Trade Program by CBP

The Free and Secure Trade (FAST) program is a professional clearance program for identifying limited-risk cargo shipments coming into the United States from Canada and Mexico. Launched soon after the 9/11 terrorist attacks, this groundbreaking trusted traveler/trusted shipper platform enables quick processing times for professional carriers who have performed criminal background checks and satisfy specific eligibility prerequisites. Enrollment in FAST necessitates that each and every link in the supply chain, from raw materials to manufacturers, service providers, operators, and importers, is certified under the C-TPAT program.

The FAST employs transponder technologies and prearrival cargo data to clear importing commercial transport trucks when they reach the US border. For inbound rail shipments brought in from Canada, CBP has the capability to target, monitor, and inspect these commodities.

CBP regularly performs onsite visits to local and international C-TPAT member establishments to assess and verify their supply chain security procedures. In excess of 10,000 organizations around the world are certified C-TPAT members. Over 78,000 commercial drivers are signed up for the FAST program across America.

FAST registration is accessible to truck drivers within the United States, Canada, and Mexico. FAST vehicle lanes expedite freight at land border ports of entry exclusively for commercial cargo, namely, 17 locations on the northern border (mostly in the states of Michigan, New York, and Washington state) and 17 on the southern border (mostly in Texas and California) (DHS FAST 2014).

3.4.3 The Megaports Initiative, NNSA by the US DOE

The Megaports Initiative is a project by US DOE that works jointly with international customs officials, port authorities and operators, and pertinent agencies in partner nations to consistently improve scanning functions for specific nuclear or radioactive substances in maritime containerized cargo of global supply chains. Focused in this objective, the Megaports Initiative assists its global partners to supply their leading national ports with radiation scanning devices and alarm transmission equipment. Furthermore, to guarantee the resilience and stability of these scanning technologies, the Megaports Initiative offers its global partners all-inclusive training, servicing, and technical support.

The purpose of the Megaports Initiative is to ensure that the maximum amount of containerized cargoes has been scanned, for imported, exported, and transshipped cargoes, with negligible delays or other effects to seaport functions. By 2015, the Megaports Initiative aims to supply 100 global ports with radiation scanning equipment capable of checking around half of the international maritime containerized freights.

From the inception of the Megaports Initiative in 2003, scanning technologies have been applied to 27 ports to date in 23 countries: Bahamas, Belgium, Colombia, Dominican Republic, Greece, Honduras (SFI port), Israel, Jamaica, Malaysia, Mexico, the Netherlands, Oman (SFI port), Pakistan (SFI port), Panama, the Philippines, Portugal, Spain, Singapore, South Korea (SFI port), Sri Lanka, Taiwan, Thailand, and the United Kingdom (SFI port). Furthermore, the new partnerships include 16 ports in 13 nations: Bangladesh, China, Djibouti, Dubai–United Arab Emirates, Egypt, Japan, Jordan, Kenya, Lebanon, Malaysia, Mexico, Panama, and Spain (DOE/NNSA 2006, 2014; GAO 2012).

3.4.4 CBP Collaboration with the US Food and Drug Administration to Prevent Bioterrorism and Agroterrorism

This initiative aims to screen high-risk imported food shipments in order. More than 2200 CBP agriculture professionals make an effort to mitigate the illegal import and propagation of hazardous insects and flora and fauna infections that could possibly damage America's harvesting and nutrition sources or even trigger bioterrorism and agroterrorism.

3.4.4.1 US Emergency Response Systems

3.4.4.1.1 National Terrorism Advisory System

In 2011, the National Terrorism Advisory System, or NTAS, substituted the color-coded Homeland Security Advisory System. Its purpose and mission are to convey critical information regarding terrorist risks by conveying well-timed, in-depth information to federal and state authorities; emergency responders; sea, land, and air transportation networks; and the public and private sectors.

NTAS is aware that all citizens are in charge of the nation's security and ought to continually be mindful of the increased probability of terrorist attack in the United States (DHS, NTAS 2014a,b).

By employing readily accessible data, the security notifications will share a succinct overview of the possible threat; details about measures being taken to establish public safety; and suggested procedures and actions that persons, communities, organizations, and authorities can follow to protect, minimize, or actively mitigate a security threat incident.

The NTAS alerts will depend on the characteristics and special circumstances of the danger. In certain instances, notifications will be sent instantly to law enforcement officials or impacted areas of the nonpublic sector. In other instances, general notifications will be released more extensively to the US citizens by means of both established and mass media avenues. These types of notifications will consist of a straightforward announcement that there is an imminent threat or elevated threat:

- An imminent threat cautions of a tangible, precise, and approaching terrorist threat against the United States.
- An elevated threat cautions of a credible terrorist risk against the United States (DHS NTAS 2014a,b).

3.4.4.1.2 Emergency Planning and Community Right-to-Know Act

The US Congress passed the Emergency Planning and Community Right-to-Know Act to address ecological and basic safety threats presented by the transportation, handling, and warehousing of hazardous substances, acknowledging that an accidental or intentional release of a chemical may harm humans, flora, fauna, and the environment. The act verifies that the communities need to be informed of any dangerous goods handled regionally (EPA EPCRA 2014). The federal government, state, tribal, and industrial compliance pertain to the monitoring, controlling, and reporting of the carriage, storage, or handling of hazardous and toxic chemicals.

- Emergency planning: As stipulated in Sections 301–303, local authorities must put together chemical emergency response plans, as well as evaluate these plans every year at least. State authorities should support this initiative by supervising and working with the local authorities in this respect. In the private sector, it is mandatory for emergency plans to be produced for commercial amenities that retain, store, or handle *extremely hazardous substances* (EHS) in volumes in excess of related threshold planning levels.

- Emergency notification: As stipulated in Section 304, amenities should instantly report accidental emissions of EHS to local and state authorities, if the volumes released are in excess of related reportable quantities as outlined in the Comprehensive Environmental Response, Compensation, and Liability Act.

3.4.4.2 Private Sector Initiatives

3.4.4.2.1 ISO/PAS 28000

The International Organization for Standardization (ISO) have launched a group of standards for the development, administration, and monitoring of supply chain security. The ISO became officially affiliated with the Smart and Secure Trade Lanes (SSTL) system in 2003 in an effort to establish global supply chain security and monitoring standards. Among the numerous global security initiatives, the ISO/PAS 28000:2005 standard is considered as the "security management systems specification for the supply chain" by the ISO. The ISO/PAS 28000 Specification for Security Management Systems for the Supply Chain provides general public and privately owned businesses an administration tool for standardization that allows agencies and corporations to utilize a global systematic procedure to ensure supply chain security. It covers a number of security activities related to information management, production, finance, and the establishments for packaging, warehousing, and hauling merchandise globally. Furthermore, the WTO aims to expedite global trade by sharing data among the federal, state, and public sector throughout the administration, monitoring, and inspection process.

3.4.4.2.2 Transported Asset Protection Association

The Transported Asset Protection Association (TAPA) is a distinctive forum that unites key stakeholders from the private and public sector, such as law enforcement agencies, international producers, manufacturers, transportation and logistics professionals, freight forwarders, and others, with the purpose of collectively cutting down losses and damage from global supply chains.

Over 600 members have joined TAPA, the majority of which include major global leaders of supply chains, logistics, and manufacturing corporations, with combined yearly revenue exceeding US$900 billion (TAPA 2014a).

Based on the EU statistics, the theft of high-risk and high-value commodities being transported through supply chains in Europe imposes a cost of over US$10.5 billion each year. Based on the fact that global and regional trade volume increases each year, the value of commodities also increases. Subsequently, global organized crime imposes increasing risks of theft, illegal activities, and violence and must be monitored and controlled at a national level.

- TAPA's security requirements have been accepted at a global level as the security standards that support global facilities and transportation companies to mitigate illegitimate freight activities.
- TAPA's Incident Information Service continuously gathers records and distributes critical information pertaining to freight crime intelligence. Increased awareness of security incidents in real time helps federal, state, and commercial entities to safeguard transportation operations. Furthermore, it helps identify illegitimate activities and track down compromised or stolen cargoes.

TAPA security standards are compatible with the C-TPAT conformity recommendations. The C-TPAT is a US federal government program created to decrease the threat of terrorist activities relating to the global supply chain. International, non-US service providers are not eligible to officially engage in the C-TPAT program; however, compliance to TAPA standards helps to ensure the companies' harmonization with the C-TPAT standards.

TAPA-certified organizations need to undergo a comprehensive physical audit in their premises to verify concurrence with a variety of freight security requirements. These stipulate the bare minimum security standards for conformity within the entire supply chain and the techniques used to sustain those specifications, such as

- A designated security manager and frequent ongoing security training for all personnel.
- Security vetting inspections for cargoes.
- Background checks of all personnel.
- Closed-circuit security cameras installed at virtually all entrance points to monitor illegitimate activities.
- Circumference barriers with security illumination and security alarm systems.
- Biometric fingerprint entry control to property and designated security areas.
- Planning and control-discrepancy switches used to control system vulnerabilities and guarantee the security and accuracy of records.
- Vehicle security is ensured with actual-time GPS and AIS monitoring.
- Security seals and locks for containers and trucks.

TAPA (2014b) was established with the purpose of enhancing security within the entire supply chain system, while creating more robust and reliable global trade, transport, and warehousing systems, and therefore assists to facilitate global growth and economic development.

3.4.4.2.3 The SSTL Program

SSTL is a supply chain security pilot program initiated and funded by the industry, since its inception in 2002, with the purpose of ensuring the security of cargo containers globally. SSTL's objective is to recognize the corrupt containers during transit by applying non-intrusive inspections. It entails container security technologies systems such as RFID, real-time satellite tracking systems, alerts and monitoring devices, anti-intrusion sensors, and computer software to encompass all these capabilities. The SSTL effort started off from three port and shipping conglomerates that control over 70% of the global container trade: (i) Hutchison Port Holdings, (ii) PSA Corporations, and (iii) P&O Ports. Due to these companies' influence in the industry, it now covers over 65 members headquartered in major centers of North America, Europe, and Asia. The high percentage of containerized cargo involved in this initiative enables holistic supply chain security coverage through the Department of Defense *Total Asset Visibility* initiative, which expands through the entire supply chain (GAO 2014; Hutchison-Whampoa 2014).

In 2003, a memorandum of understanding was formed between the ISO and the SSTL initiative in order to set global supply chain security standards (SCST 2014).

CASE STUDY: INTER-AMERICAN COMMITTEE ON PORTS (CIP) ORGANIZATION OF AMERICAN STATES

Interview: Jorge Durán
Chief of the Secretariat, OAS

The Organization of American States (OAS) is the world's oldest regional organization. Central to its purpose are the four pillars stated in the 1948 OAS Charter—democracy, human rights, development, and security. Today, the OAS brings together all 35 independent states of the Americas and constitutes the main political, juridical, and social governmental forum in the hemisphere. In terms of maritime and port safety and security, the CIP and the Inter-American Committee on Terrorism (CICTE) seek, within their respective mandates, to promote effective dialogue and cooperation.

Under the structure of the OAS, the CIP is part of the Executive Secretariat for Integral Development, whereas CICTE works as part of the Secretariat for Multidimensional Security. The CIP and CICTE have their own independent mandates and work collaboratively in areas where they have common objectives. The mandate of CIP is to strengthen the CIP Technical Secretariat's role as a facilitator of policy dialogue, promote hemispheric cooperation on port sector issues, and foster effective public and private cooperation throughout the Americas. By comparison, the main purpose of CICTE is to promote and develop cooperation among member states of the OAS to prevent, combat, and eliminate terrorism in accordance with both inter-American and international agreements.

A key aspect of CIP's mandate involves the exchange of successful experiences among member states. Reinforcing earlier CIP resolutions, the Declaration of Cartagena established six priority areas that, among other topics, included port protection and safety. Following up in June 2014, during its IX Ordinary Meeting, the CIP approved a proposal by the Delegation of Barbados to create a working group focusing on maritime security in ports under the Technical Advisory Group (TAG) on Port Protection and Safety. The objectives of this working group are to (1) establish an efficient and direct communication system between safety and security port officials and (2) implement modern, internationally recognized training programs for ports throughout the Wider Caribbean Region (WCR). Most importantly, this TAG incorporates not only representatives from member states but also CIP associate members that include administrative, academic, commercial, and developmental organizations related to port sector activities.

Through effective dialogue and cooperation, private sector firms and associations can become effective partners in development, making ports both easier and safer to use for all. However, implementing policies that modernize port facilities requires greater investment that can only arrive through modernizing initiatives by member states. One example of an effective public–private partnership facilitated by the CIP is between Rightship-Americas and the port authority of Barbados, Barbados Port Inc. During the CIP First Hemispheric Seminar of Port Legislation held on November 24 and 25 in Montevideo, Uruguay, an incentive program for reducing carbon emissions was introduced. By rewarding vessels that had higher standards of energy efficiency, this program reduced the overall carbon footprint created from both vessels and port facilities.

However, enhancing maritime security practices while ensuring continuous and efficient flows of trade requires a regional framework for both public and private sector actors throughout the hemisphere. Common guidelines—incorporating everything from boarding procedures, loading fuel, storing food and water, disposing waste and residues, and even safety on deck—are needed not only to deal with accidents and mishaps but also, perhaps more importantly, to prevent them. One key approach that the CIP uses is organizing capacity-building events to promote international security standards, such as the 2004 International Ship and Port Facility Security Code. In April 2014, 17 member state officials from the WCR participated in the First Workshop on Maritime Security held in Washington, DC. Furthermore, the CIP organized three Hemispheric Conferences on Port Security, which involved more than 350 participants from 34 member states and trained over 180 Caribbean port security officials.

Likewise, since February 2007, CICTE and the Inter-American Drug Abuse Control Commission formed the Port Security Assistance Partnership (PSAP) to foster greater synergy within the OAS. PSAP's objectives are to assess security-related procedures within a target country's major port facilities, identify vulnerabilities, and develop a comprehensive and tailored package of training and capacity-building activities for areas of need. Currently, PSAP organizes ongoing Crisis Management Exercises and Best Practices Workshops, as well as other training events for all member states. These workshops are designed to promote a better understanding of maritime security threats and vulnerabilities within each subregion and to increase coordination, cooperation, and the exchange of information and best practices among those responsible for maritime security. Notably, technical assistance and expertise are provided by Transport Canada and the United States Coast Guard, as well as several private sector companies partnered with CICTE.

In conclusion, improving hemispheric port safety and security standards requires a combination of modernizing policies from member states with greater public–private partnerships throughout the Americas. Through effective dialogue, cooperative involvement, and above all constant maintenance of working relationships, private sector firms can become partners in development, making ports both easier and safer for all.

INTERVIEW AND CASE STUDY

Durán, Jorge, Chief of the Secretariat, Case Study: Inter-American Committee on Ports (CIP), Organization of American States.

REFERENCES

APEC. 2014. APEC Asia Pacific Economic Cooperation. Available at http://www.apec .org/Groups/Committee-on-Trade-and-Investment/Sub-Committee-on-Customs -Procedures.aspx). Accessed December 30, 2014.

Burns, M. 2013. Estimating the Impact of Maritime Security: Financial Tradeoffs between Security and Efficiency. *Journal of Transportation Security*, December, Volume 6, Issue 4, pp. 329–338.

Burns, M. 2014. Building Resilient Supply Chains through Policies, Partnerships and Technologies. DHS Supply Chain Security Workshop, Houston—April 23, 2014.

CBP ISF 102. 2014. Importer Security Filing (ISF) "10 + 2" Rule. Available at http://www .cbp.gov/border-security/ports-entry/cargo-security/importer-security-filing-102. Accessed December 12, 2014.

CSI Brief. 2014. Container Security Initiative (CSI), 2014. Available at http://www.cbp .gov/border-security/ports-entry/cargo-security/csi/csi-brief. Accessed December 12, 2014.

DHS. 2014. US Department of Homeland Security Overview. Available at http://www.dhs .gov. Accessed November 4, 2014.

DHS FAST. 2014. FAST: Free and Secure Trade for Commercial Vehicles, 2014. Available at http://www.cbp.gov/travel/trusted-traveler-programs/fast. Accessed December 30, 2014.

DHS ICE. 2014. DHS Immigration and Customs Enforcement. Available at http://www .ice.gov/hsi. Accessed January 28, 2015.

DHS NEXUS. 2014. Trusted traveler programs, NEXUS. Available at http://www.cbp.gov /travel/trusted-traveler-programs/nexus. Accessed December 30, 2014.

DHS OBIM. 2014. The Office of Biometric Identity Management (OBIM). US Department of Homeland Security. Available at http://www.dhs.gov/obim. Accessed December 19, 2014.

DHS RFID. 2014. Radio Frequency Identification (RFID): What is it? Available at http:// www.dhs.gov/radio-frequency-identification-rfid-what-it. Accessed December 30, 2014.

DHS SFI. 2014. The Secure Freight Initiative (SFI). Available at http://www.dhs.gov /secure-freight-initiative. Accessed December 30, 2014.

DHS, CSIP. 2014. Container Security Initiative Ports. Available at http://www.dhs.gov /container-security-initiative-ports. Accessed December 12, 2014.

DHS, NTAS. 2014a. National Terrorism Advisory System (NTAS). Available at http:// www.dhs.gov/national-terrorism-advisory-system. Accessed December 30, 2014.

DHS, NTAS. 2014b. National Terrorism Advisory System (NTAS). Available at http:// www.dhs.gov/topic/ntas. Accessed December 30, 2014.

DOE/NNSA. 2006. DHS and DOE Launch Secure Freight Initiative. $60 Million Effort Begins at 6 Foreign Ports to Scan for Nuclear Material Overseas. Press Release December 7, 2006. Available at http://www.nnsa.energy.gov/mediaroom/pressreleases /dhs-and-doe-launch-secure-freight-initiative. Accessed December 30, 2014.

DOE/NNSA. 2010. The Second Line of Defense Megaports Initiative. National Nuclear Security Administration. Office of the Second Line of Defense. Megaports Initiative. U.S. Department of Energy's National Nuclear Security Administration (DOE/ NNSA) September 2010. Available at http://nnsa.energy.gov/sites/default/files/nnsa /inlinefiles/singlepages_9-15-2010.pdf. Accessed December 12, 2014.

DOE/NNSA. 2014. Stockpile Stewardship and Management Plan. Fiscal Years 2014, 2015, and 2016. Available at http://nnsa.energy.gov/ourmission/managingthestockpile/ssmp. Accessed February 8, 2015.

EAPIS. 2014. Electronic Advance Passenger Information System. Available at https://eapis .org; https://eapis.cbp.dhs.gov/. Accessed December 19, 2014.

EPA EPCRA. 2014. Emergency Planning and Community Right-to-Know Act (EPCRA). Available at http://www2.epa.gov/epcra/what-epcra. Accessed December 30, 2014.

Europa. 2002. Council of the European Union. Available at http://europa.eu/legislation
_summaries/justice_freedom_security/fight_against_terrorism/l33168_en.htm. Accessed
January 10, 2015.

EU TCU. 2014. AEO Policy (Authorized Economic Operators) established by the Taxation
and Customs Union. Available at http://ec.europa.eu/taxation_customs/customs
/policy_issues/customs_security/aeo/index_en.htm. Accessed December 30, 2014.

FBI. 2014. US Joint Terrorism Task Forces. Available at http://www.fbi.gov/about-us
/investigate/terrorism/terrorism_jttfs. Accessed December 19, 2014.

FEMA. 2014. The Federal Emergency Management Agency (FEMA). Available at http://
www.fema.gov. Accessed December 12, 2014.

GAO (US General Accounting Office). 2003. GAO-03-616T. Transportation Security.
Post-September 11th Initiatives and Long-Term Challenges. Available at http://www
.gao.gov/new.items/d03616t.pdf. Accessed December 30, 2014.

GAO. 2007. The SAFE Port Act and Efforts to Secure Our Nation's Seaports. GAO-
08-86T: Published: Oct 4, 2007. Publicly Released: Oct 4, 2007. US Government
Accountability Office.

GAO. 2012. US Government Accountability Office. Combatting Nuclear Smuggling.
Megaports Initiative Faces Funding and Sustainability Challenges. Report to
Congressional Requesters. October 2012, GAO-13-37. Available at http://www.gao
.gov/assets/650/649759.pdf. Accessed December 30, 2014.

GAO. 2014. US Government Accountability Office. DOD could improve total asset visibility initiative with results act framework. Available at http://www.gao.gov/products
/GAO/NSIAD-99-40. Accessed December 30, 2014.

GPO. 2006a. Security and Accountability for Every Port Act of 2006 Public Law 109-347-
Oct. 13, 2006. 120 Stat. 1884 Public Law 109-347-Oct. 13, 2006. US Government
Printing Office, Available at http://www.gpo.gov/fdsys/pkg/PLAW-109publ347/pdf
/PLAW-109publ347.pdf. Accessed December 30, 2014.

GPO. 2006b. Security and Accountability for Every Port Act of 2006 or the "SAFE Port
Act 2006." Available at http://www.gpo.gov/fdsys/pkg/PLAW-109publ347/pdf/PLAW
-109publ347.pdf. Accessed December 12, 2014.

GPO, DHS, USDA. 2002. The Public Health Security and Bioterrorism Preparedness and
Response Act (Bioterrorism Act or PHSBPRA). Available at http://www.gpo.gov/fdsys
/pkg/PLAW-107publ188/html/PLAW-107publ188.htm. Accessed December 12, 2014.

Huddy, L. and Feldman, S. 2011. Americans Respond Politically to 9/11: Understanding the
Impact of the Terrorist Attacks and Their Aftermath. American Psychologist, 66, 455–467.

Hutchison-Whampoa. 2014. Overview. Available at http://www.hutchison-whampoa
.com/en/media/press_each.php?id = 1086. Accessed December 12, 2014.

IMO. 2013. International Convention for the Safety of Life at Sea (SOLAS). Available at
http://www.imo.org. Accessed January 18, 2015.

Kant, I. 1795. "Perpetual Peace: A Philosophical Sketch" (*Zum ewigen Frieden. Ein philosophischer Entwurf*). Germany. Available at Constitution Society, http://www
.constitution.org/kant/perpeace.htm. Accessed December 30, 2014.

MTSA. 2014. Maritime Transportation Security Act. Available at http://www.uscg.mil/d8
/msuBatonRouge/mtsa.asp. Accessed December 12, 2014.

NATO. 2014a. North Atlantic Treaty Organization (NATO). Available at http://www
.nato.int/nato-welcome/index.html. Accessed December 30, 2014.

NATO. 2014b. North Atlantic Treaty Organization (NATO). Available at http://www
.nato.int/cps/en/natolive/official_texts_17120.htm. Accessed December 30, 2014.

NBAA. 2014. National Business Aviation Association. Advance Passenger Information System (APIS). Available at http://www.nbaa.org/ops/intl/customs-regulatory/apis /history.php. Accessed December 19, 2014.

NSA. 1947. The National Security Act of 1947. Available at https://history.state.gov/milestones /1945-1952/national-security-act. Accessed April 9, 2014.

NZ Customs. 2014. New Zealand Customs Service: SES (Secure Export Scheme). Available at http://www.customs.govt.nz. Accessed December 12, 2014.

Rousseau, J.-J. 1754. *Discourse on Inequality.* Marc-Michel Rey: Holland (reprinted in 2013, Kessinger Legacy, USA).

Rousseau, J.-J. 1762. *The Social Contract.* E.P. Dutton: New York (translated with Introduction by G.D.H. Cole, reprinted in 2013, Bartleby Publishers: USA).

SCST. 2014. The Strategic Council on Security Technology. Available at http://www.scst .info. Accessed December 12, 2014.

SENTRI, DHS. 2014. SENTRI Program Description. The Secure Electronic Network for Travelers Rapid Inspection program (SENTRI), An Overview, Department of Homeland Security. Available at http://www.cbp.gov/travel/trusted-traveler-programs /sentri/sentri-overview. Accessed December 19, 2014.

Singapore Customs. 2014. Supply Chain Security. Singapore Customs, Supply Chain Security. STP (Secure Trade Partnership). Available at http://www.customs.gov.sg. Accessed December 12, 2014.

TAPA. 2014a. Profile. Transported Asset Protection Association (TAPA). Available at http://www.tapaonline.org/. Accessed December 12, 2014.

TAPA. 2014b. Profile TAPA Europe. Transported Asset Protection Association (TAPA). Available at http://www.tapaemea.com/. Accessed December 12, 2014.

The United Nations Office on Drugs and Crime (UNODC). Overview. Available at http:// www.unodc.org. Accessed December 30, 2014.

TSA. 2014a. Overview. Transportation Security Administration. Available at http://www .tsa.gov. Accessed December 12, 2014.

TSA. 2014b. Risk-Based Security Initiatives. Available at http://www.tsa.gov/traveler -information/risk-based-security-initiatives. Accessed December 19, 2014.

TSA Blog. 2013. Year in review, 2013. Available at http://blog.tsa.gov/2014/01/tsa-blog -year-in-review-2013.html. Accessed December 12, 2014.

TSA Blog. 2014. Year in review, 2014. Available at http://blog.tsa.gov/2015/01/tsa-blog-year -in-review-2014.html. Accessed January 28, 2015.

UCTC. 2014. TWAEO (Taiwan Authorized Economic Operator), issued by the Directorate General of Customs, Ministry of Finance. Universal Container Terminal Co. Ltd. Available at http://www.uctc.com.tw/english/english.htm. Accessed December 12, 2014.

UN CTITF. 2014. Terrorism. The Counter-Terrorism Implementation Task Force (CTITF). Available at http://www.un.org/en/terrorism/ctitf/. Accessed December 30, 2014.

UN. 2004. UN Launches Container Control Program to Fight Illicit Trafficking. Available at http://www.un.org/apps/news/story.asp?NewsID=12292&Cr=unodc&Cr1=#.VDnK QE3jjcc. Accessed December 30, 2014.

UNCTAD. 2013. UNCTAD's Review of Maritime Transport. 2013. Available at http:// unctad.org/en/publicationslibrary/rmt2013_en.pdf. Accessed December 30, 2014.

UNODC. 2006. Press Release. Available at https://www.unodc.org/unodc/en/press/releases /press_release_2006_05_05-1.html. Accessed December 30, 2014.

UNODC. 2011. Countering the world of smuggling through container control. United Nations Office on Drugs and Crime (UN ODC). Available at http://www.unodc.org /unodc/en/frontpage/2011/May/countering-the-world-of-smuggling-through-container -control.html. Accessed December 12, 2014.

UNODC. 2014a. Global Container Control Program Delivers Solid Successes against Global Illicit Trafficking. Available at http://www.unodc.org/unodc/en/frontpage /2014/July/global-container-control-programme-delivers-solid-successes-against -global-illicit-trafficking.html. Accessed December 30, 2014.

UNODC. 2014b. Organized Crime. Available at http://www.unodc.org/documents/organized -crime/generalbrochureEN.pdf. Accessed December 30, 2014.

UNODC. 2014c. Overview, Drugs and Crime. United Nations Office on Drugs and Crime (UN ODC). Available at http://www.unodc.org/. Accessed December 12, 2014.

UNODC. 2014d. Piracy. Maritime Crime Program (MCP). Available at http://www.unodc .org/unodc/en/piracy/index.html?ref = menuside. Accessed December 30, 2014.

UNODC. 2014e. United Nations Office on Drugs and Crime (UN ODC), Maritime Program. Available at http://www.unodc.org/unodc/en/piracy/index.html?ref=menuside. Accessed December 12, 2014.

UNSC. 2014. United Nations Security Council (UNSC). Available at http://www.un.org/en /sc, 2014 and http://www.un.org/en/peace. Accessed December 12, 2014.

US DOD. 2014. Department of Defense, Mission. 2014. Available at http://www.defense .gov/about/#mission. Accessed December 19, 2014.

US DOS. 1947. US Department of State, Office of the Historian. 1947. National Security Act of 1947. Available at https://history.state.gov/milestones/1945-1952/national -security-act. Accessed December 19, 2014.

US Senate. 1947. US Senate selected committee of intelligence, National Security Act of 1947 (Chapter 343; 61 Stat. 496; approved July 26, 1947) [As Amended through P.L. 110–53, Enacted August 3, 2007]. Available at http://www.intelligence.senate.gov /nsaact1947.pdf. Accessed December 19, 2014.

WCOOMD. 2014. World Customs Organization (WCO). Available at http://www .wcoomd.org/. Accessed December 12, 2014.

WHO. 2014. Substance Abuse. Available at http://www.who.int/substance_abuse/en/. Accessed December 30, 2014.

CHAPTER 4

Critical Infrastructure Security
Resilience in Action

By nature we have no defect that could not become a strength, no strength that could not become a defect.

Johann Wolfgang Goethe (1749–1832)
German writer and statesman

4.1 INTRODUCTION

Critical infrastructure and key resources (CIKR) is the powerhouse of national security, economy, and well-being. We recognize it as the power and water used for industrial and residential use; the transportation that enables trade, mobility, and prosperity; and the communication networks that ensure our connectivity with the world. Critical infrastructure (CI) comprises tangible and intangible assets, technologies, and networks so vital for the nation that their incapacitation or damage would have a devastating effect on nations, industries, and communities alike (DHS 2013).

While different nations may have established different sectors of CI, there seems to be a correlation between the crucial areas of a country based on its national priorities, national resources, production, and so on. Table 4.1 compares and contrasts the CI sectors in six nations, i.e., the United States, Canada, the European Union, Australia, Japan, and South Korea.

In the United States, the Department of Homeland Security (DHS) has identified 16 sectors of CI, which are all instrumental for resilient logistics and transport activities.

4.2 CI SECURITY

According to the Presidential Policy Directive 21 (PPD-21) pertaining to *Critical Infrastructure Security and Resilience*, CI represents "systems and assets, whether physical or virtual, so vital to the United States that the incapacity or destruction of such systems and assets would have a debilitating impact on security, national economic security, national public health or safety, or any combination of those matters." The national plan recognizes that the nation's CI is primarily owned and controlled by private entities. Nevertheless, federal entities as well as state, local, tribal, and territorial authorities and international interests also own and control CI.

TABLE 4.1　Critical Infrastructure Sectors in Six Nations

	United States (16)	Canada (10)	European Union (11)	Australia (7)	Japan (10)	Korea (7)
1	Chemical sector		Chemical industry	Chemical industry		
2	Commercial facilities					
3	Communications	Information and communication technology	See IT	Communications*	Information and communications	Broadcasting; national network
4	Critical manufacturing	Manufacturing				
5	Dams					
6	Defense industrial bases					National defense technology
7	Emergency services					
8	Energy	Energy and utilities	Energy	Energy*	Two sectors: —Electricity —Gas	Energy
9	Financial services	Finance	Finance	Banking and finance	Finance	
10	Food and agriculture	Food	Food	Food chain		
11	Government facilities	Government			Governmental/administrative services (including local governments)	
12	Healthcare and public health	Health	Health	Health	Medical services	
13	IT		Information, communication technology (telecoms, internet, satellite systems, computers/software)	Expert group: IT security		

(Continued)

TABLE 4.1 (CONTINUED)   Critical Infrastructure Sectors in Six Nations

	United States (16)	Canada (10)	European Union (11)	Australia (7)	Japan (10)	Korea (7)
14	Nuclear reactors, materials, and waste		Nuclear industry			Nuclear energy
15	Transportation systems security	Transportation	Transport	Transport	Three sectors: Logistics Civil aviation Railways	Three Sectors: Roads Subway Airports
16	Water and wastewater system	Water	Water	Water services*	Water works	Water resources
17			Space			
18			Research facilities			Government research institutions
19				Expert group: resilience		
20				Energy, water, and communication sectors form the Oil and Gas Security Forum		
21		Safety				

Source: The author, adapted from DHS, Critical Infrastructure Security, available at http://www.dhs.gov/topic/critical-infrastructure-security, accessed December 2, 2014, 2014; PPD-21, The White House, Office of the Press Secretary, February 12, Presidential Policy Directive—Critical Infrastructure Security and Resilience, Presidential Policy Directive/Ppd-21, available at http://www.whitehouse.gov/the-press-office/2013/02/12/presidential-policy-directive-critical-infrastructure-security-and-resil, accessed August 5, 2014, 2013; EC, "Critical infrastructure security and resilience" and council directive 2008/114/EC, 2008; OECD, OECD, available at http://www.oecd.org/sti/40761118.pdf, 2008; Australia TISN, Development of policies and protection of critical information infrastructures, available at http://www.tisn.gov.au/Documents/Australian+Government+s+Critical+Infrastructure+Resilience+Strategy.pdf, 2008; PSC Canada, Public Safety Canada. Government of Canada. National Strategy for Critical Infrastructure, available at http://www.publicsafety.gc.ca/cnt/rsrcs/pblctns/srtg-crtcl-nfrstrctr/index-eng.aspx, 2014.

Note: Number next to each country, aims to underline the number of critical infrastructure sectors in each nation respectively.

TABLE 4.2   United States: 16 CI Sectors and SSAs

	SSA	CI Sector(s)
1	Department of Agriculture	Food and agriculture (meat, poultry, and processed egg products)
2	Department of Defense	Defense industrial base
3	Department of Energy	Energy (production, refining, storage, and distribution of oil, gas, and electric power)
4	Department of Health and Human Services	Healthcare and public health (also in charge of food other than meat, poultry, and processed egg products)
5	Department of the Treasury	Financial services
6	Environmental Protection Agency	Water and wastewater services
7	Department of Homeland Security	Chemical facilities Commercial facilities Communications Critical manufacturing Emergency services IT Dams Commercial nuclear reactors
8	Department of Homeland Security, Department of Transportation	Transportation systems
9a	Department of Homeland Security, General Services Administration	Government facilities[a]
9b	Department of Education	Education facilities
9c	Department of the Interior	National monuments and icons

Source: The author, adapted from DHS, Critical Infrastructure Security, available at http://www.dhs .gov/topic/critical-infrastructure-security, accessed December 2, 2014, 2014; The White House, Presidential Policy, Directive on Critical Infrastructure Security and Resilience, available at http://www.whitehouse.gov/the-press-office/2013/02/12/presidential-policy-directive -critical-insfrastracture-security-and-resil, accessed December 11, 2014, 2014, 2013; DHS, The National Strategy for the Physical Protection of Critical Infrastructures and Key Assets, February 2003, available at http://www.dhs.gov/xlibrary/assets/Physical_Strategy.pdf, accessed December 12, 2014, 2003; DHS, Critical Infrastructure, available at http://www.dhs.gov /critical-infrastructure, accessed December 4, 2014, 2013; EO, Executive Order 13010.2010. Critical Infrastructure Protection. Federal Register, July 17, 1996. Vol. 61, No. 138, pp. 37347–37350, 1996; "Partnering for Critical Infrastructure Security and Resilience."
[a] Government facilities subsectors.

The US national policy's mission is to reinforce and retain secure, operating, and resilient CI. The US National Plan identifies a federal division or agency as the lead administrator (sector-specific agency [SSA]) for the 16 sectors of CI, which are identified in Table 4.2.

4.2.1 The Nation's CIKR

The nation's CIKR entails buildings, transportation structures, cyber networks, commodities, and processes. Mitigating the risk of CIKR is crucial to maintain national security, socioeconomic stability, and optimum standards of living. For this reason, the 16 CI sectors

(Table 4.2) ought to be resilient, secure, and in a position to mitigate risks. The DHS (2014) has developed a sector-specific plan for each sector, which contains information for each of the subsectors, as well as information on the interaction between all CIKR sectors. In order to reinforce and sustain secure, operating, and resistant CI, synchronized initiatives should include a federal–state–private, community, tribal, and territorial collaboration (DHS 2014).

The 16 CI sectors are as follows:

1. Chemical sector

   This sector consists of five chemical types: agricultural chemicals, basic chemicals, specialty chemicals, consumer products, and pharmaceuticals. This sector is vital to national growth and the economy. Despite their different qualities, development mechanisms, market cycles, technologies, and practices, all five chemical types are closely interrelated with most other CI areas (see Table 4.3).

2. Commercial facilities sector

   Most facilities in this sector are owned, managed, and controlled by the private sector with minimum public (federal, state, and regional) intervention. This implies that access to these facilities is available to the public with minimum security measures. This sector contains eight subsectors, some of which may be overlapping:

   a. Entertainment and media (such as television channels, movie studios, radio stations, and theaters)
   b. Gaming (such as casino sites)
   c. Lodging (including convention centers and hotels)
   d. Outdoor events (such as athletic, cultural, or religious events; energy parks; recreational areas; festivals; campsites; and parades)
   e. Public assembly (such as churches, museums, and convention centers)
   f. Real estate (including industrial facilities, warehouses, business, residential, storage, and mixed utilization facilities)
   g. Retail (e.g., retail centers and districts, shopping malls)
   h. Sports leagues

3. Communications sector

   The communications sector encompasses all national socioeconomic aspects bridging the public and private sectors while facilitating all CI areas. Modern communication achieves interoperability through the use of advanced satellite, wireless, and land-based technologies.

   While the private sector is the major entity accountable for safeguarding communication facilities and resources, collaboration with the public sector is elementary to ensure the integrity and resilience of communication systems especially during a disaster.

4. Critical manufacturing

   The resiliency of critical manufacturing at a federal and private level is essential, more so during a security threat, as it ensures the continuity of CI sectors. The seven key industries involved include

   a. Aviation and aerospace product and parts manufacturing
   b. Electrical machinery manufacturing
   c. Machines manufacturing
   d. Primary metals and minerals
   e. Railroad rolling stock manufacturing
   f. Transportation equipment manufacturing
   g. Vehicle manufacturing

TABLE 4.3   The CI Connectivity Matrix

CI	1. Chemical Sector	2. Commercial Facilities	3. Communications	4. Critical Manufacturing	5. Dams	6. Defense Industrial Bases	7. Emergency Services	8. Energy	9. Financial Services	10. Food and Agriculture	11. Government Facilities	12. Healthcare and Public Health	13. IT	14. Nuclear Reactors, Materials, and Waste	15. Transportation Systems Security	16. Water and Wastewater System
1. Chemical sector	X	X	X	X		X	X	X	X	X	X	X	X	X	X	X
2. Commercial facilities	X	X	X	X	X	X	X	X	X	X	X	X	X	X	X	X
3. Communications	X	X	X	X	X	X	X	X	X	X	X	X	X	X	X	X
4. Critical manufacturing	X	X	X	X		X	X	X	X		X	X	X	X	X	X
5. Dams		X	X	X	X	X	X	X	X		X	X	X	X	X	X
6. Defense industrial bases	X			X	X	X	X	X	X		X	X	X	X	X	X
7. Emergency services	X	X	X	X	X	X	X	X	X	X	X	X	X	X	X	X
8. Energy	X	X	X	X	X	X	X	X	X	X	X	X	X	X	X	X
9. Financial services	X	X	X	X		X	X	X	X	X	X	X	X	X	X	X
10. Food and agriculture	X	X	X			X	X	X	X	X			X		X	X
11. Government facilities		X	X	X	X	X	X	X	X		X	X	X	X	X	
12. Healthcare and public health	X	X	X	X	X	X	X	X	X	X	X	X	X	X	X	X
13. IT	X	X	X	X	X	X	X	X	X	X	X	X	X	X	X	X
14. Nuclear reactors, materials, and waste	X	X	X	X	X	X	X	X	X		X	X	X	X	X	X
15. Transportation systems security	X	X	X	X	X	X	X	X	X	X	X	X	X	X	X	X
16. Water and wastewater system	X	X	X	X	X	X	X	X	X	X		X	X	X	X	X

Source: The author.

5. Dams

The dams sector consists of dam constructions, hydropower generation infrastructure, maritime locks, dikes, hurricane barriers, manufacturing waste facilities, and water preservation and management amenities.

The United States has at least 87,000 dams; hence, this is an essential area of the nation's infrastructure and offers numerous socioeconomic benefits, including entertainment, flood management, hydroelectric energy, inland maritime, waste control, water supply, and preservation of wildlife.

6. Defense industrial bases

In collaboration with the Department of Defense (DoD), this global sector supplies equipment and services necessary in organizing, deploying, and maintaining army operations. It focuses on the R&D, modeling, manufacturing, distribution, and repair of military technologies and weapons in compliance with the national military specifications. The sector includes over 100,000 defense industrial base businesses and their supply chains in the United States and abroad, occasionally operated in collaboration with the private sector or foreign contractors.

7. Emergency services sector

The emergency services sector (ESS) signifies the government's first line of protection in risk mitigation from both deliberate and accidental man-made accidents along with natural catastrophes. Its mission is to safeguard lives, the environment, and assets; support communities during catastrophes; and assist their recoveries. Therefore, it serves as the main shield of all the other CI sectors through the disciplines of (i) emergency management, (ii) emergency medical services, (iii) fire and emergency services, (iv) law enforcement, and (v) public works.

8. Energy sector

The energy sector (ES) focuses on the production, refining, storage, and distribution of oil, gas, and electric power and basic chemicals, specialty chemicals, agricultural chemicals, pharmaceuticals, and consumer products.

9. Financial services

Founded in 2002, the Financial Services Sector Coordinating Council for Critical Infrastructure Protection and Homeland Security is the sector administrator for financial services to safeguard CI centered on functional risks. Serving as a bridge between the public and private sector, this sector aims to boost safety and security in all the CI areas (FSSCC 2014).

10. Food and agriculture

This sector amounts to around one-fifth of the US financial activities and is to a large extent owned by the private sector. It consists of about 2.2 million farms, almost a million restaurants, and around 400,000 licensed food making, handling, and storing facilities. While it is related with most sectors, its closest interdependencies entail

a. Agriculture and food processing
b. Chemicals
c. Dams
d. Energy
e. Financial services
f. Transportation systems
g. Water and wastewater systems

11. Government facilities

This sector comprises facilities owned and operated or rented nationally or abroad by government, state, regional, and tribal authorities. It contains numerous structures, many of which are available to the general public for commercial functions and financial and trade dealing, as well as facilities where public access is restricted, due to the private and confidential technologies, data, activities, and supplies they contain. This sector also entails cyber components that help safeguard the sector properties: technological, structural, or knowledge-based.

12. Healthcare and public health

Operational sustainability and resilience are essential for this sector, which deals with human health, and safeguards all 16 sectors from risks like terrorism, contagious disease outbreaks, and natural disasters. The sectors closely affiliated pertain to communications, emergency services, energy, food and agriculture, IT, transportation systems, and water and wastewater systems. Since most resources of this sector belong to the private sector, it is necessary to ensure a public–private collaboration.

13. IT

This sector is vital to all other CI areas and ensures national safety, security, health, well-being, and economy. It encompasses public and private sectors and universities in an effort to improve the development and distribution of hardware, software, and IT techniques and services always in close connection with the communications sector. A public–private coalition is strongly required.

14. Nuclear reactors, materials, and waste

The nuclear sector manages and controls industrial nuclear energy reactors that supply energy in the public, private, and domestic sectors nationwide. It consists of the subsequent main subsectors: atomic facilities, materials, and waste. The sector encompasses
  • Atomic fuel-cycle space and equipment
  • Non-energy atomic reactors employed for research, education, and radioisotope generation
  • Nuclear and radiological equipment applied to healthcare, manufacturing, commercial, and educational environments
  • The transporting, warehousing, and waste management of atomic and radioactive materials

15. Transportation systems security

Transportation is a vital socioeconomical drive. Human survival, communication, and growth are directly related to our capacity to transport people and commodities around the globe. The history of mankind would have never reached the modern levels of sustainable growth without smart mobility systems to move people and commodities in a cost-effective, environmentally friendly, and energy-efficient manner (WBCSD 2002).

The term transportation security pertains to the legitimate or illegitimate trade and movement of passengers, commodities, and substances. Due to the interconnectivity of all the supply chain and logistics components, transportation security threats cannot be considered as remote incidents. The appearance of an isolated threat in transportation is most likely to have a ripple effect throughout the nation, the society, and the economy. Globalization and the introduction of advanced technologies have not only benefited the industry in the efficient transportation of goods; they have also led to the increase in transportation-related security threats and criminal activities.

16. Water and wastewater systems

With almost 155,000 community drinking water systems and 16,500 widely available wastewater treatment plans in the United States, this sector is crucial to general public health and welfare while offering risk-free drinking water and appropriate wastewater treatment and management.

Each nation's CI sector is interrelated with all other segments. Table 4.3 shows the CI Connectivity Matrix for the US CI. Furthermore, the CI sectors influence the supply chain throughout its stages, as indicated in Table 4.4.

Under the principle that a supply chain and transportation network is as strong as its weakest link, the presence of a sustainable systemic weakness damages the entire supply chain and leads to increased threats affecting both the public and private sectors.

While examining the 16 CI segments covered in this section, it seems that these identify resources that are necessary for survival, socioeconomic operations, and growth. Figure 4.1 demonstrates how these 16 sectors are highly interconnected with the society's needs, as reflected in the theories of Abraham Maslow and Clayton Alderfer.

From a security viewpoint, this graph associates each CI sector, and their risks, with the consequences in a specific national, social, and/or psychological sector.

4.2.1.1 Level 1: Lower Level: Existence Sector

The pyramid's foundation, or primary human needs, is built on resource deficiencies and the human desire to feel safe and secure and have one's survival needs met. The CI sectors associated with survival are (#7) emergency services, (#12) healthcare, and (#16) water and wastewater systems. This explains why during a disaster or wartime, these sectors are protected by nations, and attacked by enemies, more than any other sector. It is worth noting that the survival needs are a prerequisite for the next level in Maslow's pyramid, which is growth.

4.2.1.2 Level 2: Middle Level: Relatedness Sector

Once the basic needs of nations, societies, and individuals are met, it is necessary to use communication, transportation, and information exchange in order to not only ensure survival but also grow into the upper level of achievements and growth. The CI sectors associated with relatedness are (#3) communications, (#9) financial services, (#13) IT, and (#15) transportation systems security. This level does not outgrow survival but serves as a bridge that connects existence and growth.

4.2.1.3 Level 3: Upper Level: Growth Needs

Once the basic needs of nations, societies, and individuals are met, they strive to meet the needs of the pyramid's upper level by being increasingly engaged in growth and accomplishments. A nation's power and growth can be clearly determined by the following CI sectors: (#1) chemical sector, (#2) commercial facilities, (#4) critical manufacturing, (#5) dams, (#6) defense industrial bases, (#8) energy, (#10) food and agriculture (as a trading commodity and as survival), (#11) government facilities, and (#14) nuclear reactors.

What these CI sectors have in common is that their level of growth and innovation outline the nation's power status. Moreover, once these resources are depleted, reduced, or eliminated, relatedness tools, services, and technologies are used, i.e., information, communication, and transportation. Once any and all of these bridges fail to restore the previous growth level, the nation or individual's survival may be at stake.

CI should be secure and in a position to mitigate and rapidly recuperate from all security threats. Planning ahead to establish robust, well-organized infrastructures is

TABLE 4.4   The Supply Chain CI Matrix

Supply Chain CI	1. Decision-Making Centers: Political, Commercial, and Economic Activities	2. Supply	3. Trade	4. Transport	5. Storage: Physical or Cyber Storage	6. Communications
1. Chemical sector	X	X	X	X	X	X
2. Commercial facilities	X	X	X	X	X	X
3. Communications	X	X	X	X	X	X
4. Critical manufacturing	X	X	X	X	X	X
5. Dams	X	X	X	X	X	X
6. Defense industrial bases	X	X	X	X	X	X
7. Emergency services	X	X	X	X	X	X
8. Energy	X	X	X	X	X	X
9. Financial services	X	X	X	X	X	X
10. Food and agriculture	X	X	X	X	X	X
11. Government facilities	X	X	X	X	X	X
12. Healthcare and public health	X	X	X	X	X	X
13. IT	X	X	X	X	X	X
14. Nuclear reactors, materials, and waste	X	X	X	X	X	X
15. Transportation systems security	X	X	X	X	X	X
16. Water and wastewater system	X	X	X	X	X	X

Source: The author, based on the DHS website.

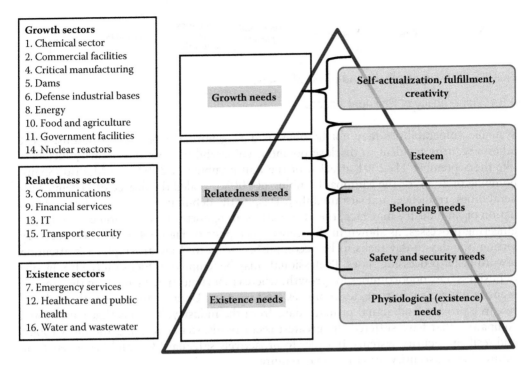

Growth sectors
1. Chemical sector
2. Commercial facilities
4. Critical manufacturing
5. Dams
6. Defense industrial bases
8. Energy
10. Food and agriculture
11. Government facilities
14. Nuclear reactors

Relatedness sectors
3. Communications
9. Financial services
13. IT
15. Transport security

Existence sectors
7. Emergency services
12. Healthcare and public
    health
16. Water and wastewater

Growth needs

Relatedness needs

Existence needs

Self-actualization, fulfillment, creativity

Esteem

Belonging needs

Safety and security needs

Physiological (existence) needs

FIGURE 4.1   The 16 CI sectors in Alderfer's existence, relatedness, and growth theory and Maslow's pyramid of human needs. (From the author.)

essential to boost and retain secure, operating, and resilient systems. It is necessary to build public and private partnerships with a common goal to foster the security and resilience of the nation's CI. This collective effort requires commitment, know-how, and continuous efforts from all stakeholders (The White House 2013; DHS 2014).

As we examine the supply chains and transportation industries both before and after significant industry disasters, we realize that such events have served as wake-up calls to identify our supply chains' shortcomings, vulnerabilities, and areas for improvement. Most importantly, such events show the interconnectivity between all the CI sectors and between governments, the industry, and the society.

4.3 PHYSICAL ASSETS AND KEY ASSET PROTECTION

Physical assets are defined as tangible products or resources of financial, industrial, or trade value. Within a supply chain, such items, as indicated in Figure 4.2, may include

a. Land and capital among the factors of production, investment funds, and cash flow
b. Buildings and warehouses
c. Office equipment, machinery, spare parts, and inventory
d. Transportation vehicles
e. Commodities, be they raw materials or finished goods

Physical assets are measurable so their value can be appraised, though it may fluctuate as goods become obsolete, depreciated, damaged, contaminated, stolen, etc.

FIGURE 4.2   Supply chain and physical assets.

4.3.1 Vulnerability of Physical Assets

Systemic vulnerabilities may not be obvious during normal working operations, yet it takes a security incident to disclose potential vulnerabilities. Serious security incidents like the September 11, 2001 attacks, or the Bali bombing of 2002, the Madrid (Spain) bombing of 2004, or the Mumbai bombing of 2008 revealed the degree of systemic vulnerabilities, resilience, and sustainability. Despite the debilitating effects of losses that a nation or an industry may face, the aftermath is an opportunity of awareness, and reengineering processes, as shown in the iceberg metaphor of Figure 4.3. In a real-industry setting, the day-to-day tasks to be accomplished seem to draw an employee's attention toward faster processing times. Professionals may be tempted to focus on the bright side of business, i.e., opportunities for growth, whereas shortcuts may be made in the areas of security investment in time, technologies, and training. Upon examining both academic research projects and actual primary data from the industry, it seems that nations and companies that have suffered the greatest security disasters can build the most robust and resilient security systems. In order to proactively safeguard CIs and key assets from future threats, security initiatives may require

1. More stringent implementation of security regulations
2. Strategic alliances with industrial, national, and global security organizations and networks

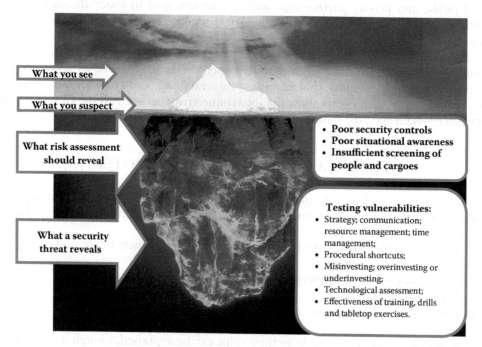

FIGURE 4.3   Tip of the Iceberg.

3. Private and public sector coalitions
4. Integration and visibility throughout the entire supply chain
5. Scrutinized background checks for employees, vendors, and partners
6. Investment in security technologies, i.e., area monitoring, cargo screening, geo-mapping, and satellite systems
7. Monitoring and logging technologies and processes and so on

4.3.2 Physical Assets' Evaluation

Physical assets are independent security targets whose intentional damage could bring about severe short- and long-term effects from loss of life, environmental impact, asset damage, and company collapse. Another characteristic of physical assets is that although they may not be of critical significance during normal business operations, their vulnerability could be the Trojan horse to compromise the security of the entire supply chain.

Table 4.5 can be used as an *asset-evaluation* template in any industrial, logistics, or supply chain segment. The same table could be used to number the significance of an asset or group of assets for buildings, vehicles, cargoes, or machinery for a single company, a group of companies, or the entire supply chain.

TABLE 4.5   Asset Evaluation for Significance and Vulnerability for CI Sectors

Supply chain and logistics

Single asset	Group of assets	Single company	Group of companies	Supply chain

Cargoes	Buildings	Warehouses	Vehicles	Pipelines and refineries	Machinery	Innovative assets

A. Asset Significance Level		B. Asset Vulnerability Level	
Very high	10	Very high	10
High	8–9	High	8–9
Medium high	7	Medium high	7
Medium	5–6	Medium	5–6
Medium low	4	Medium low	4
Low	2–3	Low	2–3
Very low	1	Very low	1

Measuring Commercial and Financial Value
CI value
Financial value
Commercial value
Innovation value

Measuring Exposure to Security Risks
Structural vulnerability
Geographical vulnerability
Surveillance vulnerability
Technology vulnerability
Regulatory vulnerability
Human factor vulnerability
(training, motivation, fatigue)

Source: The author.

4.4 TRADE AND TRANSPORT DOCUMENTATION

4.4.1 Electronic (Paperless) Trade

Every logistics or transportation project needs the right input, i.e., the right proportion and usage of the factors of production, in order to generate the desired output that meets the industry standards and the customers' requirements.

In order for the industry to stipulate what resources (factors of production = input) are needed to attain specific commercial, operational, technical, and regulatory requirements (output), the industry uses specific contracts of carriage of goods and a plethora of commercial documents. Security threats may appear both in hard-copy documents and in electronic contracts of affreightment. In fact, security threats may appear at any stage of the logistics process, throughout the supply chain, from input to output.

These contracts of carriage of goods may be industry-, carrier-, commodity-, and/or company-specific. They may involve the multimodal or intermodal transportation of goods for door-to-door transportation or just a fragment of the trip. They may stipulate the desired performance of two or more entities concerned or may orchestrate the actions of numerous supply chain players such as the carriers, manufacturers, vendors, suppliers, importers, exporters, and so on.

For the past centuries, the commercial documentation pertaining to trade agreements and the transportation of commodities and passengers have been issued in paper form. The modern trade and transport industry has enjoyed a sustainable growth over the past decade or so. The benefits associated with this growth have brought about increased demands upon the industry on behalf of the end users, the law enforcement agencies, and other key players within the supply chain:

- The cargo receivers need faster shipping times, reduced costs, and increased cargo safety and punctuality.
- Government bodies need more security and require fast and valid data well in advance of the carrier's arrival, i.e., in electronic form.
- If the industry fails to deliver in this high-speed commercial race, this will lead companies to reduced market share and reduced earnings.

Nowadays, the trade and transport sectors still depend upon paper-based methods to process the cargoes or passengers, which means increased work load in a rapidly increasing industry. A typical global cargo load involves intermodal transportation, the processing of which requires more than 30 commercial documents. Increased regulations pertaining to customs clearance, security, and safety increase the requested data and the volume of this documentation, thus raising both the cost and the processing times.

Nevertheless, over these past decades, the trade and transport stakeholders have been exploring the possibility of a secure cyberspace that would enable the fast processing of commercial transactions and legally binding documents through the issuance of electronic documentation.

While the concept of electronic signatures and electronic contracts has been widely discussed since the 1980s, the wide adaptation of electronic trade and transport documents has been halted for security reasons. During the times where fraudulent documentation exceeded 33% globally, the issuance of electronic contracts seemed unachievable.

The aspirations for electronic documentation were finally materialized, as new cyber technologies and new web and IT platforms now empower the industry by generating and transferring official binding contracts. A series of legally binding documents of financial and commercial significance is now possible, which enable global trade and transport operations to process at a much faster pace.

The electronic documents resemble the formats and clauses stipulated in the original, paper documents and are therefore user-friendly. Some of the commercial documents that are available in electronic forms include

- *Contract of affreightment*—a binding contract that stipulates the obligations and legal rights between the carrier (owner of an aircraft, ship, or truck) and the charterer (freight forwarder, cargo seller, or buyer). The carrier engages in providing cargo space at a specified time, via a specified route, for a specified freight, to the charterer who is accountable for reimbursement regardless of whether the freight is ready for transport. This agreement deals with issues connected specifically with a ship (carrier), its crew, and the designated trade routes that it has to follow.
- *Charter party (C/P)*—also known as charter agreement or charter contract, a C/P pertains to the hire or lease contract leasing or hiring agreement between the carrier (owner of an aircraft, ship, or truck) and the charterer (freight forwarder, cargo seller, or buyer). Under a C/P, a ship is leased (full cargo load or parcel cargoes for multiple charterers).
- *Voyage charter party (Voy C/P)*—pertains to an agreement for a single voyage or consecutive voyages.
- *Time charter party (TC/P)*—pertains to an agreement for a fixed period of time, i.e., 1 year to 10 or more years.

Typically, in Voy C/P and TC/P, the shipowner maintains rights of ownership and management, while the charterers have the right to select the ports of call.

- *Bareboat charter party (BB C/P)*—In BB C/P, the shipowner retains the legal ownership of the asset; however, all commercial, technical, recruiting, insurance, and other functions are undertaken by the bareboat charterers.

4.4.2 Contract of Carriage

A binding contract (confirmed typically by an air waybill [AWB], bill of lading [B/L], or traveler admission) pertains to clauses of carriage that stipulate the responsibilities and privileges of a carrier and a shipper/passenger. The carrier engages in delivering commodities or passengers from a specific port of departure to a specific destination in exchange for a fee expressed as freight rate for cargoes or fare for passengers. This agreement addresses concerns associated particularly with the nature of cargo that is being carried (cargo type, weight, volume, specific handling requirements such as HazMat; restrictions such as time- or temperature-sensitive cargoes). In addition, through the clause stipulation, there is an evaluation on how the responsibility and settlement for damage or loss of the cargoes or the injury of passengers are carried out. An explicit set of clauses evaluates performance and allocates funds, performance bonuses, fees, and penalties. In other transportation segments such as commercial passenger airlines or cruise ships, the document also stipulates the carrier's policy pertaining to luggage fees, ticket validity, loss, damage, cancellation and delays, insurance and claims, and so on.

4.4.3 Bills of Lading

A B/L stipulates the name of the ship's captain; the place of origin (loading port) and destination (discharging port); the type, weight, and volume of the cargoes; the name of the consignee; and the freight rate agreed.

An electronic bill of lading (eB/L) should evidently reflect the primary features of a paper bill of lading, specifically its usefulness as a receipt and proof of delivery, as verification of or comprising the contract of carriage, and, if negotiable, it will serve as a document of title. Nevertheless, a B/L is also a document that is flexible enough to enable merchants to buy and sell freight globally and frequently as the carrier with the cargo are in transit (UK PANDI 2014).

4.5 E-COMMERCE TRANSFORMING TRANSPORTATION

Increasingly, more companies are using electronic freight documentation for sea, land, and air transportation.

In aviation, International Air Transport Association (IATA) has announced the launching of the electronic airway bill and its rapid expansion in over 600 trade routes. In the commercial aviation industry, IATA e-freight is an effort that benefits the entire cargo supply chain. It encompasses carriers, freight forwarders, ground handlers, shippers, customs brokers, and customs authorities. As shown in Figure 4.4, paper documentation is now replaced with electronic information, thus minimizing expenses, improving transportation times, reliability, and the commercial competitiveness of air transportation (IATA 2014).

Industries and governments seek to cut paper documentation and speed up the processing of deals. Goods that are shipped by sea require a B/L document, which lays out the terms of a contract between a shipper and a transportation company. Increasingly, more companies are using electronic cargo documentation, which, as shown in Figure 4.5, enables the rapid issuance of cargo papers (Cargo Docs).

The new possibilities will provide tremendous support to hectic industry segments, such as the maritime transportation, which represents over 80% of global trade. It is worth noting that in this hectic industry sector, the importation of a single cargo by sea requires an average of 36 original paper documents and 240 copies from 27 separate parties.

To produce a legitimate eB/L, it should have three primary characteristics:

1. *Legal framework*: i.e., the Rotterdam Rules, to make certain that the eB/L reserves the rights and obligations of the parties within a paper B/L. Providers of eB/Ls should verify that their program satisfies all its users' insurance coverage prerequisites, especially those of shipowners' protection and indemnity insurance.
2. *IT framework*: pertinent to which the eB/L should be safeguarded. There should only be an individual original eB/L and an individual entity who is in charge of that electronic document. No one should minimize this right of power or the validity of the eB/L.
3. *Practical framework*: the eB/L should have the essential number of functions:
   a. *The inherent functionality to allow the progress of an eB/L from issue to production in a manner similar to a paper B/L*, such as the ability to (i) endorse the eB/L to a different party, shifting the right to ownership and control of the cargo; (ii) offer a security interest in the freight transported; and (iii) request a modification of the eB/L.

b. *The new functionality required by its creation in electronic form*: for an eB/L to be completely functional, it should also be in a position of being transformed into paper, e.g., in case the eB/L must be endorsed to an individual or entity who is not willing to recognize it in an electronic form or if it is needed by a court (IATA 2013; CNSC 2014; UK PANDI 2014).

- Commercial invoices—commercial, pro-forma, consular
- Packing lists—dock, or warehouse, receipt
- Bills of Lading (B/L)—ocean B/L, or motor/truck or air bill, or way bill
- Electronic Export Information (formerly the Shipper's Export Declaration, or SED) is not an actual document but still a very important part of the export process
- Certificates of Origin (C/O), sometimes country-specific—NAFTA C/O, Israel C/O
- Declaration of Dangerous Goods (DGD)—HazMat, placards
- Certificates—insurance, free sale, inspection, phyto-sanitary, authentication (apostile)
- Miscellaneous—letters of credit, ATA carnet, duty drawback

FIGURE 4.4 E-documents by IATA. (From IATA, 2014 targets: Grow global e-AWB penetration to 22%, available at http://www.iata.org/whatwedo/cargo/e/freight/Pages /index.aspx, accessed December 5, 2014, 2014.)

Typical process:
Minimum total time: 65 minutes
✓ Draft printing time: 0 minutes
✓ Reviewing time: 1–60 minutes
✓ Signing time: 1 minute
✓ Issue time: 1–5 minutes
✓ Receive-endorse-amend: 1–60 minutes
✓ Produce: 1–60 minutes

E-process:
Real time data sharing to all entities simultaneously
Total time: 5 minutes

FIGURE 4.5 Cargo Docs by ESSDOCS. (From Cargo Docs, CargoDocs by ESSDOCS, available at http://www.essdocs.com, 2014.)

This section examined new technologies such as e-commerce, and their impact upon the entire supply chains, through uninterrupted flows of cargoes and information. While the industry significantly benefits from such novelties, at the same time, its cloud-based electronic environment makes it more vulnerable to security threats. Cyber security is a significant threat harbored by e-technologies, and Section 4.6 will analyze both the threats and the statistics. Furthermore, Section 4.7 will examine the resilience opportunities through the business continuity/disaster recovery (BC/DR) methods.

4.6 CYBER SECURITY

Cyberspace seems to control all modern activities of the public and private sectors: from confidential banking and corporate data to commercial contracts, energy supply, and even security monitoring of physical assets. Cloud-based technologies may vary in terms of vulnerability, and cyber criminals have both the tools and the capacity to identify the weakest links. Among cyber attacks, the most vulnerable seem to be the CI-related functions that heavily depend not only on cyber platforms, such as public electricity, energy pipelines, and water distribution, but also supply chains and logistics.

As much as some virtual databases promote integration of activities, they become more vulnerable by attracting cyber security attacks. In the past decade or so, cybercrime has accelerated, disclosing confidential government and corporate data, hampering vital functions, while causing tremendous financial losses.

Expansion is another trend for cyber criminals with the purpose of maximizing the intrusion while allocating their hacking tasks according to each individual or group area of specialization. Therefore, a mass systemic attack would benefit in multiple ways, i.e., identity theft, banking and commercial fraud, commercial intelligence, and so on.

Modern hacking activities seem to be driven by the following motives:

- Cyber crime
- Cyber espionage
- Cyber warfare
- Banking fraud; credit card and financial/commercial document scheming

The motivations behind the attacks are as follows:

- Cyber intelligence, cyber espionage—at a political, commercial, religious, or socioeconomic level
- Theft of proprietary information—at a political, commercial, and personal level
- Cyber-identify theft, hacking, identity spoofing, password-based access control, data modification, etc.
- Cyber propaganda, infiltration to radical terrorist groups, with the purpose of propagandizing, orchestrating, and facilitating organized attacks and providing codified instructions to global members
- Hacktivism, the promotion of political, religious, or other beliefs, and punishing cyber users that may not have the same views

Logistics and transport companies need to eliminate cyber risks throughout the supply chains and develop skills to address the rapidly growing threats, be it cyber crime, IP infringement, accounting, banking, or commercial fraud.

One of the reasons for concern is the monetary, commercial, and branding/reputation costs affiliated with cybercrime. It has been estimated that the stock market can severely punish or reward companies' tolerance and resilience against cyber attacks. Especially in cases where companies are unable to protect their clients' financial and personal data, the economic and stock market impact is both imminent and long-lasting.

According to PwC's 2014 Global Economic Crime Survey, 7% of US businesses lost at least $1 million as a result of cybercrime attacks in 2013 in comparison with 3% of international organizations. In addition, 19% of US companies experienced monetary losses from $50,000 to $1 million in comparison with 8% of global companies.

Both in the United States and globally, energy seems to be the industry sector and the CI sector that is most targeted by hackers for many good reasons. When it comes to other industry segments that are frequently attacked, these include trade and transport companies, medical/healthcare companies, and the education sector. In the United States, the navy can detect about 110,000 cyber attacks every single hour, and yet the number of attacks over the years seems to go up steadily. Breaking down the costs associated with annual losses due to cybercrime for nations, US companies are first globally with losses of over $8.9 million, whereas German businesses lose $6 million and UK firms $5.2 million with reasonable variations for costs concerning discovering cybercriminal activities and recovery (FBI 2009–2014; Ponemon statistics 2012–2014; GoGulf 2014).

The top 15 countries where cyber attacks originated in 2013–2014 include the United States, China, Russia, Taiwan, Germany, Brazil, Ukraine, Italy, Australia, Hungary, Romania, Argentina, Israel, Poland, and Japan. Based on the cyber security report released by *MarketsandMarkets research*, the international cyber security network is anticipated to expand from $63.7 billion in 2011 to $120.1 billion in 2017 at a projected annual rate of growth of around 11.3% (MarketsandMarkets 2012–2014).

Classification of the costs related to annual damage from cyber crime for countries is led by US firms with $8.9 million, followed by German companies at $6 million and UK firms third at $5.2 million with sensible differences for cost repartition between, for example, detecting activities and recovery.

The Royal Canadian Mounted Police distinguishes cybercrime in two types:

a. *Technology-as-target*—criminal violations aimed toward computer systems and other information technologies, including the unauthorized use of computer systems or data access mischief.

b. *Technology-as-instrument*—criminal violations where cloud-based systems, the Web, and IT systems are critical for committing the crime. These violations include money laundering, financial fraud, identity fraud, intellectual property infringements, organized crime activities, drug trafficking, human trafficking, cyber bullying, and so on.

Based upon the law enforcement observations from these two classifications of cyber crime, the following observations were made:

a. *Technological advancements generate new possibilities for criminals.* Online marketplaces and Internet-facing systems offer even more prospects and rewards for organized criminal communities as they do for legitimate businesses, as these groups have no geographical boundaries and are physically remote from their victims, enabling them to conceal their identities.

b. *Cybercrime is growing.* Whereas cybercrime used to be a *criminal niche*, modern security attacks have expanded to other criminal groups that attack cyber systems simultaneously.

c. *Cybercrime needs new ways of policing.* The criminal exploitation of innovative and rising technologies—including cloud computing and social media—demands new regulating actions to keep abreast with the new cybercrime networks.

It is worth noting that an accurate evaluation of the cyber crime losses is not easily achievable, as companies of all sizes are reluctant to report such attacks in order to avoid further damage of their public image. Nevertheless, the existing statistics are still alarming: each year, 232.4 million identities are exposed, whereas there are about 556 million targets (companies or individuals), which equals to about 1.5 million people each day.

Dealing with cyber attacks is a mutual responsibility for the public and private and nonprofit sectors and all levels of federal government. It is imperative to create robust public–private coalitions in order to defend the cyber systems from attacks that could potentially create large-scale damage to our systems.

4.7 RESILIENCE IN ACTION: BC/DR

Business continuity encompasses all the actions necessary to maintain the company's resilience from a commercial and security/emergency response perspective. Accordingly, a business continuity plan (BCP) is defined as the selection of methods and processes based on company- and industry-specific data that have been processed, compiled, and made available in case there is a security threat or other emergency incident. The requirement for business continuity planning has expanded rapidly in the twenty-first century, powered by both the regulatory conformity requirements and the stakeholders' needs. Prerequisites for business continuity recommend that companies evaluate security and emergency plans, as well as assess the outcomes of specific company plans or even compare them with other company plans within their supply chain. The goal here is to reduce any delays or interruptions within the supply chain and thus ensure the company's reliability within the industry. Administration should be able to integrate enterprise continuity concerns at an early stage, in the general business model, in order to reduce the likelihood of cargo flows or other service disruptions.

While focusing but not being limited to security threats, the BCP in logistics and transportation should deal with the occurrence of incidents such as

a. Mechanical failure of machinery, cargo-handling equipment, the carrier itself, and so on

b. Power failure or satellite systems/web connectivity that impacts the energy supply or IT and telecommunications

c. Intentional damage leading to application malfunction or database loss or damage

d. Sabotage

e. Cyber threats and hacking

f. Intentional damage or assault by the use of fire, explosives/blasting agents, nuclear or chemical weapons, and so on

g. Intentional causing of loss or damage to assets, cargoes, or CI components

4.7.1 Disaster Recovery Plan

Disaster recovery is the method of restoring the functions or facilities after the catastrophe has ended. A disaster recovery plan (DRP) or BCP or business process contingency plan explains how a corporation is to cope with possible security threats or other catastrophic events.

A DRP or manual typically stipulates corporate protocols, methods, and procedures that should be complied with in the case of a catastrophe. It is a detailed declaration of sustainable measures to be applied prior to, during, and after an incident.

4.7.2 The DRP Stages

The purpose of a DRP is to continue regular company operations with minimum possible delays. A standard DRP has various levels, such as the following:

- Comprehending the company's operations and scope of business and the interconnectivity of internal and external logistics
- Assessing the risks and identify the vulnerability of a company segment, the entire company, or the entire supply chain in numerous sectors, such as working processes, physical assets, CI, and contingency planning
- Realizing the effects of a security threat to each and every tier of the corporate pyramid
- Establishing a short-term restoration strategy
- Establishing a long-term restoration strategy, entailing the fast recovery into *business as usual*, by proactively identifying the commencement of operations in order of significance
- Evaluating and regularly sustaining and upgrading the strategy to encompass changes or threats in the market, the company, the economy, and so on. An essential component to an effective DRP is to adopt preventive measures in order to eliminate the occurrence of strategic threats.

A DRP is designed in a proactive manner that helps avert any security attack and eliminate its impacts. It is crucial for the protocols to guide the company's resilience, i.e., rapid recovery, in order to either sustain or rapidly commence objective-critical capabilities. Generally, disaster recovery planning entails an evaluation of business functions, sustainability capabilities, and facilitating tools. It may also incorporate a substantial part of its proactive strategy in incident prevention.

Disaster recovery is the course of action through which you continue business after a disruptive incident, such as a security threat. *Disaster recovery* seems to be an area frequently neglected or inadequately performed for three reasons:

a. Based on human nature and the propensity of being optimistic, incidents appear to be improbable.
b. Despite the time and efforts, professionals typically do not get credit for an averted catastrophe unless an incident actually happens.
c. Similarly, professional efforts cannot be measured unless an incident actually happens; for example, professionals typically do not get credit for allocating the right budget portion to the right investment for the right type of threat.

Business continuity planning recommends a more thorough method of resilience and sustainable operations during a plethora of security and other incidents.

Disaster recovery and business continuity planning are functions that assist businesses to plan ahead in order to mitigate any security incident or other incidents. This section examined their usefulness, as well as differences and principles they have in common. Regardless of these variances, the two terms are frequently applied together as BC/DR due to their positive contribution to resilience.

REFERENCES

Australia TISN. 2008. Development of policies and protection of critical information infrastructures. Available at http://www.tisn.gov.au/Documents/Australian+Government+s+Critical+Infrastructure+Resilience+Strategy.pdf.

CNSC. 2014. IATA E-Freight. What you need to know. Available at http://www.cnsc.net/Documents/IATA%20e-freight%20%20What%20you%20need%20to%20know.pdf. Accessed December 5, 2014.

Cargo Docs. 2014. CargoDocs by ESSDOCS. Available at http://www.essdocs.com.

DHS. 2003. The National Strategy for the Physical Protection of Critical Infrastructures and Key Assets, February 2003. Available at http://www.dhs.gov/xlibrary/assets/Physical_Strategy.pdf. Accessed December 12, 2014.

DHS. 2013. Critical Infrastructure. Available at http://www.dhs.gov/critical-infrastructure. Accessed December 4, 2014.

DHS. 2014. Critical Infrastructure Security. Available at http://www.dhs.gov/topic/critical-infrastructure-security. Accessed December 2, 2014.

EC. 2008. "Critical infrastructure security and resilience" and council directive 2008/114/EC.

EO. 1996. Executive Order 13010.2010. Critical Infrastructure Protection. Federal Register, July 17, 1996. Vol. 61, No. 138, pp. 37347–37350.

FBI. 2009–2014. Financial Crimes Report to the Public. Federal Bureau of Investigation. FBI. Available at http://www.fbi.gov/stats-services/publications/financial-crimes-report. Accessed December 21, 2014.

FSSCC (Financial Services Sector Coordinating Council). 2014. Protecting Critical Financial Infrastructure. Available at https://www.fsscc.org/. Accessed February 2, 2014.

GoGulf. 2014. Go-Gulf Cyber Crime Blog. Available at http://www.go-gulf.com/blog/cyber-crime/. Accessed December 1, 2014.

IATA. 2013. International Air Transport Association 2013. E-Freight Fundamentals. Available at http://www.iata.org/whatwedo/cargo/e/efreight/Documents/e-freight-fundamentals.pdf. Accessed December 5, 2014.

IATA. 2014. 2014 targets: Grow global e-AWB penetration to 22%. Available at http://www.iata.org/whatwedo/cargo/e/efreight/Pages/index.aspx. Accessed December 5, 2014.

MarketsandMarkets. 2012–2014. Cyber Security Market report. MarketsandMarkets. Available at http://www.marketsandmarkets.com. Accessed December 5, 2014.

OECD. 2008. OECD. Available at http://www.oecd.org/sti/40761118.pdf.

Ponemon statistics. 2012–2014. On cost of cybercrime-security affairs. Ponemon statistics. Available at http://www.securityaffairs.com. Accessed December 18, 2014.

PPD-21. 2013. The White House, Office of the Press Secretary, February 12. Presidential Policy Directive—Critical Infrastructure Security and Resilience, Presidential Policy Directive/Ppd-21. Available at http://www.whitehouse.gov/the-press-office /2013/02/12/presidential-policy-directive-critical-infrastructure-security-and-resil. Accessed August 5, 2014.

PSC Canada. 2014. Public Safety Canada. Government of Canada. National Strategy for Critical Infrastructure. Available at http://www.publicsafety.gc.ca/cnt/rsrcs/pblctns /srtg-crtcl-nfrstrctr/index-eng.aspx.

PwC. 2014. Global Annual Economic Crime Survey. Available at http://www.pwc.com/. Accessed January 10, 2015.

RCMP. 2014. Cybercrime: An overview of incidents and issues in Canada-Royal Canadian Mounted Police. Available at http://www.rcmp-grc.gc.ca. Accessed December 21, 2014.

UK PANDI. 2014. Paperless Trading Electronic Bills of Lading. Available at http:// www.ukpandi.com/knowledge/article/paperless-trading-electronic-bills-of-lading -frequently-asked-questions-faqs-6167/. Accessed December 16, 2014.

The White House. 2013. Presidential Policy, Directive on Critical Infrastructure Security and Resilience. Available at http://www.whitehouse.gov/the-press-office/2013/02 /12/presidential-policy-directive-critical-infrastructure-security-and-resil. Accessed December 11, 2014.

WBCSD (World Business Council for Sustainable Development). 2002. Business & Biodiversity: A Handbook for Corporate Action. Available at http://www.wbcsd .org/pages/edocument/edocumentdetails.aspx?id=26&nosearchcontextkey=true. Accessed November 1, 2014.

Classifying Security Threats through the Nine Hazardous Materials (HazMat or Dangerous Goods) Categories

Alfred Nobel's discoveries are characteristic; powerful explosives can help men perform admirable tasks. They are also a means to terrible destruction in the hands of great criminals.

Pierre Curie (1859–1906)
Nobel Prize winner in physics

5.1 INTRODUCTION

In the previous chapters of the book, we examined the different security threats that are typically encountered in transportation, and the critical infrastructure sectors that need to be safeguarded in order to mitigate such threats. This chapter examines the possibility of the cargo itself being intentionally used as a security threat due to its hazardous nature. Security offenders may use conventional weapons, bomb vests and other explosive substances, flammable liquids, nuclear power, or even biological hazards such as viruses, invasive species, or fertilizers. What these weapons have in common is that they are all classified as hazardous materials (HazMat), which can be carried by sea, land, pipelines, and, under certain restrictions, air transport.

HazMat cargoes may be transported in the following forms:

- Containers (ammunition, uranium, plutonium, chemicals, biohazards)
- Tanks as liquid bulk commodities (chemicals, oil, gas)
- Holds in dry bulk commodities (fertilizers)
- Pipelines (oil, gas)

Although these are commodities of high usefulness and high value, they are susceptible to sabotage and/or intentional, improper use. Once security offenders gain access to HazMat at any stage of the supply chain, they may impose considerable security risk. It is imperative for security professionals to be aware, proactive, and knowledgeable about the identification, labelling, handling, and transportation of different classes of HazMat. This will reduce any security vulnerabilities while protecting the nation, the community, the industry, and the environment.

5.2 HAZARDOUS MATERIALS (HazMat): AN OVERVIEW

HazMat, also referred to as "chemicals" or "dangerous goods" (DG), are elements or substances (physical, chemical, biological) that, when released, discharged, or activated, have the potential of becoming a threat to human life, health, the environment, flora and fauna, and or property and assets due to their biological, chemical, or physical composition (WMD/EMD HazMat 2014; WMD/EMD.Chemicals 2014). Security vulnerabilities are derived not only by the increasing volume of global trade and logistics activities but also by the hazardous nature of the cargoes carried. According to the United Nations (UN) and all international and national regulations, there are nine HazMat classifications, which may become potential security threats.

In the United States, DG are more generally referred to as HazMat, whereas in England, Canada, and Australia, they are called DG.

In the United States, HazMat goods are identified and controlled by a regulatory framework implemented by the US Department of Transportation (DOT), the US Environmental Protection Agency (EPA), the US Occupational Safety and Health Administration (OSHA), and the US Nuclear Regulatory Commission. Each has its own definition of a "hazardous material" (IHMM 2014).

HazMat commodities may belong to one or more of the nine HazMat classifications established by the UN, i.e., can be flammable, explosive, combustible, corrosive, radioactive, poisonous, toxic, biological agent, and/or reactive. HazMat goods are considered as the backbone of the global economy, and their trade and transport are both necessary and beneficial. Despite their increased requirements for safe handling, storage, and transport, most HazMat include commodities of high demand and high value, such as oil and gas, plutonium, uranium, and numerous chemicals and blasting agents used in the industry, the military, and scientific research. This chapter discusses the nature of these commodities and explains why the trade and transport of HazMat may impose security threats.

The effect, duration, intensity, and final outcome of every incident is determined by a wide variety of connected parameters that include the HazMat distinct chemical composition, volume spilled, the circumstances of the discharge, the incident's location, and population afflicted. Small-range spills or releases can be promptly addressed with nearby emergency response available in the vicinity or surge to disastrous levels with long-range repercussions that demand a large number of officials of federal government, regional, and local authorities at the incident location (WMD/EMD HazMat 2014).

Depending on the HazMat nature, the risk to safety can be flammable, explosive, combustible, corrosive, radioactive, poisonous, toxic, biological agent, and reactive.

A discharge can happen accidentally or intentionally:

a. Accidentally, as the outcome of a natural disaster, equipment failure, human error or negligence; or
b. Intentionally, i.e., by serving as terrorism, piracy, illegitimate trade and travel, and any other criminal activity

A discharge may occur as an outcome of any action and operation that allows the HazMat to flow freely into the atmosphere and generate a prospective risk to safety or security. HazMat incidents, regardless of the intentional or unintentional motive, may occur

a. Due to change in temperature or pressure
b. Due to interaction with other compounds or chemicals, hazardous or not
c. Due to incidents resulting to splattering, leakage, overflowing, or emissions of volatile organic compounds or noxious vapors (Burns 2012, 2014)

According to the US DOT, HazMat or DG can be defined as "Any substance which may pose an unreasonable risk to health and safety of operating or emergency personnel, the public, and/or the environment if not properly controlled during handling, storage, manufacture, processing, packaging, use, disposal, or transportation" (FMCSA/DOT 2013, 2014).

The US DOT defines HazMat as any compound or commodity that when moved or relocated imposes threat to the environment or the society and is governed according to the Hazardous Materials Regulations 49 CFR 100-180 related to the International Maritime Dangerous Goods Code, Dangerous Goods Regulations of the International Air Transport Association, Technical Instructions of the International Civil Aviation Organization, US Air Force Joint Manual, and Preparing Hazardous Materials for Military Air Shipments (49 CFR 100-180).

OSHA describes hazardous goods as compounds that impose a health or physical hazard and may encompass substances that are toxic, corrosive, allergens, irritants, cancer agents, and generally as damaging to the vital bodily organs; their chemical manifestation may be a flammable, explosive, volatile, reactive, combustible, oxidizing, or pyrophoric agent (29 CFR Code of Federal Regulations [CFR] 1910.1200).

EPA supports the OSHA characterization by specifying that the damage to life, health, flora, and fauna is caused when HazMat are discharged by leakage, overflow, emissions, drainage, insertion, pumping in or out, waste disposal, spills, and so on (40 CFR 355 includes a directory of more than 350 harmful and highly harmful substances).

Training for DG/HazMat is mandatory to all personnel involved with HazMat cargoes at any stage of the supply chain, i.e., from raw materials, extraction, refinery, manufacturing, transportation, warehousing, distribution, packaging, labelling, staffing, and unstaffing. The US DOT also stipulates mandatory training in line with the DOT HazMat regulations (49 CFR Part 172, Subpart H). HazMat specialists should be adequately trained and competent to handle hazardous goods and DG (US DOT 2014a,b, 49 CFR 172 H).

5.2.1 HazMat Statistics

For the average transportation or supply chain professional operating in a fast-paced industrial environment, the likelihood of being exposed to HazMat is considerable. In the United States alone, well over 60,000 products are produced and distributed each year, among which the US DOT classifies somewhere around 2000 as HazMat. Well over 4 billion tons of hazardous and chemical materials are transported on an annual basis by sea, land, air, and pipelines. These commodities involve over 100,000 distinct supply chain nodal points, such as areas of origin, transit, and destination. In this supply chain procedure, literally millions of professionals are involved in the haulage, storage, marking, and labelling of 500,000 HazMat shipments on a daily basis, amounting to over 1.5 billion tons per year.

Unfortunately, an accurate statistical analysis of the instances concerning HazMat incidents, vulnerabilities, and damages may not be feasible because a systematic registration and reporting program is not available at a global, national, state, or industry level. While making an effort to outline the value of such information, the US "Agency for Toxic Substances Disease Registry" created the Hazardous Substances Emergency Events Surveillance program in 1990 (ATSDR CDC, 1990–2014). Fifteen state occupational safety and health departments actively engage in this HazMat reporting initiative, whereas some interesting statistical facts and figures were derived from their research:

- Each year, over 9000 emissions and spills of HazMat take place, with 75% manifesting at HazMat and/or chemical industrial locations, whereas about 25% of these incidents happen in motion, i.e., during haulage.
- The vast majority of transport-linked occurrences, i.e., 85%, are related to land haulage, and 15% of the incidents were related to sea and air transport. Furthermore, 26% of these incidents took place in residential areas, whereas 74% of these events occurred on highways, industrial zones, and remote locations where communities were not endangered.
- The root cause analysis revealed that most HazMat spills occurred unintentionally, i.e., either because of human error (negligence, improper judgment, lack of experience, lack of training, fatigue) or due to machinery malfunction.
- The most frequent health impact types entail eye problems and respiratory system complications.
- The most frequent HazMat associated with incidents were inorganic materials (24%), and the second most frequent occurrence relates to volatile organic compounds (20%).

5.2.2 Hazard Classification: Physical, Health, and Environmental Threats

Incident management pertains to the safeguarding of human life, flora and fauna, the environment, corporate resources and property, and networks and information systems from security hazards—both intentional and unintentional. An incident is defined as a situation resulting from human action, and the motive can be of vital significance when an occurrence is the result of vicious intentions.

HazMat-related incidents may be typically categorized as intentional and unintentional. When a HazMat accident occurs, it may be likely that the authorities, the emergency responders, and the communities may not be aware of the motive and cause that has triggered the occurrence. It is therefore essential for all key players involved to have in place a root cause analysis and risk management methodologies that incorporate the role of HazMat as a cause and impact for both intentional and unintentional incidents.

This categorization will determine the federal and state agencies and law enforcement specialists who will be involved, the emergency response, and the contingency planning protocols adopted.

Such occurrences may be *intentional* or *unintentional*:

a. *Intentional occurrences*: Criminal groups or individuals may use HazMat in order to impose their will and intentionally cause damage and social turmoil. Such incidents are typically described as criminal acts of illegitimate activities, such as terrorism, extremism, sabotage, arson, and so on. Intentional events are classified as security HazMat (or DG) incidents yet may differ in terms of the motive:

    i. *Noncompliance*, i.e., unlawful behaviors that are initiated with the purpose of avoiding the financial burden of compliance, for example, the purposeful disposal of industrial waste or any HazMat type and class in order to shun the investment of resources, funds, time, and effort.

    ii. *Criminal but nonterrorist incidents*: In these cases, the destructive behavior where HazMat is used to destroy human life or the environment but for personal motives against specific individuals.

    iii. *Terrorist attacks*, which involve actions that threaten the homeland security, and are categorized in terms of the motive, i.e., politics, faith-based, or belief/ideological reason (see also Chapter 2, Section 3).

b. *Unintentional occurrences* are classified as Safety HazMat (or DG) incidents and are a result of (i) natural disasters; (ii) engineering or electronic malfunction; or (iii) human error, negligence, or fatigue.

According to the current US law as stipulated in the USA Patriot Act, behaviors of domestic terrorism are the ones that "(A) include activities hazardous to human life, and violate the international, national, state, tribal or regional criminal laws; (B) seem to be designed with the purpose of (i) forcing, influencing or frightening a social segment or the general population; (ii) having an impact on the diplomatic, political, religious, cultural or socioeconomic decisions of a political, religious or other regime, through fear, intimidation or emotional abuse; and/or (iii) impacting the operations, functions, performance, and overall decisions of a political, commercial or religious group by acts of violence, abduction, mass destruction or injuries" (see also Chapter 2, Section 3).

In addition to the conventional weapons, HazMat can also be used to create similar effects with weapons of mass destruction. Such HazMat substances may be utilized to poison foodstuffs, livestock, and plans.

It is possible for HazMat-related disasters, incidents, and/or near misses to occur in any and all of the supply chain components, from raw materials and mineral extraction to manufacturing, warehousing, transportation, and distribution.

Both deliberate and accidental occurrences related with HazMat may have identical consequences.

5.2.3 HazMat Incidents

HazMat incidents are defined as materials that when released are capable of damaging humans, flora and fauna, the environment, and properties. Such incidents involve substances or compounds that impose threats to safety and the environment and require the operations of professional, well-trained HazMat emergency responders. These DG belong to one or more of the nine HazMat classifications and may include organic or inorganic materials, gas, liquids, or solids.

5.2.3.1 Mens Rea: Criminal Act or Incident

The majority of crimes need to have what legal professionals describe as "*mens rea*," and that is Latin for a "guilty mind." To put it differently, what an offender was planning, reasoning, and intended when the crime was committed makes a difference. "Mens rea" enables the criminal justice mechanism to distinguish among an individual or group who did not plan or intend to create an incident and someone who deliberately attempted to commit a crime.

5.3 HazMat CLASSIFICATIONS

5.3.1 Global and National Regulatory Framework

The following global organizations have developed a set of HazMat rules and regulations for the carriage and handling of DG. Some of these rules are all-encompassing, whereas others focus on industry segments, i.e., sea, land, and air transport. Nevertheless, the overall idea here is to create a harmonized system that can be easily recognized by all HazMat professionals, carriers, and emergency responders.

5.3.1.1 Global HazMat Regulations

The *UN Recommendations on the Transport of Dangerous Goods* constitute the foundation and regulatory model upon which the global HazMat regulations are based, i.e.,

  a. **Air transport:**
  - The *International Civil Aviation Organization* (adopted to meet the air transportation HazMat standards)
  - The *International Air Transport Association* (IATA) has developed the *IATA Dangerous Goods Regulations* to accommodate the private airline industry and domestic federal requirements.
  b. **Sea transport:**
  The International Maritime Organization (IMO), which is an instrument of the UN, has produced the International Maritime Dangerous Goods Code (IMDG Code), as a component of the International Convention for the Safety of Life at Sea (SOLAS), to facilitate ship safety when carrying HazMat (see Section 5.3.9).
  c. **Rail transport:**
  The Intergovernmental Organization for International Carriage by Rail has created the "Regulations Concerning the International Carriage of Dangerous Goods by Rail" (RID), as a component of the Convention Concerning International Carriage by Rail (COTIF), which is enforced in Europe, Maghreb, and the Middle East.

5.3.1.2 US HazMat-Related Departments, Agencies, and Regulations

In the United States, HazMat involve a number of departments and federal agencies, each of which mitigate the 9 categories of hazardous materials threats, from different scopes. These scopes include but are not limited to: security (terrorism, piracy), safety, sea, land and air transportation, customs clearance, warehousing, emergency response, communities protection, social responsibilities, and so on.

All HazMat professionals, be they laboratory or refinery workers, truck drivers, ocean carriers, or port stevedores, need to work in a safe environment, use the suitable personal protective equipments (PPEs), be trained, and be aware of the HazMat dangers. For this reason, the US Department of Labor (DOL) has established the Occupational Safety and Health Administration (OSHA) to oversee the working conditions and establish safety and security.

The Department of Transportation (DOT) and its federal agencies have developed an efficient set of HazMat rules to assist the transportation of HazMat, at a domestic and global level, through the following agencies, whose functions are self-explanatory.

5.3.1.2.1 Pipeline and Hazardous Materials Safety Administration   The Pipeline and Hazardous Materials Safety Administration (PHMSA) has a toll-free hotline (1-800-467-4922) to facilitate shippers with filled-in documentation, i.e., HazMat cargo manifests, identify the appropriate shipping names and select the appropriate package type and make for specific HazMat cargoes to be transported by sea, land, and air, which amount to over 1 million shipments in the United States. In addition, the PHMSA is in charge of the US pipeline networks, which in the United States alone covers at least 2.6 million mi or 64% of the energy transportation (PHMSA 2014).

Other US federal agencies that deal with specific transport segments, and therefore may be involved in the transportation of HazMat, in collaboration with the PHMSA, include

- National Highway Traffic Safety Administration (NHTSA)
- Federal Highway Administration (FHWA)
- Federal Motor Carrier Safety Administration (FMCSA)
- Federal Aviation Administration (FAA)
- Federal Railroad Administration (FRA)
- Federal Transit Administration (FTA)
- Maritime Administration (MARAD)

It is worth noting that in case of an actual security threat, the Department of Homeland Security, and potentially the Department of Defense (in case of a critical national security threat), will play a crucial role in the mitigation and investigation of such security threats.

5.3.2 OSHA'S Hazard Communication Standard (HCS HazCom)

The Hazard Communication Standard (HCS), also referred to as the "Right-to-Know Law," was introduced in 1983, by the US Occupational Safety and Health Administration (OSHA), and in 1994, its improved, amended version was enforced.

The scope of the HCS is to ensure the classification of all HazMat or chemicals, imported, exported, or produced and transported domestically. Furthermore, all details pertaining to these risks should be shared among company management and personnel. Communication through the corporate chain of command should be achieved through the implementation of HazCom, a sophisticated "hazard communication" program that involves container marking, labeling, the understanding of safety data sheets (or material safety data sheets [MSDSs]) and HazMat/HazCom training.

According to the HazMat Communication Standards (OSHA), any substance that imposes a physical or health risk is classified as a HazMat, namely,

a. HazMat imposing *physical risk* entails a substance whose chemical composition as proven by scientific evidence is flammable, explosive, combustible liquid, oxidizer, compressed gas, organic peroxide, pyrophoric, reactive, or water reactive.

b. HazMat imposing *health risk* entails a substance whose chemical composition, as proven by a minimum of one study in line with proven scientific evidence, causes severe (acute) or long-term (chronic) health impact to personnel exposed to these substances.

The health risk may be related to HazMat that are scientifically proven carcinogens, toxic irritants, corrosives, toxic or highly toxic agents, reproductive toxins (reproductive system damage), neurotoxins (nervous system damage), hepatotoxins (liver damage), nephrotoxins (kidney damage), agents that damage the hematopoietic system (blood cell and circulatory damage), or the eyes, brain, lungs, skin, or mucous membranes (lubricating epithelial tissues).

The HCS categories of physical and health hazards are demonstrated in Table 5.1. Furthermore, the nine HCS categories containing the pertinent health or environmental hazard are shown in Figure 5.1 (OSHA HazCom 2012a,b; OSHA HazMat 2014a,b).

5.3.3 UN Committee of Experts on Transport of Dangerous Goods

The UN Committee of Experts on Transport of Dangerous Goods was selected to guide physical hazards research in partnership with the International Labor Organization (ILO). Based on their scientific findings in the assessment of hazardous and chemical substances, the Organization for Economic Cooperation and Development (OECD) further investigated the health/environmental hazards and organic compounds. ILO is also a leader in HazCom. The OECD and ILO groups are represented from governments, industry, and workers.

TABLE 5.1   HCS Categories of Physical and Health Hazards

Physical Hazards HCS	Health Hazards HCS	Other Health Hazards
Fire Hazards	**Systemic Effects**	Cardiovascular toxicity
Combustible liquids	Carcinogen	Immunotoxicity
Flammable liquids	Toxic agent	Connective tissue effects
Flammable aerosols	Highly toxic agent	Sensory organ toxicity (sight, hearing,
Flammable gases	Corrosive	taste)
Flammable solids	Irritant	Gastrointestinal toxicity
Oxidizers	Sensitizer	Skeletal/muscular effects
Pyrophorics		Endocrine system toxicity
Explosion Hazards	**Target Organ Effects**	
Compressed gas	Hepatotoxin	
Explosives	Nephrotoxin	
Reactive Hazards	Neurotoxin	
Organic peroxide	Blood/hematopoietic toxin	
Unstable (reactive)	Respiratory toxin	
Water reactive	Reproductive toxin	
	Cutaneous hazard	
	Eye hazard	

Source: OSHA, available at https://www.osha.gov/dsg/hazcom/ghd053107.html, 2014a.

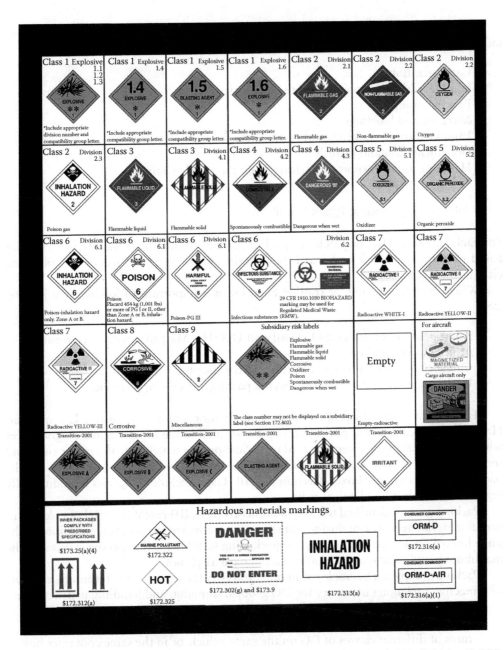

FIGURE 5.1 Hazardous materials warning labels. (From US DOT, 2014, 49CFR CH.1.2014. Code of Federal Regulations #49. US Government Publishing Office; US DOT, 2014, Hazardous Materials Regulations. Available at http://www.dot.gov, accessed August 18, 2014; US DOT, 2014, U.S. Department of Transportation, HazMat. Available at http://www.usdot.gov. Accessed July 30, 2014.)

The UN Committee investigates the principal stages of a supply chain and transportation where HazMat handling is crucial:

1. Categorization
2. HazMat identification and limited quantities
3. Packing group
4. Marking and labelling
5. Familiarization, training, and certification
6. Documentation and records
7. Handling and transportation throughout the supply chain

5.3.4 UN Packing Groups: Types I, II, III

For each HazMat (DG) dispatch, a "packing group" should be designated to HazMat based on the level of risk or hazard they entail. These are prioritized in the following classification:

When shipping, storing, or trading HazMat, it is important to follow the following steps:

1. Appropriately recognize and classify all DG (HazMat) that will be transported or need to be handled
2. Categorize each cargo type according to the nine hazard classes
3. Designate each cargo type to a specific packing group if appropriate

Typically, a material's proper shipping name (noncommercial name), UN number, HazMat classification, and packing group are located in the MSDS. Some cargoes meet with the specification of several hazard classifications, in which case the major risks and secondary risks should be both stipulated in the MSDS and the HazMat labels on the package or the container boxes. Certain hazard classes include categories to additionally segment materials with identical risks.

Packing groups identified in Roman numerals (I, II, III) reveal the level of risk a dangerous material may present during transportation compared to other commodities in the same hazard class. These can verify the packaging suitable for the specific goods and the maximum permissible quantities allowed onboard airplanes.

Packing groups can be employed in order to verify the reason for determining the level of protective packaging necessary for DG groups, shipping, and handling instructions:

- *Group I*: High risk and maximum protective packaging needed. Various mixtures of different classes of DG on the same vehicle or in the same container box are not allowed if one or more of the goods carried belong to Group I.
- *Group II*: Medium risk.
- *Group III*: Low risk among regulated goods and minimum protective packaging within the transportation requirement (IMO 2014).

5.3.5 The Nine Classes of HazMat

There are nine distinct "class" designators to specify the type of hazard for each commodity based on their chemical composition and behavior, as stipulated in Table 5.2.

TABLE 5.2   Nine (9) Classes of Hazardous Materials

Class 1 Explosives
Examples: Ammunition; pyrotechnics; detonators; primers; flares; Rockets; nitroglycerine.

Division 1.1—Compounds and chemical substances with a mass explosion hazard.
Example: Dynamite.

Division 1.2—Compounds and chemical substances with a blasting/projection hazard, yet not a mass explosion risk.
Example: Flares.

Division 1.3—Compounds and chemical substances with a fire hazard, a minor blast hazard, and/or a minor projection hazard, yet not a mass explosion risk.
Example: Fireworks; rocket propellants.

Division 1.4—Compounds and chemical substances imposing no significant risk (explosion dependent upon hazmat quantity, storage conditions and packing arrangements.)
Example: Consumer fireworks, Ammunition.

Division 1.5—Very insensitive substances having a mass explosion hazard.
Example: Blasting Agents.

Division 1.6—Extremely insensitive substances which do not impose a mass explosion hazard.
Example: Explosive devices.

Class 2 Gaseous Products
This category consists of components that are Dissolved under Pressure, Compressed, or Pressurized Cryogenic Liquids, and Liquefied Gases.
Behavior: Flammables, asphyxiates, oxidizers, toxic or corrosives.
Examples: Aerosols; Fire extinguishers; Petroleum & Gaseous products; Refrigerant gases; Acetylene; Carbon oxides; nitrogen, hydrogen, oxygen compounds, Methane, Ethane, Propane, Butane.

Division 2.1—Flammable Gases, that kindle when in contact with an ignition source.
Example: Propane, Acetylene, Hydrogen.

Division 2.2—Non-flammable, non-poisonous gases, such as cryogenic gases or liquids with temperatures below −148°F (−100°C).
Examples: materials used for cryopreservation and rocket fuels, such as nitrogen and neon.

(Continued)

TABLE 5.2 (CONTINUED)   Nine (9) Classes of Hazardous Materials

Class 2 Gaseous Products

Division 2.3—Poisonous, Toxic Gases. If inhaled, may impact
   health or cause death.
Examples: fluorine, chlorine, hydrogen cyanide.

Class 3 Flammable or combustible

Liquids fluids, mixes of fluids or liquids comprising solids in solution or suspension that give off
   a flammable vapor, and whose Flash Point (FP) does not exceed 141F (60°C).
Examples: Acetone; Paints; Alcohols; Gasoline, Shale Gas, Crude oil and Petroleum products;
   Diesel fuel, Aviation fuel; Liquid bio-fuels; Resins and Tars.

Class 4 Other Flammable Substances

Class 4: Flammable solids;
Solid materials prone to spontaneous combustion; or discharge flammable gases.
Class 4.1: Flammable solids, self-reactive substances and desensitized explosives.
Class 4.2: Spontaneously combustible Solids.
Class 4.3: Spontaneously Combustible when wet. Materials that emit flammable gases when wet.

Division 4.1—Flammable Solid.
Examples: Ammonium Picrate; nitrocellulose, magnesium, safety
   matches.

Division 4.2—Spontaneously Combustible Material. Substances
   prone to spontaneous combustion.
Examples: white phosphorous, aluminum alkyls.

Division 4.3—Dangerous when wet. Substances which, in contact
   with water, emit flammable gases.
Examples: Sodium, calcium, potassium, calcium carbide.

(Continued)

TABLE 5.2 (CONTINUED)   Nine (9) Classes of Hazardous Materials

CLASS 5 Oxidizing Substances and Organic Peroxides

Division 5.1—Oxidizing agents.
Examples: ammonium nitrate, hydrogen peroxide, potassium permanganate; calcium hypochlorite.

Division 5.2—Organic Peroxides Oxidizing Agents.
Examples: Methyl; Ethyl; Ketone Peroxide; benzoyl peroxides, Cumene hydroperoxide.

Class 6 Toxic (Poisonous) and Infectious Substances

Division 6.1—Toxic (Poisonous) Materials 6.1a Toxic substances that might result in death or severe damage if inhaled, ingested or absorbed by skin.
Examples: potassium cyanide, mercuric chloride.
6.1b (Now PGIII) Toxic substances that are dangerous to human health (Note: the placard / symbol is no longer approved by the United Nations). Examples: pesticides, methylene chloride.
Division 6.2—Biohazards, Infectious Substances.

A substance recognized or likely to contain a pathogen, for instance bacteria, viruses, parasites, fungi, that can induce disease in humans, animals or environmental degradation. The World Health Organization (WHO) divides this class into two categories:
Category A: An infectious substance stored and transported in a mode that allows exposure leading permanent impairment or life-threatening or lethal disease in healthy humans or animals. Examples: Anthrax virus, Ebola Virus.
Category B: An infectious substance stored and transported in a mode that does not lead to permanent impairment or life-threatening or lethal disease in healthy humans or animals once exposure occurs.

Class 7 Radioactive (Nuclear) Materials

Division 7—Radioactive substances or a combination of substances that emit ionizing radiation. This is a random (stochastic) process by which a nucleus of an unstable atom decays, i.e. spontaneously emits energy, i.e. ionizing radiation. Examples: uranium, plutonium, alpha particles, beta particles, gamma rays.
All radioactive atoms decay at some point yet not at the same level. The time required for decay depends upon the type of atom.

(Continued)

TABLE 5.2 (CONTINUED)   Nine (9) Classes of Hazardous Materials

Class 8 Corrosives

Division 8—Corrosive Materials can dissolve organic tissue or significantly corrode particular metals:

8.1 Acids: sulfuric acid, hydrochloric acid.

8.2 Alkalis: potassium hydroxide, sodium hydroxide.

Corrosive materials can attack and chemically destroy metals, and other materials. Inhalation, absorption or pure contact of a corrosive material can harm the eyes, skin, the tissue beneath the skin, as well as the respiratory and gastrointestinal tracts. Direct exposure causes chemical burns.

Examples: Battery fluid, caustic soda, potash.

Class 9 Miscellaneous Hazardous Materials (Dangerous Goods)

Environmentally hazardous substances; wastes; Polychlorinated Biphenyls (PCB); Magnetized material.

Dry ice; Asbestos; Engines of internal combustion; air-bag inflators, self-inflating life rafts; Battery-powered equipment or vehicles; Zinc Dithonite.

*Category includes Environmentally Hazardous Substances, Elevated Temperature Material, Hazardous Wastes, and Marine Pollutants.

Miscellaneous Hazardous Materials previously known as "Other Regulated Materials."

CONSUMER COMMODITIES

Consumer commodities are materials that are packaged and distributed in a form intended for, or suitable for sale through retail sales. In order to determine if a particular hazardous material may qualify as a consumer commodity, refer to the section number in Part 173 identified in column 8 of the 172.101 Table for that material.

EXCEPTIONS:

Agricultural Operations

The haulage of agricultural merchandise (see 49 CFR171.8) by freeway could be excepted from certain or all of the prerequisites of the Hazardous Materials Regulations when carried in compliance with the provisions of 49 CFR 173.5.

Materials of Trade

The haulage of materials of trade (see 49 CFR 171.8) by freeway could be excepted from a number of the prerequisites of the Hazardous Materials Regulations when carried in compliance with the provisions of 49 CFR 173.6.

http://environmentalchemistry.com/yogi/hazmat/placards/

US DOT HazMat Placards

Class 1 Explosives—49CFR 173.50

1.1   1.2   1.3

(*Continued*)

TABLE 5.2 (CONTINUED)   Nine (9) Classes of Hazardous Materials

US DOT HazMat Placards

Class 1 Explosives—49CFR 173.50

Class 2 Compressed Gasses—49CFR 173.115

Class 3 Flammable Liquids—49CFR 173.120

Class 4 Flammable Solids—49CFR 173.124

Class 5 Oxidizers—49CFR 173.127

Class 6 Poisons—49CFR 173.132

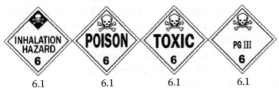

(Continued)

TABLE 5.2 (CONTINUED)   Nine (9) Classes of Hazardous Materials

US DOT HazMat Placards

Class 7 Radioactive Materials—49CFR Subpart I

7

Class 8 Corrosive Liquids—49CFR 173.136

8

Class 9 Miscellaneous—49CFR 173.140

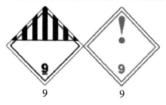

9   9

Other Related Markings

Source: Compiled by the author, based on Burns, M., *HazMat Regulations Training Manual (40 Hours)*. US Coast Guard, National Maritime Center-Approved Manual. Texas Southern University, Houston, TX, 2012; Burns, M., *HazMat Training Manual (40 Hours)*. US Coast Guard, National Maritime Center-Approved Manual. University of Houston, Houston, TX, 2014; FMCSA.DOT, 2013, Available at http://www.fmcsa.dot.gov/sites/fmcsa.dot.gov /files/docs/Nine_Classes_of_Hazardous_Materials-4-2013.pdf, accessed August 14, 2014; FMCSA/DOT, 2014, Federal Motor Carriers Safety Administration, U.S. Department of Transportation, Hazardous Materials. Available at http://www.fmcsa.dot.gov/regulations /hazardous-materials, accessed August 14, 2014; WMD/EMD HazMat. 2014. Washington Military Department, Emergency Management Division. 2014. Hazardous Materials. Available at http://www.emd.wa.gov/hazards/haz_hazardous_materials.shtml, accessed May 26, 2014; US DOT, 2014, 49CFR CH.1.2014. Code of Federal Regulations #49. US Government Publishing Office; US DOT, 2014, Hazardous Materials Regulations. Available at http://www .dot.gov, accessed August 18, 2014; US DOT, 2014, U.S. Department of Transportation, HazMat. Available at http://www.usdot.gov, accessed July 30, 2014.

5.3.6 United Nations (UN) Identification Numbers

UN identification numbers are the four-digit ID numbers used for global trade and transport to verify HazMat, their classification, chemical composition, and behavior. The UN numbers typically range from UN0001 to around UN3506 and usually come after the letters "UN" (for example, UN1830, i.e., sulfuric acid with over 51% acid) in order to avoid misunderstanding between several other numeric identification codes.

The UN identification numbers are assigned by the UN Committee of Experts on the Transport of Dangerous Goods. They are designated and published as a component of their Recommendations on the Transport of Dangerous Goods, also referred to as the Orange Book. These official guidelines are implemented by a plethora of global and national regulatory organizations in charge of the diverse modes of transport (UN Model Regulations; see UNECE 2001–2013; DG; see UNECE 2014).

5.3.7 North American (NA) Identification Numbers or DOT Numbers

North American (NA) identification numbers, or DOT numbers (US DOT numbers), serve the same purpose as the UN numbers. HazMat that may not be designated a UN identification number are likely to be designated an NA identification number.

The reference of UN and/or NA identification numbers is mandatory for the shipping and distribution of HazMat. Placards with the appropriate UN/NA numbers are seen on maritime containers, 18-wheeler trucks, railway transport systems, and so on.

5.3.8 UN Markings of Containers

One of the most significant duties of HazMat professionals is their ability to select a suitable container for HazMat cargo shipments. According to the international UN packaging requirements, and the UN-harmonized national and state regulations, professionals who handle HazMat shipments should be familiar with HazMat identification, documentation, marking, labelling, and packaging. In the United States, the professional requirements for handling HazMat are stipulated in the Code of Federal Regulations Number 49, as specified by the US DOT, 49 CFR 172.704. To enable safe packaging, handling, shipping, and unstuffing of global and local HazMat cargo shipments, the US DOT implemented the "performance-oriented packaging (POP)" guidelines in line with the UN packaging requirements (US DOT 2014a,b,c).

POP was launched into global packaging rules in 1989, and on January 1, 1991, it became mandatory for US shipments outside the continental United States. It was introduced in the US federal regulations within the following five years, whereas in 1996, it took over as legislation of the property for labeling and packaging of all HazMat-regulated shipments. POP markings are placed on cargo packaging that has successfully passed a number of checks and tests that emulate the moving and transportation strains and pressures and comprise of leakage, vibration, drop, hydrostatic pressure, pile up tests, and so on.

These kinds of tests that are prescribed by the US DOT, CFR 49 is in accordance with UN guidelines and is harmonized with the global and other national standards.

Cargoes that are containerized, palletized, in barrels, and so on, once subjected to testing and evaluated for shipping HazMat, should be marked, labeled, and specified in line with the UN DG specification to signify the attributes and restrictions of the

TABLE 5.3   HazMat Marking 1B1/Z120/S/15/USA/NC1

1	Package identification	1—Drum/Pail 2—Barrel 3—Jerrican 4—Box 5—Bag 6—Composite packaging (i.e., steel/plastic)
B	Material	A—Steel B—Aluminum C—Wood G—Fiber H—Plastic
1	Package type	1—Closed Head 2—Open Head
Z	Signifies packaging group for which the package was tested	X—Groups I, II, and III Y—Groups II and III Z—Groups III (Refer to 49 CFR 172.101 for Packing Group information)
120	Maximum weight in kilograms that the container and package may weigh in shipment	
S	Rated for shipping solids	
15	Year of manufacture	
USA	Country of origin	
NC1	Name or symbol of manufacturer	

Source: The author.

package. The marking process entails specific letters and numbers to ensure safe stuffing, shipping, handling, and unstuffing.

A HazMat package for solid cargoes should have a marking similar to Table 5.3.

5.3.9 The International Maritime Dangerous Goods (IMDG) Code

HazMat professionals should consult the IMDG Code for goods that are traded internationally. The greatest part of Volume II of the IMDG Code incorporates the *Dangerous Goods List* (DGL). This list relates to the UN numbers that are specified for each distinctive type of DG. As discussed in Section 5.1, national regulations for the carriage of HazMat goods are harmonized with the UN's rules, as to the classification, UN numbers, and lists. This is demonstrated by comparing the UN Dangerous Goods List, as shown in Table 5.4, and the US DOT's HazMat table, as shown in Table 5.5.

5.3.10 The Dangerous Goods List, IMDG Code

The list of DG consists of the following 18 columns:

1. *Column 1: UN No.*—this column shows the UN number used on a specific HazMat or commodity, as allocated in the UN List of the Transport of Dangerous Goods, developed by the UN Experts Committee.

TABLE 5.4 Dangerous Goods List (International)

					Dangerous Goods List			Packagings and IBCs			Portable Tanks	
UN No.	Name and Description	Class or Division	Subsidiary Risk	UN Packing Group	Special Provisions	Limited Quantities	Packing Instruction	Special Provisions		Portable Tank Instruction	Portable Tank Special Provisions
(1)	(2)	(3)	(4)	(5)	(6)	(7)	(8)	(9)		(10)	(11)
0004	Ammonium picrate dry or wetted with less than 10% water, by mass	1.1D				None	P112(a) (b) or (c)	PP26			
0005	Cartridges for weapons with bursting charge	1.1F				None	P130				
0006	Cartridges for weapons with bursting charge	1.1E				None	P130 LP101	PP67 L1			
0007	Cartridges for weapons with bursting charge	1.2F				None	P130				
0009	Ammunition, incendiary with or without burster, expelling charge or propelling charge	1.2G				None	P130 LP101	PP67 L1			
0010	Ammunition, incendiary with or without burster, expelling charge or propelling charge	1.3G				None	P130 LP101	PP67 L1			

Source: UNECE, United Nations Economic Commission for Europe Dangerous Goods List and Limited Quantities Exceptions. Part 3. Available at http://www.unece.org/fileadmin/DAM/trans/danger/publi/unrec/English/part3.pdf, accessed May 26, 2014, 2003a; UNECE, United Nations Economic Commission for Europe Recommendations on the Transport of Dangerous Goods. Nature, Purpose and Significance of the Recommendations. Available at http://www.unece.org/fileadmin/DAM/trans/danger/publi/unrec/rev13/English/00E_Intro.pdf, accessed October 13, 2014, 2003b.

TABLE 5.5   HazMat Table in the United States

Symbols	HazMat Descriptions and Proper Shipping Names	Hazard Class or Division	Identification Numbers	PG	Label Codes	Special Provisions (§ 172.102)	Packaging (§ 173.***) Exceptions	Packaging (§ 173.***) Nonbulk	Packaging (§ 173.***) Bulk	Quantity Limitations (See §§ 173.27 and 175.75) Passenger Aircraft/Rail	Quantity Limitations (See §§ 173.27 and 175.75) Cargo Aircraft Only	Vessel Slow-Age Location	Vessel Slow-Age Other
(1)	(2)	(3)	(4)	(5)	(6)	(7)	(8A)	(8B)	(8C)	(9A)	(9B)	(10A)	(10B)
	Acellerene, see p-Nitrosodimethylanline.												
	Accumulators, electric, see batteries, wet etc.												
	Accumulators, pressurized pneumatic or hydraulic (containing non-flammable gas), see Articles pressurized, pneumatic or hydraulic (containing non-flammable gas).												
	Acetal	3	UN1088	II	3	IB2, T4, TP1	150	202	242	5 L	60 L	E	
	Acetaldehyde	3	UN1089	I	3	A3, B16, T11, TP2, TP7	None	201	243	Forbidden	30 L	E	
A	Acetaldehyde ammonia	9	UN1841	III	9	IB8, IP3, TP7, T1, TP33	155	204	240	200 kg	200 kg	A	34
	Acetaldehyde oxime	3	UN2332	III	3	B1, IB3, T4, TP1	150	203	242	60 L	220 L	A	
	Acetic acid, glacial *or* Acetic acid solution, *with more than 80% acid, by mass.*	8	UN2789	II	8.3	A3, A5, A7, A10, B2, IB2, T7, TP2	154	202	243	1 L	30 L	A	

(Continued)

TABLE 5.5 (CONTINUED) HazMat Table in the United States

Symbols	HazMat Descriptions and Proper Shipping Names	Hazard Class or Division	Identification Numbers	PG	Label Codes	Special Provisions (§ 172.102)	Packaging (§ 173.***)			Quantity Limitations (See §§ 173.27 and 175.75)		Vessel Slow-Age	
							Exceptions	Nonbulk	Bulk	Passenger Aircraft/Rail	Cargo Aircraft Only	Location	Other
(1)	(2)	(3)	(4)	(5)	(6)	(7)	(8A)	(8B)	(8C)	(9A)	(9B)	(10A)	(10B)
	Acetic acid solution, *not less than 50% but not more than 80% acid, by mass.*	8	UN2790	II	8	A3, A5, A7, A10, B2, IB2, T7, TP2	154	202	242	1 L	30 L	A	
	Acetic acid solution, *with more than 10% and less than 50% acid, by mass.*	8	UN2790	III	8	IB3, T4, TP1	154	203	242	5 L	60 L	A	
	Acetic anhydride	8	UN1715	II	8.3	A3, A5, A7, A10, B2, IB2, T7, TP2	154	202	243	1 L	30 L	A	40
	Acetone	3	UN1090	II	3	IB2, T4, TP1	150	202	242	5 L	60 L	B	
	Acetone cyanohydrin, stabilized	6.1	UN1541	I	6.1	2, B9, B14, B32, B76, B77, N34, T20, TP2, TP13, TP38, TP45	None	227	244	Forbidden	Forbidden	D	25, 40, 52, 53
	Acetone oils	3	UN1091	II	3	IB2, T4, TP1, TP8	150	202	242	5 L	60 L	B	
	Acetonitrile	3	UN1648	II	3	IB2, T7,TP2	150	202	242	5 L	60 L	B	40
	Acetyl acetone peroxide *with more than 9% by mass active oxygen.*	Forbidden											

Source: US DOT. 49CFR CH.1.2014. Code of Federal Regulations #49.US Government Publishing Office, 2014a.

2. *Column 2: Proper Shipping Name (PSN)*—this column offers the PSNs in upper case characters that may be followed by clarifications in lower case characters. The PSNs will be shown in plural in case of isomers. Unless otherwise stated, the word "SOLUTION" in a PSN within a HazMat (DG) List shows one or more specified DG contained in a liquefied substance that may not be typically controlled by this code. If a flashpoint is mentioned in this column, the data are in line with closed-cup methods.

3. *Column 3: Class*—this section refers to the HazMat division, e.g., for class 1, it further shows the HazMat class and the compatibility group pertaining to the substance or compound of the HazMat group.

4. *Column 4: Subsidiary risk*—this column relates to the classification number(s) of any subsidiary hazards pertaining to the cargoes' classification system (nine categories). This column also identifies HazMat (DG), e.g., marine pollutants or severe marine pollutants, as follows:

   P – Marine pollutant (only if it contains at least 10% of material(s) defined with "P" or at least 1% of materials defined with "PP" in this column or the index)
   PP – Severe marine pollutant

5. *Column 5: UN packing group*—entails the packing group classification in Latin numbers 1, 2, 3 (i.e., I, II, or III) designated to the HazMat, compound, or substance. If one or multiple packing groups are indicated for the entry, the packing group of the material or components to be transported should be determined, in line with its properties, by using the HazMat classification criteria.

6. *Column 6: Special provisions*—this section entails a number designated for any special provision(s) related to the HazMat. Special provisions relate to all packing groups permitted for a particular substance or article unless the guidelines and HazMat data are self-explanatory. If a special provision is no longer required, this special provision is removed, but the special provision number is not allocated for a new HazMat type to avoid confusion when handling HazMat. For this reason, once a HazMat number is allocated to an obsolete substance, it is not used again.

7. *Column 7: Limited quantities*—it presents the maximum quantity per interior packaging permitted for the HazMat to be transported as per the conditions for limited quantities. The word "None" in this column demonstrates that the HazMat is not permitted to be carried.

8. *Column 8: Packing instructions*—it features alphanumeric codes that are connected with the pertinent packing instruction(s). These describe the packages (i.e., large) that may be used for the carriage of materials and components. A code including the letter "P" is the term for packing directions for the usage of packages.

   A code comprising the letters "LP" describes packing instructions for the usage of large packages. If a code for the letter(s) "P" or "LP" is NOT given, it ensures that the substance is not allowed in that form of packaging.

9. *Column 9: Special packing provisions*—this column consists of alphanumeric codes that refer to corresponding special packing provisions presented. The distinctive packing provisions indicate the packages (which may include large HazMat packages).

   A particular packing provision such as the initials "PP" identifies a special packing provision similar to the use of a packing guidance showing the code "P."

   A distinctive packing provision that contains the letter "L" identifies a special packing provision appropriate for packing instruction showing the code "LP."

10. *Column 10: International Code for the Construction and Equipment of Ships carrying Dangerous Chemicals in Bulk (IBC Code) packing instructions*—it consists of alphanumeric codes that pertain to the pertinent IBC instruction, which signifies the kind of IBC that will be used for the carriage of the material under reference. A code containing the letters "IBC" is the term for packing instructions for the use of IBCs. If a code is not provided, it indicates that the substance is not permitted in IBC.

11. *Column 11: IBC special provisions*—it relates to an alphanumeric code, such as the letter "B," which usually describes the special packing provisions appropriate for the use of packing instructions displaying the code "IBC."

12. *Column 12: IMO tank instructions*—it is only appropriate for IMO portable tanks and road tank vehicles constructed as outlined by the requirements of Amendment 29 of the code in line with the adjusting provision. This column incorporates T codes and in some cases TP notes. When no T code is presented in this column, the T code presented in column 13 will apply.

13. *Column 13: UN tank and bulk package guidelines*—this column features "T codes" appropriate for the transport of DG in portable tanks and road tank vehicles. When a T code is not provided in this column, it signifies that the DG are not authorized for transportation in tanks unless specifically authorized by the competent authorities.
    * *Bulk container code*—the code "BK2" identifies closed bulk containers used for the transportation of commodities in bulk containers. When a bulk container code is not offered, it means that the material is not permitted in a bulk container. Transport in sheeted bulk containers (BK1), i.e., pen-top bulk containers with rigid bottoms, such as hopper-type bottoms, side and end partitions, and a nonrigid top, are not allowed in this code.

14. *Column 14: Tank special provisions*—consists of TP notes suitable for the transport of HazMat in portable tanks and road tank vehicles. The TP information presented in this column relate to the portable tanks laid out in both columns 12 and 13.

15. *Column 15: EmS*—this column denotes relevant emergency schedules for FIRE and SPILLAGE in the "The EmS Guide—Emergency Response Procedures for Ships Carrying Dangerous Goods." Furthermore, the initial EmS code denotes the pertinent fire schedule (e.g., Fire Schedule Alfa "F-A" General Fire Schedule).

    The subsequent (2nd) EmS code signifies the relevant "spillage schedule" (e.g., Spillage Schedule Alfa "S-A" Toxic Substances).

    Underlined EmS codes describe special situations, i.e., a product or chemical substance for which further advice is provided in the emergency response procedures.

    For HazMat provided for transportation under N.O.S. entries or other common items, the most relevant emergency response procedures may vary from the features of the hazardous components. Due to this fact, shippers may have to declare diverse EmS codes from those indicated if, to their awareness, these codes are more appropriate.

    The provisions in this column are not compulsory.

16. *Column 16: Stowage and segregation*—it offers the stowage and segregation terminology as suggested in part 7.

17. *Column 17: Properties and observations*—it consists of properties of and observations on the DG detailed. The provisions in this column are not compulsory. The properties of most gases provide an indication of its thickness with regards to air. The figures in brackets provide the density in comparison to air

- "Lighter than air" if the vapor density is down to half that of air
- "Much lighter than air" if the vapor density is less than 50% of air
- "Heavier than air" if the vapor density is up to double compared to air, and
- "Much heavier than air" when the vapor density is more than twice that of air
  When explosive limitations are presented, these relate to the volume percentage of the vapor of the substance when mixed with oxygen.

The ease of use and level to which various liquids mix with water varies widely, while most of the entries are indicators of miscibility, i.e., a substance's ability to mix in all proportions, forming a homogeneous solution. In these cases, "miscible with water" would mean "able to be mixed with water in all amounts to form an entirely homogeneous liquid."

18. *Column 18: UN No.*—see column 1.

5.3.11 HazMat Identification System

The *HazMat Identification System* (HMIS), as featured in Figure 5.2, is a numbered color bar, or a hazard score table, that features the use of labels with color-coded bars and pertinent training in order to identify the hazard risks of DG. It was developed by the American Coatings Association as a conformity aid for the OSHA Hazard Communication Standard. By the use of labels and placards, these reveal data pertinent to the hazardous shipment, by way of symbols and colors, which are useful to identify the cargo, and mitigate threat during the HazCom process.

5.3.12 Shipping Documentation

Shipping documentation is issued as an indicator of what is labeled as dangerous on placards. These should state the commodity's "shipping name" (which is the proper chemical name, and not the commercial name); HazMat classification; ID number and quantity, and where appropriate, specify if the material is toxic, waste, and so on. It is mandatory for shipping documentation to accompany all HazMat shipments, and are required to provide with a 24-h emergency information telephone number. The location where the shipping papers are stored can be problematical; often, they are found in close proximity to the HazMat or in other locations not easily accessible during an emergency. Shipping papers should remain at the incident scene for use by all response personnel.

FIGURE 5.2   The HMIS color bar.

5.3.13 Identifying HazMat Leakage

The existence of HazMat can be distinguished by odor, vapor clouds, dead animals or fish, fire, and skin or eye irritation. Typically, if one identifies a distinctive odor of HazMat, it should be assumed that some sort of leakage has occurred, and the person is still in the danger area, even though some chemicals have a noticeable odor at levels below their toxic concentrations. Some chemicals, however, can impair an individual's sense of smell (e.g., hydrogen sulfide), and others are odorless, colorless, or tasteless (e.g., carbon monoxide). During cargo inspections and regular transport operations, binoculars can be used for professionals to obtain observable information from a safe distance.

5.3.14 HazMat in the Maritime Industry

Since around 90% of global trade is being carried by sea, the IMO and the maritime industry have also established specific rules, regulations, and guidelines for HazMat (Table 5.6). Since the IMO is an instrument of the UN, ensuring compliance with the transportation and handling of hazardous cargoes not only facilitates companies to operate in safety and environmental protection but also eliminate fines.

TABLE 5.6   HazMat Regulatory Requirements and Standards

The regulatory framework stipulating the HazMat requirements, transportation, and handling includes the following standards whose compliance is mandatory by the industry:

GLOBAL
- International Maritime Organization of the United Nations
- International Maritime Dangerous Goods Code
- 1960 International Convention for the Safety of Life at Sea
- IMO Maritime Safety Committee and the Marine Environment Protection Committee, the Sub-Committee on Bulk Liquids and Gases
- Facilitating the transport of radioactive material

UNITED STATES
The US Coast Guard
A. The STCW Convention, Regulation II/2, Sections A-II/2, B-V/b, B-V/c and Chapter 5, STCW-95 Endorsement, the Manila Amendments effective as of January 1, 2012.
B. The US DOT Hazardous Materials Regulations
C. 29 CFR Part 1910, Occupational Safety and Health Standards, Subpart H, HAZMAT. 29 CFR 1940.120: Occupational Safety and Health Standards, Toxic and Hazardous Substances (http://www.gpo.gov).
D. 33 CFR Part 155, Oil or Hazardous Material Pollution
E. 40 CFR Parts 260–279 Hazardous Wastes
  40 CFR 311 Environmental Protection Agency
      Subchapter J—Superfund, Emergency Planning, and Community Right-To-Know Programs
      Part 311—Worker Protection (http://www.gpo.gov).
F. 49 CFR Parts 100–185 The Hazardous Materials Regulations (HMR), which entails four key provisions: (i) HazMat handling, processes, and policies; (ii) HazMat descriptions and labeling; (iii) HazMat packaging prerequisites and; (iv) Operational guidelines.
G. NFPA: Standard 473 National Fire Protection Association. Standard for Competencies of EMS Personnel Responding to Hazardous Materials Incidents.

Source: The author.

International Code for the Construction and Equipment of Ships carrying Dangerous Chemicals in Bulk (IMO 2015). Bulk transportation of chemical substances is dealt with by the IMO Regulations of

i. SOLAS Chapter VII—Carriage of DG and
ii. Marine Pollution (MARPOL) Annex II—Regulations for the Control of Pollution by Noxious Liquid Substances in Bulk.

SOLAS and MARPOL both mandate hazardous chemicals to be transported onboard chemical tankers constructed after July 1, 1986 to conform with the International Code for the Construction and Equipment of Ships carrying Dangerous Chemicals in Bulk (IMO 2015).

The IBC Code offers a global standard for the safe maritime transportation of dangerous and noxious liquid chemicals in bulk, which stipulates the ship design, construction, operations, and machinery needed to ensure safety and environmental protection.

Ships in line with the IBC Code must be built in accordance with one of the following specifications:

- A type 1 vessel is a chemical tanker meant to carry Chapter 17 of the IBC Code products with high-risk environmental and safety hazards that demand the highest possible safety measures to prevent a leakage of such cargo.
- A type 2 vessel is a chemical tanker meant to carry Chapter 17 of the IBC Code products with moderate-risk environmental and safety hazards that demand significant preventive measures to prevent a leakage of such cargo.
- A type 3 vessel is a chemical tanker meant to carry Chapter 17 of the IBC Code products with low-risk environmental and safety hazards that demand a moderate degree of containment to increase survival capability in a damaged condition.

Thus, a type 1 vessel is a chemical tanker meant for the carriage of products considered to present the highest overall threat and type 2 and type 3 for products of gradually lesser dangers. Consequently, a type 1 vessel will endure the highest standard of risk, and its cargo tanks will be found at the maximum recommended space inboard from the shell plating (IMO 2014).

5.4 HAZMAT SECURITY AND HEALTH IMPACT

5.4.1 HazMat Chemicals and Health Hazards

The intentional release and use of hazardous chemical substances are typically categorized based on the health impact in accordance with the major body organ that is impacted by exposure.

These harmful substances that have been utilized or have been intended for use as chemical weapons in military combat, civil wars, political unrest or terrorist attacks (see also Chapter 2) may be classified as

i. Respiratory (pulmonary or choking agents),
ii. Blistering agents (vesicants),
iii. Blood/circulatory agents, and
iv. Nerve agents.

i. *Respiratory, pulmonary, or choking agents* typically either penetrate the body through inhalation and harm the respiratory system or are ingested locally and trigger negative health impacts. They cover a wide range of toxic gases, such as chlorine, phosgene, organohalides, ammonia, nitrogen oxides, and so on. These are regarded as inorganic chemicals that infiltrate and invade lung cells, mainly leading to pulmonary edema (lung swelling). They enter the respiratory system in liquid, gaseous, vapor, or aerosolized forms. Within their gaseous form, they function predominantly by causing inflammation and discomfort in the respiratory system, including the nasal passage, throat, lungs, and airways, as well as the mucous membranes. In the case of splash or vapor exposure, they can enter the eyes, mouth, or nostrils. All of these are available for public use and may very well be acquired and made use of by terrorist groups.

These chemicals have low boiling points, which means they can promptly become gaseous components once they are exposed to natural room temperatures. They are classified as nonpersistent agents, indicating that they will rapidly evaporate. Related signs or symptoms may involve breathing problems, a suffocating feeling, coughing, chest and heart pain, as well as pulmonary fluid that can lead to asphyxiation.

These chemical substances have played a notable role in historic military combats, in particular during the US Civil War (1861–1865), World War I (1914–1918), the war in Bosnia and Herzegovina (1992–1995), and the Iraq War (2003–2011). During the First World War, over 70,000 instances of gas poisoning occurred among US soldiers. As opposed to alternative chemical weapons, choking agents are extremely useful to the society and the industries. For instance, suppliers use chlorine and ammonia to refrigerate foodstuff; purify drinking water; and manufacture detergents, cleaning solutions, and other household items (Pike 2011; Shea 2012; UPMC Center for Health Security 2013).

ii. *Blistering agents* (vesicants) are assimilated through skin absorption or by causing damage to the skin tissue (e.g., mustard gas, lewisite). They induce systemic damage, such as in the nerve agents and various body parts. Vesicants are chemical substances that may induce serious chemical burns, severe skin and eye soreness, and irritation. These are extremely hazardous substances as they may cause painful blisters and large-scale burns. Due to their severe health impacts, they are used in warfare as chemical agents.

iii. *Blood, circulatory agents, gases, or systemic agents* (e.g., hydrogen cyanide) enter the blood and attack the circulatory system both directly or indirectly as they are moved through the entire body. Their effects are felt immediately. Some of the main symptoms include headaches, apnea, convulsions, heavy breathing, loss of consciousness, or even death. Due to their severe health impacts, they are used in warfare as chemical agents.

iv. *Nerve agents* (e.g., VX, VR) tabun (GA), sarin (GB), soman (GD) belong to a highly toxic class of chemicals, the "organophosphates," which poison the nervous system and disrupt bodily functions that are vital to an individual's survival. They were originally produced in a search for insecticides, but because of their toxicity, they were evaluated for military use. There are large stockpiles of nerve agents that, if obtained by terrorists, could be released using bombs, explosives, spray tanks, or rockets.

Nerve agents have a physiological effect similar to that of many insecticides commonly found in the community, such as malathion, diazinon, and chlorpyrifos. The nerve agents enter the body typically via the skin tissue (dermis, pores) or respiratory system and attack the nervous system. If organophosphate poisoning is not treated with appropriate antidote, the effect on cholinesterase is permanent (OSHA 2014a,b,c).

Nerve agents, depending on their purity, are clear and colorless or slightly colored liquids and may have no odor or a faint, sweetish smell. They evaporate at various rates and are denser than air, so they accumulate in low areas. Nerve agents include GA, GB, GD, and VX.

The health impact may vary according to the intensity and time period that the subject(s) are exposed to the chemicals. Health impacts may involve short-term sickness or personal injury, long-term, irreversible health problems, or even death.

5.4.2 Radiation and Health Hazards

The health effects of radiation depend on many factors, including the type of radiation, exposure pathway, concentration and amount of exposure, and duration of exposure. Large exposures delivered over a short period of time can cause acute radiation sickness, and, in some cases, death. Lower exposures to radiation over time (e.g., over a working lifetime) increase the probability of developing chronic health problems, birth defects, and cancer especially if the cumulative dose is significant.

Different forms of electromagnetic radiation may vary in frequency and wave length, and include infrared light, visible light, ultraviolet light, heat waves, radio waves, x-rays, and gamma rays. The general rule here is that "longer wave length, lower frequency waves (i.e., heat and radio) release less energy than shorter wave length, higher frequency waves (i.e., X-rays and gamma rays)" (WHO 2014). The penetrating powers of alpha and beta particles and gamma rays are shown in Figure 5.3.

Ionizing radiation is generated by energy of radioactive decay. During an atomic interaction, the atom is charged with ample energy in a manner that releases tightly formed electrons from the atomic orbit, thus charging or ionizing the atom. This energy is released as radiation in three primary forms: alpha particles, beta particles, and gamma rays, as demonstrated in Figure 5.4.

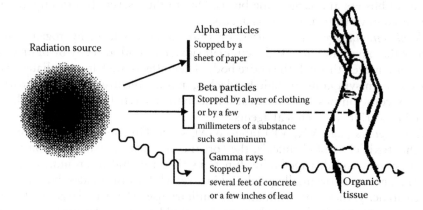

FIGURE 5.3 The penetrating powers of alpha and beta particles and gamma rays. (Courtesy of North Dakota Department of Health, 2014, What is ionizing radiation? Available at http://www.ndhealth.gov/AQ/RAD/ionize.htm, accessed August 23, 2014.)

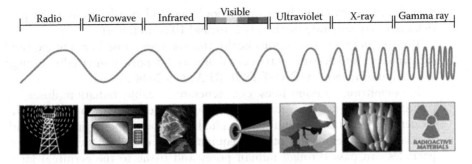

FIGURE 5.4   Types of radiation. (From US EPA, Global Climate Change, available at http://www.epa.gov/climatestudents/images/1-2-1-radiationpop.gif, accessed December 1, 2014.)

Alpha, beta, and gamma radiation particles are typical radioactive elements that are widely used in the industry, medicine, and military operations. On the other hand, terrorists may also use these particles to impose severe health, environmental, commercial, and financial damage.

- The *health perils* associated with radioactive isotopes (e.g., emitting alpha, beta, or gamma radiation) are determined by the quantity of radiation and the time of exposure. In other words, the larger the radiation dose, the greater the health and environmental impact.
- *Acute versus chronic radiation exposure*: An acute exposure to radiation entails a large amount of radiation obtained in a short period of time, whereas a chronic exposure to radiation pertains to a small amount of radiation obtained over a long period of time.
- *Safeguarding from radiation*: The three key principles to safeguard from radiation are specified as (i) time, (ii) distance, and (iii) protective gear and equipment.
  a. Alpha radiation
      Alpha particles move in straight lines via matter and transfer their energy in short travel, i.e., 2–7 in. Therefore, their damage is intense yet confined in a limited area. Their principal method of interaction is ionization, the process where neutral atoms or molecules are converted to electrically charged atoms or molecules.
      Alpha radionuclides that are alpha-emitting radioactive elements include plutonium, uranium, and americium. Once alpha radiation penetrates the body through inhalation, skin absorption, or ingestion, biological damage occurs, thereby increasing the likelihood of lung cancer and other types of cancer (EPA Radiation 2014).
      Radiation can be prevented with slim layers of protective material. Nevertheless, they can be very harmful if swallowed or enter exposed wounds, as they can transfer high volumes of energy in a limited surface and totally destroy living tissue (UK Royal Society of Chemistry 2014).
  b. Beta radiation
      Beta emitters are high-energy, high-speed negatrons, i.e., singly negatively charged electrons, or positrons, i.e., singly positively charged electrons. Beta

particles are negatively charged, less ionizing, and smaller than alpha particles but can penetrate further, i.e., around 10 ft. in the air.

Beta particles impose serious health threats: they cause burns to exposed skin and eyes and destroy vital internal organs if deposited internally through inhalation or ingestion (ORISE DOE REAC/TS 2014).

Beta-emitting radionuclides can generate sizeable radiation doses, in particular when used in radiological weapons. Beta radiation particles are moderately penetrating, and if individuals are not properly protected with HazMat suits, personal protective equipment, or even heavy clothing, beta particles can pass through human pores and tissue to the germinal layer, the area where new skin cells are generated. Due to their light weight, they do not move in predictable range patterns, such as straight lines, but pursue a randomly selected path through substance. Beta radionuclides that are beta-emitting radioactive elements include tritium, cobalt-60, strontium-90, iodine-129 and -131, cesium-137, and so on.

Beta emitters can be employed in a plethora of industrial activities, including manufacturing, construction, and industrial thickness assessments, by employing their penetrating capability into thickness measurement. Furthermore, beta particles are successfully used in healthcare, i.e., clinical diagnosis, radiation, and therapy. As an example, iodine-131 is employed to cure hyperthyroidism and cancer; phosphorus-32 is commonly employed in the fields of genetics and molecular biology; strontium-90 is used to find radiation as part of medical, biological, and agricultural research (EPA Radiation 2014). Tritium is used to create fluorescent signs, i.e., emergency signs and lamps used in industries, transportation modes, public signs, watches, gauges, and dials. It is also used to verify drug safety during the research and approval of new medicine.

c. Gamma radiation

Gamma radiation entails electromagnetic energy of short wave but of significant penetrating power and high frequency. It travels at a distance of about 1 mi at the speed of light. Gamma radiation moves by air up to a mile and has the capacity to permeate most materials, including tissue, deeper and at a greater distance compared to beta or alpha particles. Only robust, compacted materials like steel or concrete can absorb some of the gamma radiation. When gamma rays pass through the human body, they impose both an external and internal health risk. Exposure to gamma rays or contact with a contaminated area or materials may cause tissue damage, radiation toxicity, cancer, or death.

5.4.3 CBRN: Chemical, Biological, Radiological, or Nuclear Release

Chemical, biological, radiological, and nuclear (CBRN) materials are referred to as an umbrella definition for chemical, biological, and radiological substances in any physical condition and type, which could result in potential risks to communities, regions, and armed forces. It may also pertain to chemical weapon precursors and establishments, machines, or chemical substances that can be employed for improvement or implementation of weapons of mass destruction or weapons and devices that are classified as CBRN (CIA, NATO CBRN 2014).

A CBRN HazMat incident may pertain to DG discharge or leakage, be it chemical, biological, radiological, or nuclear. The effects and consequences of such accidents may be severe regardless of the unintended or deliberate act leading to the incident. CBRN occurrences may be unintentional or intentional.

5.4.4 Chemical Hazards

Chemical threats entail intentionally released substances and are often classified according to their effect on the body based on the primary organ system affected by exposure. Nerve agents (e.g., GB, VX, and VR) enter the body through the skin or lungs and affect the nervous system. Blood gases or systemic agents (e.g., hydrogen cyanide) enter the bloodstream either directly or indirectly and are transported throughout the body. Respiratory agents (e.g., chlorine, phosgene) are inhaled and can cause damage to the lungs. Blister agents (e.g., mustard gas, lewisite) damage the skin, and if they get absorbed, they can also affect other parts of the body. Depending on the severity of exposure, impacts may include temporary illness or injury, permanent medical conditions, or death.

5.4.5 Biological Hazards

Biological hazards include disease-causing microorganisms and pathogens, such as bacteria and viruses. The distinguishing characteristic of these substances is their ability to multiply within a host and cause an infection. Some bacteria and viruses can be spread, or transmitted, from one individual to another. Infections typically occur as a result of airborne exposure, skin contact, or ingestion. In general, exposure to bacteria and viruses can occur through inhalation (as is the case with airborne *Bacillus anthracis* spores, which cause anthrax), ingestion of contaminated food or water (the case with *Escherichia coli*, which causes gastrointestinal infection), contact with infected individuals, or contact with contaminated surfaces (which may be harboring, for example, viruses that cause influenza). Ricin, a toxin found in castor beans, is also classified as a biological agent with the potential for use in an intentional attack. The HazMat emergency responders attend CBRN occurrences indistinguishably, in order to protect human life, safety of flora, fauna, the environment and property, regardless of the intentional or unintentional character. Nevertheless, the investigation and legal protocol may vary at a global, national, or state level, whereas the entities involved and measures to be taken also depend on the motive or intention entailed.

When used for detonation, CBRNs are used to create conventional bombs (e.g., pipe bombs), enhanced explosives (e.g., fuel oil–fertilizer mixture), and fortified blast agents (e.g., dirty bombs) (Hrdina et al. 2009; Aruna et al. 2010).

5.4.6 Radiological Dispersal Devices (RDDs)

Radiological dispersal devices (RDDs), also known as "dirty bombs," consist of radioactive material combined with conventional explosives developed to employ explosive pressure to spread out the radioactive material within a sizeable area. The materials used for dirty bombs are both inexpensive and commercially available, making it easy for terrorist groups to acquire. The terrorists' predominant goal is to generate social turmoil and psychological damage by causing anxiety and fear in selected social segments. Another impact is to cause loss of resources and financial and commercial damage throughout the emergency response, cleanup, and resiliency timeline. Harmful effects deriving from the explosion may include death, bodily injuries, spread of radioactive dust, and other harmful particles.

The unintended consequences and effects of an RDD, commonly referred to as "dirty bomb," has the potential to generate health damage due to explosion, high temperatures, debris, and radiological particles. An RDD is made up of radioactive substances placed on a traditional explosive device. The short- and long-term radiation emissions, together with the health, environmental, and safety impact, depend upon the level of radioactive substances and the discharged volume. The overall damage and consequences can typically be established after the blast has occurred. Radiation is typically associated with the body's exposure to gamma rays and beta particles.

To assess the health impact pursuant to contact with radioactive substances, it is necessary to measure a number of elements: the quantity of the radiation dose, i.e., level of exposure, and the duration of exposure.

5.4.7 Toxic Industrial Chemicals (TICs)

Toxic industrial chemicals are chemical substances classified as HazMat. They are considered dangerous due to their flammable, explosive, poisonous, radioactive, or reactive nature. Exposure routes may entail skin contact, inhalation, ingestion, or injection. These categories of chemicals include petroleum and gaseous products, fertilizers, cleaning, painting and lubricating substances, pesticides, and so on. Due to their extensive application in a plethora of utilities, such as in manufacturing and infrastructure processes, global trade, transport, etc., an accidental discharge or leakage is always a possibility:

- *Medical use and inhibiting agents.* While certain toxic chemicals and their fore-runners are widely employed in the global industry as a primary raw material, in medicine, they are utilized as inhibiting agents that stop metastatic cancer or the reproduction of malignant cells.
- *Gaseous chemicals and fumigants.* These are used in pest control as disinfectants, pesticides, insecticides, or herbicides. Typically associated with unintended large-scale contamination and poisoning, fumigants and disinfectants are naturally harmful chemicals for human life, animals, plants, and the environment. Extremely volatile, they are employed in large volumes to sanitize garden soil prior to planting seeds and plants. Regardless of whether the incidents manifest or not, the use of these harmful toxins has considerable side effects.
- *Chemical weapons.* These hazardous chemicals are classified as chemical weapons in cases where they are developed and stored in quantities that surpass legal requirements' stipulations regarding the permissible limits and uses. In this respect, the term chemical weapon is employed to describe any kind of harmful chemical substance or its by-products that could potentially lead to loss of life, personal injury, mutilation, immobilization, or any type of physical discomfort due to its chemical nature.
- *Military weapons* and any transportation, storage, and distribution units intended to manufacture, store, and supply chemical weapons, regardless of whether loaded or unloaded, are also regarded as weapons on their own.

HazMat incidents may also be classified in terms of *proactive and reactive action*:

1. *Predisaster HazMat plans* pertain to the preventive action focused on identifying and averting potential threats or attacks.
2. *Postdisaster HazMat contingency plans* relate to the reactive action whose goal is to attend and mitigate hazard incidents.

HazMat countermeasures pertain to procedures followed in response to a HazMat incident with the purpose of mitigating the safety, environmental, or socioeconomic consequences and entail

a. *Technological mitigation,* which entails technologies used for HazCom software, i.e., to ensure communication during a HazMat incident, HazMat treatment, and mass casualty decontamination
b. *Health mitigation,* which includes preventing measures (prophylaxis) and actual medical treatment of HazMat-related injuries
c. *Legal and regulatory framework,* which focuses both on preventive and mitigation measures, such as
   - The Hazardous Materials Transportation Act (1975)
   - The Hazardous Materials Transportation Uniform Safety Act (1990)
   - The Hazardous Materials Transportation Authorization Act (1994)
   - EPA's Emergency Management Program, including
      i. The Clean Air Act
      ii. The Clean Water Act
      iii. The Oil Pollution Act
      iv. The Comprehensive Environmental Response, Compensation, and Liability Act
      v. The Superfund Amendments and Reauthorization Act
      vi. The Emergency Planning and Community Right-to-Know Act
      vii. The Chemical Safety Information, Site Security and Fuels Regulatory Relief Act (EPA 2014) http://www.epa.gov/osweroe1/lawsregs.htm
d. *Corporate strategies,* including intelligence systems, contingency plans, training, familiarization, and standard operating procedures (OSHA RDD 2014)

REFERENCES

ATSDR CDC. 2014 US Agency for Toxic Substances Disease Registry created the Hazardous Substances Emergency Events Surveillance program in 1990. Available at http://www.atsdr.cdc.gov/, 1990–2014. Accessed January 2, 2015.

Burns, M. 2012. *HazMat Regulations Training Manual (40 Hours).* US Coast Guard, National Maritime Center-Approved Manual. Texas Southern University, Houston, TX.

Burns, M. 2014. *HazMat Training Manual (40 Hours).* US Coast Guard, National Maritime Center-Approved Manual. University of Houston, Houston, TX.

CIA, NATO CBRN. 2014. Combined Joint Chemical, Biological, Radiological and Nuclear Defence Task Force. The Alliance's multinational CBRN defense capability. Updated Aug. 28, 2014.

EPA. 2014. Global Climate Change. Available at http://www.epa.gov/climatestudents /images/1-2-1-radiationpop.gif. Accessed December 1, 2014.

EPA Radiation. 2014. Alpha Particles. Available at http://www.epa.gov/radiation/understand /alpha.html. Accessed September 15, 2014.

FMCSA.DOT. 2013. Available at http://www.fmcsa.dot.gov/sites/fmcsa.dot.gov/files/docs /Nine_Classes_of_Hazardous_Materials-4-2013.pdf. Accessed August 14, 2014.

FMCSA.DOT. 2014. Federal Motor Carriers Safety Administration, U.S. Department of Transportation, Hazardous Materials. Available at http://www.fmcsa.dot.gov /regulations/hazardous-materials. Accessed August 14, 2014.

Hrdina, C.M., Coleman, C.N., Bogucki, S., Bader, J.L., Hayhurst, R.E., Forsha, J.D. et al. 2009. The "RTR" medical response system for nuclear and radiological mass-casualty incidents: A functional TRiage-TReatment-TRansport medical response model. *Journal of Pre-Hospital and Disaster Medicine*. 24:167–178.

IHMM. 2014. What Are Hazardous Materials. Institute of Hazardous Materials Management. Available at http://www.ihmm.org/about-ihmm/what-are-hazardous -materials. Accessed September 24, 2014.

IMO. 2014. The IBC Code, Environmental Pollution Prevention, Chemical Pollution. International Maritime Organization. Available at http://www.imo.org/OurWork /Environment/PollutionPrevention/ChemicalPollution/Pages/IBCCode.aspx. Accessed August 26, 2014.

IMO. 2015. IBC Code. Available at http://www.imo.org/en/OurWork/Environment /PollutionPrevention/ChemicalPollution/Pages/IBCCode.aspx. Accessed January 12, 2015.

North Atlantic Treaty Organization. 2014. Available at https://www.cia.gov/library /reports/general-reports-1/terrorist_cbrn/terrorist_CBRN.htm. Accessed August 14, 2014.

North Dakota Department of Health. 2014. What Is Ionizing Radiation? Available at http://www.ndhealth.gov/AQ/RAD/ionize.htm. Accessed August 23, 2014.

ORISE DOE REAC/TS. 2014. Guidance for Radiation Accident Management. Radiation Emergency Assistance Center, Training Site. Beta Radiation. Oak Ridge Institute for Science and Education. Department of Energy. Available at https://orise.orau.gov /reacts/guide/beta.htm. Accessed April 10, 2014.

OSHA. 2014a. HazMat Communication (HazCom). Available at https://www.osha.gov /dsg/hazcom/ghd053107.html. Accessed August 23, 2014.

OSHA. 2014b. Emergency Preparedness Guide. Available at https://www.osha.gov. Accessed August 23, 2014.

OSHA. 2014c. Nerve Agents Guide. Available at https://www.osha.gov/SLTC/emergency preparedness/guides/nerve.html. Accessed August 14, 2014.

OSHA HazCom. 2012a. OSHA Hazard Communication Standards. Available at https:// www.osha.gov/dsg/hazcom/. Accessed June 19, 2014.

OSHA HazCom. 2012b. HazMat Communication (HazCom). Available at https://www .osha.gov/dsg/hazcom/ghd053107.html. Accessed August 23, 2014.

OSHA HazMat. 2014a. Available at https://www.osha.gov/dsg/hazcom/ghd053107.html. Accessed September 12, 2014. What Are the Classifications of HAZMAT? How Will I Know if My Chemical Is "Hazardous"?

OSHA HazMat. 2014b. Chemical Pollution Prevention. Available at https://www.osha .gov/pls/oshaweb/owadisp.show_document?p_table=standards&p_id=9765), http://www.imo.org/OurWork/Environment/PollutionPrevention/Chemical Pollution/Pages/IBCCode.aspxIMOIBCCode.2014. Accessed May 17, 2014.

OSHA RDD. 2014. Radiological Dispersal Devices (RDD)/Dirty Bombs. Available at https://www.osha.gov/SLTC/emergencypreparedness/rdd_tech.html. Accessed June 4, 2014.

Pike, J. 2011. Choking Agents. GlobalSecurity.org Web site. 2011. Available at http://www.globalsecurity.org/wmd/intro/cw-choking.htm. Accessed April 10, 2014.

Shea, D.A. 2012. *Chemical Weapons: A Summary Report of Characteristics and Effects*. Washington, DC: Congressional Research Service 2012. Available at http://www.fas.org/sgp/crs/nuke/R42862.pdf. Accessed April 10, 2014.

UK Royal Society of Chemistry. 2014. Alpha, Beta and Gamma Radioactivity. Radio-chemical Methods Group, Essay #3. Available at http://www.rsc.org/images/essay3_tcm18-17765.pdf. Accessed May 8, 2014.

UNECE. 2001–2013. UN Model Regulations; UN Recommendations on the Transport of Dangerous Goods—Model Regulations. Twelfth revised edition; © 2001 United Nations Publications; United Nations Economic Commission for Europe. Available at http://www.unece.org/trans/danger/publi/unrec/12_e.html. Accessed April 10, 2014.

UNECE. 2003a. United Nations Economic Commission for Europe Dangerous Goods List and Limited Quantities Exceptions. Part 3. Available at http://www.unece.org/fileadmin/DAM/trans/danger/publi/unrec/English/part3.pdf. Accessed May 26, 2014.

UNECE. 2003b. United Nations Economic Commission for Europe Recommendations on the Transport of Dangerous Goods. Nature, Purpose and Significance of the Recommendations. Available at http://www.unece.org/fileadmin/DAM/trans/danger/publi/unrec/rev13/English/00E_Intro.pdf. Accessed October 13, 2014.

UNECE. 2014. Dangerous Goods; United Nations Economic Commission for Europe. Available at http://www.unece.org/trans/danger/danger.html. Accessed October 13, 2014.

UPMC Center for Health Security. 2013. Pulmonary or Choking Agents. December 01, 2013. Available at http://www.upmchealthsecurity.org/our-work/publications/choking-agents-fact-sheet. Accessed October 13, 2014.

US DOT. 2014a. 49CFR CH.1.2014. Code of Federal Regulations #49. US Government Publishing Office.

US DOT. 2014b. Hazardous Materials Regulations. Available at http://www.dot.gov. Accessed August 18, 2014.

US DOT. 2014c. U.S. Department of Transportation, HazMat. Available at http://www.usdot.gov. Accessed July 30, 2014.

WHO. 2014. Ionizing Radiation. World Health Organization. Available at http://www.who.org. Accessed August 18, 2014.

WMD/EMD HazMat. 2014. Washington Military Department, Emergency Management Division. 2014. Hazardous Materials. Available at http://www.emd.wa.gov/hazards/haz_hazardous_materials.shtml. Accessed May 26, 2014.

WMD/EMD.Chemicals. 2014. What to do during chemical emergencies. Washington Military Department, Emergency Management Division. 2014. Available at http://www.emd.wa.gov/publications/pubed/know_what_to_do_during_chemical_emergencies.pdf. Accessed May 26, 2014.

CHAPTER 6

Supply Chain Security
Mind the Gap!

> All courses of action are risky, so prudence is not in avoiding
> danger (it's impossible), but calculating risk and acting decisively.
> Make mistakes of ambition and not mistakes of sloth.
> Develop the strength to do bold things, not the strength to suffer.
>
> **Niccolo Machiavelli (1469–1527)**
> *The Prince*

6.1 INTRODUCTION

While the previous chapters of this book focused on different security threats, and the various global and national agencies, initiatives, and programs dedicated in combating security, it became apparent that there are certain systemic gaps that need to be addressed.

This chapter addresses these gaps, namely, Section 6.2 aims to identify the systemic gaps of different technologies, methodologies, and protocols implemented with the goal of improving logistics management to optimum levels of security and resilience.

Section 6.3 uses a number of case studies of leading companies of different supply chain segments. The purpose of these case studies is to demonstrate the challenges and opportunities of the industry to ensure business continuity and overcome any security challenges.

Section 6.4 sets the security standards by proposing the implementation of protocols like 5S, Kaizen, Lean and Agile, Kanban, Six Sigma, Total Quality Management (TQM), Deming's 14 points on Quality Management, define–measure–analyze–improve–control (DMAIC), and 4D as federal and commercial tools for developing a more robust, efficient system to raise security to higher standards. The proposed tools ensure measurable improvement of the existing system, which leads to resilience through controlled input and output, elimination of waste, elimination of error, and so on.

6.2 MIND THE GAP: THE IMPACT OF SECURITY ON TRADE FLOW, TRADE ROUTES, AND THE ECONOMY

6.2.1 Supply Chain Disruptions and Potential Security Gaps

Modern supply chains tend to adopt lean inventory models with the purpose of enhancing responsiveness, minimizing costs, eliminating waste, and duplication of efforts. However, their hazard exposure tends to increase for two different reasons:

a. As companies go global, they outsource and shift their center of production further away from their corporate headquarters; limitations are encountered in the spheres of visibility, real-time information, and intervention.

b. As an antipode, companies try to increase visibility, simplify processes, and minimize cost by consolidating their supply chain networks. Nevertheless, this strategy is detrimental in cases of man-made security attacks, natural catastrophes, socioeconomic factors, bottlenecks and production disruptions, and so on.

Considering that every single company, industry, and supply chain is distinct, the risk mitigation techniques ought to be customized accordingly to be in line with the whole supply chain. Nevertheless, there are 12 major categories that classify most operational supply chain risks; these include

a. *Forecasting risks*: These are typically associated with all of the following risk divisions and may entail accurately predicting market cycles; financing, return on investment; sales forecasting associated with supply and demand, pricing strategy, competition, new market entrants, substitute markets, products that will be obsolete, innovations, strikes, cost and availability of factors of production; and so on.

b. *Time delays*: These are considered as waste and may affect any loss or misuse of time throughout the supply chain, from input to output.

c. *Supply chain disruptions*: These may be related to internal or external causes, and accidental or deliberate disturbances, affecting the strategic, operational, technical, or tactical processes and goals.

d. *Production capability*: This risk entails the quantity of services or merchandise developed, manufactured, or distributed by using corporate factors of production, i.e., entrepreneurship, labor, land, and capital; risk may entail any and all of the factors of production or the process of production.

e. *Inventory or stock*: This risk may entail the raw materials and/or merchandise stored in corporate warehouses with the intention of being distributed, sold, repaired, upgraded, and/or resold.

f. *Sale and purchase, procurement*: This risk could pertain to the process of buying or selling services or commodities while aiming to attain the corporate vision and mission.

This risk could also be related to the main goals of buying and selling, which include (1) retaining the value proposition (value for money) for corporate services and/or products, (2) retaining optimum investment and lean inventory, (3) ensuring input efficiency as a means of optimizing output efficiency, and (4) retaining and enhancing the company's market share.

g. *Technologies*: This risk entails systemic vulnerabilities from input to output; overinvestment or underinvestment (rate of return); financing, mortgage repayment; expected versus actual life cycle; innovative vs. obsolete technologies; overutilized vs. underutilized technologies; operational failure, maintenance, repairs, retrofitting, etc.

h. *Supply chain visibility and integration*: Visibility and integration are critical components of a sturdy and resilient supply chain. They ensure the capability to form integrated alliances that monitor and control the flow of information, services and commodities. Visibility and integration entails real-time data exchange throughout each stage from raw materials to production, distribution, warehousing, and final consumer. To minimize risks and ensure optimum performance, modern supply chains use a set of tools including integrated strategies and holistic real-time communication. Facilitating technologies for real-time tracking and information exchange include satellite- and cloud-based systems, radio-frequency identifications (RFIDs) and software tracking through Global Positioning System, Automatic Identification Systems, etc.

i. *Copyright infringement*, where the associated risks include the unauthorized use, copy, and reproduction of patents and intellectual property.

j. *Purchasing and procurement*: These are risks related to the investment and budget allocation; the decision to buy inappropriate, low-quality, or faulty service or commodity; the timing of purchase (too early or late); volume bought; unfavorable contractual stipulations; additional costs; misuse of resources; and so on.

k. *Account receivables (turnover ratio)*: This risk entails an accounting evaluation employed to quantify a company's efficacy in terms of obtaining financial credit from vendors and suppliers, and also collecting money owned. The receivables turnover ratio reveals how effectively a company employs its resources.

l. *Account payables (turnover ratio)*: This is a risk associated with calculating the short-term liquidity, i.e., assessing the rate by which a business repays its vendors and suppliers.

6.2.2 The Swiss Cheese Model for Security

The Swiss cheese model of incident causation demonstrates that, despite the numerous tiers of defense being strategically located among risks and incidents, each layer contains gaps or vulnerabilities, and when aligned, incidents may occur. Figure 6.1 demonstrates how the Swiss cheese model can be applied on supply chain and logistics security threats in a global setting where multiple layers of defense are aligned and vulnerabilities are exposed.

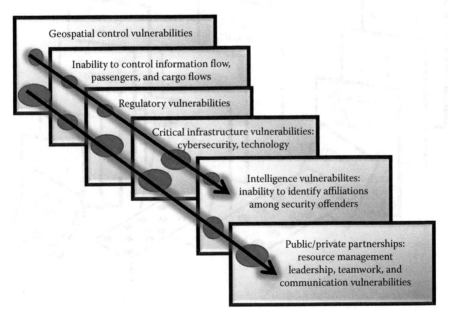

FIGURE 6.1 The Swiss cheese model applied on supply chain and logistics security. (From the author.)

6.2.3 The Security Threat Domino Effect

According to the "domino theory," certain challenges or threats within one nation, region, or industrial segment tend to disperse and negatively influence nearby areas. The original "falling domino principle" was first suggested by the 34th US president, Dwight "Ike" Eisenhower in 1954:

> You have a row of dominoes set up, you knock over the first one, and what will happen to the last one is the certainty that it will go over very quickly. So you could have a beginning of a disintegration that would have the most profound influences.

The "domino principle" was used by President Eisenhower to express his concerns over the spread of communism in Indochina and how this could affect democracy, freedom, and rights throughout neighboring Asian countries. However, this theory could well represent challenges in global security and reflect the manner in which a single security vulnerability could be the Trojan horse where an entire system may suffer.

This growing intricacy in a globalized environment tends to increase risk, as visibility is limited, and the control span is significantly diminished. In instances where disruptions are inadequately controlled, the domino effect phenomenon occurs, as a single threat manifesting at a single component of a supply chain can significantly influence other parts. Governments and companies alike use risk assessment methods in order to proactively recognize, monitor, and control possible risks as they occur.

Figure 6.2 expresses the potential impacts of a security threat at a horizontal and vertical level, affecting societies, industries, and nations. The domino effect explains the significance in rectifying security vulnerabilities at a company and industrial level.

FIGURE 6.2   The domino effect applied on supply chain and logistics security. (From the author.)

6.2.4 The Pareto Principle

This is the "80–20 rule," also known as "The Pareto principle," named after Vilfredo Pareto, an Italian economist. This theory is further named as "the law of the vital few," as it has been observed that approximately 20% of our efforts lead to the 80% of the outcomes. While this law is quite popular among risk assessment methodologies, in a security framework, it can be estimated that

- 20% of supply chain disruptions will affect 80% of the freight;
  80% of supply chain disruptions will affect 20% of the freight.
- 20% of the security personnel will cause 80% of the human errors;
  80% of the security personnel will cause 20% of the human errors.
- 20% of the security personnel will produce 80% of the required deliverables;
  80% of the security personnel will produce 20% of the required deliverables.
- 20% of our security partners will provide us with 80% of intelligence data;
  80% of our security partners will provide us with 20% of intelligence data.
- 20% of the security attacks may damage 80% of a target;
  80% of the security attacks may damage 20% of a target.
- 20% of the security attackers may execute 80% of the attack;
  80% of the security attackers may execute 20% of the attack.

Figure 6.3 reflects the Pareto principle, which describes the correlation between the "significant few" of 20% (or Pareto efficient), and the "insignificant many" of 80% (or Pareto inefficient).

The Pareto principle can also be applied in the following security-related processes:

- Supply chain disruptions
- Consistency or effectiveness of security measures
- Cargo screening and inspecting during loading and unloading or shipment and receipt process
- Effectiveness of innovative technologies
- Visibility and integration of supply chains
- Illegitimate activities during trade and transport in a particular route and so on

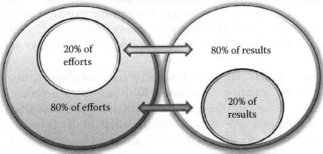

The significant few: 20% of efforts will generate 80% of the results.
The insignificant many: 80% of efforts will generate 20% of the results.

FIGURE 6.3 Pareto principle: the 80%–20% rule. (From the author.)

6.3 LOGISTICS NETWORKS: STRENGTHENING OUR SUPPLY CHAINS

This section introduces a number of case studies of different industry segments, and shows the efforts and systems put in place to ensure resilient and sustainable operations.

CASE STUDY: CYBER SECURITY THREATS IN SUPPLY CHAINS

Interview: Michael G. Dinning

Director, Multimodal Programs and Partnerships, Volpe, the National Transportation Systems' Center

As supply chains become more dependent on information systems and networks, they may face increased risks from cyber attacks that could disrupt trade and the movement of goods. A comprehensive approach to cyber security should be followed by public and private entities in the supply chain to reduce cyber security risks and to ensure that supply chains are resilient to disruption from cyber attacks.

DEPENDENCE ON INFORMATION

Freight supply chains are becoming increasingly dependent on information, computer systems, and communication networks. Information systems are critical to supply chain operations, the associated financial transactions, and the management of virtually every enterprise and process in the chain. Intermodal cargo terminals depend on computer software for loading ships, managing container movements, controlling access, and many other functions. The equipment used at terminals, such as container cranes, depends on industrial control systems and computer processors to operate efficiently. In some ports, material handling has been automated using robotics technology.

All modes of transportation are adopting digital information technologies to increase system safety and efficiency. E-enabled aircraft, ships, trains, and trucks are becoming the norm. Traffic management systems are used to provide situational awareness, manage transportation networks, and respond to disruptions. Positive train control, satellite-based digital air traffic management systems, and digitally connected cars and trucks are being developed and implemented. Every mode of transportation depends on satellite-based navigation systems, such as the Global Positioning System, for position and timing information. Vehicle operations are becoming more automated, with innovations like automated truck platooning being considered to increase safety and fuel efficiency.

Supply chain partners, such as manufacturers, distributors, and retailers, are also dependent on information technology. With just-in-time processes prevailing, accurate and timely information on supply chain movements is critical. Urban congestion is stimulating new approaches to retail distribution of goods, and these new processes depend on information systems. Consumers use e-commerce and mobile communications to select and order retail goods. Consumers, shippers, and carriers expect access to real-time shipment status information.

POTENTIAL VULNERABILITIES AND RISKS

This increased dependence on digital technology can result in potential vulnerabilities and risks. Widespread use of the Internet and remote access to computer systems can increase the "attack surface" and vulnerability of transportation and logistics information systems. Information is often shared among a wide variety of organizations, and vulnerabilities in any part of the network may be exploited, resulting in both local and systemic impacts.

The consequences of a successful cyber attack on supply chains could be significant. Disruptions to the availability or integrity of information supporting the supply chain could compromise supply chains in many ways. Virtually every physical movement in the supply chain has corresponding information and financial transactions, which are essential to processes such as electronic manifesting and e-commerce. Just-in-time logistics processes could be significantly impacted if accurate delivery times and the availability of supplies are not known. Security assessments and customs prescreening of manifests could be delayed if shipment information is not available. Without automated terminal management tools, cargo handling would be difficult and time consuming. Material-handling equipment could be rendered inoperable if embedded industrial control systems were compromised. In many cases, manual procedures no longer exist or would be inadequate to meet the demands of today's supply chains.

GROWING CYBER THREATS

Threats of cyber attacks are growing at a rapid rate. Cyber attacks can originate from cyberterrorists, hacktivists attempting to disrupt operations to make a political statement, or criminal enterprises. Automated hacking tools make cyber attacks easier to accomplish, and illegal cyber hacking services can be purchased on the Internet. More sophisticated advanced persistent threats have been mounted against some information and control systems in other critical infrastructure sectors, such as energy and finance. The potential for disruption and profit in transportation and supply chain systems makes them a potential target.

AN ILLUSTRATIVE EXAMPLE—THE PORT OF ANTWERP HACKING INCIDENT

From 2011 to 2013, drug smugglers reportedly hacked into the terminal management system that controlled container movements at the Port of Antwerp (BBC News, October 16, 2013). The smugglers were able to obtain information about the placement and security details of containers that contained illegal drugs hidden in legitimate cargo from South America. They then mounted a physical attack, sending truck drivers to steal the containers from the port. When apprehended, the smugglers had over $200 million in heroin and cocaine along with numerous firearms.

The hackers initially got access into the container management information system by sending malicious software to terminal workers, possibly as part of a phishing attack where the employee is tricked into clicking on a phony Internet link or attachment. This enabled the smugglers to gain access to container data. The initial attacks were discovered, and the vulnerability was eliminated with firewalls. The

Port of Antwerp, Nocrdzee Terminal. (Courtesy of Volpe.)

Port of Antwerp. (Courtesy of Volpe.)

Port of Antwerp Containers. (Courtesy of Volpe.)

criminals then physically broke into the terminal offices. They installed devices on the computers that logged what the staff keyed into their computers and the information they displayed on their computer monitors and transmitted this information outside the port. The smugglers again gained access to the port and made off with additional containers before the second attack was discovered.

The drug smugglers' attack on the Port of Antwerp was an example of a hybrid attack, a combination of cyber and physical attacks. This attack illustrates the need for a comprehensive systems approach to cyber security. Cyber security controls, such as firewalls, malware detectors, logical (or network) access control, and intrusion detection systems all could reduce the risks of this type of attack. These mitigation measures must be accompanied by continuous training and awareness campaigns with employees to warn them about potential attack methods, such as phishing. Physical security methods, such as secure identification credentials and physical access controls, are needed to protect the facilities where computer equipment is located.

MITIGATING SUPPLY CHAIN CYBER SECURITY RISKS

Every organization in a supply chain must adopt good security policies, procedures, and technologies. The processes and functions of supply chains are so tightly interrelated that disruptions in one activity could have impacts throughout the supply chain. In addition, a cyber attack on one organization could compromise their information and could also be used to pivot to other locations that are networked to the attacked site. In addition, supply chains depend on other infrastructures, such as communications and energy, and these must also be protected to avoid cascading risks.

Comprehensive cyber security programs must include four types of activities:

1. Identify critical information and systems.
2. Assess the risk of cyber and other disruptions.
3. Implement measures to protect critical information, systems, and networks.
4. Deploy capabilities to detect, respond, and recover if cyber attacks or other types of cyber disruptions occur.

Security programs should take a systems approach that will address physical and personnel security as well as cyber security. Coordinating with personnel security efforts is important to ensure that adequate screening of new employees is conducted and that employee access privileges to information are appropriate for their responsibilities. Coordinating with human resources functions may also ensure that potential problems with disgruntled employees are detected before they can become insider threats.

Organizations in the supply chain must be able to respond quickly and effectively to cyber attacks or other disruptions. Automated intrusion detection and information screening measures can detect anomalies and prevent or respond to minimize damage. Supply chain organizations should establish relationships with the intelligence community, computer emergency response teams, law enforcement agencies, and information sharing and analysis centers (ISACs) to obtain information on threats, incidents, and mitigation methods. ISACs have been formed to facilitate information exchange for many modes of transportation, including surface, public transit, aviation, and maritime transportation. Since the supply chain is multimodal, access to information on several modes may be needed. In addition, many organizations communicate with the Multi-State ISAC, which exchanges information among regions in the United States. Since supply chains are often global, similar exchange of information on incidents and threats is needed with international organizations.

Cyber security should be part of an all-hazards approach. An all-hazards approach addresses the risks of accidental failures, natural disasters, extreme weather, and disruptions due to equipment reliability problems, in addition to risks from deliberate cyber attacks.

Cyber resilience is critical to achieve overall supply chain resilience. Cyber resilience includes three elements: (i) cyber security measures should be "baked in" as part of robust system and network designs; (ii) redundant methods should be employed to store, process, and transmit information; and (iii) adaptive policies, procedures, and technologies should be in place to enable supply chain organizations to rapidly respond and recover from cyber incidents. Measures that could improve resilience include automated backup systems and remote storage of information. In case of information system failure, employees should be capable of using downtime procedures that do not depend on fully capable computer and communications systems.

IMPLEMENTING CYBER SECURITY PROGRAMS

Supply chain cyber security and resilience depends on an organizational commitment to create and maintain a culture of cyber security. Cyber security should be included in international security initiatives, such as the voluntary Customs-Trade Partnership Against Terrorism. The guidelines in the *Framework for Improving Critical Infrastructure Cybersecurity* developed by the National Institute of Standards and Technology (NIST) are a good summary of what should be included in a comprehensive security program. The *Roadmap to Secure Control Systems in the Transportation Sector* (2012) recommends a broad set of activities to reduce control system risks in all modes of transportation. At the local level, cyber security should be addressed as part of programs such as facility security plans for ports and terminals. Cyber security should also be addressed by collaborative regional efforts, such as those coordinated by the US Coast Guard and Area Maritime Security Committees.

CYBER SECURITY RESOURCES

Many resources are available to assist supply chain organizations in formulating and implementing their cyber security programs. The guidance from NIST, the International Standards Organization, the US Computer Emergency Readiness Team, and commercial organizations such as the SANS Institute are all useful sources of information on general cyber security strategies. The Volpe National Transportation Systems Center, part of the US Department of Transportation, has extensive experience in transportation cyber security and physical security in all modes and can provide research and technical support under interagency funding agreements. Information-sharing opportunities specific to transportation are available from the Surface Transportation ISAC, as well as the ISACs of other transportation modes and other sectors (i.e., financial services, electricity). The Transportation Security Administration sponsors information exchange through the Transportation Systems Sector Cyber Working Group. The Transportation Research Board sponsors cyber security research programs and hosts information exchange at their annual meeting and through the Cyber Security Subcommittee of the Critical Transportation Infrastructure Protection Committee. This subcommittee exchanges information on threats, incidents, and mitigation strategies and maintains the Cyber Security Resource Center website at http://trbcybersecurity.erau.edu/.

CASE STUDY: THE PORT OF HOUSTON: A SUCCESS STORY

Interview: John A. Moseley
Senior Director, Trade Development, Port of Houston Authority (POHA)

PORT OF HOUSTON AUTHORITY

The Port of Houston is a 25-mi-long complex of varied private and nonprivate amenities situated only a few hours by sea from the US Gulf. The port's sustainable success ranks first in the United States in foreign seaborne tonnage, first in domestic imports, first in domestic export tonnage, and second in total domestic tonnage. It is furthermore the country's leading break bulk hub port, receiving 65% of all major US project cargoes. Foremost, the port is a leader in security management.

Strategically positioned on the Gulf Coast, the city of Houston is an ideal passage for cargo imported or exported from the US West and Midwest. The city is located near a significant cluster of markets, manufacturers, and consumers. Over 17 million people reside within 300 mi of the city, whereas almost 60 million people reside within 700 mi. Global and inland transport is facilitated by intermodal transportation by sea, air, rail, and highway routes that connect the region with global and inland destinations.

The Port of Houston (Figure 6.4) is a vibrant economic and commercial center comprising the general public terminals owned, managed, and operated by the Port of Houston Authority, while its activities generate profit for the 52 mi long Houston Ship Channel and the 150+ corporations in its vicinity. The port involves over 200 million tons of freight, which is moved by over 8000 ships and 200,000 barge voyages. The Port of Houston Authority's executives recognize the significance of combining business with security, safety, and environmental stewardship (POHA 2015a).

EXCEEDING THE MARKET'S COMMERCIAL EXPECTATIONS

Due to its location and subtropical climate, Houston is an area that experiences heavy rain during certain periods of the year and is also subject to hurricanes from time to time. For example, during hurricanes Ike and Sandy, the port authorities curtailed the hours of operation for safety reasons in advance of the storms, and subsequently, the hours of operations were able to resume normally in as little as two days with minimal to no damage to cargo or infrastructure. The position and

FIGURE 6.4   The Port of Houston and the Houston Ship Channel. (From POHA, Port of Houston Authority Overview, available at http://www.portofhouston.com, accessed November 23, 2014, 2015b.)

design of the facilities have taken into account storm surges, high water levels, etc., in order to minimize the impact of inclement weather. Other considerations include redundancy designed into the IT and telecommunications network and emergency power generation to ensure minimal disruptions to the port's customers.

CASE STUDY: ENERGY NETWORKS AND RESILIENCE

Interview: Hirini Reedy

Specialist Indigenous Energy Partner, TOA Inc., EECA, Maori Alliances & Indigenous Energy Networks, New Zealand

COMPANY PROFILE

Maori Alliances & Indigenous Energy Networks (MAIEN) is a small but growing collective of Maori Holistic Energy Partners, which is interested in partnerships with other indigenous energy partners in Southeast Asia and Pacific Islands. It draws inspiration from the United Nations Declaration of Rights of Indigenous Peoples 2007. MAIEN takes a wider indigenous definition of energy to include human energy potential as well as industrial age energy definitions derived from fossil fuel, electricity generation, and other energy sector types. MAIEN is still in its seedling phase in New Zealand, but it intends to focus on the growing sustainable energy and environmental sector in all major economies over the next five years.

MAIEN AND RENEWABLE ENERGY

From a New Zealand and a Maori point of view, approximately 70% of their electricity is renewable sources, no coal or nuclear, mainly hydrothermal and geothermal. We must put in new energy-efficient technologies, sustainable energy supply, and evolved consumer behaviors. We must expand our definitions and import new ones.

"CRITICAL INFRASTRUCTURE SECURITY" AND STRATEGIC ALLIANCES

The energy industry is considered by governments as a "critical infrastructure security" sector. There have been alliances among New Zealand, Australia, the United States, Canada, Japan, South Korea, the European Union, and many other nations. However, since private industries are characterized by commercial competition, companies may be reluctant to share critical data.

We are still seeing post-World War II tensions happening. We are still seeing religious tensions, tribal tensions, and terrorist tensions still happening. We must expand our definitions around partnerships and see all the cost benefits of our actions and nonactions not just economically and financially but also from a planetary sense. We need to transcend such debates sooner because we are reaching a critical point for certain regions of the planet. So MAIEN is an alternative approach to the current trajectory that the human race is heading along.

6.4 SETTING THE SECURITY STANDARDS THROUGH QUALITY IMPLEMENTATION

This section aims to establish resilient security standards by the use of quality management protocols like 5S, Kaizen, Lean and Agile, Kanban, Six Sigma, TQM, Deming's 14 points on Quality Management, DMAIC, and 4D as tools for bridging the security gaps.

6.4.1 Bridging the Security Gaps

Although a variety of security threats need to be mitigated, most of the vulnerabilities can be classified into categories, as reflected in Figure 6.5.

The impact of the aforementioned security gaps entails industrial and transportation disruptions, as depicted in Figure 6.6.

The consequences of these disruptions impose severe impact upon supply chains. In the case of severe disruptions, loss of life, social turmoil, environmental damage, or asset damage may occur. From a strictly commercial perspective, producers/manufacturers are not in a position to offer the "just-in-time" services to their assembly lines.

In the event of a major disruption, i.e., when a hub port is closed, the regional logistics companies may lose about US$3–4 million a day. When a major port is closed, e.g., LA, Long Beach, the losses reach tens of millions of dollars per week (Pritchard 2014).

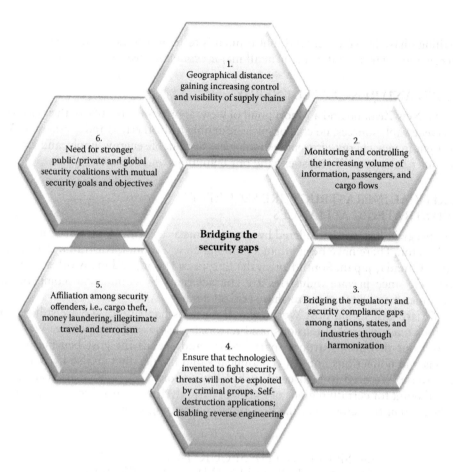

FIGURE 6.5   Bridging the security gaps.

FIGURE 6.6   Supply chain: industrial and transportation disruptions. (From the author.)

The use of quality management tools can bridge such security gaps and eliminate the damage incurred.

6.4.2 "5S"

"5S" is a lean manufacturing method that can be applied in each and every stage of the supply chain and logistics. The standardization technique uses the initial "S," which in the English and Japanese language, respectively, are as follows:

1. *Sort (Seiri 整理)*

   Sort out pertains to eliminating clutter and objects or processes that are not needed whereas retaining and segregating the processes and items that are vital for the operations.

2. *Straighten (Seiton* 整頓)

Streamlining focuses on organizing the processes and tools used for input in such a way that eliminates waste, delays, and obstructions leading to bottlenecks.

3. *Shine (Seiso* 清掃)

This quality stage relates to thoroughly and regularly sanitizing the area and maintaining the equipment in a manner that prolongs the assets' life span and performance while promoting occupational health, security, and safety. In such an environment, systemic vulnerabilities will be revealed and easily identified.

4. *Standardize (Seiketsu* 清潔)

Once the above stages have been mastered, the next process item is standardization. This refers to consistent actions put in place in a manner that eliminates deviation of movements and therefore eliminates error and waste. The working process is both predictable, safe, and secure, while performance deviations or threats simply stand out.

5. *Sustain (Shitsuke* 躾)

Sustainability pertains to retaining the "5S" methodology and promoting a culture of quality management through training, drills, and inspections based on these standards that are adopted in a company- and industry-specific manner.

6. *Safety (Anzen-sei* 安全性)

Safety is the sixth "S" added more recently and refers to both the company's safety management plan and the element of efficiency and elimination of waste.

7. *Security (Sekyuriti* セキュリティ)

Security is finally the seventh "S" and relates to the corporate risk management and risk assessment protocols that ensure the "total security management" (TSM) compliance. TSM actually not only encompasses all the supply chain security threats covered in this book, i.e., terrorism, piracy, cargo theft, illegitimate trade, and travel, but also includes financial and commercial losses.

6.4.3 "Kaizen" 改善

In Japanese, Kaizen refers to the philosophy of continuous improvement as a daily habit. The professionals who practice Kaizen are asked to audit and critically evaluate their own job, department, and corporation in an objective manner and seek for daily improvements of a smaller or larger extent. To adopt this daily working method, professionals are asked to follow the plan–do–check–act (PDCA) cycle, which consists of the PDCA stages, as shown in Figure 6.7.

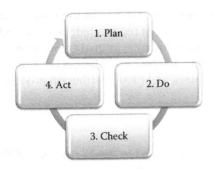

FIGURE 6.7   Kaizen and the plan–do–check–act stages. (From the author.)

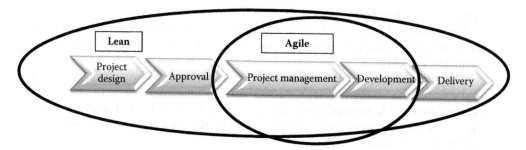

FIGURE 6.8   The lean and agile methodology. (From the author.)

6.4.4 "Lean and Agile"

This term refers to an efficient and effective supply chain where optimum use of resources is achieved, combined with flexibility or adaptability toward any internal or external disruptions, threats, or changes.

As demonstrated in Figure 6.8, lean encompasses the entire supply chain from the innovation or research and development (R&D) stage to the manufacturing, value-adding, and distribution stages. Agile, on the other hand, is focused on the production of goods or services and describes a continuous improvement methodology of methods, processes, and company culture that must be adopted.

6.4.5 "Kanban"

Kanban (which means "billboard" in Japanese) is one of the keys of lean and agile and just-in-time logistics systems. It was designed to create optimum production levels through the use of a number of cards or signals in critical stages of the supply chain:

   a. Raw materials from the vendors/suppliers to the manufacturers
   b. Manufactured segments to the assembly lines
   c. Finished goods through the logistics, distribution, and consumption stages

The cards facilitate the smooth, efficient, lean, and agile flow of goods.

6.4.6 "Six Sigma"

Six Sigma is a quality tool where companies aim to promote standardized processes and avoid deviations from excellence. It is a regimented, process- and data-intensive technique for reducing flaws or variations in the product quality. Six Sigma products are only allowed a minimum deviation in quality and process, whereas the whole process entails the assembly line, manufacturing, logistics, and final distribution process of goods or services.

6.4.7 "TQM"

TQM is a corporate tool widely applied in the 1980s and 1990s. It was developed based on other quality control systems that aim to achieve sustainable improvement of a product's quality. Though other systems such as Six Sigma and ISO 9001 have gained

FIGURE 6.9 "TQM." (From the author.)

increasing popularity, TQM is still a respected quality management method applied both for services and products, and, as shown in Figure 6.9, it aims at

- Ensuring continuous improvement
- Responsibility throughout the corporate pyramid, from top management to entry-level staff
- Achieving clients' needs
- Minimizing production costs
- Minimizing production time
- Just-in-time/demand flow manufacturing
- Personnel motivation, empowerment and rewarding, and so on

6.4.8 "Deming's 14 Points on Quality Management"

Deming's 14 points on quality management is a central TQM method for industries to boost performance and quality.

These points include

1. Standardization and continuous improvement of goods and services.
2. Implementation of the 14 points.
3. Stop reliance upon evaluation processes to attain superior quality.
4. Do not select vendors, partners, or tools exclusively on price. Cost can be reduced by selecting fewer suppliers.
5. Pursue continuous improvement and standardization of quality, development, and services.
6. Establish a training protocol and hands-on experience.
7. Promote leadership.
8. Eliminate fear.
9. Reduce segmentation among departments and functions.
10. Do not use catchy phrases, goals, and compliments to motivate employees.

11. Do not use metrics to evaluate the performance of employees or the targets of the administrators.
12. Eliminate boundaries that deprive the team's self-esteem, and remove the yearly evaluation process.
13. Encourage lifelong education and professional development for all employees.
14. Involve all managers and employees toward this corporate re-engineering.

6.4.9 "DMAIC"

The DMAIC process is a component of the Six Sigma philosophy, yet it can be used independently as a quality-improvement, problem-solving tool. It consists of six principal stages, as shown in Figure 6.10:

- Defining the risk, obstacle, or challenge
- Measuring the quality process presently used
- Analyzing the root cause of the risk, obstacle, or challenge
- Modifying design, if appropriate
- Improving the situation by identifying a solution to the problem
- Controlling and monitoring the process by eradicating the problem

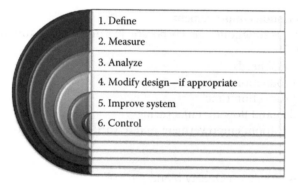

FIGURE 6.10   The DMAIC process applied in "TQM." (From the author.)

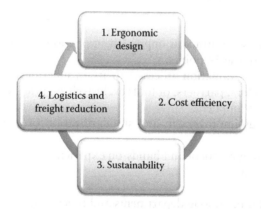

FIGURE 6.11   The 4D methodology. (From the author.)

6.4.10 The "4D" Methodology

This is a widely used method used in packaging and assembly lines, which is shown in Figure 6.11, and focuses on (a) ergonomics, (b) cost efficiency, (c) sustainable systems, and (d) logistics and freight reduction.

6.5 CONCLUSIONS

This chapter dealt with the prevailing quality standards that are currently used in supply chain and transportation quality systems. A wider use of such tools can be successfully implemented in the security management and risk assessment protocols of the private and public sectors in order to ensure that resilient, sustainable, and reliable security systems are in place.

INTERVIEWS AND CASE STUDIES

Dinning, Michael G., Director, Multimodal Programs and Partnerships, Volpe, the National Transportation Systems' Center, Case Study: Cyber Security Threats in Supply Chains.

Moseley, John A., Senior Director, Trade Development, Port of Houston Authority (POHA), Case Study: The Port of Houston: A Success Story.

Reedy, Hirini, Specialist Indigenous Energy Partner, TOA Inc., EECA, Maori Alliances & Indigenous Energy Networks, New Zealand, Case Study: Energy Networks and Resilience.

REFERENCES

BBC News. 2013. Police warning after drug traffickers' cyber-attack, Bateman, T. Available at http://www.bbc.com/news/world-europe-24539417. Accessed January 1, 2014.

Eisenhower, D. 1954. "Domino Theory Principle by President Dwight D. Eisenhower." Public Papers of the Presidents Dwight D. Eisenhower, pp. 381–390, USA.

POHA. 2015a. Port of Houston Authority Overview. Available at http://www.portofhouston .com/about-us/overview/. Accessed January 1, 2015.

POHA. 2015b. Port of Houston Authority Overview. Available at http://www.portofhouston .com. Accessed January 1, 2015.

Pritchard, J. 2014. Slowdown at Los Angeles, Long Beach ports won't impact holiday products. Associated Press and Press Telegram. December 2014. Available at http:// www.presstelegram.com/business/20141204/slowdown-at-los-angeles-long-beach -ports-wont-impact-holiday-products. Accessed December 30, 2014.

Public and Private Partnerships

In order to develop a successful public–private partnership,
government representatives would do well to focus on the
operational concerns of their private sector partners.
Listen to them. Identify those issues impacting the security and
resilience of the private sector. Determine "what keeps them up at
night." Solicit the ideas and recommendations of corporate leaders
and stakeholders. Ask them where they feel government and state
agencies can be of assistance in resolving their concerns—and then
work with them to develop reasonable solutions. That's where the
government can show "value added."

Kevin Clement CEM®, TEM®, MCP
Strategic Planner, Texas Homeland Security
Texas Department of Public Safety

7.1 INTRODUCTION

Public–private partnerships are described as the strategic alliance between the government (federal and state agencies) and the private sector, with the purpose of (a) proactively designing a contingency plan, (b) mitigating threat or responding during an emergency, and (c) supporting the rapid recovery after an incident.

Public–private partnerships were probably formed millennia ago during social emergencies, such as extreme geophysical events, wars, or security threats. During the twentieth century's World Wars I and II, national defense depended on such partnerships for financial, technological, and intelligence support. Governments, industries, and civilian volunteers worked closely in manufacturing military equipment.

Moreover, the mass training of civilians in recognizing rival forces, evacuating public spaces, and hiding in bomb shelters may be considered as outcomes of public–private partnerships.

The significance of such security partnerships was reestablished in the twentieth century, when numerous large-scale terrorist attacks occurred around the world. It is conceivable that globalization facilitated not only large-scale trade and transport but also the orchestration of such large-scale security attacks. Events such as the September 11, 2001 terrorist attack in the United States, the 2002 Bali bombings, the 2003 and 2007 Casablanca bombings, the 2004 Madrid train bombings, and the 2005 London and Bali

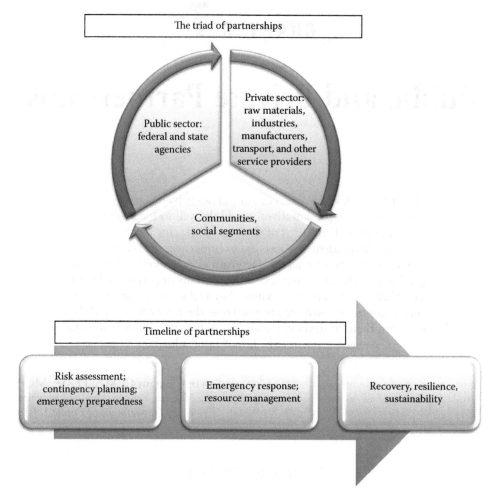

FIGURE 7.1   Security public/private partnerships. (From the author.)

bombings all revealed the significance of public–private partnerships in a holistic, consistent, and sustainable manner.

Figure 7.1 reflects the interaction among the public, private, and community sectors within an incident timeline, i.e., from risk assessment and preparedness to emergency management and recovery/resilience and sustainability.

An evaluation of the private sector preparedness before such terrorist events showed that industries, the banking system, and the insurance/underwriting system may not have been prepared for such events, perhaps because such high-impact events had not previously occurred.

Such alliances resemble elaborate supply chains, as they work best in achieving the following objectives:

    a. Creation of think tanks for information exchange and public/private network visibility.
    b. Resource management, i.e., synergistic use of resources during the risk assessment, risk mitigation, and recovery stage of a security incident. These resources

typically involve all the factors of production, i.e., entrepreneurship, labor, capital, and land.

c. Understanding the best practices or lessons learned. Arguably, the best practices are industry-, nation-, and company-specific. For this reason, it can be debated that there has been an extensive and rather generic use of the "best practices" and "lessons learned" concepts. On the other hand, one cannot fail to observe that the investigation of a security incident can provide valuable lessons to both the private and public sector as to the strategy, objective, and means used by the offenders. For example, the Boston Marathon attacks were conducted by lone wolves, involved bombings and shootings, and were motivated by extremist religious beliefs. Although these attacks did not affect the supply chain or trade and transport activities directly, the private sector was both alarmed by such an incident and was able to learn from the best practices, i.e., during the emergency response, technologies used such as face recognition, and subsequent investigation.

7.2 MODELS OF PUBLIC AND PRIVATE PARTNERSHIPS

> There's no way government can solve the challenges of a disaster
> with a government-centric approach. It takes the whole team.
> And the private sector provides the bulk of the services every
> day in the community.
>
> **Craig Fugate**
> *FEMA administrator*

Due to their complexity, supply chains and logistics activities are by nature susceptible to delays and disturbances, since the malfunction of a single component may create the entire system's failure. A number of security threats that occurred at a global level highlighted the necessity of forming public–private partnerships in key areas such as

a. Homeland security
b. Critical infrastructure sectors
c. Global supply chains, i.e., from raw materials to manufacturing and value-added goods to hub-ports and final distribution channels
d. Logistics and transport services not only for sea, land, air, and pipelines but also areas of minimum security disruptions so far, such as offshore drilling and space/interplanetary logistics
e. Public- and private-sector intelligence
f. Cyber security, information technology (IT), and cloud technology
g. Emergency management and emergency response during an incident; and
h. Recovery, resilience, and sustainability

Figure 7.2 demonstrates in detail these key areas and how these interact in the risk assessment–response–recovery timeline.

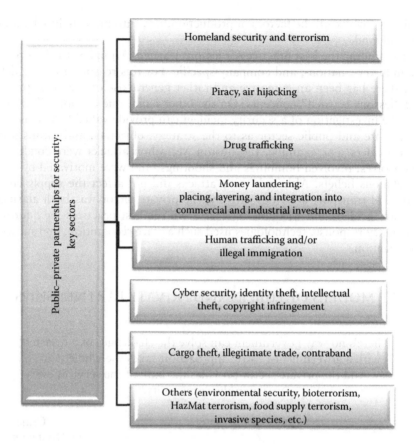

FIGURE 7.2   Public/private partnerships and key sectors.

7.3 THREAT PREVENTION, MITIGATION, AND RESPONSE

There is a plethora of highly effective public–private partnership models, and according to most of these have the pursuant fundamental characteristics: widely accessible, committed, resourced, involved, and resilient/sustainable.

Despite these common attributes, the nature of each partnership may dictate a different model architecture, such as

a. Discussing information on situational awareness
b. Determining accessible emergency resources and resilience strategies
c. Defining the scope of their collaboration by signing memoranda of agreement or memoranda of understanding
d. Ensuring preparedness, response, and resilience by participating in mutual drills, tabletop exercises, and security training
e. Establishing long-term partnerships of commitment
f. Adopting interactive protocols and effective communication channels
g. Assuring that the private sector is duly represented in an emergency operation center
h. Ascertaining that these business emergency operations centers are adequately manned

Some of the benefits that arise from such partnerships include

a. Once these public/private partnerships have been effectively established at a regional and national level, it is adequately proven that the communities located in the geographical vicinity of such partnerships are due to be benefited.
b. Highly effective partnerships are established when numerous supply chain and critical infrastructure sectors are well-represented in the public/private sector partnership. Such configurations are likely to build the muscle memory and formulate common defense lines through information exchange, drills, training, and tabletop exercises.
c. Optimum resource management, optimum investment strategies, and return on investment are most likely to be achieved through these partnerships.
d. When these security coalitions are formed, and intelligence/information is properly exchanged, all parties get to learn from past incidents or near misses. Visibility and real-time alerts can help this coalition to identify vulnerabilities, strengthen the entire network, and achieve resilience and sustainability.

CASE STUDY: PUBLIC/PRIVATE PARTNERSHIPS AND RISKS TO INFRASTRUCTURE

Interview: Thaddeus M. Bielecki*
Assistant Master, Dredge Potter (US Army Corps of Engineers)

Risks to infrastructure such as navigation has been reduced by measures established by the Department of Homeland Security through the US Coast Guard and other agencies under its direction. With such a vast inland waterway system as the United States, it is almost impossible to have a vulnerability-free infrastructure, yet there is a compelling need to protect our nation from terrorist attacks, sabotage, and illegitimate trade and transport in a sustainable manner. At any given time, there are many different commodities traveling on the US waterways bound for a variety of facilities from off-loading and transfer facilities to factories and power plants. With such a complex network to protect, the task is daunting.

One basic means of reducing the risk of an internal threat was initiating a system of background checks and requiring workers to obtain a Transportation Workers Identification Credential (TWIC). Prior to 9/11, only licensed masters, licensed engineers, and able seamen were fingerprinted and had background checks performed. Today, by contrast, every person working on a vessel or a marine facility is required to be fingerprinted and have a background check performed as part of the TWIC program. Without the TWIC, a person cannot gain employment at a marine facility or vessel. The card has a chip inside it and a PIN associated with the card in order to prevent anyone but the cardholder from using the card to gain access to a facility.

---

* The views expressed are solely Mr. Bielecki's personal opinion and do NOT represent policy or views of the US Army Corps of Engineers or any other employer or organization that he has worked for or has been associated with.

The requirement that a marine facility and vessels maintain a security plan have helped facility operators and vessel masters become more effective in protecting their facility or vessel. A vigilant watch for suspicious activity—especially of people observing and photographing routine events such as commodity transfer—needs to be reported. Homeland security tracks these reports and determines if there is a pattern of suspicious activity and alerts facility operators of the activity so there is a greater awareness for all facilities. Without reporting and collaboration between the public–private sector, all of the matrixes and models in the world are useless. Industries and civilians on the boats at the facility are the eyes and ears on the front line, and they are the ones that must report and pass the word upward. In short, the saying "if you see something, say something" carries so much weight since this information is lost if it is not passed up to a higher level, so it can be analyzed and relayed to other facilities to heighten awareness.

CASE STUDY: PUBLIC/PRIVATE PARTNERSHIPS FOR ENVIRONMENTAL SECURITY THREATS

Interview: Carleen Lyden-Kluss

Co-Founder and Executive Director, North American Marine Environment Protection Association

CORPORATE PROFILE

North American Marine Environment Protection Association (NAMEPA) was founded in 2007 as a nonprofit organization with 501c(3) status. NAMEPA is a marine industry-led initiative that works cooperatively with businesses; federal, state, and local government agencies; maritime professionals; educational institutions; and the general public to protect the marine environment by promoting the education of seafarers, port communities, and students from grade school to university level and beyond.

NAMEPA designs, develops, and leads enriching educational programs on the marine environment and maritime industry, fosters discussion between and among members of the maritime industry and the general public at national maritime conferences, and creates and disseminates comprehensive original materials that address the need and strategies for protecting our marine environment and preserving our national maritime heritage.

At the core of NAMEPA's organizational mission is an imperative to increase the safety and security of maritime operations and serve as a resource for maritime professionals and the industry as a whole. NAMEPA works with federal agencies including the US Coast Guard, including the Reserve and Auxiliary, and the National Oceanic and Atmospheric Administration to develop and disseminate high-quality educational programming on the marine environment and maritime safety. NAMEPA members include domestic and international companies within shipping, as well as wider land-based industries such as oil companies, banks, and insurance companies—all of which share NAMEPA's desire to "Save Our Seas."

FIGURE 7.3   HOUSTON, TX—February 20, 2014. NAMEPA accepts the 2014 Environment Award at the Inaugural Lloyd's List North American Awards Event. Pictured (left to right): Gail Nicholas, development director; Lyn Harris, chief operating officer; Clay Maitland, co-founder; Carleen Lyden-Kluss, co-founder and executive director; Caitlin Colon, former events coordinator; and Elise Avallon, education and outreach manager.

NAMEPA has worked hard to increase awareness about the vitality of the maritime industry to our global economy and society as a whole and to promote it as a very efficient and relatively environmentally friendly means of transportation and trade. As stated by our founding chairman, Clay Maitland, we at NAMEPA strive to "reach out and engage communities to protect the marine environment, while teaching them the importance of our industry to their daily lives."

NAMEPA was honored to receive the Lloyd's Register Environment Award in 2014 for our impact on the maritime community and our commitment to delivering high-quality educational programming on the marine environment and the maritime heritage of the United States (Figure 7.3). We acknowledge and share the commitment by the maritime industry to "Save Our Seas" and are honored to work with our members to promote the immense value of maritime trade, commerce, transportation, and services to students, regulators, environmental groups, and the public in general. In 2014, NAMEPA welcomed 69 new student members at the University of Houston's Center for Logistics and Transportation Policy.

ENVIRONMENTAL SECURITY THREATS

Halfway through the second decade of the twenty-first century, addressing and preventing security threats to maritime transportation systems is absolutely essential. In addition to the substantial threat to human safety and the prevention of loss of life at sea, a breach in the security system of a shipping cargo vessel could bring harm, perhaps intentionally, to the marine environment and constitute an act of "ecoterrorism." One cause for concern is the possibility that ships could be sabotaged through breaches in cyber security, resulting in a vessel "going rogue" and running aground, thus creating a pollution incident.

NAMEPA is working hard with the industry to foster an educated and knowledgeable maritime workforce that adheres to the strict environmental and safety regulations imposed upon ships globally by the International Maritime Organization (IMO) and that is able-bodied and prepared to mitigate any potential emergency situation on the water. While most environmental disasters, including oil spills, are accidental in nature, we at NAMEPA and the industry as a whole have a vested interest in preventing these and any other avoidable casualties to the marine environment and coastal communities. As the century continues to unfold, the shipping and maritime industry will continue to operate according to policy as the world's most environmentally benign form of transporting goods from place to place.

ENVIRONMENTAL SECURITY PARTNERSHIPS

One of NAMEPA's most significant contributions to marine environmental conservation and the protection of human life at sea is the *NAMEPA MARPOL International Convention for the Prevention of Pollution from Ships* handbook, published in 2014. The handbook was created through a grant provided by the National Fish and Wildlife Foundation, funded by oily water separation violations in North Carolina and Massachusetts. Sensing the imperative to condense and clarify the MARPOL regulations to seafarers working daily under these laws, NAMEPA successfully created and published this 24-page handbook that, according to the IMO, constituted the first material in which MARPOL regulations were clearly linked with their impact on the marine environment. In essence, this publication—which has been widely distributed to thousands of mariners (through the North American Maritime Ministry Association), recreational boaters (through the US Coast Guard Auxiliary), and industry through our own conferences and events—presents not only the "what" of MARPOL regulations but also the "why."

This publication has been well received due to its ease of use and illustrated explanations of the environmental obligation to follow the MARPOL regulations related to pollution from ships. The document summarizes the main points of the legislation in a format that is usable aboard a vessel and easy to reference when any questions arise or in procedural training. This protects industry members from incurring fines and avoids confusion when it comes to MARPOL regulations. Having access to this resource is integral in maintaining and growing an informed workforce and safeguards both ships and individual mariners from the consequences of inadvertently disregarding environmental laws. In turn, their good actions protect our shared marine environment and help secure the shipping industry's place as a relatively benign and efficient means transporting goods overseas and domestically.

NAMEPA was formed around a very strong commitment to education. Through a collaborative effort with NOAA, in 2014, NAMEPA published the *NAMEPA and NOAA Educator's Guide to Marine Debris*, which was released in 2014. It is comprised of nine STEM-focused lessons on reducing physical pollution in the marine environment and includes a multimedia component, corresponding activities, and a student survey to guide learning. NAMEPA has had success in creating and disseminating similar high-quality materials including videos, posters, brochures,

FIGURE 7.4 BRIDGEPORT, CT—Students learn about marine debris during a workshop led by NAMEPA.

and more on subjects including sustainable fisheries, marine debris, ocean acidification, climate change, marine exploration, and the maritime industry and heritage. NAMEPA educational materials have been widely distributed throughout the United States, the Caribbean, and throughout the Americas.

Some of NAMEPA's other recent programs and activities include *participation in and promotion of beach cleanups* nationwide, including participation in International Coastal Cleanup Day 2014 in San Francisco, CA; *sponsorship of a cadet award* for commitment to marine environment protection; *sponsorship of an annual science contest* among harbor schools, maritime academies, and universities relevant to marine environment protection, in partnership with the American Salvage Association; *sponsorship of an annual children's drawing contest* with a theme of environmental protection in partnership with The Jason Project and the US Coast Guard, reaching 2.5 million students; and *development and distribution of a MARPOL/marine science training handbook* and distribution to seafarers and recreational boaters in the United States (Figures 7.4 through 7.6).

OTHER ACTIVITIES

In 2015, NAMEPA—together with partners at the US Power Squadrons and marinas all over the country—will organize the first annual Clean Marina Day to take place in June. This event will help boaters get important information about the environmental and safety precautions necessary to ensure that US coastal waterways stay clean and healthy for all to enjoy for generations to come.

Also, in 2015, NAMEPA will release a brand new Marine Environment Learning Guide, new short films on leaders in conservation, policy and management of coastal and marine resources and sustainability in the maritime industry, host seminars and discussions on current marine environmental issues, present at national educational and environmental conferences, and lead workshops for groups of all ages on all our Marine Environmental Education material all over the United States.

FIGURE 7.5   PENNFIELD BEACH, Fairfield, CT—Students learn about the harmful effects of marine debris and pollution by participating in a NAMEPA-led beach cleanup—and make some very unusual finds.

FIGURE 7.6   MEXICO—In honor of North American World Maritime Day on October 22, 2014, NAMEPA visited with our new chapter in Mexico and met with some fantastic student marine environmental conservation enthusiasts.

7.4 SECURITY VULNERABILITIES IMPACTING LOGISTICS, TRADE, AND TRANSPORT NETWORKS

There is a number of different security threats that may potentially harm the logistics, trade, and transport networks and, as an extension, distress the private and private partnerships' structures, resources, and connectivity. While the many faces of security have been extensively discussed in Chapter 2 (e.g., sea piracy, illegitimate trade, and transport,

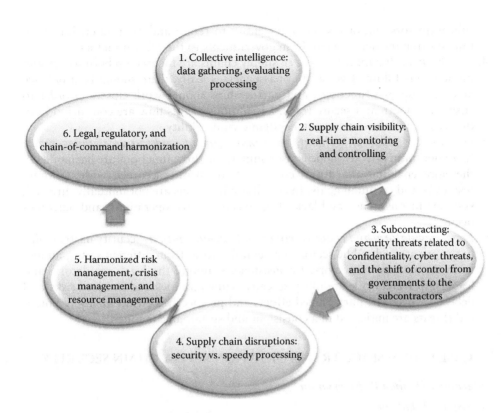

FIGURE 7.7 Security vulnerabilities impacting logistics, trade, and transport networks. (From the author.)

cargo theft, and so on), this section classifies the types of security vulnerabilities that could appear in a typical supply chain or logistics network. These risks or systemic vulnerabilities are also reflected in Figure 7.7.

7.4.1 Security Vulnerabilities

1. *Collective intelligence*: This element entails data gathering, evaluating, and processing. Based upon the principle that the output's quality and accuracy directly depends on the input, intelligence-gathering partnerships should safeguard their data-collection process from cyber security, compromised or inconsistent data, or information leaks.
2. *Supply chain visibility*: which pertains to integration of supply chain activities. Lack of visibility creates segmented systems and problematic data sharing among partners. When present and consistent, visibility can facilitate the smooth functions and operations throughout the entire supply chain, and enable the real time monitoring and controlling. Most important, it may reveal systemic vulnerabilities, security threats and safeguard mechanisms of the entire system in real time.
3. *Subcontracting*: This security vulnerability is also related to confidentiality and cyber threats. Moreover, in certain cases, the federal agreement with the

subcontractors authorizes the latter entity to retain and manage critical data, thus shifting the data control from governments to the subcontractors.

4. *Supply chain disruptions*: Modern supply chains are focused on both secure and uninterrupted flow of goods and passengers. Ideally, there should be a balance among these two functions, and partnerships should work closely in order to ensure a smooth and secure trade. Disruptions of this flow are considered both the reason and the outcome of a systemic vulnerability.

5. *Harmonized risk management, crisis management, and resource management*: In an optimum private/public consortium, these three functions are harmonized, therefore enabling all entities concerned to operate securely, with optimum resources and common goals. In case these functions are not mutually directed, systemic inconsistency and lack of balanced actions, operations, and outcomes occur.

6. *Legal, regulatory, and chain-of-command harmonization*: Security partnerships in the private and public sectors may entail entities from different states, municipalities, nations, or sectors. Inconsistencies among the legal, regulatory, and leadership framework are likely to cause vulnerabilities and increase risks and delays. Conversely, harmonized efforts and perspectives ensure that any potential threats are mitigated in a consistent and sustainable manner.

CASE STUDY: SPACE TRANSPORTATION SUPPLY CHAIN SECURITY

Interview: Stephen R. Merryman

Aerospace Engineer

Space transportation involves highly interdependent resources and processes working along multiple paths. The space transportation supply chain can be subject to many of the same security issues as any terrestrial supply chain. Indeed, most space transportation networks include participation by conventional terrestrial assets at some point in their deployment. There are, however, some unique aspects of space transportation that lead to extreme sensitivity to supply chain disruptions and other security issues. This work addresses some of the characteristics of these processes and their associated vulnerabilities when considered as part of an overall supply chain framework.

INTRODUCTION

In its simplest form, a space transportation architecture can be treated as a construction project. A customer wanting to fly a satellite approaches a launch provider and negotiates a service that will place the satellite into a desired orbit. The launch provider will procure an expendable launch vehicle (LV), assemble it at the launch site, and integrate the customer's satellite onto it. The launch provider will then certify the readiness of the vehicle, while the customer certifies the readiness of the satellite within strict demarcations of responsibility. Then the satellite is launched placing it into an agreed-upon orbit at which time the customer will take over its operations. The launch vehicle itself will be destroyed in the operation. The advent of reusable space vehicles along with complex human and robotic space missions to earth orbit and beyond raises the complexity of a space architecture with two-way flights and on-orbit assembly nodes that add to the security concern.

The concepts of integrity, availability, and confidentiality commonly used in the information security[1] discipline are useful for developing an understanding of the supply chain security issues that apply to space transportation and can be shown to be among the dominant concerns in the field. What follows is a description of the services and assets supplied by a space transportation network leading to a discussion of the security concepts that apply (Andress 2011).

CASE STUDY: THE SPACE SHUTTLE

When the Space Shuttle (hereinafter referred to as the "STS") ended its last mission, the United States lost a multicapable vehicle that will more than likely never be replicated. This is because the STS provided several different services with one orbiting vehicle. These included

a. Crew transportation to and from the low earth orbit (LEO)
b. A construction platform offering robotic crane operations assisted by spacewalking astronauts
c. Delivery to orbit of free flying satellites including checkout and deployment and vehicle utilities supporting health and status monitoring, electrical power, and thermal control
d. The capture, repair, and return back to orbit or to earth of satellites
e. Support services to the International Space Station (ISS) in the form of resupply, maintenance, and return to earth of components, experiments, and payloads
f. Use of the STS orbiter as an orbiting laboratory itself with the Spacelab missions
g. Propulsion for reboost and orbit shaping for the Hubble Space Telescope

With the exception of weather delays, at least up until the STS-51L accident in 1986, the STS was the most reliable launch vehicle in the world for getting satellites into orbit. Crewed space vehicles by design and fault tolerance are inherently more reliable than uncrewed vehicles. Various government and commercial satellite users gravitated to the STS as a launch provider in lieu of the traditional expendable rockets.

So useful and reliable was the STS that the *Challenger* accident in January 1986 rocked the satellite community that had grown dependent upon it for its transportation needs. This led to the development of the Atlas V and Delta IV Evolved Expendable Launch Vehicles (EELVs) for the uncrewed carry of payloads as a replacement for aging rockets and as an alternative to using the STS for these tasks (Zapata 2008).

The use of the STS for launching commercial satellites ended at that time, deemed too great a risk to crewed flight, as did the proposed transportation of planetary probes with cryogenic liquid fueled stages in the shuttle payload bay.

Throughout the rest of its career, the STS dominated in the construction and logistics chain for the ISS and other high-priority missions, such as the servicing and repair of the Hubble Space Telescope, SpaceHab lab module missions, and Mir space station rendezvous missions. Reliance on the STS for these sort of missions came to a hiatus with the loss of the *Columbia* in February 2003.

The STS experience demonstrates the danger of putting all of a supply line into a single transport asset or class. Such dependencies on availability represent another security vulnerability. This is similar to the issue in terrestrial transportation when a specific aircraft type is grounded due to an accident or incident. However, in the case of aircraft, the cargo to be transported is on standard containers or pallets and is easily accommodated by alternate types that are in service. There is revenue loss to the carrier, but the customers have alternate means that are readily available. When a single space shuttle had a problem, the entire fleet was subject to being grounded until the problem was identified and fixed or at least ruled out as a concern for the other shuttles.

While the STS was originally hoped to offer an airline-like form of routine access to LEO, the lessons learned suggest a system that, while very capable, was also relatively fragile and extremely labor-intensive in its operation and processing. During its commercial phase, communications satellites were being carried at freight rates that were lower than the expendable rocket competition and also may not have been reflective of the actual costs being borne by the government for the services being supplied. Despite fanciful notions about routine human space flight, it remains a very risky undertaking that requires strict discipline treating each mission as unique and also maintaining considerable budgetary margin to address unforeseen problems.

Elements of the Space Transportation Supply Chain

A space exploration mission takes years of planning, and over that time span, funding sources can turn on and off, and be redirected or repurposed, and the resulting stated direction and goals can evolve at the expense of inadvertently deprioritizing activities that may suddenly surface down the road as availability and supply issues.

This discussion will examine different assets in a space architecture along with their attributes, interdependencies, and vulnerabilities. It is not the goal of this work to develop a supply chain model or an optimal configuration. Rather, it is desired to provide the reader with an understanding of the characteristics of the various assets, their limitations, and their role in supporting the end-to-end architecture: It is desirable to have redundant transportation assets that are compatible with the cargo to be transported and the shared facilities required for processing but with as few common critical components with competitive vehicles as possible.

1. The *ground segment* consists of all of the ground-based systems required to support launch vehicle and spacecraft/payload operations, prelaunch test and checkout, and recovery. Typically, it includes all of the network and data communication facilities, the command and control systems, and tracking stations. In some cases, the simulation and training facilities required to prepare the crew and operators for the mission are also included in the ground segment. The ground segment may be a long lead item in the successful execution of a space mission and in some cases can be the cause of delays in the mission. In one case, a satellite program was delayed significantly due to unavailability of the proposed ground control system required for its operation. At least one shuttle launch experienced a delay due to a control center issue.

Ground systems are susceptible to all of the cyber-security issues of any large-scale real-time system that would impact their availability, integrity, or confidentiality. Often incorporating commercial off-the-shelf products and subject to their release and update schedules, these systems can be compromised by faulty updates or incompatible versions of code embedded in different components. Since these elements uplink commands to the spacecraft, they are of the highest criticality in the command and control structure of the architecture. They can also include some of the non-real-time tools and applications used by flight planners to establish timelines and maneuver the vehicle to planned altitude orientations and trajectories. An error in these calculations that is not caught prior to uplinking commands based on them can result in loss of a mission.

The extent of distribution of the control center functions, along with the adoption of object-oriented programming techniques in the development of their software, can present challenges to replicating undesirable behaviors for troubleshooting and getting systems to function repeatably.

Similarly, flaws in the assumptions made in the development of simulation software can result in a lack of understanding by the crew or operator trainees on the behavior of the system being modeled and result in "negative training" that can affect operational safety.

The security of communications going to and from the ground segment is obviously necessary to prevent potential takeover of the vehicle by an outside entity spoofing the control center. It is also of particular importance in crewed missions to allow confidentiality of discussions between crewmembers and medical personnel on the ground. Early shuttle missions were letting out some of these communications to the point where crewmembers' medical conditions became public knowledge in violation of federal law.

The availability of the ground segment can also be impacted by anything in the physical facility, such as power loss (ordinarily backed up with an uninterruptible power supply) or natural disaster affecting one or another ground station or the control center itself. Backup control centers maintained by international partners can help to mitigate this hazard.

The security concerns of the ground segment, then, are similar to the integrity vulnerabilities of any large-scale integrated information system. Software errors can compromise the system's integrity. Cyber threats can attack the system in such a way as to deny it to the mission user at a critical time. Failure of the system's firewalls can allow sensitive data to be accessed and compromised by unauthorized entities. Uplinked commands and data could also be compromised in such a way as to seriously endanger a mission in progress.

2. The *launch element* is the vehicle and associated infrastructure that carries the payload into orbit. Expendable launch vehicles carrying satellites constitute the majority of all launch assets. Much of the supply chain of interest here is primarily on the ground and relates to the transactions required to get all of the components of the integrated launch stack together. The primary purpose of the launch vehicle is to provide uplift to a payload. It

typically also provides communications, power, and data services to the payload during mated operations.

The launch element includes the ground facilities used to assemble, check out, and launch the vehicle. The launch element is susceptible to all of the vulnerabilities and malfunctions that are known to happen with any rocket-propelled vehicle. The sizing of the launch vehicle for a given mission is often a trade between the number of launches required to achieve the goals of the mission with the additional complexity of using rendezvous and on-orbit assembly of components uplifted on different launches against the vulnerability of losing the entire project in one launch failure. It may be desirable to break down a large payload into separately launched components such that the loss of any one component in a launch failure would not impact a program as severely as the loss of a single billion-dollar payload on a single launch vehicle.

The availability of a launch vehicle can be impacted by accidents or incidents that result in grounding of the vehicle family until the cause is known. Loss of one type of EELV that uses a similar component to another type might rule out the flight of all launch vehicles using that component until it is ruled out as a cause of the loss. Different vehicles that have commonality with each other also suffer from the same issue: different expendable rockets that might use the same engine in one of their stages would suffer the same sort of constraint, with the failure of one rocket grounding the others until the common elements are ruled out as root cause of the failure.

It is desirable from a payload owner standpoint for enough standardization in mating and adaptor fixtures to allow multiple launch vehicle types to be used for a given payload.

Each shuttle accident was followed by a long period of time (32 months in the case of STS-51L and 30 months in the case of STS-107) during which the STS was unavailable to support any ongoing missions. Considerable re-planning and workaround was necessary after the *Columbia* loss because there was a crewed ISS in orbit at the time dependent on the STS and Russian *Progress* vehicles for resupply. Conservation of consumables onboard the ISS became a significant issue. A longer-term issue was the replacement and repair of some of onboard electronic components known as orbital replacement units (ORUs) on the ISS that had originally been procured assuming a supply line that had an STS to get them up to the ISS and back down to earth for scheduled maintenance. This was factored in to the original production run of that hardware assuming that they would be returned by the STS for repair and refurbishment on the ground. There were not enough spares on the ground to accommodate the planned supply chain. Certain items that had been designed for transport onboard the shuttle had to be adapted for accommodation by alternate vehicles.

3. The *orbiting element* can be a satellite, a crewed spacecraft, a crewed space station, an orbiting depot, an orbital transfer vehicle, or a payload within a crewed spacecraft. It can be a customer or provider of services to other elements of the architecture. A data relay satellite might be required to provide continuous communication links with the ground element for other orbiting elements. A transfer vehicle is used to move the payload from one established

orbit to another. It could simply be an upper stage of the launch vehicle that is not used until the launch vehicle has already established an initial orbit. Conversely, the transfer vehicle might spend its life on orbit rendezvousing with other satellites and providing propulsive orbit shaping services to maintain their proper orbits. The OTV might, in turn, rendezvous with depots on orbit to take on propellants to continue its mission and service other satellites.

A satellite is typically placed in its destination orbit by the launch element, although it may also supply its own propulsion or transfer stage for its destination orbit once free of the launch vehicle. Once in position and checked out, it is turned over to the end user who may be a commercial or government customer. Further support to the satellite is via the ground segment.

A crewed spacecraft may rendezvous and dock with another orbiting element or conduct operations by itself. Control of the crewed spacecraft can be by uplink from the ground element or directly by the crew. The crewed spacecraft may also be carrying and operating payload experiments on behalf of a ground customer. Missions that use the transportation vehicle itself as an operational lab, such as the STS Spacelab missions, are a useful interim measure in the absence of a crewed station or dedicated lab. However, these scenarios also remove what is essentially a transport vehicle from the logistical flow all the time they are functioning as a lab.

The design and equipment layout of the orbiting element should also reflect a sparing and maintenance strategy that is as flexible as possible and capable of using any supporting launch or repair elements that are likely to be encountered. Once in place, an orbiting platform such as a space station depends on support from transportation assets. Any disruption on the availability of the transportation vehicles can have a severe impact on the long-term viability of the platform. Placement of standard grapple fixtures on satellites to allow their retrieval and repair by a shuttle equipped with a remote manipulator system was proven on the STS program. Standardization of tools and fasteners used for attaching external equipment by EVA crewmembers can facilitate maintenance across interfaces between different national elements.

4. The *return element* brings the downmass cargo or crew or both back to earth. It can be a space probe landing with parachutes in the desert following a sample gathering mission to deep space. It can be any of several different crew module families landing by parachute. It could be a rescue vehicle or a winged lifting body that lands on a runway. It is also a significant element of the repair and maintenance supply chain allowing the return and repair of components that may not be repaired on orbit. It is also important in this discussion to note that not all resupply vehicles are capable of reentry. Expendable rockets are uplift only. The Russian *Progress* resupply vehicles for the ISS burn up on reentry but can be used in that manner for waste disposal. The Japanese *HOPE* and former European ATV supply vehicles are also disposable with no return capability. At this time, the SpacEx *Dragon* module is the only resupply vehicle that can safely carry payloads back to earth. The Air Force X-37 orbiter is another carrier that can return for landing on a runway, but its payload handling characteristics are unknown. All

crewed missions require an assured return element, whether it is a shuttle, a Soyuz, or other reentry-capable vehicle. This can also include the prepositioning of backup return vehicles on earth that can be flown up into orbit on relatively short notice: In 1973, the Apollo Command and Service Module (CSM) used to take the crew up to the Skylab space station encountered a thruster malfunction that resulted in a loss of redundancy that might preclude safe return of the crew to earth. The follow-on mission CSM and Saturn IB launch vehicle was prepositioned and kit made available to take some of the interior lockers out and install extra seats to allow it to fly up to the Skylab with two crewmembers and return with all five, should it be necessary. It was not necessary, but the philosophy was followed on subsequent Skylab missions with a dedicated CSM and launch vehicle available. It was also used for the Apollo Soyuz Test Project (ASTP) mission in 1975.

A similar prepositioning strategy was undertaken toward the end of the STS program after the *Columbia* accident. This launch on demand strategy would have been invoked if the initial shuttle experienced a malfunction that would preclude its ability to reenter the atmosphere and land. In such a case, it would dock with the ISS and wait for the LOD shuttle that would be the next shuttle in the flow on an expedited schedule.

Services of the Space Transportation Supply Chain

Services involve interactions between elements of the space transportation architecture and can be carried out by different elements. These include

1. *Upmass.* The supply of payload to a destination node, be it a position on orbit, a space station, or a heavenly body. Payload mass is the primary driver in sizing the launch vehicle, and the launch elements transact heavily with the ground segment throughout the delivery of upmass. Experience has shown, however, that the complexity of the payload and potential vehicle accommodations have additional impacts that need to be accounted for. "Cost/Pound" is a traditional metric that is used to estimate costs of uplift, but consideration needs to be given to the electrical, thermal, and communications requirements to support the payload along with any payload-specific mounting requirements, adapters, and analysis. Early shuttle missions that carried commercial satellites to orbit presented difficulties accounting for costs due to the satellites that were instead being borne by the shuttle program budget. Services provided by the launch vehicle to the upmass include electrical power, thermal control, vibration isolation, downlink of payload status data via the launch vehicle communication system, power transfer from launch vehicle power to internal payload power, checkout, and deployment. The supply of upmass to the orbiting element is contingent on the availability of the launch element and is subject to all of the launch element vulnerabilities listed above.

   The planning of large-scale on-orbit construction projects necessitates some assumptions about the vehicle types used to provide upmass. If certain components of the project are of a size or shape that they can only be accommodated by a single launch vehicle family, they can represent a significant constraint on construction should the family be rendered unavailable. It is desirable to keep payloads as "launch vehicle agnostic" as possible to preclude this limitation and also to potentially allow enough competition between competing launch providers to negotiate reasonable rates.

2. *Downmass*. Return to earth of previously lifted payloads, recovered scientific samples, or newly manufactured components. This capability plays a critical role in maintenance and upkeep activities and is a fundamental leg of the in-space manufacturing supply chain. The shuttle offered considerable downmass that has yet to be equaled by any other vehicle. There is also some interest in suborbital logistics that would involve vehicles that ascend to very high altitudes for possible microgravity studies and manufacturing processes and then return. Traditional sounding rockets can fit this model, as can the *Virgin Galactic Spaceship 2* and the Blue Origins New Shephard rocket, which ascend at suborbital speeds to high altitude before returning for a landing. Downmass retrieval can also have confidentiality issues when landing in the ocean or in areas not under national control of the payload owners. Ocean landing via parachute may require an additional extension of the supply chain across international boundaries compared with, say, landing a vehicle on land within the country of origin. In addition to the criticality of downmass services in the two-way maintenance cycle, downmass has also been shown to be an important parameter in the control of stowage onboard the orbiting element of an architecture (Evans et al. 2006).

3. *Crew time*. Interaction between the crew and the payload or supply commodity is critical enough that it needs to be considered a separate service in and of itself. It is a scheduled deliverable service and drives many other activities. The human crew can assemble via spacewalk (EVA) complex structures with the assistance of semirobotic cranes (such as the Shuttle's Remote Manipulator System) operated in turn by other crew members. Crew members can react to unusual situations and synthesize solutions to problems in ways that uncrewed vehicles cannot. These crew interactions with the payload require extensive preparation and may need to be planned months or even years in advance along a separate supply line that involves scheduled training, the manufacture of payload mockups, and extensive rehearsals to establish the exact timeline and tool requirements. The seeming routine scenes of EVA suited astronauts maneuvering themselves and working on satellites and ISS components are the end result of a long supply chain that includes planning an activity, procuring and building the simulation tools and procedures required for training for the activity, and fitting the activity into the flight timeline within all of the other planned activities.

4. *Data*. The primary mission of a probe or scientific spacecraft is to make observations and return data. While not the sort of nuts and bolts element one would expect in a logistics network, the data themselves are a product and should be managed in such a way as to not impact the vehicle data stream used by the vehicle providers for their operations. This was somewhat of a problem early in the STS program when a lot service costs that were in direct support of payload activities wound up being borne by

the transportation vehicle. It is also important to avoid interleaving payload data with vehicle data in ways that might necessitate changes to the vehicle software to accommodate a payload. Software changes on space vehicles require a detailed scheduled development and checkout process that involves multiple levels of test and verification. While data and telemetry involve a lot of handshakes and exchanges between vehicles and nodes, it is unclear whether the traditional supply chain model would apply to these sort of transactions. Security vulnerability related to data integrity and confidentiality needs to be addressed. Confidentiality is necessary not only to protect proprietary information but also to guard personal information of crewmembers such as medical or similarly sensitive material. Integrity of data is an issue because it affects the utility of observational data products downlinked to the ground but also relates to the potential corruption of vehicle commands that are uplinked from the ground.

5. *Replenishment*. Resupply of consumables such as propellant, water, food, raw materials, supplies, and spare parts. Replenishment can be via direct launch or by orbiting depot or prepositioned cache. Within the replenishment process, maintenance and upkeep represent considerable vulnerability to supply chain breakages and lack of availability. In the case of the ISS, the lack of a reliable downmass capability for returning ORUs to earth at the end of the STS program required new strategies to be developed allowing the crews to perform intermediate-level maintenance on ORUs onboard the ISS that had been designed for terrestrial depot-level maintenance. Kits for repairing things on orbit with instructions sent up from the ground along with the development of procedures that were compatible with the safety and habitability requirements onboard the ISS were necessary.

6. *Security*. Security itself can be considered as one of the services that the user may require of a space transportation provider. The ability to launch a payload for a government or industry customer and protect the confidentiality of classified information or proprietary processes is a basic necessity. Commingling of classified payloads/missions with unclassified transportation assets presents challenges in protecting confidentiality. Over the life of the STS program, 11 missions with classified payloads were flown. These missions posed challenges to confidentiality because they needed to be conducted in such a manner as to avoid disclosing their true purpose while using unclassified assets for transportation and much of the operations of the launch vehicle. New control center philosophies had to be developed with remote centers taking over operations during sensitive parts of the mission that were firewalled away from all of the support and personnel required for normal vehicle operations. Meanwhile, preparing for the launch of these missions required nominal unclassified products and vehicles to be prepared along the usual timelines. It is difficult to conceal a space shuttle launch, but in some cases, even the precise launch times were kept secret long enough to disallow foreign entities from deploying tracking assets. Extra attention also had to be paid potential revealing associations of otherwise unclassified information that, when juxtaposed, might compromise confidentiality. The crewed nature of these missions undoubtedly

contributed to success, but it also added layers of potential compromises that needed to be planned around to assure that no aspects of the payloads the crew or ground operations were training for would be divulged. In the post-shuttle era, increasing reliance on commercial launch vehicles by government agencies will present similar vulnerabilities that will need to be addressed. Containerization of payloads to preclude knowledge of their mass, dimensions, and physical appearance can help. Minimizing interfaces of all kinds between the payload and the vehicle that might allow outside entities to determine vehicle resource demand would also need to be performed, along with tight controls over the mission planning and final orbital placement of the payload. Limiting communication and data paths between the payload and the vehicle make sense not just from a cost perspective but from a security perspective as well (Cassut 2009).

The projected availability of all of these services needs to be taken into consideration early in the design phase of a space project. Major components to be carried and assembled in space must be sized in such a way that their dimensions and mass can be accommodated by the vehicle assets to be used. The ISS, for example, was designed assuming the STS would be available for its construction and logistical flow, and the components and ORUs were sized and procured accordingly. The disruption of the ISS supply chain from the 2003 shuttle accident and later removal of the shuttle from the downmass portion of the supply chain had significant effects that are still being felt.

International Partners

Teaming with international partners in a space architecture adds complexity to the venture and undoubtedly elevates the level of bureaucratic overhead. It effectively lengthens the supply chain. Having an international partner in the critical path of a project can raise availability issues that are not just technical but also diplomatic and political. Following the failure of a launch vehicle carrying an American-built satellite on a Long March rocket from the People's Republic of China, a US company, acting as part of a review committee on behalf of underwriters, inadvertently sent part of an executive summary of a review of the PRC's accident report to China. The result was a protracted criminal investigation by the US government culminating years later in a multimillion dollar fine paid by the company in question. Consider that under the US International Traffic in Arms Regulations (ITAR), a spacecraft has traditionally been considered a munition, and all technical information related to it treated under the same export controls that would apply to trade in weapons (*Space Daily* 2002).

Efforts are underway to change the US Munitions List to put commercial satellite exports under Commerce Department rather than State Department control. An international space station composed of modules developed by different countries requires firm demarcations of responsibility at the interfaces of the different modules. These interfaces are both technical hardware-related and organizational, leading to more complexity in the implementation than if it were just being done as a domestic effort. The transfer of space hardware from one country to another for integration, test, or actual launch carries the same sort of customs concerns as any other form of international shipping and requires all of the applicable export licensing and declarations. An international space station can almost be looked upon as a collection of agreements flying in formation (US Department of Commerce 2015).

Dependence on foreign suppliers for critical items needed by one of the elements can also lead to availability concerns due to international conflicts. If a country's space vehicle is designed to be lifted by another country's rocket engines, as is currently the case with at least two domestic US carriers, any discord that affects that supply line will directly affect the availability of the vehicle to the supply chain. All sorts of changes can occur in the relationships between partner nations over the duration of a space program (Morring 2014).

Obsolescence

Anyone who has worked on space systems for any length of time is familiar with the comparisons made between onboard computer processing power and that which is available to commercial and consumer users on the ground. Modern electronics are very rapidly changing, and it is not at all unusual for a new spacecraft on its first flight to be equipped with systems that might be considered at least a generation behind the state of the art for an office machine. Part of the reason for this is because space systems, when designed, must select their supporting components not from what is available at the computer store but from what is available and demonstrated to be safe and reliable for use onboard aircraft. Moreover, since it takes 10–15 years to field a new military aircraft (20 years in some recent cases), a spacecraft electronics system could easily be 20 years behind the latest technology available for terrestrial systems at the beginning of its life. Unique aspects of the spaceflight environment related to radiation, thermal, and vibration pose additional certification constraints. Obsolescence can contribute to availability problems in the space supply chain. Since many of these components are manufactured in very low volumes for unique customers, the uncertainty in the ability of industry to support the manufacture of obsolete technology once it is deployed onboard must also be taken into consideration when defining the supply line. If a particular electronics box has been upgraded by its manufacturer using new technology, it may affect the certification of the onboard system in which it is installed, requiring an extensive review process before it can be implemented. There is a similar issue with any commercial off-the-shelf software packages onboard that might be subject to updates. A long-term space program must be able to maintain traceability to its baseline configuration and plan on spare supply support over decades of existence in potentially uneven funding climates that can change with political and economic winds.

7.5 CONCLUSIONS

The various elements and services of the space transportation supply chain have been discussed along with their vulnerabilities. Space transportation can suffer immediate supply chain disruptions due to accidents, and longer-term disruptions due to reassessment of the utility of assets after accidents. With a heavy reliance on information systems, space transportation assets are particularly vulnerable to cyber threats that can compromise the integrity and confidentiality of their operation up to and including the loss of a vehicle.

The ability to carry payloads down from orbit is an often-overlooked aspect of the supply chain that is vital to the maintenance of a two-way sparing philosophy and for managing stowage aboard on-orbit assets.

Of major importance in ensuring the availability of assets for launching payloads is the maintenance of a fleet of robust dissimilar launch vehicles that can accommodate standardized payloads without modification and with as little commonality of critical components between competing systems as is practicable. Maintaining a healthy supply chain requires multiple transport vehicle types so that the failure of any one will not seriously impact any assets of the supply chain dependent on resupply. The less a payload depends on a given launch vehicle type or class, the better. It is also desirable to limit payload requirements that may require vehicle modifications or scars or any software updates to vehicle computers to the greatest extent possible. The interleaving of payload data with standard operational vehicle data should be minimized.

Commingling of classified payloads with unclassified vehicles presents security concerns with associated mitigations that need to be performed to prevent compromising the confidentiality of the payload. Commingling government assets with commercial assets may exacerbate the security concern and needs to be accounted for.

Multinational teaming introduces a high level of complexity into the overall supply chain that may threaten the availability of critical services due to nontechnical reasons.

Space programs occur over a very long time span from the initial concept, to buildup, operational life, and end. Over such a long time, many subassemblies and components that were late in the state of the art at launch will be well obsolete toward the middle of the program. This needs to be considered in sparing philosophy and maintenance and repair. It also couples with downmass availability and assessment of the levels of maintenance allowable onboard.

Over the time span of a program, relationships with partners can change and with them availability of critical components. The nature and goals of a program can change over time due to political pressures and with these pressures the relative priorities of budget items. This can contribute to supply chain disruptions as critical spares are lowered in priority and not procured in a timely manner.

INTERVIEWS AND CASE STUDIES

Bielecki, Thaddeus M., Assistant Master, Dredge Potter (US Army Corps of Engineers), Case Study: Public/Private Partnerships and Risks to Infrastructure.

Lyden-Kluss, Carleen, Co-Founder and Executive Director NAMEPA North American Marine Environment Protection Association, Case Study: Public/Private Partnership for Environmental Security Threats.

Merryman, Stephen R., Aerospace Engineer, The Space Shuttle, Case Study: Space Transportation Supply Chain Security.

REFERENCES

Andress, J. and Rogers, R. (eds.), 2011. *The Basics of Information Security,* Elsevier Inc.
Cassut, M., 2009. Secret space shuttles, Air&Space Smithsonian, August. Available at http://www.airspacemag.com/space/secret-space-shuttles-35318554/?no-ist.

Evans, W.A. et al., 2006. Logistics lessons learned in NASA spaceflight, NASA/TP
    -2006-214203, May. Available at http://strategic.mit.edu/spacelogistics/pdf/NASA
    -TP-2006-214203.pdf.
Morring, F. Jr., 2014. Replacing Russian-made atlas, Antares engines would take four years,
    Aviation Week and Space Technology, May 20, 2014. Available at http://aviationweek
    .com/space/replacing-russian-made-atlas-antares-engines-would-take-four-years.
Space Daily, 2002. Loral and US government settle 1996 Chinese launch matter, January
    11. Available at http://www.spacedaily.com/news/china-02b.html.
U.S. Department of Commerce, Export control reform, Available at http://export.gov
    /ecr/index.asp.
Zapata, E., 2008. A review of costs of US evolved expendable launch vehicles (EELV),
    February, 2008. Available at http://www.weboflife.nasa.gov/shuttle/nexgen/Nexgen
    _Downloads/EELV_Costs_Paper_r2a.pdf.

CHAPTER **8**

Security Technology and Innovation

> If you think technology can solve all your security problems, then you don't understand the problems, and you don't understand the technology.
>
> **Bruce Schneier**
> *American Cryptographer*

8.1 INNOVATIVE TECHNOLOGY AND ACCESSIBILITY: A TWO-EDGED SWORD

Globalization has increased the capabilities of global trade and logistics networks, but at the same time, it has exposed our supply chains to a multitude of risks, both natural and man-made. While the public and private sectors adopt a number of security regulations, risk assessment, and analysis protocols, technology is the catalyst to prevent, deter, and recuperate potential security threats. For this reason, modern security professionals need to assume a proactive stance in order to see the big picture; identify risks, gaps, and potential vulnerabilities in the entire supply chain; and finally avert or mitigate those risks. Innovative technologies have become a mainstream business trend and requirement that are supported to combat security threats.

Nevertheless, technologies can be as useful and as efficient as the humans who utilize them: satellite-based technologies such as Global Positioning System (GPS) or Automatic Identification System (AIS) are used to facilitate global trade and transport, yet the same tools are used to navigate criminal groups involved in illegitimate trade and transport, as well as terrorists. Fast-speed boats with powerful engines are used in the maritime industry for search-and-rescue (S&R) purposes, yet similar technologies are used by sea pirates to hijack ships and capture or kill hostages in exchange for ransom fees.

Furthermore, the efficiency of equipment heavily depends upon the security professionals. At a first stage, it is the professionals who design, calibrate, and maintain high-tech security equipment.

At a second stage, it is the security specialists who use them for surveillance, recognition, and intelligence purposes. What the industry needs are motivated and well-trained security individuals who are passionate about their jobs and are hopefully neither complacent nor overly dependent upon technologies nor discouraged by the overwhelming volume of persons, cargoes, and areas that need to be monitored.

Very simply put, a security guard may be checking upon a surveillance monitor for months, with no serious incident, and yet it only takes a minute when their back is turned for a major security incident to occur.

8.1.1 Classification of Transportation Security Technologies

Arguably, we live in the day and age of technological abundance, where inventors design "multipurpose" products, with the goal to satisfy multiple industries and market segments. This is also true in the case of logistics and transportation security:

- Satellite-based technologies are used by governments to locate, monitor, and control drones, yet their spin-off technology products can be used for commercial and security purposes, i.e., to track not only containerized cargoes but also vessels' trade routes in the middle of the ocean.
- Iris-scanning technologies that soldiers have been using to identify terrorists in the combat zone are now applied at airports and border-crossing checkpoints by border patrol agents trying to identify criminals involved in contraband, cargo theft, or illegitimate human trafficking.

Based on the multipurpose nature of technologies used for security and commercial purposes, the classification of technologies in this chapter has been a challenging task.

For the sake of efficiency, this section commences with a concise reference to other researchers' classifications followed by the new classification proposed hereby by the author of this book.

Rice and Caniato (2003) of MIT have classified technologies according to

1. The level of response as
    a. *Basic*: for routine passenger and cargo checking and
    b. *Advanced*: for suspicious or targeted individuals and cargoes or persons of interest.
2. The scope of security as
    a. Physical security (gates, guards, background checks),
    b. Information security (hardware, software, audits), and
    c. Freight security (inspections, regulations and standards, cargo seals).

In the United States, the Transportation Security Administration (TSA) distinguishes surfacing technologies to be able to stand above developing threats. TSA employs state-of-the art technological innovation to efficiently screen travelers, checked luggage, and air freight. It furthermore performs careful analysis of intelligence to figure out the optimum methods of deploying the federal and industry innovative security resources at airport terminals, hub ports, and trade routes for sea–land–air. TSA implements a variety of advanced technologies in order to ensure secure trade and transport. These typically include

a. Credential authentication technologies
b. Biometric technologies
c. Threat image projection (TIP)
d. Electronic boarding pass

    e. Scanning devices for bottled liquids
    f. Explosive-detection technologies
    g. Explosive trace–detection (ETD) systems
    h. Imaging technologies (TSA 2014a,b)

   Taking into consideration the above classifications, and the security and commercial technologies that are duly described in this chapter, we are proposing the following classification, which appears in the following table:

    a. Screening technologies,
    b. Reconnaissance technologies, and
    c. Intelligence technologies

Classification of Technologies for Supply Chain and Transport Security

  1. Screening and countersurveillance systems

This technology pertains to
    a. Visual inspection
    b. 24/7 CCTV (closed-circuit camera systems)
    c. Scanning devices for bottled liquids
    d. Explosives detection technologies
    e. Explosives track detection systems
    f. Security screening of people, premises, and cargoes
Based on surveillance data and footage that become available, the next process pertains to recognition.

  2. Reconnaissance systems

For centuries, visual inspection has been the basis of recognition, before innovative technologies were utilized, such as
    a. Imaging technologies
    b. Threat image projection
    c. Electronic boarding pass
    d. Credential and ID authentication technologies
    e. Biometric technologies: face recognition, fingerprints to verify that photo IDs or fingerprints match with people
    f. Identify suspicious behaviors within a monitored environment
Based on the findings of recognition and surveillance technologies, the next technological process pertains to recognition.

  3. Intelligence technologies have been designed to gather and process data not only from both surveillance and reconnaissance systems but also from other data available such as
    a. Cyber data through satellite, web-based, cloud-based, cellular, social media, or other electronic sources
    b. Public records; background checks; criminal records; immigration, taxation, corporate; trade and transportation records
    c. Surveillance and recognition data are evaluated and/or cross-examined with the above two information sources, i.e., cyber data and federal records
Intelligence technologies help collect and assess primary and secondary data about the security offenders' patterns and habit in order to avert security threats and combat illegitimate actions.

Source: Burns, M., Estimating the impact of maritime security: Financial tradeoffs between security and efficiency. *Journal of Transportation Security*, December, Volume 6, Issue 4, pp. 329–338, May 31, 2013, Springer, 2013.

8.1.2 Security Technologies as "Force Multipliers"

In physics, force multiplication occurs when the load force applied is larger than the energy force exerted. Therefore, the force multiplier (FM) principle describes a factor that significantly spikes, or multiplies, the performance of a person, a group, or a technology used.

The term is also used in the military to describe a function that, when applied and utilized by a military force, considerably enhances the battle outcome of that power and therefore magnifies the likelihood of successful mission fulfillment (US Army 1989). This concept is a key component of the US military motto that proclaims, "*we can fight with limited resources and win*" (Crouch 1988; US Army 1989).

The very same principles can be adopted into the global trade and transport with specific benefits in resource management and the allocation of technologies and manpower to eliminate security threats. As we decrease forces in certain low-risk, low-impact areas, and shift our focus to other regions of the world, the concept will be valuable for examining the dynamics of contingency operations.

Directing our attention to realistic security challenges, based on annual statistics and intelligence information, will help governments and industries to seek for technological and scientific solutions that will serve as FMs. Furthermore, an optimum utilization of technology resources can be achieved through the formation of strategic alliances among entrusted networks of governments and regulatory bodies, as per the initiatives discussed in Chapter 3. As a next step, strengthening the public–private coalition and an open discussion among law enforcement agencies and major key players in the supply chains.

8.2 TECHNOLOGY AND TERRORISM

8.2.1 How Technology Makes Us Vulnerable

Over the past decades or so, cargoes of a low or medium value did not need extra security measures, as threats of theft typically entailed higher-value cargoes. Recent security threats impose the risk of biological, environmental, or other contamination that may now encompass any and all cargoes in any and all transportation modes.

The security incidents during modern history, such as the September 11, 2001 (9/11) terrorist attacks, the Boston Marathon bombings, and piracy and terrorism events have revealed to the public the capacities and utility of innovative technologies used by governments and the private sector. The introduction of such technologies seems to be a two-edged sword of which one edge is the legitimate use by governments and the industry, and the other edge reflects the illegitimate use by terrorists, pirates, drug cartels, and entities that impose significant threat to our society. This chapter not only will showcase the most significant security technologies of our times but also will express valid concerns pertaining to preventing these innovations becoming available to global entities that impose threats to national and commercial security around the world. While security technologies have been designed and used to safeguard global stability, dissemination of critical information and state-of-the art technologies have become available to terrorists, pirates, and other illegitimate entities. Hence, a significant undertaking would be (a) to trace the supply chain of such illegitimate sharing of security information and technologies and (b) to prevent this flow of critical technology and information from leaking into the "other side."

Throughout the history of mankind, the basic principles and characteristics of security have remained the same regardless of the scientific, topographical, socioeconomic, and political advancements. Innovative technologies have supported both the public and private stakeholders to establish particular security strategies and tactics in order to prevent and eliminate potential security risks.

In the case of transportation and trade, almost 85% of security-related damage related to logistics and the supply chain takes place during hinterland transportation. While global trade quantities continue to grow, and national boundaries are more flexible and available, criminal and terrorist groups have grown to be highly sophisticated and organized.

Again, this is a double-edged sword for the industry, as the tools and capacities used by nations to grow and advance also become available to illegitimate entities, which impose increasing security threats to industries and nations alike.

Nevertheless high-caliber guns are rather commonly used by terrorist groups. This deadly advancement had been precisely the method of terrorists utilizing contemporary information technologies, such as geospatial systems, satellite visuals, smartphones, and night-vision goggles to identify and kill any opponents.

Furthermore, the terrorists developed their personal operations center throughout the Pakistani border where they closely watched global media broadcasts, web-based reporting, and social media in real time, utilizing the public images, videos, and social media posts to wipe out more individuals (Goodman 2012).

The harmful ability of terrorist organizations is expanding steadily as terrorists have verified over time that they are skilled at making use of innovative technologies for their own profit. As a result, NATO allies create innovative and enhanced technologies to overcome this progressively advanced risk from illegitimate groups.

The 9/11 terrorist attacks against the United States are a dreadful illustration of how scientific and technological advances intended for commercial purposes, when in the wrong hands, can turn into a lethal weapon with thousands of innocent victims. The case of more than one commercial airplanes being hijacked and transformed into lethal weapons sadly demonstrates the preparedness and synchronicity of global terrorist groups. A simple online navigation by illegitimate entities can provide dangerous information and tools that both lone wolves and terrorist groups have transformed into innovative and functional communication channels. They have furthermore shown the know-how to produce

a. Sophisticated explosive devices out of everyday items, such as mobile phone devices and door bells.
b. Hazardous components, from army explosives to industrial dynamite to improvised fertilizer blends.
c. The production of chemical, radiological, and biological weapons and nuclear systems. They achieve this through the use of reverse engineering while infringing existing patents and creating lethal weapons, radiological, and (presumably) nuclear devices.

The frontrunners of terrorist groups have been rather revealing in their aspiration to obtain and use guns of mass destruction.

All of the above patterns are rather disturbing as they impose serious security threats. They are therefore of significant concern and a risk to all nations around the world (NATO Review 2004).

CASE STUDY: THE 2008 MUMBAI ATTACKS

The terrorist groups that have been identified as responsible for serious acts of terrorism frequently surprise the authorities, media, and the public opinion due to their adaptability and ease in using modern tools to destroy for their own ends. The 2008 Mumbai attacks, which attracted extensive worldwide disapproval, commenced in November 26 and continued through November 29, 2008 and resulted in the death of 164 innocent civilians and the injuries of more than 308 people. The heavily equipped attackers, who set out for Mumbai by sea, navigated with GPS technologies in line with the Indian police reports. They used BlackBerrys, CDs possessing high-quality satellite images resembling Google Earth maps, and several mobile phones with switchable SIM cards to ensure that they would not be easily monitored (Wax 2008). This terrorist attack astonished government specialists not merely with their use of advanced weapons but additionally with their level of familiarization when using modern technology, which is depicted as follows:

a. GPS/AIS technologies: GPS and/or AIS was used for the terrorists to cross the seas from Karachi (Pakistan) to Mumbai (India), while using GPSs. Based on the actual distance, i.e., 548 mil if travelled by land, and 589 nmi if by sea, it would take the terrorists at least 48 h if navigated without deviations, with an average speed of 12 nmi.
b. Terrorists were able to identify their targets since they had observed satellite pictures from Google Earth.
c. To obtain ongoing instructions on how to further coordinate the attacks, terrorists retained ongoing communication with their presumed Pakistani terrorist group members, by employing satellite phones of unidentified ownership, and are therefore very hard to trace.
d. During the three-day siege at the two luxury hotels and a Jewish center, terrorists retained their communication with the group of attackers by using online communication that further confused attempts to track and identify calls (Kahn 2008).

8.2.2 Drones as Commercial and Law Enforcement Tools for Security

Drones are fully autonomous robotics or vehicles equipped with remotely controlled technology.

Drones are directly controlled from ground control stations and use GPS/satellite technologies to relay their position in real time. In case this communication is lost, a satellite link takes over control from the ground control. Satellite technologies are used to identify the drone.

Drones have been designed to perform a wide spectrum of "3-D tasks," i.e., dull, dirty, and dangerous. Their use and demand have grown rapidly over the past few years for a number of good reasons:

a. They can complete the most dangerous missions independently without the need to jeopardize human lives, i.e., troops, law enforcement, etc.

b. They are more durable than humans, or other man-made machines, i.e., not restricted by fatigue, no need for frequent fuel replenishments, etc. As of 2014, the world record was broken by Zephyr, a British drone that managed to fly over 82 h with no intermission.

c. They are much cheaper than conventional military technologies, helicopters, etc.

They can both perform specified missions, and convey these operations to their basis, through built-in recording and surveillance capacities, i.e., surveillance cameras are employed for intelligence and exploration data gathering.

Drones are designed in a multitude of types and are capable of accomplishing a wide range of missions and tasks, and they can be classified in terms of their spatial missions, in terms of use, and in terms of equipment.

AF describes it as a "multimission, medium-altitude, long-endurance remotely piloted aircraft that is employed primarily as an intelligence-collection asset and secondarily against dynamic execution targets."

Namely, they can be classified according to their spatial operations in sea, land, and air, as follows:

a. *Air*: Unmanned aerial vehicles (UAV), or unmanned air systems, or remotely piloted aircraft systems

b. *Land*: Unmanned ground vehicles

c. *Subsea*: Unmanned undersea vehicles

d. *Space*: Unmanned/robotic space crafts

Figure 8.1 depicts a US Air Force drone, the MQ-9 Reaper. The Federal Aviation Administration classifies three key industry segments for drones: (a) military, (b) civil government, and (c) commercial (FAA 2014). For the sake of clarity, these three classifications are hereby further analyzed as follows:

FIGURE 8.1   A US Air Force drone, the MQ-9 Reaper. (From US Airforce, available at http://upload.wikimedia.org/wikipedia/commons/3/33/MQ-9_Reaper_-_090609-F -0000M-777.JPG, accessed April 4, 2015, 2014.)

1. Military
   a. *Federal law enforcement: Defense purposes*: Military, intelligence, and special operations. Drones are used by governments on special missions such as unconventional warfare, counterterrorism, intelligence, security surveillance, and manhunting and provide medicine to remote locations in times of crisis, such as wars, political unrest, and natural disasters, and so on. Emerging technologies will empower drones not only to conduct face and iris recognition and behavior analysis but also to observe and record private conversations.
2. Civil
   a. *Government civilian law enforcement*: Police, firefighting, border patrol, security surveillance, emergency response, hostage rescue or S&R operations during natural disasters; manhunting; and so on. Potentially, such technologies have the potential to enhance public safety and national security, being capable of face and iris recognition and behavioral analysis.
3. Commercial
   a. *Industry and manufacturing applications*: These automated, unmanned robotic technologies can be specially furnished with equipment that is tailor-made for the purpose and mission of the drone(s). The commercial drone market is rapidly growing due to the high demand by the energy/offshore industry, hazardous materials (HazMat) and chemical corporations, manufacturers, and assembly lines. Some of the drones' daily tasks include inspection, security surveillance, and commercial intelligence.

      Heavy-duty construction for installation and maintenance of subsea infrastructure, including underwater power and pipeline installation; discovering deep-sea oil and gas reserves, and restoring subsea cables.
   b. *As an extension of commercial use*: Drones can also be used for domestic security, surveillance, etc.

Although market trends and structures within these three segments may considerably vary, they have similar goals: to deliver specific tasks and services that may not be achieved by traditional technologies, i.e., manned technologies, or may be able to execute a feasible manned mission at an inexpensive manner. It is worth noting that while these capabilities are initially sought by the military leadership for national defense purposes, these technologies become available to the civilian law enforcement, and, eventually, to the industry. As a result of elevated awareness and demand, drones have the capacity of becoming a key component of the commercial aerospace industry. In support of this argument, the Federal Aviation Administration anticipates that 15,000 drones will be flying the US skies in 2020 and 30,000 drones by 2030 (FAA 2014).

This new "drone" market will not only benefit the drone manufacturers and the economy overall, by generating new jobs, taxation, and so on, but also will give another dimension to the new capacities being performed.

- At a law enforcement level, the new capabilities promise to enhance homeland security, protect the borders, and minimize security threats by adopting a surveillance and risk-based proactive stance.

- At a commercial level, drones will be used for commercial surveillance, supply chain, and warehouse management. The market will eventually expand into additional commercial, civilian, and domestic utilities, all related to surveillance, security, and productivity.

This chapter makes frequent references to illegitimate groups and their capacity to quickly adopt to innovative technologies. As an antipode to the benefits of drone technologies, it is worth considering the possibility of this state-of-the-art technology to become available to entities imposing security or public safety threat: terrorists, criminals involved in drug trafficking, human trafficking, illegal immigration, or any kind of illegitimate activities. Such a possibility will impose severe security threats both at a commercial and a homeland security level.

The following examples are used to verify this possibility and its consequences:

1. Use of drones by drug cartels
   a. Certain criminal organizations have already utilized drones, such as UAVs and other robotic types, to conduct criminal activities while limiting the probability of their own arrest.
   b. Since the 1990s, Latin American drug cartels have been building fully submersible submarines to smuggle drugs into the United States. It costs about a million dollars to build a 100 ft long submarine capable of establishing a regular illegitimate trade route. According to the US Drug Enforcement Agency, Mexican drug-trafficking organizations have been purchasing and commissioning foreign-made drones for drug-trafficking purposes since 2010. However, as of 2014, the drug cartels seem to be involved in the construction of locally made drones that are larger and especially designed to accommodate larger quantities of illegitimate drugs.
   c. Colombia's Revolutionary Armed Forces in partnership with drug cartels are set to create drone submarines capable of carrying 1800 kg of cocaine in excess of 1000 mi without the need of refueling.
2. Use of drones by terrorist groups
   a. Global police forces are increasingly concerned about remotely piloted drones potentially used by terrorists to attack political events and social gatherings such as religious, sports, and commercial areas. In such events, terrorists may use explosives or chemical and biological weapons.
   b. In September 15, 2013, during a political campaign organized in Dresden, Germany by Chancellor Angela Merkel and Defense Minister Thomas de Maiziere, a Parrot AR drone flew and subsequently crashed at the chancellor's feet. Although the event had no victims and no damage whatsoever, since it served as a protest initiated by the German Pirate Party, it raised some valid concerns about the potential use of similar drones by illegal groups. Even a small quadcopter, such as the one used in Germany, could carry explosives or grenades, causing death, injuries, damages, and social unrest.

Based on a plethora of incidents that are frequently announced in the media, and upon observations of the ability of criminal groups to adopt and reproduce new technologies, it is important for the authorities to restrict, monitor, and control the use of drones.

Should these technologies become available to international or national criminal groups, they could gain access to these technologies and replicate them through reverse engineering.

8.2.3 Reverse Engineering (Back Engineering)

Reverse engineering may be defined as the procedure of obtaining information on the pattern, design, or blueprint of any man-made technology, construction, or product and reproducing it in line with the information obtained. Reverse engineering may apply to not only technologies and software but also chemical, biological, or nuclear structures.

The reverse engineering process entails taking apart or disassembling a product in order to

1. Observe how it operates
2. Duplicate it
3. Be able to improve on its existing design

The process of reverse engineering may be legitimate or illegitimate, i.e., entailing patent and copyright infringement, while its purpose and motive could entail (i) commercial and economic profitability; (ii) military and political applications, such as a nation's military buildup; (iii) commercial or military sabotage; and so on.

In order to avert any potential security threats, it is necessary for governments and policy makers to establish methods and technologies that will identify, monitor, and avert planned drone attacks from illegitimate entities or terrorist groups. A legal and regulatory framework should be implemented to criminalize the construction, possession, and use of drones with the intention to cause damages.

8.2.4 National Terrorism Advisory System, USA DHS

The National Terrorism Advisory System (NTAS) successfully conveys details about terrorist threats by offering timely, detailed data to the public, federal, and state agencies; emergency responders; sea, land, and air hub ports; and trade centers, as well as the private sector.

Every alert provides data to the public about the risk, including, if accessible, the geographic location, transportation mode, or critical infrastructure possibly affected by the threat; protective measures being taken by authorities; and procedures that people and residential areas can take to safeguard themselves and their households and help protect, alleviate, or recover from any security threat (DHS NTAS 2014).

There are two levels of security threat alert:

1. *Imminent threat alert*: Warns of a legitimate, specific, and approaching terrorist threat against the United States.
2. *Elevated threat alert*: Warns of a legitimate terrorist or security threat against the United States.

Such alerts will consist of a clear affirmation that there is an impending or elevated threat. Employing available data, the alerts will provide a concise review of the potential

FIGURE 8.2   National Terrorism Advisory System (NTAS) notification. (Courtesy of US DHS, 2014.)

security threat; details about actions being taken to ascertain public safety; and recommended actions that individuals, communities, businesses, and governments may take to help prevent, mitigate, or respond to the security danger.

The NTAS notifications will be dependent on the type of the threat: in certain cases, alerts will be sent straight to law enforcement or impacted areas of the private sector, whereas in others, alerts will be released more broadly to the public through both official and mass media stations. Figure 8.2 shows the National Terrorism Advisory System (NTAS) notification.

8.2.5 Terrorist Threats: "Anti-Access Area-Denial" Threats

At a federal level, strategies for countering biological threats have a fundamental concept or fear that biological weapons will sooner or later be used in a terrorist attack. To avoid lethal viruses from developing into weapons of mass destruction (WMDs), it is important to acquire prompt and reliable inside information related to possible threats.

There is a realistic threat of anti-access/area-denial (A2/AD) strategies where potential enemies might employ to fight coalition powers.

Anti-access is described as measures and functions, typically long range, created to protect against a rival's force from getting into a critical infrastructure or territory or a functional area. Area-denial is the term for activities and capacities that are apt to have reduced range and restrict an opponent's mobility of action inside an operational area. It emphasizes three significant tendencies in the operational conditions: (i) the development of A2/AD capacities over the world, (ii) the transforming international defense strategy of the United States over time, and (iii) the breakthrough of cyberspace and space as potential areas of conflict (Boland 2012).

Over the past decade or so, the Pentagon's investigation and research agencies developed a few counterexplosive devices, sensors, and devices that block transmission or reception of signals (jammers) that were employed in Iraq and Afghanistan. Lately, armed forces researchers assisted to deal with the "A2/AD" risks in order to avoid adversary guns from attacking or blasting US troops or US naval warships. Areas of critical infrastructure such as all computer-based systems, transportation and energy platforms, bridges, dams, significant buildings, monuments, dams, or even can also be assaulted by distant attackers (Erwin et al. 2012).

8.3 SECURITY TECHNOLOGY FOR THE LOGISTICS AND SUPPLY CHAIN INDUSTRIES

8.3.1 Intelligence Technologies: Satellite and Communication Systems

8.3.1.1 Global Navigation Satellite System and Satellite Navigation Technologies

A satellite navigation system (SatNav) uses satellite technology to deliver global geospatial positioning. It enables digital receivers to establish the 3D positioning (i.e., longitude, latitude, and altitude) with great accuracy by the use of time signals transported by radio from satellite systems. Time synchronicity is achieved by estimating each location's time zone.

When a SatNav system has global coverage, it is defined as a "Global Navigation Satellite System" (GNSS).

GNSS is a sophisticated satellite technology that is applied to identify the precise geospatial position of a user's GNSS device in any global location. As shown in Figure 8.3, GNSS platforms make use of a satellites' constellation in collaboration with surface stations. The triangulation technique is used to obtain receiving satellite indicators from several sources to accurately identify a specific position, e.g., of a vehicle or ship in motion.

8.3.1.1.1 GNSS Commercial Applications
The first GNSS commercial/civilian applications involved scientific exploration, surveying, and mapping. Over the past decade, GNSS has been used in the industry, integrated with satellite-based technologies such as GPS and radio-frequency identification (RFID), which are also examined in this chapter. Some of the GNSS applications include not only Dynamic Positioning of Deep Offshore Platforms but also transportation, maritime navigation (AIS), land vehicle navigation (GPS), equipment control, cargo tracking, security, smartphones, and a myriad of other applications.

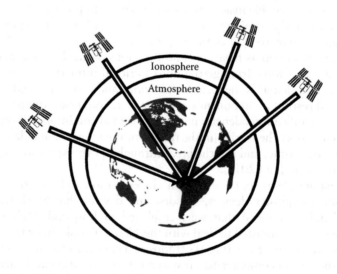

FIGURE 8.3   Global Navigation Satellite System (GNSS). (From the author.)

GNSS-receiving devices can offer users with extremely accurate time, as regional time is adjusted with the high-accuracy satellite clocks. This empowers industrial and transportation functions, e.g., in cellular technologies, power plants, web-based applications, electronic commerce, banking and so on (NovAtel 2014).

8.3.1.2 GPS

GPS is a GNSS invented in the 1970s by the US Department of Defense (US DOD), yet its technology was upgraded in 1995.

The founding fathers of the GPS are Dr. Bradford Parkinson, Roger L. Easton, and Ivan A. Getting.

The GPS program at the US Joint Program Office was established in 1974 with only about 30 officers. For a number of years, it has been the only functional GNSS on the globe; GPS utilizes a sequence of satellites that broadcast accurate microwave indicators that allow GPS devices to establish their location in real time, velocity, and course/orientation.

8.3.1.2.1 GPS-Tracking Unit
A GPS-tracking device utilizes the GPS to establish the accurate position (latitude, longitude) of an individual, motor vehicle, cargo, or any asset to which it is affixed. It has the capacity to show motion in real time and to register a target's position at frequent time periods. The device functions when a modem is attached be it portable such as SMS or PRS SMS (radio wave-based or satellite-based), thus enabling the target's position to be monitored within a map background both in real time and in the form of a report where all movements (speed, stops, route, deviations) are duly monitored and analyzed by the use of a GPS-tracking software. Additionally, data-tracking options are obtainable, such as recording and storing location data or transmitting data to a designated location.

8.3.1.2.2 Typical GPS Logger
The use of GPS as "data-pushing" technology involves surveillance/monitoring. When such a device is attached on an individual or transportation mode, it enables any motions to be tracked. This technology is used both in investigations and for commercial purposes (safety, compliance, and performance, i.e., reporting to clients or to supervisors).

In case of incidents, such data may be retrieved and examined during the "incident investigation and root cause analysis" to verify the circumstances of the incident such as possible time or causes.

8.3.1.2.2.1 Data Pullers (GPS Transponders)
In contrast to data-pushing GPS technologies, which transmit the system's position at frequent intervals, the pull concept enables the GPS transponders to be constantly switched on, while the system still tracks performance, route, speed, and other parameters continuously. This "pull technology" may not be widely utilized or available, yet it resembles computers that are nonstop connected to the Internet.

Such technologies are useful both for investigations and the industry, their utilities may include tracking items or vehicles that are possibly compromised, stolen, or hijacked or monitor the movement of cargoes and container boxes on sea, land, and air. Data pullers are widely used as systems made up of a GPS receiver and a mobile phone that, when an SMS text request is received, they can respond to the message by providing their location.

1. US NAVSTAR GPS: (1970 and 1995 upgrade)

    The US NAVSTAR GPS is the pioneer of what is known as GPS technologies. Its first satellite system was launched in 1978, and the system was fully developed in 1995.

    The fleet of NAVSTAR GPS satellites provides latitude, longitude, altitude, direction of travel, travel velocity, and correct time of day to anyone anywhere, day or night, in any weather.

    NAVSTAR is short for Navigation System using Timing and Ranging. The design of the US' extensive 24-satellite system was authorized in 1973, and the first satellite was launched in 1978. The system was used mainly by the US Government/Department of Defense, whereas a downgraded version was offered for civilian use. In 2000, commercial pressures to make this technology available to civilians for industrial and private use brought to end the "selective-availability" phase. In 2007, it was determined that the US Navstar III generation will not have the option of "selective availability."

2. Russian GLONASS (2001)

    The Russian GLONASS was developed in 2001 and is operated by the Russian authorities, the Russian Aerospace Defense Forces, and the Russian Federal Space Agency (Roscosmos or Russpace). "GLONASS K" is its recently upgraded version.

3. Chinese BeiDou (2020)

    The Chinese BeiDou Navigation Satellite System is restricted to serve as a navigation system, whereas there are efforts to upgrade it into a GNSS by 2020. In November 2014, the International Maritime Organization (IMO) officially approved the Beidou Navigation Satellite System as a Global Radio Navigation System (Beidou 2014).

4. European Union (2020)

    The launching European Union's (EU's) Galileo Satellite Positioning System is a 5-billion-euro project that was approved by the EU Ministers in 2010, with the goal of being fully implemented around 2020. In 2011, its initial four satellites were launched by the European Space Agency (ESA 2014).

    Galileo aims to differentiate from the existing US GPS and the Russian GLONASS projects by providing an enhanced global S&R function. In case of an accident, the built-in transponder will enable the satellite systems to convey a distress signal from the afflicted party, i.e., a ship in distress, to the Galileo Rescue Coordination Center in order to commence the S&R operations. The novelty here is that Galileo will be designed to transmit a feedback to the distressed party verifying that their message was conveyed and that S&R operations will soon commence. This technology is still in its initial stages, and its implementation stage is estimated to be in position after 2020.

5. Other national initiatives that aim to establish their own navigation systems are France, India, and Japan.

8.3.1.3 AIS

AIS is a computerized monitoring program used onboard vessels and by vessel traffic services (VTSs) with the purpose of tracking down the ships' position. This is achieved by digital data exchange among other nearby vessels, AIS and VTS base stations, and satellites. AIS data enhance marine radar, which remains the key method of collision deterrence within sea transportation.

The term Satellite-Automatic Identification System (S-AIS) is used interchangeably to define when satellite systems are employed to identify AIS signatures.

Data made available from AIS devices (for instance, the ship's IMO unique identification number; latitude and longitude [position], navigational route, and speed) could be shown on a monitor or an "Electronic Chart Display and Information System" (ECDIS). ECDIS is a computer-based map-reading data program that conforms with the regulations of the IMO and may be utilized as a substitute for hard-copy navigational charts. AIS technologies are designed to support a ship's safety, security, compliance, and operations in a plethora of ways:

1. AIS technologies enable not only the ships but also the coast guard, the authorities, the shipowners, the freight forwarders, etc., to monitor a ship's course both in real time and in later time in order to verify the performance, location, course taken, speed, etc.
2. Safety—through selecting a safe navigational route as opposed to taking shortcuts in draft-restricted or tidal waters and through monitoring in real time the ships' traffic at any given location through facilitating situational awareness and thus averting incidents, i.e., oncoming ships, offshore platform, etc.
3. Security—enabling situational awareness in war zones, terrorism- or piracy-prone areas, illegitimate trade areas, and so on.
4. Compliance—e.g., being able to prove that the ship's speed or navigational route taken is in line with the regional or international rules and/or the contract of carriage (charter party).
5. Operations—e.g., avoiding commercial disputes by being able to prove the actual time that the ship needed in order to load, unload, remain outside the hub port due to heavy traffic, etc., and proving the actual time that the ship was in a specific location or verifying if the ship deviated for commercial or other reasons.
6. Investigation and root cause analysis—in case of a breach of commercial contract, or in case of a safety, security, or environmental incident, the authorities and the parties concerned will have a clear picture of the actual vessel's movements in a specific location at a specific time.

AIS incorporates a standard VHF transceiver along with a positioning technology such as a GPS with other digital navigation devices, such as a gyrocompass (gyroscope). Each ship transmits regularly its position, together with its main ID particulars, such as the ship's name, VHF call sign, and so on. Through the use of AIS transponders equipped onboard other vessels or VTS technologies and other ashore devices, the ship's signals can be transmitted in real time, thus enabling the ship to demonstrate its position in a radar display in comparison with the other positions of vessels, boats, and offshore platforms in the vicinity.

AIS has a widespread use by federal and state authorities to monitor and keep track of the movement and operations of ships calling at ports of the world. As demonstrated in Figure 8.4, AIS allows authorities to dependably and affordably observe ships' navigational positions and operational activities throughout coastlines, with additional data from satellite-modeled networks. Especially in seaports and inland waterways characterized by heavy traffic, a regional VTS typically exists to manage ship traffic.

The AIS was created by the IMO technical committees as a system to prevent collisions between large ships at sea that are located outside the range of shore-based

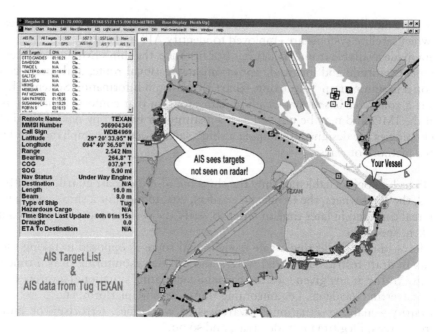

FIGURE 8.4 AIS Mapping used by the US Coast Guard. (Courtesy of Navigation Center, US Coast Guard, DHS, 2014.)

systems. This satellite technology recognizes the identification of each and every vessel in a selected region, together with its precise longitude, latitude, and navigational characteristics, facilitating an online profile of each ship to be generated. The AIS specifications incorporate a variety of automatic calculations according to these position reports, for instance, closest point of approach and collision alarms. AIS is typically used in addition to standard radar systems and may not be used by all vessels.

Current maritime rules have required the setting up of AIS devices on all SOLAS ships, i.e., ships that fit into a specific framework in line with the IMO's International Convention for the Safety of Life at Sea (SOLAS). According to SOLAS, AIS system should be in place, onboard ocean-going vessels of a gross tonnage (GT) of 300 MT or more, as well as all passenger vessels irrespective of size (IMO 2014a,b).

The regulatory requirements for port authorities or shore facilities are to have them equipped with only receivers in order to be able to view the local traffic without having to transmit their particular location. Virtually, all AIS transponder-fitted marine traffic can be monitored in an accurate and efficient manner, yet this detailed mapping is restricted to the VHF range, approximately 200 nmi.

AIS data acquired by VTS are significant for incident investigation purposes, because they provide reliable recorded data in a specific time, location, ship identification, ship's navigational route and speed, course over ground, and rates of turn as opposed to the less-precise data made available from radars.

A well-rounded snapshot of an incident, during its investigation process, may be acquired by voyage data recorder (VDR) information, subject to the ship's data maintenance, as it reveals information that can be cross-checked with the AIS technologies, such as the ship's navigational course, recordings of oral communication, and radar images depicting the actual incident. Nevertheless, VDR data may not be kept for a long time, as the IMO stipulation only needs this to be stored for 12 h.

An interesting utilization of the AIS data with both positive and negative impacts would be to allow it to be publicly shared through the Web without the requirement for an AIS receiver. Standard data include the ship's name, particulars, position, speed, and navigational course. These data are mapped, are retrievable online, and have potentially limitless international range, and the historical records are archived. Worldwide AIS transponder info gathered from both satellite- and web-based stations are becoming available on the World Wide Web via a variety of service providers. Once these aggregated data are set to be viewed on virtually any Internet-based system, they provide real-time positioning information from anywhere in the world.

Again, speaking of the pros and cons of modern technologies, it is the author's view that the ship should be able to publicly share its satellite-based data only if the readers of these data can be positively identified as registered members of a satellite system.

Some of the benefits the AIS technology offers are the following:

- If read by potential clients, such as cargo owners and freight forwarders, this exposure of the ship's real-time data can boost the ship's commercial opportunities.
- If there is an operational or legal dispute, these data can serve as evidence as to the ship's compliance to the commercial contract or regulatory stipulations.
- In case the ship navigates in piracy-prone zones, AIS technologies can help ships by possibly tracking small piracy ships approaching or identifying other commercial ships in the vicinity. In piracy-prone areas, it is common for commercial ships to navigate closely, as a group, in order to deter potential piracy attacks.
- If in an emergency, it will serve as a distress signal enabling the authorities and other ships to locate and assist the incident.
- Similarly, in case of a natural or security incident in the region, the authorities can trace the ships that need to be evacuated or ask them to participate in the S&R operations. In this instance, the authorities can use AIS-based systems as an asset management tool.

On the other hand, due to the fact that AIS-monitoring applications and regular VHF radio transceivers do not have AIS transponders, they could be used by shore-based entities that may not need to transmit information. Also, they may choose this cost-effective solution to a dedicated AIS device for smaller-sized ships to view local traffic, but the user will continue to be undetectable by other traffic on the system. When ships are publicly sharing their position online, it is necessary to ensure that visibility is mutual, i.e., the identity of the recipients and viewers of these data can also be verified. This is achieved when the viewers are members of an established AIS-based service provider. In this case, the online viewers can be positively identified if needed.

The antipode of this is a number of free online websites that offer AIS-based information. Whereas the shipowners may decide to register their fleet and make it visible to global web users, the anonymity offered in such websites may be detrimental for the ship's security, as sensitive real-time data can be viewed by any potential threat, from illegitimate cargo smugglers to pirates and terrorists.

The following table demonstrates the IMO's regulations for carriage of AISs.

Regulations for Carriage of AISs by the IMO

AIS Transponders

AISs are designed to be capable of providing information about the ship to other ships and to coastal authorities automatically.

Regulations for Carriage of AIS

Regulation 19 of SOLAS Chapter V—Carriage requirements for shipborne navigational systems and equipment—sets out navigational equipment to be carried on board ships, according to ship type. In 2000, IMO adopted a new requirement (as part of a revised new Chapter V) for all ships to carry AISs capable of providing information about the ship to other ships and to coastal authorities automatically.

The regulation requires AIS to be fitted aboard all ships of 300 GT and upwards engaged on international voyages, cargo ships of 500 GT and upwards not engaged on international voyages, and all passenger ships irrespective of size. The requirement became effective for all ships by December 31, 2004.

Ships fitted with AIS shall maintain AIS in operation at all times except where international agreements, rules, or standards provide for the protection of navigational information.

A flag state may exempt ships from carrying AISs when ships will be taken permanently out of service within two years after the implementation date. Performance standards for AIS were adopted in 1998.

The regulation requires that AIS shall

- Provide information—including the ship's identity, type, position, course, speed, navigational status, and other safety-related information—automatically to appropriately equipped shore stations, other ships, and aircraft
- Receive automatically such information from similarly fitted ships; monitor and track ships
- Exchange data with shore-based facilities

The regulation applies to ships built on or after July 1, 2002 and to ships engaged on international voyages constructed before July 1, 2002, according to the following timetable:

- Passenger ships, not later than July 1, 2003
- Tankers, not later than the first survey for safety equipment on or after July 1, 2003
- Ships, other than passenger ships and tankers, of 50,000 GT and upwards, not later than July 1, 2004

Source: IMO, available at http://www.imo.org, 2014a,b.

8.3.1.4 Cloud-Computing Technology

Cloud computing, or "the cloud" technology, pertains to the on-demand "pay-as-you-go" computing infrastructure that is based on large-scale sharing of computer resources rather than acquiring traditional servers or personal devices to manage such applications.

This is an Internet-based computing system that offers various services, including unlimited storage capacity, servers, and applications, that are available to customers via the Internet by the use of numerous servers that are allocated to global clients upon demand. Clouds are distinguished as public, private, or a mix of both.

The expression "moving to cloud" pertains to companies using the OPEX system (operational expenditures in a "pay-as-you-go" basis) versus the CAPEX system (capital expenditures in computer infrastructure), which becomes obsolete and depreciated over time.

Cloud technologies are user-friendly, enabling multinational companies to share their data, electronic contracts, and multinational group projects. Users can freely obtain remote access to data without geographical restrictions. Furthermore, the system's backup, updates, and other functions are performed automatically with no delays or without compromising the server's speed. Furthermore, cloud-based systems enable the large-scale sharing of data among supply chains, corporate consortiums, strategic allies, and so on.

8.3.1.4.1 Cloud-Computing Security and Cyber Threats Despite the many benefits of this technology, the increasing cybersecurity threats have raised questions as to the capacity of this new technology to alleviate cyber attacks and be able to store and retrieve information that could be potentially compromised.

For this reason, cloud-computing security has been developed; cloud security is a progressing subcategory that safeguards computer systems (hardware, software), networks, and data. It represents an extensive set of guidelines and innovative systems with the purpose of protecting data, programs, and the pertinent cloud infrastructure.

In brief, cloud security controls may include

- *Deterrent action* pertains to the measures aimed to decrease cloud-based cyber attacks. Deterrent controls generally minimize danger by warning prospective attackers of the undesirable repercussions that will follow if they proceed with the cyber attack.
- *Preventive action* aims to fortify the cloud platform against unwanted occurrences usually by minimizing or preferably eradicating vulnerabilities. As an example, robust authorization and access verification protocols for cloud users aim to keep away unauthorized users.
- *Threat identification* detects potential hazards and responds effectively to any incidents that take place. In the instance of a cyber attack, such a control will initiate the preventive or corrective actions needed in order to mitigate the threat. Cloud platforms and network security monitoring, such as intrusion diagnosis and deterrence measures, are usually used to detect attacks on cloud systems and assistance of communications infrastructure.
- *Corrective action* takes place during or after an incident. Though it may not completely eradicate the threat, it eliminates the consequences by reducing the damage. Furthermore, it promotes resiliency by restoring system backups.

8.3.1.5 "Cell-All": Smartphones with HazMat Detectors

Mobile phones have the capacity to monitor toxic materials in the environment, such as chlorine, carbon monoxide, and chemical warfare agents. The general public would have a new level of individual security and protection toward a range of relatively common airborne chemicals and toxic compounds, along with terrorist threats pertaining to WMDs. In cases when sensor data are controlled in an environmental detecting system for emergency responders and other entities, it will promote emergency preparedness to a higher level. The Cell-All concept was initiated and successfully tested by the US Department of Homeland Security (DHS). This technology is based on new nanotube sensors produced by NASA and Synkera Technologies and is designed to operate within the small area and power usage requirements of a mobile phone (Needs 2007).

In the same way that antivirus software is idle in the background and rises to existence in the event that it detects suspicious activity, this is how Cell-All frequently sniffs the adjacent air for particular volatile chemical substances. When a risk is detected, an alarm ensues in a couple of ways. For personal safety purposes, just like a hazardous gas leakage, an alarm notifies the user—who can choose from the settings if the alarm is an actual sound, or vibration, a phone call, or an SMS (text message). For imminent disasters where an evacuation and rapid action are needed, the instructions included may pertain to a specific place, time, and evacuation guidelines to designated areas through designated emergency operations centers.

The Cell-All initiative created by the DHS's Science and Technology Directorate is designed to empower cell phones with a sensor able to sense dangerous chemicals at negligible cost to the producer, i.e., $1 per sensor (DHS 2012).

This initiative aims to develop a lightweight, cost-effective, power-efficient alternative. While it may take a few years until the Cell-All technology of the HazMat sensors in our phones becomes commercially available, this is a technology of potentially high demand and usefulness.

8.3.1.6 Transportation Worker Identification Credential Card and Readers by the TSA

Within the United States, the Transportation Worker Identification Credential (TWIC) Card is needed by federal law for all transportation workers, including commercial workers and drivers, who require access to secure or restricted areas of maritime establishments. TWIC is implemented by the US TSA and the US Coast Guard. TWIC is a crucial security measure that will ensure people who impose a security threat do not gain unescorted access to secure areas of the nation's maritime transportation system.

In 2012, the TSA introduced a system to qualify a card reader to be harmonized with the TWIC Reader Hardware and Card Application Specification. This TWIC Card Reader technology is shown in Figure 8.5. Readers anticipated to be conformant to TSA TWIC reader specifications will be placed on a qualified technology list (QTL) preserved and made accessible to the public by the TSA. QTL qualification specifications vary by

FIGURE 8.5 TWIC Card Reader, Transportation Worker Identification Credential (TWIC®). (Courtesy of US TSA, 2014.)

reader type and claimed features of the vendor. All practical reader testings for the new QTL program will be carried out by a National Voluntary Laboratory Accreditation Program–accredited laboratory. Reader compliance and harmonization with TWIC environmental specifications, such a temperature spectrum, moisture, shock, and vibration, will need the product owner to provide to TSA certificates of conformance for all obligatory environmental requirements and any supplemental environmental qualifications (TSA 2012). Figure 8.5 demonstrates the TWIC card readers.

8.3.2 Reconnaissance/Recognition Systems: Biometrics Facial Recognition and Biometrics Technologies (2D and 3D)

8.3.2.1 Facial Recognition and Biometrics Technologies (2D and 3D)

Biometrics can be defined as intelligent computerized identification systems that recognize distinctive physical qualities, such as fingerprints, iris scans, or usually a blend of the two, therefore enabling authorities to authenticate that an individual is exactly who they claim to be by making use of their own distinctive identifiers. This technological innovation is employed at global and domestic points of entry, which include airports, hub ports for sea and land, and border-crossing locations, thus enabling the authorities to control access to significant facilities.

Biometrics are the quantifiable physiological or personality traits used for a person's identification for security purposes. Fingerprint analysis is a prevalent biometric technique used since the early twentieth century, yet modern technologies also incorporate iris and retina recognition, voice recognition, DNA, palm prints, and facial patterns (FBI 2014).

Biometrics are increasingly useful not only to verify a person's identity but also to establish a connection between security threats and illegitimate activities, with persons of interest that may be involved. The authorities can now search for a match by scanning a biometrics data bank.

8.3.2.2 Iris and Retinal Scanning (Ocular-Based Recognition)

According to the science of biometrics, iris and retinal reading are classified as "ocular-based" recognition systems, which suggests they seek to identify individuals based on their unique physiological features, i.e., iris and retinal patterns, which are unique for every person.

8.3.2.2.1 Iris Recognition
Iris scanning utilizes photographic technology with subdued infrared lighting to scan the detailed, complex patterns of the human iris. Statistical and mathematical algorithms are used to compare the digital, high-definition scan among a large iris database in order to find the best matches and eventually identify a person. Elaborate search engines look for the "perfect iris match" at a high speed. Iris recognition enjoys an increasing scientific credibility, as it provides significant benefits:

- The iris's ability to remain unaltered and protected over time unlike fingerprints or retinas
- High matching speed, i.e., several millions of iris codes per second per single-core CPU
- High accuracy rate in matching the iris scan among millions of persons of interest

8.3.2.2.2 Retinal Recognition   Retinal scanning pertains to the biometric reading of an individual's retina, i.e., the layer of blood vessels that are found at the rear side of the eye. A person's retinas may be unique just like the iris and the fingerprints yet can change over time due to health issues, pregnancy, and so on. In retinal scanning, the individual must be in front of the scanning device at a close distance, i.e., less than 3 ft. (1 m) away.

The individual must look through the eyepiece and line up a series of points. As the eye is focused on the points, the individual patterns of the retina are mapped (Seto, Y., Ed. Li S.Z. 2009).

Figure 8.6 shows the biometrics equipment used by the FBI: laptop with biometrics software, digital fingerprint, and retinal scanners.

Biometrics technologies are dependable, functional, and practically impossible to forge. They employ innovative digital techniques to recognize a person by their distinctive physical or behavioral characteristics. Improvements and functions have been amplified upon federal and public requirements to meet the expectations of safeguarding international, personal, and commercial security. Biometrics can enhance the effectiveness of security performance by reducing the risks of terrorism, or illegitimate activities, while facilitating borders and gate passing, as well as cargo-handling processes. This security technology is especially useful for the security clearance of frequent travelers both for leisure and transportation professionals. Biometric recognition tools, such as fingerprints and iris recognition technologies, could be integrated in *smart recognition cards (Smart ID)* and incorporated with online access to transport documents, such as the carrier's credentials, cargo manifest, personal ID, and so on. The Smart ID card's uses may vary from securing building access and computer security to photo ID such as passports and TWIC cards.

8.3.2.3 Facial Recognition: 2D and 3D Biometric Technologies

Facial recognition is an essential tool for to be used by the authorities for personal identification. 2D and 3D biometric techniques are used for recognition of "persons of interest"

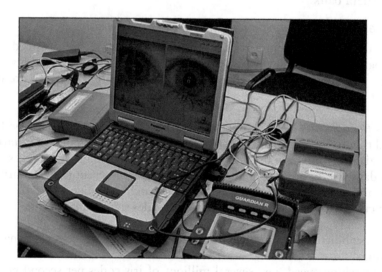

FIGURE 8.6   Biometrics equipment used by the FBI. (From US FBI, Federal Bureau of Investigation, 2014.)

or suspects from pictures or video data using 3D facial images. These tools enable the investigators in their function by making identification achievable even from partial facial image taken with low resolution. In the state-of-the-art multibiometric approach, various biometric technologies are combined.

The preceding two-dimension facial recognition is typically easier and less costly to obtain; nevertheless, it has encountered certain obstacles. This is the case if the identification of people in pictures or video series of crime scenes did not produce a clear and well-taken frontal face angle. The recognized advantages from using 3D relative to 2D data comprise less quality and definition deviation experienced due to reasons such as makeup and less sensitivity to lighting changes. This is a key reason why the 3D face recognition is to prevail over the challenges encountered with 2D recognition methods and will ensure high-resolution, easily identifiable images regardless of changes in illumination, appearance, or body posture.

These solutions help protect against identity theft and deny counterfeiters and immigration law violators of the chance to cross the national boundaries. The outcomes of these inspections are accessible to the authorities for improved security. Hence, based on biometric technologies, thousands of illegitimate travelers have been averted.

8.3.2.3.1 Facial Recognition and Biometrics in the United States The DHS is committed to developing improved facial recognition technologies that will enable authorities to identify counterfeiters and suspects within rather crowded areas through the use of closed-circuit television (CCTV) cameras. DHS aims to create a surveillance system that will connect security software with surveillance cameras to scan crowds of people and quickly recognize people by their facial features. The DHS has examined a crowd-scanning undertaking referred to as the Biometric Optical Surveillance System. This system is efficient at collecting images of humans from 164 to 328 ft. away. The program is devised to acquire images of people both in motion within a specific distance and obtain the frontal face photo of a person while they are right in front of the video camera (DHS BOSS 2012).

The Office of Biometric Identity Management (OBIM) makes use of biometrics to ensure secure and fast travel for legitimate visitors yet protects from persons who wish to harm or violate the national laws. Biometrics gathered by OBIM and connected to specific biographic information enable a person's identity to be established, then verified, by the US government.

Several federal and state agencies employ OBIM services to precisely identify individuals and establish if they present a risk to the authorities and the society.

With each encounter, from applying for a visa to searching for immigration advantages to enter the US borders, OBIM

- Compares an individual's biometrics toward a watchlist of identified or assumed criminals, terrorists, or immigration violators
- Verifies through the whole database of all the fingerprints gathered by the DHS since OBIM started to check if an individual is using an alias and trying to enter the country or a designated area with falsified identification
- Compares an individual's biometrics against those linked to the identification record made available to the authorities to make certain that that report legitimately belongs to the individual demonstrating it and not to another person (DHS OBIM 2013)

8.3.2.4 Crowdsourcing and Facial Recognition

Research focus in face recognition has shifted toward recognition of faces "in the wild" for both still images and videos, which are captured in unconstrained imaging environments and without user cooperation. Due to confounding factors of pose, illumination, and expression, as well as occlusion and low resolution, current face recognition systems deployed in forensic and security applications operate in a semiautomatic manner; an operator typically reviews the top results from the face recognition system to manually determine the final match (Best-Rowden et al. 2014).

Crowdsourcing utilizes the input of a crowd of online users to collaboratively solve problems. Modern technologies involve a computing model that uses crowdsourcing to combine and optimize human efforts and machine-computing elements. The new model uses social networks as a formal part of the criminal investigation process to efficiently perform the complex tasks of face recognition.

Scientific research pertaining to face recognition for security and forensic purposes is focused toward facial recognition while "in motion" for images or videos taken without the user's knowledge or consent. Due to restricting parameters such as low-resolution image, limited or ample brightness, positioning angle in front of the camera, and facial expression, current face recognition techniques function in a semiautomatic method; a security technology user generally compares the semifinal results of images automatically selected from the face recognition program in order to physically establish the final match (NIST Biometrics 2007).

Several security and forensic data banks have selected and utilized pertinent images and videos from social media platforms, which have been also using facial recognition tools to enable members to identify acquaintances. The Pentagon has assigned AOptix to create a smartphone application that reads and transfers biometric information pertaining to facial recognition from a distance.

CASE STUDY: THE USE OF BIOMETRICS IN BOSTON BOMBING

Through the use of an authentic law enforcement video recording from the Boston bombings, scientists discovered that one of the three face recognition technologies used by the authorities was much more accurate in providing a very accurate recognition, a perfect match of person of interest, Dzokhar Tsarnaev. On the other hand, Tamerlan Tsarnaev, the suspect who was finally killed during the shootout with law enforcement officials, could not be successfully matched, because he was wearing sunglasses. The limitations of facial recognition technologies were also identified during similar incidents with persons of interest wearing a hat, or having an object obscuring their eyes and face. For the authorities to identify persons of interest, they typically spend hundreds of hours to watch video footage, pictures, and any clues that would link them to a case. technologies

Facial recognition systems can effectively handle certain cases in which facial pictures obtained from a video recording were taken under favorable angles and conditions, such as natural light, proximity to camera, and so on. Under managed conditions, when the face is set at an angle toward the video camera, and if the illumination is sufficient, the facial recognition technologies may be up to 99% accurate. Automatic face recognition can easily identify persons of interest and attach a name to a face as the closest match is identified through an extensive search of literally thousands of suspects (Homeland Security Newswire 2013).

FIGURE 8.7   Handheld Interagency Identity Detection System (HIIDE). (Courtesy of the US ARMY [Sgt. Barrell, US ARMY, 2009].)

The US military forces have been using a single-use equipment, known as the Handheld Interagency Identity Detection System, as shown in Figure 8.7, to scan, upload, and transmit data from someone's face, eye, or thumb to their biometrics data banks.

8.3.3 Cargo-Tracking and -Monitoring Systems (Sea, Land, Air)

8.3.3.1 Radio-Frequency Identification

RFID pertains to the utilization of radio waves for automatic identification and data capture.

The RFID is a high-demand technology, and its global sales in 2014 have exceeded US$20 million.

RFID tags can be

1. Passive, i.e., passive reader active tag systems;
2. Active, i.e., active reader active tag systems; or
3. Battery-assisted passive, i.e., active reader passive tag systems

By means of a wireless use of electromagnetic fields, data are transmitted in order to automatically recognize and monitor tags attached to commodities. RFIDs consist of two key components:

1. A transponder, or tag, or label, which has a particular serial number linked to a particular item or commodity. Tags have a built-in transmitter and receiver and serve to electronically save data related to the attached object. The tag does not have to be located directly in line of sight of the reader in order to be browsed: it can be read from a moderate distance of several feet away.
2. A reader, or interrogator, which is a two-way radio transmitter and receiver that can both scan the tag, retrieve stored data, and transmit these data to the RFID software. As the RFID microchip saves the data, the antenna broadcasts and

receives transmitted data accordingly. Real-time alerts and real-time reporting are available on a 24/7 basis, to be read by designated parties concerned within a single company, or within designated key players within a supply chain, such as the cargo shippers, receivers, and so on.

The use of RFID tags is extensive, as it encompasses most industries throughout the global supply chain. Companies use this technology to ensure optimum efficiency by tracking the production progress and extending the monitoring throughout the storage, transport, and distribution process. Logistics and transportation companies use RFIDs in containerized and palletized cargoes in order to track the location of cargoes from the port of origin to the final destination. RFIDs are especially helpful in tracking time- and temperature-sensitive commodities like medicine, HazMat, food, etc. Companies that produce, sell, and transport dangerous goods and chemicals are employing RFID systems in order to locate containers or railcars transporting hazardous chemicals around the world. This ensures that both the cargoes and the communities are safe, secure, and do not impose an environmental threat.

8.3.3.1.1 Supply Chain Visibility with RFID Tags RFIDs contribute to the supply chain visibility and integration of data by providing real-time monitoring of vehicles and cargoes. Optimum security technologies are only competent when the transportation route and performance records have been monitored and recorded throughout the voyage, ensuring door-to-door visibility.

Modern RFID sensors entail a wide variety of capabilities to measure door intrusion, light, temperature, shock and vibration, and so on. Among the most significant features of RFID technologies are

a. *Real-time cargo monitoring* for container boxes, palletized cargoes, or smaller parcel cargoes.
b. *Real-time transportation monitoring*, i.e., real-time tracking of the vehicle's route, speed, inclination, and acceleration.
c. *Door intrusion and tampering sensors* to detect attempts to open container doors or any intrusion or tampering in any of the box's surfaces.
d. *Temperature, light, and humidity sensors*: these entail the monitoring of sensitive or hazardous cargoes. Several RFID tags may be installed in adjacent cargoes in order to monitor cargoes of different storage requirements. This monitoring will enable quick intervention in case of mechanical failure or cargo exposed to extreme temperatures, i.e., snow or heat affecting the carrier's temperatures.
e. *Shock and vibration sensors* to monitor shock loads while shock-sensitive cargoes are in transit. Mechanical accelerometers are used as electrical switches attached to the sensor input of an RFID tag.
f. *Cargo pressure sensors* measure pressure in compressed gases, liquids, or other hazardous cargoes.
g. *Tire-pressure sensors* for commercial trucks: these systems help avert rollover or other vehicle accidents.
h. *Acceleration sensors* used in transportation and manufacturing to monitor the equipment's or vehicle's performance for safety and/or security purposes. Accelerometers measure and report the real-time rotating equipment vibrations (including compressors, turbines, fans, or pumps) in real time.

i. *Inclination sensors/tilt sensors* determine an angular position with regards to gravity and have a wide range of utilities, from transportation security and cargo integrity to seismic monitoring in the offshore industry.

j. *Chemosensors, biosensors, and radioactive or HazMat sensors* for vehicle and cargo screening.

8.3.3.1.2 RFID Container Security Devices Container Security Devices (CSD), as shown in Figure 8.8, play a significant role in verifying that containers have not been compromised and have been transported safely and securely through the supply chain while assisting trade and customs operations. Both mechanical cargo seals and electronic seals (E-seals) can greatly improve cargo security, as they safeguard the system from potential acts of pilferage, illegitimate trade and transport, as well as terrorist attacks.

8.3.3.2 Mechanical Seals

A mechanical container seal is a gadget designated with a distinctive identifier and is frequently labeled with a specific seal and color that represents a specific entity in the supply chain, such as the cargo owner or conglomerate.

The seal is attached on the outside of the container doors and is meant to both prevent and signify potential tampering or intrusion from the container doors. Furthermore, based upon its structure and design, the seal offers different degrees of resistance to a deliberate or unintended endeavor to tamper it or violate its container doors. In case a tampered seal was to be substituted with a comparable unit after accessibility, the seal's distinctive identification number may well not match with the one that was documented when the authentic seal was attached. The sealing method for security seals is of high significance. SCS technologies for container security utilize six key types of high-security seals: electronic seals, bolt seals, barrier seals, indicative seals, padlock seals, and cable seals.

FIGURE 8.8   RFID technologies for container seals. (Courtesy of Maersk Lines.)

8.3.3.3 Electronic Seals

The necessity to increase container security especially for dispatches that entail high-value goods has resulted in the design and advancement of numerous kinds of "smart seals." These seal types have integrated actual physical security and data management abilities. An advanced level of performance is included by systems able to send electronic signals in case the seal has been tampered with, in which case these seals transmit an alarm by the use of fiber optics, radio frequency (RF), or infrared. In their most sophisticated iterations, electronic seals may be enhanced with a number of sensors, such as biological, chemical, radioactive, and so on. Their message pertaining to the container status is both registered and transmitted. In conjunction with a GPS transmitter, notifications or position information concerning the container can be transported in real time to a main processing system that can identify the location of the container box.

It is important to notice that E-seals simply monitor the seal's condition regardless of the inside status of the container box. Sometimes, the container's integrity may be compromised; however, if the seals remain intact, their sensors will not pick up the incident, still offering "false-positive" readings.

8.3.3.4 Real-Time Locating Systems Technologies

Real-time locating systems (RTLSs) provide highly accurate visibility of critical assets throughout their supply chain and transportation process. For trade and transportation companies, this information means having door-to-door visibility and the potential to identify all containerized or palletized cargoes. For the cargo manufacturers, this technique facilitates smart supervision, cargo flow, and procurement management of all corporate critical assets, both the ones located in the facility and at an expansive storage yard. From a security perspective, this technology empowers the company by monitoring and controlling workforce access while making certain that their operations are in compliance with the regulatory and industrial framework. RTLS features different automated identification systems that implement wireless indicators to establish the exact location of tagged property or staff. RTLS devices comprise "active" transponder tags that convey a long-range transmission at standard intervals, position sensors that obtain and transmit tag signals, and a position device that gathers and conveys the information.

8.3.3.5 Smart Container Technologies (United States)

Modern smart containers, as shown in Figure 8.9, entail a map-reading and tracking system, satellite positioning, interior sensors, and RF recognition in order to protect the container and its contents throughout its multimodal travel.

Most respected shipping companies offer container tracking track and trace options available online. While microchip transmitter-equipped containers may be costly, they facilitate the real-time electronic monitoring of the boxes. As specific carrier companies customarily deal with exclusive or tailor-made software and applications for this sort of services, cargo recipients need to get in touch with each carrier separately, which is a time-consuming task. Nevertheless, shipping websites progressively improve the manner in which cargo shippers, receivers, carriers and customs' brokers coordinate the transportation operations, by offering access via a single platform. Additional service instruments will be comprised of bills of lading, navigational schedules, container reservations, and event announcements. Conglomerates and larger companies may be granted access to these portals and could operate entirely with electronic data, such as bills of lading. Gradually, such Internet sites may also connect with both e-commerce and digital commercial services.

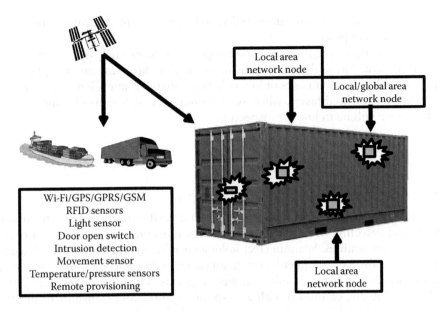

FIGURE 8.9 Smart containers' data exchange network for monitoring and tracking. (From the author.)

Based upon their intricacy, container seals, in contrast to RFID systems, can monitor, record, and broadcast all key activities that might take place throughout a commercial journey, especially the opening and closing of container doorways. These data become available via scanning possibly accessed remotely by the use of RFID technologies. These valuable technologies not only enhance global cargo security but also facilitate trade flow by minimizing customs procedures and eliminating trade disruptions. Increased security issues are further requiring the use of digital seals in the leading edge of antiterrorism actions.

The Smart Container project launched by US Customs represents an attractive approach to ensure higher security measures. However, the financial investment required is always a decisive factor. The industry needs to balance the security likelihood and impact on one hand and the financial cost on the other. Shippers who make use of the smart box initiative, and engage in the DHS initiatives such as the Customs-Trade Partnership against Terrorism and the Container Security Initiative, can enjoy considerable monetary benefits. Their compliance to the DHS initiatives suggests that they will undergo less inspections and less delays, making them more attractive commercially and more unlikely to be targeted for security checks by the authorities.

Containers that qualify as smart boxes will need to utilize container security devices and high-security, tamper-evident seals that satisfy the International Organization for Standardization standards.

Smart container sensors have the ability to identify defects or tampering, such as

- Door tampering, such as opening, breakage, or removal
- Cracks or openings on any side of the container
- Carriage of persons or animals in the containers
- Carriage of undeclared HazMat of nonpermissible quantities, i.e., cargoes that may impose biological, chemical, or nuclear threat

Furthermore, the container's location and speed can be verified through efficient GPS-based technologies in place.

In case a violation, inconsistency, or tampering is suspected, the container will be due to be inspected. The authorities are using an efficient targeting and sampling method according to which the containers of low risk and nonapparent evidence of tampering or damage will be expedited faster, whereas the containers with signs of tampering, theft, or other damage will be in line for inspection.

8.3.4 Non-Intrusive Inspections

8.3.4.1 Cargo Scanning or Non-Intrusive Inspection

Cargo scanning or non-intrusive inspection (NII) describes nondamaging techniques of examining and detecting illegitimate or dangerous substances during the transportation of humans or commodities. Scanning technologies are frequently used in globalized transportation, especially for container boxes, in an effort to detect hazardous substances, i.e., biological, radioactive, toxic, or other dangerous goods. The increasing security and terrorist threats globally, combined with an expanding trade and transport of illegitimate humans, drugs, and nuclear weapons or potentially harmful cargoes, necessitate more stringent scanning protocols and the use of advanced technologies.

a. *Targeting protocols*: The screening process involves targeting of the increased threat cargoes based on an intelligence database that contains the company history, supply chain affiliations, and other factors.
b. *Non-intrusive scanning technologies* are used to verify whether the actual cargo type and quality (and quantity) are in line with the shipping documents, such as contracts of affreightment, bills of lading, cargo manifests, etc.
c. Visual inspections based on intelligence gathered through item (a) and/or (b).

8.3.4.2 In-Motion Scanning Technologies

While governments and the industry currently use non-intrusive scanning (passive) technologies, the high volume of cargo to be scanned, combined with the alarming statistics of security threats globally, urge the industry to upgrade their technologies and use fast scanning, i.e., while the cargo is in motion.

Such technologies will greatly benefit the industry as they ensure security without compromising the trade flows by causing bottlenecks and long waiting lines.

8.3.4.3 Special Nuclear Material Detection

In accordance with Title I of the Atomic Energy Act of 1954, "special nuclear material" (SNM) pertains to fissile materials, i.e., materials that decompose by spontaneous fission, thereby producing neutrons. SNMs include uranium-233, plutonium, or uranium-235, whereas source materials are excluded (NRC 2013).The products from these reactions, such as protons, alpha particles, gamma rays, and fission proponents, can initiate the detection process. Some reactions require a minimum neutron energy (threshold), but most take place at thermal energies. Detectors exploiting thermal reactions are usually surrounded by moderating material to take maximum advantage of this feature.

Neutrons detectors can be used for monitor for SNM in commerce. Detectors can use solid-, liquid-, or gas-filled detection media (Crane and Baker 2013).

8.3.4.4 Neutron Radiation Detectors

Neutron detectors are widely used for security purposes. Neutron detection refers to the successful screening of fast neutrons. Current technologies used for the neutron detection include both software and hardware. Detection software comprises analysis applications including visual analysis to quantify the neutrons' number and energies reaching the sensor. On the other hand, detection hardware pertains to the equipment such as scintillation detectors and other types of neutron detectors.

A neutron is a neutrally charged chemical compound located in the nucleus of an atom or typically within a proton inside the nucleus.

The detection of neutrons suggests the potential presence of nuclear energy. National customs authorities increasingly require neutron scanning technologies, as shown in Figure 8.10, to be located in hub port areas in order to improve cargo and passengers' security.

There is a variety of neutron scanner technologies. For example, radiation portal monitors frequently use helium-3-filled gas detectors to look for neutron traces. However, the global shortage of helium-3 has resulted in the search of other elements suitable for neutron detection. Boron trifluoride (BF_3) has been widely used, yet its applications were restrained, especially in larger detection units, due to its high toxicity levels. Among the elements that have been successfully used for neutron scanning are (a) lithium-6, which has been used in crystal scintillator compounds, and (b) a stable isotope of boron (boron-10) in powder form (Knoll 2010; Lam 2012; DOE Patents 2013).

Enhancing the efficiency of radiological and nuclear technologies is essential for the scanning and aversion of nuclear hazards. The inactive diagnosis of fast neutrons is a

Neutron moderator
Neutron detector
Gamma detector

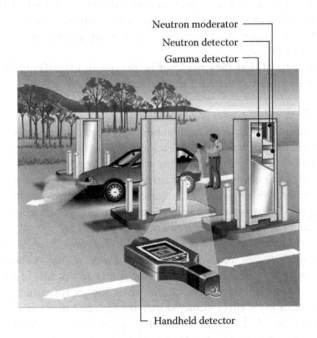

Handheld detector

FIGURE 8.10 Neutron moderator, neutron detector and gamma detector, and handheld detector. (From GAO.GOV, available at http://www.gao.gov/technology_assessment/key _reports, excerpted from GAO-11-753, p. 18.)

warning of the existence of specific nuclear components such as plutonium weapons. Prompt neutron scanning further facilitates increased detection of protected particular nuclear substances in diverse active scanning techniques.

8.3.4.5 Radiation Portal Monitors

A radiation portal scanner is a passive detection equipment for nuclear and radiological substances that offers Customs and Border Protection (CBP) with a passive, non-intrusive method to screen people, industrial and private vehicles, freight consignments, and any place where illegitimate trade and transport is suspected. Such technologies can detect different types of radiation from dirty bombs, nuclear weapons, and any HazMat that are used in the marketplace.

In order to mitigate terrorist attacks, CBP is investing in radiation portal screens at logistics hubs, seaports and airports, rail hubs, border points of entry, and land border area seaports in order to detect the potential existence of hazardous and radioactive substances. This is a passive technology that detects and notifies the authorities of any hazardous cargoes, yet this monitor does not generate images (CBP 2014).

8.3.4.6 Gamma-Ray Radiography for Nuclear Threats: Gamma and Neutron Radiation Detectors

Gamma-ray radiography is used to identify nuclear components. Due to their high atomic numbers and densities, nuclear elements highly absorb gamma rays while firmly deflecting muons. Therefore, nuclear components are relatively solid to gamma rays and are identified as dark areas in radiographs of cargoes and sea and land transportation containers.

A gamma-ray scanning device utilizes a radioactive pellet to generate gamma rays that have the capacity to scan the largest shipping dispatch in a short time. Despite the minimal dosage of radiation, the process entails the scanning of cargoes, while the carriers may not be present during scanning. Gamma-ray radiography creates 2D cargo images (LANL Muon 2003).

Their characteristic is that they may not be precise in identifying HazMat especially when used to scan cluttered areas with numerous objects.

8.3.4.7 Muon Tomography

The fast-neutron radiography, or muon tomography, method is an efficient device for screening freight for illegitimate cargoes including drugs or HazMat. Neutrons tend to connect with matter in a supporting manner to gamma rays, and they have the capacity to establish the chemical composition of cargoes, i.e., identify the hazardous ones. In comparison to gamma-ray radiography, neutron radiography systems are considerably more effective especially in sensing nuclear materials, where the conventional methods like x-rays or gamma rays are not precise (Yousri et al. 2012).

This is a passive radiation, which is harmless to humans. Hence, when used, transportation professionals do not have to exit the area. Muon scans, as shown in Figure 8.11, are considered to be more efficient compared to gamma-ray scans, in terms of radiation, and offer more "value for money," considering their longer life and less service requirements. Muon radiography's three-dimensional images are more accurate and efficient than the two-dimensional detection method of gamma-ray radiography. Cosmic-ray muons are more penetrating, which suggests that this technology can identify nuclear materials even if they are hidden beneath other cargoes or protective barriers (LANL Muon 2003; Wolverton 2007).

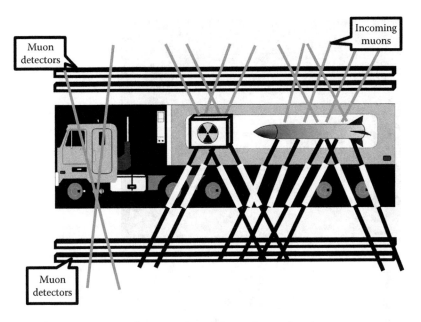

FIGURE 8.11   Muon tomography scanning. (From the author.)

8.3.4.8 X-Ray Radiography: Backscatter X-Rays

Due to growing security and terrorist risks, the scanning of humans for HazMat is significant. X-ray radiographic inspection, as shown in Figure 8.12, is a method used to inspect blasting agents and weapons. These units can be employed by the customs and border patrol authorities within airports, ports, nuclear power plants, and other critical infrastructure areas.

Although x-ray radiography shares certain similarities with the gamma-ray radiography, it is more effective for the detection of particular nuclear materials as compared with gamma-ray technologies, as it distinguishes between organic vs. inorganic materials (Strellis 2004).

Customs and other law enforcement agencies carry out inspections in which the x-ray technologies pass through the container boxes and subsequently generate images of the contents with minimum delay.

8.3.4.9 Biosurveillance

Biosurveillance is significant to ensure health situational awareness, especially when combined with other health-related methods and instruments, such as intelligence technologies, supply chain operational activities, lab/diagnostics, and so on (HSS 2015). Biosurveillance is a technique of collecting, combining, analyzing, and communicating important information that may possibly connect with biological hazards and threats to human, animal, or plant health. Biosurveillance functions cover anything from conventional epidemiological procedures to sophisticated state-of-the-art technologies.

8.3.4.10 Thermal Imaging

Infrared thermography, thermal video, and imaging technologies are illustrations of infrared imaging technology. Thermographic cameras identify radiation in the infrared spectrum of the electromagnetic range (approximately 9000–14,000 nm or 9–14 µm) and generate thermograms, i.e., radiation-based image. Thermal imaging cameras accentuate

(a)

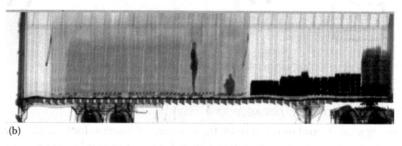

(b)

FIGURE 8.12   (a) Portal VACIS gamma-ray radiography device designed to take x-ray like images of cargo containers. (Courtesy of Thufir, 2005. Available at http://commons .wikimedia.org/wiki/File:Portal_VACIS_x-ray.JPG, accessed March 5, 2015.) (b) VACIS Gamma-ray image of a shipping container showing two stowaways. (Available at https:// upload.wikimedia.org/wikipedia/commons/d/d7/VACIS_Gamma-ray_Image_with _stowaways.GIF, accessed March 5, 2015.)

preexisting security systems in the entire supply chain, i.e., transportation, manufacturing, power plants, and so on.

These technologies provide well-defined visuals and video footage of what cannot be seen in the naked eye or what normal CCTV systems cannot define. This technology perceives infrared energy, as opposed to visible light, in order to create images based on the slightest temperature variations. This enables thermal imaging systems to observe in the greatest detail at night or in foggy, dusty, or humid atmosphere.

Thermal imaging surveillance cameras as shown in Figure 8.13 are used for traffic monitoring purposes in order to identify illegitimate trade or transport of humans, animals, or cargoes.

8.3.5 Aviation Security Technologies

8.3.5.1 Credential Authentication Technology

Credential authentication technology (CAT) instantly authenticates personal identification documents that passengers demonstrate to TSA throughout the security gate-screening

(a)

(b)

FIGURE 8.13   (a) Thermal Imaging Technology. Central Command Area of Responsibility —
Fire Controlman 3rd Class John Hunt views an Iranian merchant ship using thermal
imaging on board the guided missile destroyer USS Paul Hamilton (DDG 60). Hamilton
is currently conducting Maritime Interception Operations (MIO) in the region. MIO
operations are performed by specially-trained personnel who board and inspect vessels
to ensure they are in accordance with U.N. resolutions and to prevent transportation
of illegal cargo. Hamilton is deployed and conducting a variety of mission in support of Operation Enduring Freedom. (Courtesy of U.S. Navy, Photographers Mate
2nd Class Jeffrey Lehrberg. Available at https://commons.wikimedia.org/wiki/File:US
_Navy_021209-N-0331L-001_viewing_an_Iranian_merchant_ship_using_thermal
_imaging.jpg, accessed March 5, 2015.) (b) Thermography of a Steam Locomotive.
Radiant Power visible by Thermography = Emitted Radiant Power + Transmitted Radiant
Power + Reflected Radiant Power. (Courtesy of Wikicommons, https://upload.wikimedia
.org/wikipedia/commons/2/25/ParowozIR.jpg, accessed March 5, 2015.)

procedure. It improves security and offers optimum efficiency by instantly validating
passenger ID as recognition while acquiring the traveler's vetting status (TSA 2014a,b).

The Credential Authentication Technology/Boarding Pass Scanning System (CAT/
BPSS) ensures the authenticity of travelers' personal identification papers and/or board-
ing passes at TSA security checkpoints. TSA is modernizing its privacy impact assessment
(PIA) to mirror its intention to network CAT/BPSS so that they can transfer information

from the Secure Flight1 database to CAT/BPSS systems at security checkpoints. This PIA-upgraded system relates to all areas where TSA will start and set up Secure Flight connections. Wherever TSA carries on operating CAT/BPSS systems devoid of Secure Flight connectivity, the formerly published PIAs of November 2007 and August 2009 are in effect. This process will not modify the personal privacy bearing of the data acquired formerly by TSA for the Secure Flight system (DHS/TSA/PIA, 2013).

8.3.5.2 Advanced Imaging Technology

Advanced imaging technology (AIT) is a nonintrusive system that securely monitors individuals for metal and nonmetal risks, such as firearms and blasting agents, that could be concealed beneath garments to assist TSA in maintaining the traveling public secure. TSA commenced screening the innovative AIT back in 2007 and commenced setting up systems to airport terminals in 2008. These systems can recognize a wide variety of hazards to transport security in real time, within just a few seconds, to safeguard travelers and crews. Imaging technologies are an essential component of TSA's attempt to continuously search for innovative systems that make certain that travel continues to be secure by remaining ahead of developing risks.

TSA presently employs nonintrusive "millimeter-wave AIT" to securely screen travelers for metal and nonmetal threats. About 740 AIT units are stationed at approximately 160 airports across the country.

All AIT systems stationed at airports are created to strengthen and safeguard passenger level of privacy by removing passenger-specific visuals and as an alternative auto-detecting possible threats and displaying their position on a generic format of a traveler that is similar for all individuals.

AIT screening process is risk-free for all travelers, and the technologies employed satisfy the government's safety and health requirements. Considering that imaging technology has been implemented at airports, an excess of 99% of passengers prefer to get processed through security by this technology over different screening processes (TSA AIT 2014).

8.3.5.3 Bottled Liquid Scanners

Bottled liquid code reader and screening techniques are employed throughout the country by transportation security authorities to identify likely liquid or other solution hazards that could be found in a traveler's baggage. These systems distinguish fluid explosives from typical yet potentially hazardous liquids and is employed to screen safe yet common fluids that are used by airline passengers if the quantities are exceeding 3.4 oz., i.e., the maximum permissible limits. BLS systems employ a range of technologies such as infrared, electromagnetic resonance, lasers, and so on (TSA 2014a).

8.3.5.4 Explosive-Detection System

All luggage and bags boarding on the plane, regardless of whether allowed as carry-on or taken as baggage, are screened for explosives. With approximately 2 million individuals traveling on a daily basis, the security officers have a difficult task to achieve. This is accomplished by utilizing blasting sensors and pertinent technologies that operate in a similar manner like the CT equipment used in the medical science. By way of an advanced assessment of every checked luggage, the explosive-detection system (EDS) equipment can rapidly record an impression of an individual bag and establish if this luggage includes a possible risk item. If further screening is needed, it could be instantly redirected to a resolution area where security authorities will thoroughly examine it to make certain it does not impose a security risk; in that situation, law enforcement officers or HazMat, fire department, or other specialists may be contacted. While employed in addition to an airport's computerized inline luggage-handling program, remarkable benefits in terms of both security and effectiveness are accomplished.

8.3.5.5 ETD

ETD is a method employed at security checkpoints globally to check luggage and travelers for remnants of explosives. ETD technologies are utilized on an arbitrary time frame. Authorities may swab a part of the carry-on or examined luggage or a traveler's palms and subsequently position the swab within the ETD device to examine it with the purpose of identifying the existence of possible explosive deposits. ETD technologies are widely utilized in airport terminals ever since 2010 as an element of TSA's multidimensional strategy to aviation security while also keeping travelers secure.

8.3.5.6 Paperless Boarding Pass

The paperless boarding pass (PBP) innovative program allows travelers to acquire a downloadable copy of their boarding pass on their mobile phones or individual digital software. This progressive method simplifies the client encounter with security authorities while elevating the chance to identify falsified boarding passes. Every digital boarding pass is exhibited as an encoded two-dimensional barcode together with traveler and flight data. TSA security officers utilize scanning devices to verify the genuineness of the boarding pass at the gate. At the checkpoint gate, a TSA travel document-checking official will direct the traveler on how their mobile phone can be used in order for TSA to easily verify the genuineness of the boarding pass. Travelers will always be needed to display photo ID so authorities can authenticate that the name stated on the boarding pass fits with the name on the ID.

8.3.5.7 TIP: Security Training Software

On top of the educational drills and theories, the authorities use hands-on coaching to maintain the security officials' capabilities heightened. Within the everyday utilization of TIP computer software, the security authorities are consistently examined on their capability to sense weapons and blasting agents by the use of x-ray. Likely risks, such as carrying weapons and blasting agents, are demonstrated as x-ray scanned pictures of carry-on hand luggage so our security specialists continue to be concentrated and receptive. This variety of assessments enable authorities to assess personal efficiency, and real-time response, and as a result improve and restructure the instructional package as deemed suitable. Due to the fact that x-ray devices are connected to a huge interior system, every single airport and x-ray screening system obtains computerized impression updates from the technology lab. In turn, this is demonstrated to the security authorities throughout the country for investigation and intelligence purposes.

8.3.6 Maritime Technologies

Multimodal transportation arrangements require the harmonization of security measures among sea, land, and air transport. However, maritime transportation accounts for about 80% of global transportation in terms of sheer volume (Burns 2013). This suggests that all transportation modes share similar security challenges, such as terrorism patterns, illegitimate trade (contraband), cargo theft, illegitimate travel, and immigration by the use of hidden areas in carriers. Among these threats, hijacking—which in the maritime industry is called "piracy"—will be duly examined hereby.

In the aftermath of the 9/11 attacks in the United States, the IMO, under the umbrella of the United Nations, founded the International Ship and Port Facility Security Code (ISPS Code). This is a compulsory set of security protocols and regulations that aim to improve the security of ships and port facilities. Both the requirements of the ISPS Code and pressures deriving from the criminal activities of pirates (kidnapping or killing of seafarers in order to leverage higher ransom money) have urged the maritime industry to produce and employ unique technologies for the protection of human life, the environment, the ship, and its cargo. These technologies, as seen in Figures 8.14 and 8.15, will be concisely stated in this section.

What all these technologies have in common is that they help reduce the carriers' insurance premiums, and their uses are also used in military combatting.

8.3.6.1 Technologies in Ships' Panic Rooms (Citadels or Safe Rooms)

Among the countermeasures against piracy, citadels are the bulletproof, air-conditioned, remotely located rooms where crew members can hide in case their ship has been hijacked.

The panic room serves two main purposes:

1. To serve as a refuge for the ship's crew, thus eliminating the possibility of an attack leading to hostage-taking, fatalities, or injuries.
2. To provide emergency technologies where the crew may
   a. Transmit distress signals and await for rescue operations by military and other forces and

FIGURE 8.14 USS Boxer tows the lifeboat from the Maersk Alabama to Boxer to be processed for evidence after the successful rescue of Captain Robert Phillips. (From US Navy photo courtesy of Mass Communication Specialist 2nd Class Jon Rasmussen.)

FIGURE 8.15   M/V Maersk Alabama of Maersk Lines using high-pressure hoses to deter pirates from boarding the vessel. (Courtesy of Maersk Lines.)

b. Remotely monitor and control ship's functions, such as turning off the vessel's engines and automated systems, thus disabling the pirates to navigate the ship to a region they have planned

Eventually, the pirates may decide to loot the ship, and disembark on their own will, while rescue operations are on their way.

8.3.6.2 Armed Security Guards

Pursuant to a number of serious piracy incidents that led to the kidnapping, abduction, or even torture and death of seafarers, the IMO has made provisions for the use of Armed Maritime Security Guards onboard ships. Typically, the shipowners or the cargo owners hire the guards from specialized maritime private military companies or private security companies. The guards are highly trained professionals, frequently military veterans or former law-enforcement officers.

Despite the fact that the use of firearms onboard ships for self-defense purposes is legally authorized, each maritime company has established different security provisions depending on their national regulations, company culture, and the perception of security threats that will dictate what type of guards they will hire for their ships. In some cases, the company may hire well-equipped military veterans, whereas companies with antigun policies may only hire men of limited training to serve mainly for watch-keeping purposes (Sea Security 2014). In both cases, the purpose of the security guards is not to assault but to prevent pirates from boarding the ship. In both cases, the daily fees for a team of four armed guards is approximately $5000 per day, whereas the duration of a trip could range between 5 and 25 days (Burns 2013).

8.3.6.3 Active Denial System (Nonlethal)

This technology, also called "Vehicle-Mounted Active Denial System," was first developed by Raytheon in 2000 in collaboration with the US DOD.

The system sends a not visible, narrow beam of 95-GHz millimeter electromagnetic waves toward any target within 700 yd. As the waves travel at the speed of light, they can penetrate the target's skin to a superficial depth of 1/64 of an inch. While this causes a heat sensation, no visible or permanent injury is caused.

The purpose of this weapon is to deter pirates from boarding the vessel.

8.3.6.4 Optical Laser Distractor (Dazzler; Antipiracy Laser Device) (Nonlethal)

Dazzlers or optical distracters are being used in the maritime industry as nonlethal piracy preventive measures. These systems, as shown in Figure 8.16, send a narrow beam of intensive light in order to catch the pirates' attention and intimidate them from approaching the vessel. Another purpose of this weapon is to temporarily impair their vision by the intense light.

This is a high-performance laser beam created to dazzle and temporarily blind the pirates without causing permanent eye or other health damage.

This nonlethal technology can be used through day and night and reaches targets of over half a mile away (2 km). The beam can be linked with the ship's radar and sensor

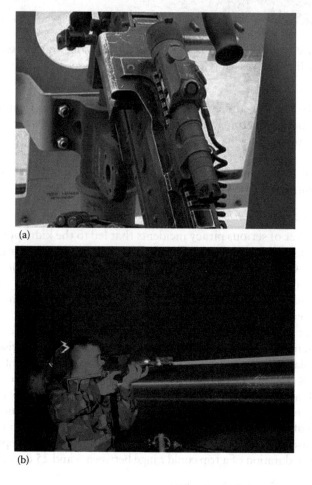

(a)

(b)

FIGURE 8.16   (a) Optical (Green) Dazzler mounted on M-240B in Iraq. (Courtesy of Wikimedia. Available at https://upload.wikimedia.org/wikipedia/commons/thumb/7/7e /Dazzler_mounted_on_M-240B_in_Iraq.jpg, accessed March 12, 2015.) (b) US Navy Master-at-Arms 2nd Class Victor Arroyos, from San Antonio, fires the Navy's optical dazzler on the fantail of the aircraft carrier. (Courtesy of Wikimedia. Available at https:// en.wikipedia.org/wiki/Master-at-arms#/media/File:US_Navy_101016-N-2218M-027 _Master-at-Arms_2nd_Class_Victor_Arroyos_from_San_Antonio_fires_the_Navy%27s _Dazzler_on_the_fantail_of_the_aircraft_carri.jpg, accessed March 12, 2015.)

technologies in order to identify targets both mechanically and with human intervention. Dazzlers are used not only for maritime security and supply chain security but also for critical infrastructure protection.

8.3.6.5 Boat Trap (Net) (Nonlethal)

This is a self-protection mechanism consisting of nets and/or wires used to seize and inactivate (jam) the propellers of fast-speed pirate boats that may attack commercial vessels. These nets are thrown by helicopters or kept on side booms onboard the vessels and can expand for over 30 ft. (10 m) from the ship.

The mechanism operates even while the vessel operates in full speed or is heavily maneuvering, i.e., unlike previous patents that were operable under certain speed or maneuvering restrictions. This is especially useful, as a ship typically increases speed and increases maneuvering in order to keep the pirates away from the vulnerable locations on the ship's sides (port and starboard).

8.3.6.6 Long-Range Acoustic Device (Nonlethal)

The Long-Range Acoustic Device (LRAD), or sound canon, is a high-intensity directional sonic weapon developed for long-range transmission and delivering potent alert tones.

This innovative technology is intended for military, public safety, and emergency use when forewarnings, alerts, directions, or emergency response messages need to be conveyed.

LRAD systems are user-friendly via a straightforward, recognizable, and consistent interface. Hand-operated or independent systems are developed for 24/7 performance in extreme environments.

The system broadcasts with focused sonar technology to convey their messages from 164 ft. (50 m) of other, less effective technologies, to 9800 ft. (3000 m) with the use of LRAD systems (LRAD 2014).

8.4 CONCLUSION

Among a plethora of supply chain and transportation security technologies, this chapter examined the ones mostly used by federal governments and the industry. The impact of technology in eliminating security threats seems to be one of paramount significance. However, its impact also depends on other factors, such as risk assessment (Chapter 9) and the human factor (Chapter 10), during an incident. Risk assessment methodologies are necessary to evaluate threats and allocate the right resources at the right time and the right location in order to mitigate the risk, whereas the human factor is the catalyst in utilizing all the technologies, regulations, and security protocols discussed herein.

REFERENCES

Beidou. 2014. Chinese Beidou Navigation Satellite System Officially into Global Radio Navigation System. Available at http://www.beidou.gov.cn/. Accessed December 20, 2014.

Best-Rowden, L., Bisht, S., Klontz, J.C., and Jain, A.K. 2014. Unconstrained face recognition: Establishing baseline human performance via crowdsourcing. *Proceedings of IEEE IJCB. Institute of Electrical and Electronics Engineers.* Available at http://openbiometrics.org /publications/bestrowden2014unconstrained.pdf. Accessed November 7, 2014.

Boland, R. 2012. Military Counters Anti-Access Threats. Armed Forces Communications Electronics Association (AFCEA). Available at http://www.afcea.org. Accessed November 7, 2014.

Burns, M. 2013. Estimating the impact of maritime security: Financial tradeoffs between security and efficiency. *Journal of Transportation Security*, December, Volume 6, Issue 4, pp. 329–338. May 31, 2013, Springer.

CBP. 2014. Radiation Portal Monitors Safeguard America from Nuclear Devices and Radiological Materials. US Customs and Border Protection. Available at http://www.cbp.gov/border-security/port-entry/cargo-security/cargo-exam/rad-portal1. Accessed November 7, 2014.

Crane, T.W. and Baker, M.P. 2013. Neutron Detectors. Available at http://energy.gov/sites/prod/files/2013/07/f2/hdbk-1122-04_lp216_0.pdf. Accessed December 14, 2014.

Crouch, T.T. 1988. *Compilation of LIC References and Bibliography*, Vol. II. Langley Air Force Base, VA, Army-Air Force Center for Low Intensity Conflict.

DHS. 2012. Cell-All: Super Smartphones Sniff Out Suspicious Substances. Available at http://www.dhs.gov/cell-all-super-smartphones-sniff-out-suspicious-substances. Accessed December 14, 2014.

DHS BOSS. 2012. Privacy Impact Assessment Update for the Standoff Technology Integration and Demonstration Program: Biometric Optical Surveillance System Tests. DHS/S&T STIDP/PIA-008(b) December 17, 2012. Available at http://www.dhs.gov/sites/default/files/publications/privacy/PIAs/privacy_pia_st_stidpboss_dec2012.pdf. Accessed December 14, 2014.

DHS NTAS. 2014. The National Terrorism Advisory System (NTAS). Available at http://www.dhs.gov/ntas-public-guide. Accessed December 14, 2014.

DHS OBIM. 2013. Office of Biometric Identity Management (OBIM) Identification Services. Available at http://www.dhs.gov/obim-biometric-identification-services. Accessed December 6, 2014.

DHS/TSA/PIA. 2013. Credential Authentication Technology/Boarding Pass Scanning System. DHS/TSA/PIA-024(b). January 18. Available at http://www.dhs.gov/sites/default/files/publications/privacy/PIAs/privacy_pia%20update_tsa_cat%20bpss_20130118.pdf. Accessed December 6, 2014.

DOE Patents. 2013. Patent Assignee: Los Alamos National Security, LLC (Los Alamos, NM). Inventors: Wang, Zhehui; Morris, Christopher; Bacon, Jeffrey Darnell; Makela, Mark F; Spaulding, Randy Jay. Available at http://www.osti.gov/doepatents/biblio/1083974. Accessed December 1, 2014.

Erwin, S.I., Magnuson, S., Parsons, D., and Tadjdeh, Y. 2012. Top Five Threats to National Security in the Coming Decade. Available at http://www.nationaldefensemagazine.org/archive/2012/August/Pages/default.aspx. Accessed December 14, 2014.

ESA. 2014. European Space Agency. Available at http://www.esa.int. Accessed December 1, 2014.

FAA. 2014. FAA Aerospace Forecast Fiscal Years 2010–2030. Unmanned Aircraft Systems. Federal Aviation Administration (FAA). Available at https://www.faa.gov/data_research/aviation/aerospace_forecasts/2010-2030/media/Unmanned%20Aircraft%20Systems.pdf. Accessed November 7, 2014.

FBI. 2014. Fingerprints and other biometrics. US Federal Bureau of Investigation. Available at http://www.fbi.gov/about-us/cjis/fingerprints_biometrics. Accessed December 1, 2014.

GAO. 2013. Combating Nuclear Smuggling: Lessons Learned from Cancelled Radiation Portal Monitor Program Could Help Future Acquisitions. GAO-13-256: Published: May 13, 2013. Publicly Released: Jun 11, 2013. Available at http://gao.gov/products /GAO-13-256. Accessed November 7, 2014.

Goodman, M. 2012. How technology makes us vulnerable. CNN, July 29, 2012. Available at http://www.cnn.com/2012/07/29/opinion/goodman-ted-crime. Accessed December 6, 2014.

Goodman, M. 2013. Criminals and Terrorists Can Fly Drones Too. Remote-Controlled Aircraft and Robot Technology Can Be Used for Bad Just As Easily As For Good. Jan. 31, 2013. Available at http://ideas.time.com/2013/01/31/criminals-and-terrorists-can -fly-drones-too. Accessed December 14, 2014.

Homeland Security Newswire. 2013. Facial Recognition Biometric Technology Identifies One of the Boston Marathon Bombers. Published May 28, 2013. Available at http:// www.homelandsecuritynewswire.com/dr20130527-biometric-technology-identifies -one-of-the-boston-marathon-bombers. Accessed December 14, 2014.

IMO. 2014a. Regulations for carriage of Automatic identification systems (AISs). International Maritime Organization. Available at http://www.imo.org. Accessed November 7, 2014.

IMO. 2014b. Safety of Life at Sea Convention, SOLAS 1974 December 2000 amendments. Available at http://www.imo.org. Accessed November 7, 2014.

Kahn, J. 2008. Mumbai Terrorists Relied on New Technology for Attacks. December 8, 2008, India. The New York Times. Available at http://www.nytimes.com /2008/12/09/world/asia/09mumbai.html. Accessed December 6, 2014.

Knoll, G.F. 2010. Radiation Detection and Measurement, 4th Ed. Fowley D. Publishers, USA.

Lam, S. 2012. Helium-3 Proportional Counters and Alternatives for Neutron Detection. Stanford University. March 19, 2012. Available at http://large.stanford.edu /courses/2012/ph241/lam1/. Accessed October 12, 2014.

LANL Muon. 2003. Los Alamos. Available at http://www.lanl.gov/quarterly/q_spring03 /muon_text.shtml. Accessed November 7, 2014.

LLNL. 2014. Mono-Energetic Gamma-ray (MEGa-ray). Laurence Livermore National Laboratory. Available at https://lasers.llnl.gov/science/photon-science/mega-ray. Accessed December 14, 2014.

LRAD 2014. LRAD System. LRAD Corp. Available at http://www.lradx.com/site/. Accessed October 23, 2014.

NATO Review. 2004. Military Matters: Combating Terrorism through Technology. Marshall Billingslea examines how NATO is developing technology to counter increasingly sophisticated terrorism. Available at http://www.nato.int/docu /review/2004/issue3/english/military.html. Accessed December 6, 2014.

Needs, C. 2007. Disaster Preparedness 2011: Smart Phones Enhanced with Nanotube Hazmat Detectors Bring a New Dimension to Preparedness. Available at http:// www.cbrne-terrorism-newsletter.com/resources/Winter%202011%20NSL%20 PART%202.pdf. Accessed December 14, 2014.

NIST Biometrics. 2007. Biometric Automated Toolset (BAT) and Handheld Interagency Identity Detection Equipment (HIIDE). Overview for NIST XML & Mobile ID Workshop. Biometrics Task Force. September 19, 2007. Available at http://biomet rics.nist.gov/cs_links/standard/archived/workshops/xmlandmobileid/Presentations -docs/Vermury-BAT-HIIDE.pdf. Accessed November 7, 2014.

NovAtel. 2014. GNSS Applications. NovAtel Inc. Available at http://www.novatel.com /an-introduction-to-gnss/chapter-1-gnss-overview/section-3/#sthash.BGBOJkqO .dpuf. Accessed November 12, 2014.

NRC. 2013. Special Nuclear Material. US Nuclear Regulatory Commission. Available at http://www.nrc.gov/materials/sp-nucmaterials.html. Accessed December 14, 2014.

Rice, J. and Caniato, F. 2003. Building a secure and resilient supply chain network. SCMR. MIT. Available at http://web.mit.edu/scresponse/repository/Rice_SCResp _Article_SCMR.pdf.

SCST. 2014. Hutchison-Whampoa 2014. Available at http://www.hutchison-whampoa .com/en/media/press_each.php?id=1086. Accessed December 14, 2014.

Sea Security. 2014. The rise of private maritime security companies. Sea Security Organization. Available at http://www.seasecurity.org/mediacentre/the-rise-of-private -maritime-security-companies/#sthash.RPIbFbQ6.dpuf. Accessed December 2, 2014.

Seto, Y. 2009. Retina recognition. In Li, S.Z. (ed.) *Encyclopedia of Biometrics*, pp. 1128– 1130. Springer Publishers.

Strellis, D.A. 2004. "Protecting our Borders while Ensuring Radiation Safety." Presentation to the Northern California Chapter of the Health Physics Society. Retrieved September 2007.

TSA AIT. 2014. Advanced Imaging Technology. Available at http://www.tsa.gov/traveler -information/advanced-imaging-technology. Accessed December 6, 2014.

TSA. 2012. Reader Qualified Technology List (QTL). Available at http://www.tsa.gov /stakeholders/reader-qualified-technology-list-qtl. Accessed December 14, 2014.

TSA. 2014a. Credential Authentication Technology (CAT). Available at http://www.tsa .gov/about-tsa/security-technologies. Accessed December 6, 2014.

TSA. 2014b. Technology. Available at http://www.tsa.gov/about-tsa/technology. Accessed December 6, 2014.

US Airforce. 2014. MQ-9 Reaper. Available at http://www.af.mil/AboutUs/FactSheets /Display/tabid/224/Article/104470/mq-9-reaper.aspx. Accessed December 6, 2014.

US Army. 1989. U.S. Army Field Manual 100-20, Military Operations of Low Intensity Conflict. Washington, DC. 1989. P.1-10.

Washington Post Foreign Service. 2008. Wednesday, December 3, 2008. Available at http:// www.washingtonpost.com/wp-dyn/content/article/2008/12/02/AR2008120203519 .html. Accessed December 6, 2014.

Wax, Emily. 2008. Mumbai Attackers made sophisticated use of technology. Washington Post Foreign Service. December 3, 2008. Available at http://www.washingtonpost.com /wp-dyn/content/article/2008/12/02/AR2008120203519.html. Accessed August 1, 2014.

Wolverton, Mark. 2007. "Muons for Peace." *Scientific American*, September 2007, Volume 297 No. 3, pp. 26–28. doi:10.1038/scientificamerican0907-26

Yousri, A.M., Osman, A.M., Kansouh, W.A., Reda, A.M., Bashter, I.I., and Megahid, R.M. 2012. Scanning of cargo containers by gamma-ray and fast neutron radiography. *Armenian Journal of Physics*, Vol. 5, Issue 1. Laboratories for Detection of Landmines and Illicit Materials, Nuclear Research Centre, Atomic Energy Authority, Cairo, Egypt.

CHAPTER **9**

Security Risk Analysis

Wise men say, and not without reason,
That whoever wished to foresee the future
Might consult the past.

Niccolo Machiavelli (1469–1527)

9.1 IDENTIFYING SECURITY VULNERABILITIES

This section pertains to risk analysis, risk assessment, and risk management. Governments and companies alike try to create resilient systems as security-related interruptions have the power to immobilize global production and supply and therefore affect the entire supply chain. Over the past few decades, global supply chains grew immensely through forming complex networks in order to boost performance and cost efficiency and satisfy customers' demands. This growing intricacy of supply chains tends to increase risk, as visibility is limited, and the control span is significantly diminished. In instances where disruptions are inadequately controlled, the domino effect phenomenon occurs, as a single threat manifesting at a single component of a supply chain can significantly influence other parts. Governments and companies alike utilize risk analysis tools and protocols in order to manage and control risky events as they occur.

9.1.1 Security in a "High-Risk, High-Reward" Industry

Risk can be described as the likelihood that an incident will take place and negatively impact the attainment of the company's strategies, goals, and objectives. Based upon the "high risk, high reward" principle, the industry's need for security seems to be as strong as the need for expansion. The primary functions of global trade and transport networks are based upon this principle, where resilient and secure systems also need to be flexible, reliable, and capable of functioning with limited delays or obstructions. The role of the modern risk manager is therefore increasingly challenging, as nations and industries can only achieve rewards through their exposure to certain risks.

Globalization has brought about a number of opportunities for strategic partnerships enabled through sizable and intricate supply chains. These opportunities for growth are likely to harbor security risks. Some of these risks may pertain to not only cargo theft, illegitimate trade, human trafficking, sea piracy, and money laundering but also sabotage and terrorist activities. Global logistics and supply chains involve high-risk, high-intensity, and high-profit activities, and therefore, risk analysis should be implemented as a nonstop, sustainable process.

9.1.2 Security Risk Analysis and Its Components

Security risk analysis is a method employed to recognize and evaluate security risks that may endanger the integrity of a system, venture, or activity at a corporate or national level. The method is utilized in order to develop proactive security tools that will eliminate and/or mitigate threats.

As demonstrated in Figure 9.1, risk analysis is made up of three primary components, i.e.,

i. *Security risk management (SRM)*, which can be defined as the monitoring and controlling of security risks; it is the methodical technique of comprehending, analyzing, and dealing with such risks to increase the levels of corporate or national resilience and sustainability. Furthermore, SRM reveals new security paths, alternatives, and resources that are derived out of change, thus offering new avenues and opportunities. Ultimately, successful SRM supports corporate growth by promoting awareness, classification, and mitigation of security risks;

ii. *Security risk assessment (SRA)*, which is defined as the method to recognize potential security risks and assess the potential outcomes of such an incident in terms of risk factors, such as vulnerabilities, intensity, duration, and so on. A security impact analysis (SIA) could be implemented in order to verify the possible effects caused by security threats, which could cause loss of life, damage or loss of assets, commodities, trade interruptions, corporate performance, and so on; and

iii. *Security risk communication (SRC)*, which is defined as the information exchange before, during, and after a security threat has occurred. When used proactively, SRC helps promote preparedness, intelligence, and avoidance of risk, whereas during a security attack, SRC facilitates the emergency response process and general public announcements. Most importantly, SRC builds resilience as it helps minimize the probability, impact, and recovery time.

FIGURE 9.1   Risk analysis and its components. (From the author.)

9.1.2.1 Risk Management

> Because it is not feasible to secure our homeland against every conceivable threat, we have instituted risk management as the primary basis for policy and resource allocation decision making.
>
> **DHS Strategic Plan 2012–2016**

Since the only way to eliminate risks would be to eliminate sustainability and growth, nations and the global industry have developed a set of risk management tools, with the purpose of handling risks.

Risk management can be defined as an ongoing process that is achieved during the entire life span of a project, system, or supply chain operations. It is a well-structured technique for pinpointing and measuring unidentified factors that may influence the outcomes and create appeasement strategies. Risk management helps mitigate risk through carefully determining, choosing, preparing, and applying case-specific risk mitigations. Successful risk management is determined by the effectiveness of risk management planning, prompt detection, recognition and evaluation of risk, prompt response and corrective actions, ongoing evaluating, monitoring, re-evaluation, risk communication, documentation, and coordination (DOD 2006).

Risk management is the procedure of risk recognition, evaluation, and handling of those risks. The two main steps of risk management pertain to understanding the existing risks and dealing with them in a manner that the corporate goals and objectives are met.

The complete risk management process involves strategic and synchronized procedures that are designed to

  i. Reduce the risk impact created by an event–outcome combination
 ii. Reduce the likelihood of that event–outcome combination
iii. Strengthen, guide, and assist emergency responders
 iv. Facilitate incident investigation, root cause analysis, and crisis management and eventually assist in systemic recovery

9.1.2.1.1 The Stages of Risk Management   As seen in Figure 9.2, risk management is conducted in the following key steps:

1. Threat evaluation: External risks
   Security threats, in particular, pertain to the intention of an offender to inflict harm or damage upon a company, industry, a society segment, or a nation.
2. Assessment of systemic vulnerabilities: Internal risks
   While the first stage focuses on the external risk factors, i.e., the intention of criminals to attack, this stage pertains to the internal risk factors or weaknesses: risk managers are hereby asked to evaluate tangible and intangible vulnerabilities:
   a. *Tangible vulnerabilities* may include land, capital, technologies, merchandise, energy, buildings, and other infrastructure or superstructure.
   b. *Intangible vulnerabilities* may include strategies and tactics, partnerships, innovation, entrepreneurship, labor, skills and training, information technology, and so on (see Figure 9.2).

FIGURE 9.2 The stages of risk management. (From the author.)

3. Threat classification based on probability and impact

   Some threats may be very likely and of low or moderate impact (such as cargo theft), whereas others may be of low probability yet of high impact (such as a terrorist attack).

4. Resource management

   Resource management is used to employ the right tools and resources needed to avert or reduce risks. Once internal and external risks are evaluated and classified, as per steps 1–3 of the risk management methodology, resource allocation and management is essential for the next two steps to be successful. Efficient resource allocation is needed both to prevent and mitigate a security threat. If the threat cannot be averted, resources are also needed to respond during the security incident.

   Resource management can be defined as the effective and efficient usage of a nation's or company's resources as and when required. These resources can be tangible and/or intangible.

   a. *Tangible resources* may include land, capital, technologies, merchandise, energy, buildings, and other infrastructure or superstructure.

   b. *Intangible resources* may include strategies and tactics, partnerships, innovation, entrepreneurship, labor, skills and training, information technology, and so on.

   It is worth noting that the same tangible and intangible assets that serve as a system's resources are at the same time a system's vulnerabilities (see Figure 9.2).

5. Proactive risk elimination

   By cultivating and sustaining a proactive culture, risks can be avoided or limited. The level of preparedness depends upon the company's ability or desire to allocate time, funds, resources, and efforts in risk elimination. Also, accurate forecasts (output) depend on the accuracy of input in the risk assessment process.

6. Risk mitigation and crisis management

While risk management primarily aims to be proactive, in order to avoid risks, crisis management tools and processes are also in position to be used during emergency response, i.e., in case the risk cannot be avoided, and hence has to be addressed and overcome.

7. Building resilient systems

These are systems that have the capacity, resources, and strength to recover fast after a security attack.

8. Building sustainable systems

Sustainability moves beyond resilience, as the system is robust enough to withstand security attacks, with minimum vulnerabilities and/or the capacity to recover with minimum disruptions and losses.

Concurrently, these elements address the three key aspects of hazard: (i) probability, (ii) consequences, and (iii) impacts. In the last few years, the approach to risk analysis has been progressively improved and refined from segmented procedures and company performance to a holistic approach encompassing a group of allied companies, supply chains, an industry, or a nation. The practices of risk analysis are anticipated to further develop and expand in order to encircle the global trade activities and the increasingly complex supply chains.

Risk assessment and risk management support both nations and industries in evaluating and comprehending the possible risks, and vulnerabilities exist. When a proactive culture is adopted, risks can be predicted and can therefore be prevented or reduced before they severely affect the national or commercial security.

9.1.2.2 Risk Assessment

Risk assessment can be defined as the methodical procedure for pinpointing and analyzing occurrences such as probable risks and possibilities that may impact the desired results in a negative or positive manner. These incidents or trends may be

a. *Internal*, which may include but are not limited to human error, negligence, fatigue, lack of training, lack of familiarization, inefficiency, lack of cash flow, shortage or problems with any and all of the factors of production, strikes, and so on. Internal risks can be further classified as strategic, tactical, and operational.

b. *External*, including but not limited to supply versus demand changes, new market entrants, competition, market cycle and economic cycle fluctuations, substitute trade routes, transportation modes or emerging hub ports, and new legislation or regulation.

Risk assessment aims to identify the potential events that may interfere with the company's strategies, goals, and objectives.

An efficient risk assessment methodology employed as a component of the company's culture enables administrators to better recognize, assess, and make the most of corporate risks while sustaining the proper configurations to guarantee optimum performance and regulatory compliance.

Risk assessments need to be focused in the company's drivers, which could be commercial, operational, technological, safety, security, environment, quality, and so on. Figure 9.3 demonstrates the risk assessment methodology adopted for trade and transport security in particular.

Hazard identification	Vulnerability assessment	Impact analysis
Hazards: probability and impact	Assets at risk: vulnerabilities	Impacts
• Terrorism • Marine piracy • Land and air hijacking • HazMat/biological/nuclear threat • Money laundering • Cyber attack • Illegitimate trade • Illegitimate travel	• National security • Populations • Environment: flora and fauna • Critical infrastructure and IT • Supply chains • Factors of production • Copyright infringement • Commercial disruptions • Loss of reputation • Growth	• National security damage • Fatalities, injuries, permanent total disability (PTD) • Environmental pollution • Critical infrastructure damage • Supply chain disruptions, delays, material losses • Loss of reputation • Growth hindrance

FIGURE 9.3 Risk assessment methodology for trade and transport security. (From Burns, M., adopted by "The Ready Campaign" of US Government, available at http://www.ready.gov, accessed December 12, 2014, 2014.)

Proactive risk indications improve the capacity to mitigate true threats and take advantage of opportunities well in advance. Since risk assessments are time sensitive, and industry specific, tailor-made amendments are likely to ensure the most beneficial results.

Risk assessment employs a combination of strategic tools in order to establish a robust, resilient system. Such tools may include

   i. Risk identification and forecasting
  ii. Risk communication
 iii. Risk management
  iv. Risk deterrence
   v. Risk monitoring and controlling
  vi. Risk transfer
 vii. Risk mitigation
viii. Risk acceptance
  ix. Risk outsourcing
   x. Risk sharing, i.e., to third parties or allied organizations that are designated, available, and willing to support the port's risk mitigation by providing financial, technical, operational, or other forms of assistance

9.1.2.2.1 The Purpose of Risk Assessment   The purpose and utility of risk assessment is to

- Generate understanding of potential threats and hazards
- Recognize the vulnerability of each key player and each function within a supply chain in the public and private sectors
- Ascertain whether current preventive actions and contingency plans are sufficient or whether increased action is needed to eliminate vulnerabilities
- Avert consequences, losses, systemic failures, or delays
- Classify risks and preventive action based on probability and vulnerability-based impact

9.1.2.2.2 Examples of Risk Assessment   Risk assessment can be conducted at various levels of the organization.

Examples of frequently performed risk assessments include

a. *Strategic risk assessment.* Top managers typically assess threats concerning the company's vision and strategic plans.
b. *Supply chain risk assessment.* This is conducted by the key players within a supply chain with the purpose of identifying systemic vulnerabilities and ensuring visibility and integration.
c. *Security risk assessment* entails intentional threats such as terrorist attacks, piracy, sabotage, and so on. Systemic vulnerabilities include individuals, critical infrastructure, physical assets, systemic continuity, and so on.
d. *Operational risk assessment.* Assessment of internal or external factors that may cause operational delays or damage related to the factors of production and the flow of people, goods, and services throughout the supply chain.
e. *Product risk assessment* entails the risk factors connected with a company's product management process.
f. *Information technology risk assessment* examines the likelihood and possible impact of technological investments, performance, reliability, profitability, and systemic failures related to information technology, input and output, cyber-attacks, and cyber protection.
g. *Project management risk assessment* involves a project-specific evaluation, key players' contribution and projected gains, processes, time frames, cost–benefit analyses, and so on.

9.1.2.2.3 Risk Assessment Formulas   The level of security risk depends on two factors: (a) the likelihood and (b) the severity of outcomes. Therefore, the equation to assess the security risk based on a single hazard is

$$\text{Security risk assessment} = \text{probability} \times \text{single hazard} \tag{9.1}$$

Security or safety risk may be composite, i.e., entails multiple hazards. These hazards could all pertain to security or could combine safety and security threats.

a. *Composite security hazards.* For instance, the illegitimate transport of bio-hazardous substances or illegitimate immigration could serve as segments of a planned terrorist attack.
b. Likewise, composite safety hazards could entail unintentional damages due to a combination of, e.g., natural disasters and human error.
c. *Composite safety and security hazards.* In this case, a natural disaster such as a hurricane could create systemic vulnerabilities and increase the security risk.

A Composite Risk Index reflects the possibility of an incident with more than one motives or risk impacts and is assessed as follows (Burns 2014a):

$$\text{Composite Risk Index} = \text{probability} \times \text{impact of multiple-hazard event} \tag{9.2}$$

Logistics and supply chains are designed based on a harmonized and standardized system of processes, which are also called "standard operating procedures" (SOPs). Risk

FIGURE 9.4   SOPs for logistics and supply chains. (From the author.)

managers are asked to explore these standardized procedures at an internal and external level and identify both their strengths and vulnerabilities. Figure 9.4 depicts the SOPs within the logistics and supply chains.

9.1.3 Risk Communication

Risk communication can be defined as the data interchange related to a risk, its probabilities, and impact. The practices of risk communication are associated with crisis management and emergency response, which all play a pivotal role in informing the general public about an imminent or potential threat. It promotes leadership and teamwork, and when implemented effectively, it supports human life, facilitates evacuation procedures, and eliminates the possibility of false information.

The National Research Council (1989–2015) describes risk communication as "an interactive process of exchange of information and opinion among individuals, groups, and institutions." The description also entails "discussion about risk types and levels and about methods for managing risks." Particularly, this procedure is characterized by degrees of involvement in choices, actions, or guidelines aimed at handling or coping with security, safety, or other types of risks. Risk communication may be comprised of public engagement interweaved with risk assessment and risk management practices.

9.1.3.1 *The Key Principles of Risk Communication*

According to the US Environmental Protection Agency (EPA 2014), there are seven primary guidelines for the application of risk communication:

1. Recognize and include the general population as being a respectable team member and stakeholder
2. Strategize and assess your initiatives with diligence
3. Pay attention to the community's particular considerations
4. Be truthful, trustworthy, and receptive
5. Work well and team up with other legitimate entities
6. Meet the requirements of the mass media
7. Communicate clearly with tenacity and empathy

9.1.4 Risk Analysis: Challenges and Opportunities

The practices of risk analysis are essential to alleviate modern security threats and entails a number of opportunities and challenges that need to be overcome:

1. Balancing resilience and growth

    As the global commercial stage becomes more promising and more challenging at the same time, it is the role of risk managers to design and apply a framework of specific strategic and tactical tools that will help companies to both mitigate threats and enhance their expansion goals. Risk management is therefore a critical tool that balances resilience with growth.

2. Building a proactive risk management culture

    Risk management needs to be proactive as opposed to reactive. Its goal is to promote a culture of preparedness and active readiness in order to protect the system's resiliency.

    While at a theoretical level, preventing a catastrophe is a priority or a desirable objective for any and all nations and corporations, in the real world, it is difficult to be achieved: risk managers need to identify systemic vulnerabilities even before problems actually arise. Based upon the principle that our security systems are as strong as our weakest link, modern security professionals need to extend their monitoring and controlling activities throughout the entire supply chain and identify the vulnerabilities among hundreds or even thousands of partners, allies, vendors, employees, and clients.

3. Monitoring and controlling complex supply chains

    Globalization has offered modern managers numerous cost-reduction opportunities, such as outsourcing, focus on low-cost, high-volume, and so on. Over time, these activities have created increasingly vulnerable and more complex supply chains, thus complicating the risk assessment and risk management tasks. Outsourcing and global operations have limited the managers' control and visibility. Just-in-time, lean and agile techniques were implemented with the goal of eliminating waste and optimum allocation of resources. However, the improper use of these tools may deplete the company of resources and therefore hinder growth and productivity. Similarly, while the pattern of eliminating the number of vendors and suppliers with the purpose of ensuring product standardization, quality, and price efficiency during a supply chain disruption incident, such as extreme weather, business continuation, or the change of diplomatic relations between countries, companies with a limited number of vendors may be deprived of potential substitute collaborators, which may eventually lead to delays in manufacturing, distribution, and delivery.

A risk pertains to the level of potential vulnerability to damage, which may take place within a specific time, place, and circumstance. The risk severity index, as shown in Figure 9.5, is calculated by multiplying the likelihood of a risk manifesting, with the magnitude of impact if a risk incident takes place. A scale of 1–10 may be used to evaluate the risk likelihood and the potential magnitude of impact, respectively. The following image demonstrates how risk is quantified.

During the risk assessment process, a risk matrix is employed to establish the different levels of risk as the consequence of likelihood and severity. The accuracy and reliability of risk metrics is directly proportionate to the quality of data input, in which case

FIGURE 9.5   Risk severity index.

it serves as a useful tool for the public and private sector that helps improve visibility of risks and justify management strategic decision making. Risk matrices need to be modified to accurately forecast specific risks entailed in individual tasks, projects, and industry segments. Table 9.1 shows the security threat probability ratio, whereas Table 9.2 demonstrates the severity and likelihood categories for risk assessment.

TABLE 9.1   Security Threat Probability Ratio

Level	Security Threat Probability	Likelihood of Occurrence Ratio
1	Improbable	~10%
2	Low probability	~30%
3	Medium probability	~50%
4	High probability	~70%
5	Almost certainty	~90%

TABLE 9.2   Severity and Likelihood Categories for Risk Assessment

	Mishap Risk Assessment Values and Severity Categories			
	Catastrophic	Critical	Marginal	Negligible
Severity and Likelihood	Severity Category I Major Loss/ Damage	Severity Category II Significant Disability or Damage	Severity Category III Minor Disability or Damage	Severity Category IV Limited or No Damage
Almost certainty	1	3	7	13
High probability	2	5	9	16
Medium probability	4	6	11	18
Low probability	8	10	14	19
Improbable	12	15	17	20

Source: U.S. Department of Defense, *Standard Practice for System Safety*, MIL-STD-882D, available at https://acc.dau.mil/CommunityBrowser.aspx?id=255833, 2000; Defense Contract Management Agency, available at http://guidebook.dcma.mil/49/index.cfm, accessed December 14, 2014, 2014.

Note: The table outlines severity and probability categories for risk assessment.

TABLE 9.3   Risk-Informed Decision Making

Part #	Risk Process
Part 1	Evaluating risks, options, and alternatives
Part 2	Risk analysis of alternatives
Part 3	Risk-informed alternative selection: Final decision of paths and performance based on risk analysis

Source: NASA, Risk Management Handbook. NASA/SP-2011-3422, Version 1.0, November 2011, NASA. National Aeronautics and Space Administration, NASA Headquarters, Washington, DC, available at http://www.nasa.gov, accessed December 8, 2014, 2011.

9.1.5 Risk Matrices

Different public and private organizations have developed variations of risk matrices:

1. Risk Matrix, US Department of Defense
   The US Department of Defense has developed and adopted the "Risk Management Process Model," which entails specific steps to be taken for the risk management process:
   i.   Risk identification
   ii. Risk analysis
   iii. Risk mitigation planning
   iv. Risk mitigation plan implementation, and
   v.   Risk tracking (DOD 2006)
2. NASA Identification of Alternatives
   During the decision-making and risk assessment process, a detailed method of performance measures is evaluated for each of the following sectors:
   * *Security and safety*, including the elimination of security and safety threats, injury, fatality, destruction, or total loss of critical infrastructure.
   * *Technical*, including innovative and obsolete technologies, manufacturing, supply chains, vendors, spares, repairs, financial or technological limitations, training and employability, investment choices, and so on.
   * *Cost*, pertaining to investment choices and the risks of overinvesting, underinvesting and misinvesting. Also banking and budget allocation.
   * *Schedule*, pertaining to deadlines, time constraints, and so on (NASA 2011).

NASA has also established the Risk-Informed Decision Making (RIDM) process for risk-informed decision making, which is demonstrated in Table 9.3.

9.1.6 ISO 31000:2009 for Risk Management

The International Organization for Standardization (ISO) has established the ISO 31000:2009 Code to harmonize risk management procedures in established and upcoming standards. It offers a common strategy in support of standards coping with particular risks and/or sectors, while it does not modify or substitute those standards. ISO 31000:2009 can support companies to minimize risk, which consequently helps them identify weaknesses, and attain their strategic corporate goals.

FIGURE 9.6   The ISO 31000:2009 Matrix for Risk Management.

ISO 31000:2009 addresses the entire management program in a comprehensive manner while improving the structure, performance, safeguard, and ongoing advancement of risk management methods. When implementing ISO 31000, it is fundamental to incorporate current risk management methods with the new ISO model. Figure 9.6 demonstrates the ISO 31000:2009 Matrix for Risk Management.

9.2 INCIDENT REPORTING AND RISK MANAGEMENT SOFTWARE

This section examines the role of Maritime Security Risk Analysis Model (MSRAM) and Dynamic Risk Management Model (DRMM) in supporting US Coast Guard's mission to forecast and alleviate "generic attack" security risks within US ports and waterways via evaluating threats, consequences, and key vulnerability areas. MSRAM is used during the risk assessment process, whereas DRMM is used to develop risk management for optimum decision making (Burns 2012, 2014a,b).

9.2.1 MSRAM

The MSRAM is a Microsoft Access methodology that facilitates the US Coast Guard's mission to comprehend and minimize the risk of terrorist attacks on US targets mainly in national seaports and waterways. Namely, its role is to support the US Coast Guard's mission to forecast and alleviate "generic-attack" security risks within US ports and waterways. It evaluates threats, consequences, and key vulnerability areas.

According to the USCG-CREATE (2010), MSRAM offers a "best practice" among probabilistic risk assessment (PRA)–based risk assessment tools and "is a standard by which other PRA tools could be judged." MSRAM is a security risk analysis tool used to assist in the prioritization and protection of Critical Infrastructure and Key Resources (CIKR). It is selected as the tool that best complies with the National Infrastructure Protection Plan's risk assessment requirements. Recurring requests for access to MSRAM have been made by numerous public and private entities at a global level. The MSRAM data analysis capabilities enhance the federal and state decision making throughout the chain of command at a strategic, tactical, and operational level.

The MSRAM aims to

- Alleviate terrorist attacks within the United States
- Reduce the nation's vulnerability to terrorism
- Eliminate the resulting consequences, i.e., damages
- Recuperate from potential threats/attacks while ensuring socioeconomic security and sustainability

MSRAM commenced as a USCG port–captain risk tool created soon after the terrorist attacks of September 11, 2001. By 2005, the USCG commenced improvement and execution of MSRAM in an effort to reap the benefits of previous incidents, near misses, vulnerabilities, and past experience, both related to the waterways and at an administration level. The initial MSRAM program was launched in 2006, yet, since then, the system has become increasingly efficient and detailed, with over 100,000 scenarios and 30,000 potential targets and vulnerabilities.

Table 9.4 demonstrates the USCG Security Risk Evolution, as reflected in the ongoing MSRAM progress and efficiency from 2006 to 2014, as thousands of security targets and threat scenarios have been added in the system's database.

Tables 9.5 and 9.6 show the different target types and attack modes that have been added in the MSRAM database from 2006 to 2014.

TABLE 9.4   MSRAM Targets and Scenarios from 2006 to 2014

Year	Targets	Scenarios
2006	15,862	16,599
2007	18,741	56,660
2008	22,594	67,381
2009	22,996	68,059
2010	28,319	85,259
2014	30,000	100,000

Source: Burns, M. Ensuring Optimum Resilience in Marine Transportation: Extended Applications of the Maritime Security Risk Analysis Model and the Dynamic Risk Management Model. Conference: Innovative Technologies for a Resilient Marine Transportation System. 3rd Biennial Research and Development Conference—June 24–26, The National Academy of Sciences Building, Washington, DC, available at http:// onlinepubs.trb.org/onlinepubs/conferences/2014/MTS2014 /Burns.pdf, accessed December 8, 2014, 2014b.

TABLE 9.5   MSRAM Target Types and Attack Modes from 2006 to 2014

Target Types	Attack Modes	Attack Modes	Attack Modes
Barge	Truck bomb	Attack by hijacked vessel	
Facility	Assault team	Swimmer/diver	
Infrastructure	Passenger	Sabotage	
Key asset		Attack by hijacked large aircraft/small suicide aircraft	Standoff weapon launched from water and land
Vessel	Boat bomb while vessel present	Multiple boat bomb	Chemical, biological, radiological, nuclear
Other		Cyber attack	Mines (aquatic and land)

Source: Burns, M. Ensuring Optimum Resilience in Marine Transportation: Extended Applications of the Maritime Security Risk Analysis Model and the Dynamic Risk Management Model. Conference: Innovative Technologies for a Resilient Marine Transportation System. 3rd Biennial Research and Development Conference—June 24–26, The National Academy of Sciences Building, Washington, DC, available at http://onlinepubs.trb.org/onlinepubs /conferences/2014/MTS2014/Burns.pdf, accessed December 8, 2014, 2014b.

TABLE 9.6   MSRAM Scenarios: Target Types and Attack Modes

Target Types	Attack Modes
• Targets in the vicinity of military outloads	• Boat attack
• Strategic assets: Nuclear power plants	• Attack by hijacked aircraft
• Infrastructure (bridges, pipelines, tunnels, dams)	• Attack by hijacked vessel
• Offshore platforms, MTSA-regulated facilities	• Assault team/suicide attack
• HazMat carriers, barges, and ships	• Sabotage
• High-rise buildings and nonregulated high-consequence targets in the port and waterway vicinity	• Bomb (boat, truck, aircraft, submarine) • Bomb (swimmer/diver) • Mines (aquatic and land) • Chemical, biological, radiological, and nuclear weapons
• Historical buildings, monuments, and events	• Passenger ship/explosive devices

Source: Burns, M. Ensuring Optimum Resilience in Marine Transportation: Extended Applications of the Maritime Security Risk Analysis Model and the Dynamic Risk Management Model. Conference: Innovative Technologies for a Resilient Marine Transportation System. 3rd Biennial Research and Development Conference—June 24–26, The National Academy of Sciences Building, Washington, DC, available at http://onlinepubs.trb.org/onlinepubs/conferences/2014/MTS2014/Burns.pdf, accessed December 8, 2014, 2014b.

9.2.1.1 Timeline of MSRAM

Post-September 11, 2001:
- *Protect US potential targets of attack*: seaports, waterways, ships, and refineries
- *USCG (DHS)* federal agency for maritime security, encompassing the protection of US ports, coasts, and inland waterways as part of its ports, waterways, and coastal security mission
- *Economic impact*: cargoes of $700 billion/annum
- Impact on global trade, transport, and society

21004: USCG commitment to design and implement risk management and risk assessment:
- Progress in assessing maritime security risks using MSRAM

2005: MSRAM development:
- The Coast Guard had begun to address the limitations of its previous port security risk model

2012–2014: USCG risk management is implemented through MSRAM:
- Prioritizing port security resource allocation
- Recognizing competences essential to alleviate potential threats
- Identifying key targets (Burns 2014b)

Table 9.7 illustrates the MSRAM timeline from 2001 to 2015. Table 9.8 shows the methodology that employs target risk data and threat/vulnerability scenarios to evaluate the possible consequences.

TABLE 9.7 MSRAM Timeline from 2001 to 2015

2001–2005 PSRAT—Port Security Risk Assessment Tool	2006—MSRAM 1	2007—MSRAM 2	2008–2015—MSRAM +
Aim: Enhancing COTP risk security management Improve • Consistency + threat • Consequence data to support ONS • Port risk data supported port security risk assessment GAO = Good start—improvements needed	Aim: Sustain field + headquarters. Addresses threat element from USCG ICC + consistency issues Supported • COTP/sectors • ONS • TWIC • Fight maritime terrorism GAO = Address concerns. Addresses 13 of 18, critical infrastructure and key resources	Aim: Advance training, support and information assessment • Expanded range of scenarios Supported COTP/sectors • ONS—special training for port security teams • TWIC • Combatting maritime terrorism • Mounted automatic weapon project GAO = Most efficient tool for risk management in DHS	Aim: Address full scope of CBRN threat Improve • Consequence/vulnerability analysis Address 18 of 18 CIKR. Support DHS, OGA, states, and other nation's risk analysis The Government Accountability Office (GAO) is an independent United States agency which provides to the US Congress services related to audit, evaluation and investigation. According to GAO, maritime security is the transport and industrial sector that has achieved significant progress in terms of prevention, mitigation and resilience. GAO offers third party validation, right after the MSRAM upgrades have been validated by the DHS/US Coast Guard

Source: Burns, M., Ensuring Optimum Resilience in Marine Transportation: Extended Applications of the Maritime Security Risk Analysis Model and the Dynamic Risk Management Model. Conference: Innovative Technologies for a Resilient Marine Transportation System. 3rd Biennial Research and Development Conference—June 24–26, The National Academy of Sciences Building, Washington, DC, available at http://online pubs.trb.org/onlinepubs/conferences/2014/MTS2014/Burns.pdf, accessed December 8, 2014, 2014b.

Note: CBRN, Chemical, Biological, Radiological and Nuclear Risk Assessments; COTP, Captain of the Port; GAO, Government Accountability Office; ICC, Intelligence Coordination Center; ONS, Operation Neptune Shield; TWIC, transportation worker identification card.

TABLE 9.8   MSRAM Risk Information and Scenario Assessment

Target Risk Data	Scenarios = Target and Attack Mode	Consequences
Target name	Threat	Primary consequences
• Area (port, waterway, lat/long, county)	• Ideology intent	• Death/injury
• DHS MCI/KR station (maritime critical infrastructure/key resource)	• Capability	• National security
	• Geographic intent	• Symbolic
• DHS critical port infrastructure		• Economic, direct
• USCG station		• Health and environmental, direct
Risk assessment/mitigation	Vulnerability	Secondary consequences
• USCG role (lead, support, other)	• Feasibility	• Economic, indirect
• Maritime Transportation Security Act (MTSA 2002) equivalent to ISPS	• Target vulnerability	• Health and environmental, indirect
	• Max consequence	
• Port captain		

Source: Burns, M. Ensuring Optimum Resilience in Marine Transportation: Extended Applications of the Maritime Security Risk Analysis Model and the Dynamic Risk Management Model. Conference: Innovative Technologies for a Resilient Marine Transportation System. 3rd Biennial Research and Development Conference—June 24–26, The National Academy of Sciences Building, Washington, DC, available at http://onlinepubs.trb.org/onlinepubs /conferences/2014/MTS2014/Burns.pdf, accessed December 8, 2014, 2014b.

9.2.2 DRMM

While the MSRAM serves as a risk assessment model, the DRMM was created as a risk management tool for optimum decision making in view of terrorist threats. The role of DRMM is to utilize MSRAM's risk assessment data and methodology in likely scenario-based drills that reflect likely threats and expose vulnerabilities. It accurately evaluates timelines, investment needs, and prioritizes risk. Moreover, it serves as a "risk-based decision-making tool" for terrorism.

DRMM evaluates different yet interrelated security strategies by predicting how they are prone to minimize risk vulnerability gradually. DRMM additionally estimates the outcome of what-if scenarios, supposing that different aspects of the security "landscape" might change in the future. In effect, DRMM provides virtual conditions for exercising different risk management techniques and gaining knowledge from simulations instead of expensive investment decisions with unforeseen performance. In order to secure the critical infrastructure protection, federal departments will identify, prioritize, and coordinate protective measures through shifting from a consequence- to a risk-based system (Burns 2014b; FEMA 2013).

In essence, DRMM

- Helps consolidate and allocate resources, capabilities, and competencies
- Promotes communication and coordination between federal–state–private sectors
- Helps develop risk management and contingency plans
- Prioritizes investment and helps develop risk reduction strategies
- Helps carry out in-depth risk assessment scenarios
- Justifies risk management decisions at tactical, operational, and strategic levels

9.3 CONCLUSION

As a conclusion, both MSRM and DRMM serve as useful tools in the risk assessment process. Figures 9.7 and 9.8 demonstrate how resilience and sustainability are achieved with the use of both these tools.

This chapter dealt with risk asessment methodologies and software that may identify systemic vulnerabilities. The next step for security professionals is to safeguard our physical and cyber security systems, through a number of countermeasures that prevent terrorism, or any intentional attack that compromises the integrity of our systems. The following case study on risk assessment was developed by Paul Fuhs, a port demolitions expert and president of the Board of Directors at the Marine Exchange of Alaska. The engineering aspects of this case study were developed by John W. Pickering. PE, MBA, President, PND Engineers, Inc.

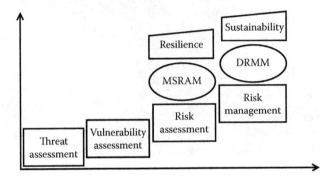

FIGURE 9.7   Security resilience and sustainability with the use of MSRAM and DRMM. (From Burns, M., "Effectiveness Evaluation of the Maritime Security Risk Analysis Model and the Dynamic Risk Management Model," Transportation Research Board of the National Academies, 2012; Burns, M., *Port Management and Operations*, CRC Publishers, Taylor & Francis Group, Boca Raton, FL, 2014a; Burns, M., Ensuring Optimum Resilience in Marine Transportation: Extended Applications of the Maritime Security Risk Analysis Model and the Dynamic Risk Management Model, The National Academy of Sciences Building, Washington, DC, 2014b.)

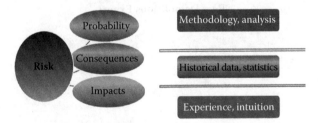

FIGURE 9.8   Security risk methodology with the use of MSRAM and DRMM. (From Burns, M., "Effectiveness Evaluation of the Maritime Security Risk Analysis Model and the Dynamic Risk Management Model," Transportation Research Board of the National Academies, 2012; Burns, M., *Port Management and Operations*, CRC Publishers, Taylor & Francis Group, Boca Raton, FL, 2014a; Burns, M., Ensuring Optimum Resilience in Marine Transportation: Extended Applications of the Maritime Security Risk Analysis Model and the Dynamic Risk Management Model, The National Academy of Sciences Building, Washington, DC, 2014b.)

If I Were a Terrorist
And You Were a Port ...

Port Vulnerabilities
And Engineering Countermeasures
To Prevent Terrorism

By Paul Fuhs
Port Demolitions Expert

(Courtesy of Paul Fuhs.)

APPENDIX: IF I WERE A TERRORIST AND YOU WERE A PORT ...

CASE STUDY: RISK ASSESSMENT: PORT VULNERABILITIES AND ENGINEERING COUNTERMEASURES TO PREVENT TERRORISM

Interview: Paul Fuhs
Port Demolitions Expert and President of the Marine Exchange of Alaska

(Courtesy of Paul Fuhs.)

Paul Fuhs is currently the president of the Marine Exchange of Alaska, a trade association for the Alaska maritime industry. He does consulting work for a variety of clients including shippers, ports, marine pilots, and marine engineering design firms.

For 12 years, Mr. Fuhs worked as a commercial diver and underwater explosives expert in the Bering Sea, headquartered in Dutch Harbor, home port for "The Deadliest Catch." He demolished a variety of civilian and former military port facilities and other structures to make way for new port construction in the rapidly developing fisheries brought about by the 200-mi Exclusive Economic Zone.

He also led emergency response work for the US Coast Guard, blasting and burning fuel on vessels that had run aground to prevent environmental damage to the rich Aleutian Islands ecosystem.

During the Vietnam War, Mr. Fuhs was trained as a military intelligence agent and a North Vietnamese linguist. During the 1990s, he served as the State of Alaska's Commissioner of Commerce and International Trade.

As mayor of Unalaska/Dutch Harbor, he implemented use of Open Cell™ bulkheads for port improvements and has been a proponent of the Open Cell system since that time.

INTRODUCTION

It goes without saying that marine ports are critical strategic assets to any country, both militarily and economically, thus making them prime targets of terrorism. Bringing down major container crane or fuel facilities would cause serious damage to a nation's or region's economy and would score a major symbolic victory for the terrorists. The 2002 West Coast longshoremen's strike demonstrated the financial damage caused by disruption of port activities. A 10-day shutdown was estimated to cost up to $20 billion in financial damages. Because of this, serious attention has rightfully been given to port security across America and other countries.

Most port security programs focus on controlling access by terrorist agents into port facilities through screening identification, fencing, security cameras, etc. While these methods are effective in reducing the risk of attack on port facilities, ports are too dynamic in their operations, and there are too many land- and water-based avenues of ingress to always guarantee physically stopping a determined terrorist.

The fact is that due to the design of many of our port structures, even a small cadre of operatives, carrying small amounts of high explosives, can inflict major damage to our ports.

This paper describes the techniques used to demolish port facilities and identifies their weakest design elements, which should receive additional security attention such as increased surveillance or physical barriers. For new facilities, or for facilities that are being replaced, designs should be used that would thwart or eliminate destruction by terrorism. Those designs are also described here.

PORT DESIGN VULNERABILITIES AND VECTORS OF ATTACK

The most vulnerable elements of any port structure are those constructed of concrete. Concrete is a tremendous building material, strong when reinforced and kept in place. It is even stronger when compressed through prestressing techniques.

However, concrete is a form of ceramic, with weak lateral strength. When subjected to high-velocity explosive shock, it shatters like glass. Once broken, the sheer weight of the broken member tends to pull the rest of the structure down with it.

We have all seen videos of buildings imploding. Such a small amount of explosives is used, and yet the whole building comes down. How does that happen? Primarily by attacking the first two or three floors of elevator shafts. Once those levels fail and began to fall, they pull the rest of the building, tied together through reinforcing rebar, down with them until the whole building collapses. The heavier the building, the easier it is to bring down.

In ports, those sections with the heaviest loads are the most subject to successful attack. Those would be the sections holding container cranes, which exert tremendous forces on the tangent points of their traveling wheels. Of course, this would also cause the most damage to the operating capability of the port.

I will describe here some of the simple methods that can be used to quickly demolish concrete pillars, piles, I-beam steel members, and prestressed deck members. This is not secret classified information. It is readily available through the Internet and specialty bookstores.

Concrete supports can be brought down by very small amounts of explosives. The key to this easily deployable device is detonating the opposing charges at exactly the same time through electric detonators or equal-length detonating primacord (Figure 9.A1). When the shockwaves meet in the center of the pillar and attempt to reflect off each other, massive structural damage is created through internal pulverization of the concrete.

Here is the formula for calculating the explosive charge:

Multiply the diameter or thickness of the target to be breached by the constant, 5, which gives the number of pounds of plastic explosive required for reinforced

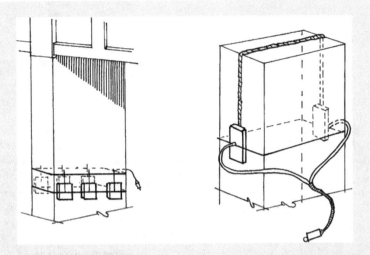

FIGURE 9.A1 Opposable charges. (From DOA, *Special Forces Demolition Techniques. US Army Field Manual FM 31-20*, Department of the US Army, USA, 1965.)

> concrete. For example, if a concrete target pier measures 1.06 meters in thickness (about 3.5 feet) the total amount of plastic explosive required is 6 pounds (2.72 kilograms). Divide the required amount of explosives in half and place the halves diametrically opposite one another on the target, using ropes or a simple wood frame. Simultaneous detonation of both charges is mandatory.

Source: DOA, 1965. Special Forces Demolition Techniques. US Army Field Manual FM 31-20. Department of the US Army, 1965. USA.

Only 6 lb. of explosives are needed to take out a 3.5 ft. thick concrete support.

Concrete piles, which are often prestressed to provide compressive strength for piledriving, have little lateral strength and can be easily attacked with small amounts of explosives using the method previously described, deployed from a skiff or from divers operating below the surface (see Figure 9.A2).

Round steel piling is the most difficult to attack. You can place charges around it, but it will only crimp the pipe. There are shaped charges available, but they are difficult to procure or manufacture and time consuming to deploy. If deployed underwater, a chamber must be purged of water to create the airspace for the shaped-charge jet to develop. This provides positive buoyancy to the charge, which must be counterweighted, etc.

Even then, the charge only cuts out about a 1/2 in. ring of the piling so the upper section tends to settle down on the lower section and not provide the movement needed to bring the superstructure down. Round steel piles should always be used in port applications due to their superior resistance to attack.

I-beam steel sections (Figure 9.A3) and tied-back steel bulkheads (Figure 9.A4) are more easily breached through the direct application of plastic explosives. When these charges are placed in strategic locations, they can cause massive failure of structures. The charge of plastic explosives (RDX) need only be as thick as the steel but never less than 1/2 in. to maintain detonating wave strength. These charges are also deployable in a short time period (see Figure 9.A3).

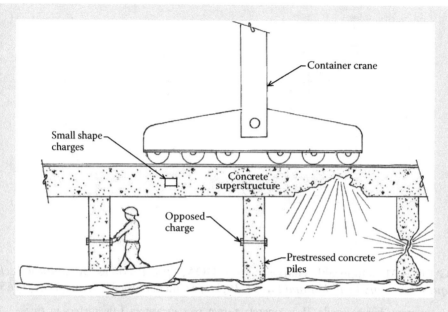

FIGURE 9.A2   Opposed charge elevation. (Courtesy of Paul Fuhs.)

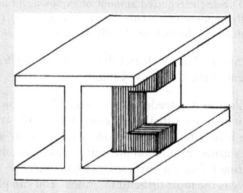

FIGURE 9.A3   RDX, plastic charge. (From *US Navy, US Navy Seal Combat Manual 0502-LP-190-0650*, UDT/SEAL, UDT Technical Training, USA, 1974.)

Traditional steel bulkheads with exposed tie rods and walers are also subject to attack due to their exposed structural elements. Although they may not experience immediate catastrophic failure such as concrete, they would be rendered essentially unusable since they would no longer support a bearing load at the face of the dock.

Concrete caisson structures consist of huge prefabricated concrete structures, resembling an open box, that are then sunk onto a prepared seabed foundation. The box is then filled in with dredged or other soil material to create a monolithic dock structure. These facilities are highly resistant to attempts to damage them through use of explosives due to the mass of concrete involved, inability to place opposing explosive charges, the sheer mass of the soil and the soil's absorption, and fracturing of the detonation wave.

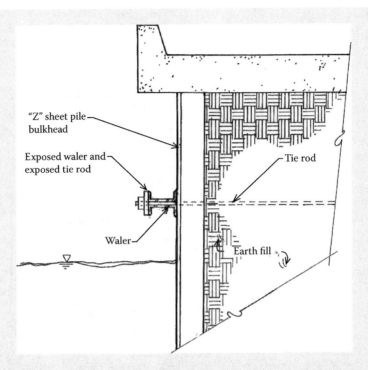

FIGURE 9.A4 Typical "Z" sheet pile bulkhead configuration. (Courtesy of Paul Fuhs.)

However, they are subject to damage from large-scale seismic events as occurred in Kobe, Japan in 1995, which caused major structural failures and shifting of foundations. They are also extremely expensive to build (See Figure 9.A12).

Wooden pile structures are very susceptible to attack using 400 grain detonating cord. Only two wraps around the piling are necessary to cut clean through the piling since the water pressure tends to concentrate the force of the charge into the piling. The detonating cord is continued from piling to piling so only one detonation point is necessary to bring down a large section of dock (see Figure 9.A5). One or two divers can wrap many pilings in a short period of time.

If a leading corner of a dock is attacked, as that corner falls down, the weight of the deck and superstructure starts to pull the rest of the dock down with it, snapping off section after section of wood piling as it goes down, particularly if cross bracing has not been meticulously maintained. I have taken down an entire 1000-ft. wooden dock by shooting only 16 wooden pilings at the leading corner.

Prestressed concrete deck members are also highly susceptible to attack. Even if a dock is built on round steel piling, it is often covered by prestressed concrete deck members. Since concrete has little lateral strength on its own, long concrete sections are "prestressed." Steel strand is stretched within a concrete form and then concrete poured over them. After the concrete has set, the strand is released, and the concrete member will camber due to eccentric compression. When dead load is placed on it, the member will return to a level position rather than sagging.

This genius technology allows for huge spans and even whole buildings resting on a single concrete pier. However, that strength is only realized within the plane

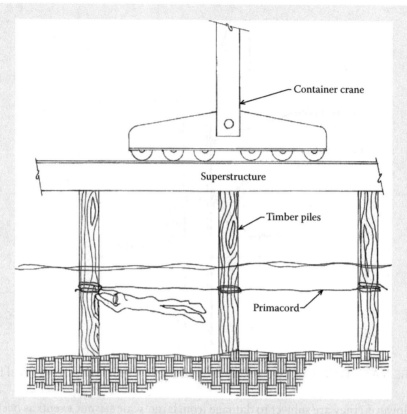

FIGURE 9.A5   Primacord charge on wooden piling. (Courtesy of Paul Fuhs.)

of the stressing. Any lateral movement whatsoever or damage to the concrete covering the stressed strand will result in the prestressed member exploding on its own as the tremendous pressure inside is released. This often occurs when construction crews incorrectly lift members into place and subject them to any lateral movement. Concrete is literally blown everywhere.

The illustration below (Figure 9.A6) shows how prestressed deck members can be attacked resulting in massive structural failure of docks.

Admittedly, all these methods of attack would require penetration of security measures by land or water. But they do not require many people or much in the way of explosives or equipment to deploy. The results would be devastating to any port.

A simpler way to create the same destruction would be to use an incoming vessel to ram the dock. An infiltrated vessel crew could take charge of the helm and use the vessel to create major damage to concrete and wooden dock structures.

Those of us who work around docks know how carefully marine pilots bring vessels to the face of a dock precisely because they know how fragile these facilities are.

A ship, or container loaded with explosives, could also be detonated at the dock causing massive structural damage.

What is the most cost-effective engineering design that could thwart all of these potential attacks to port structures and make them virtually indestructible?

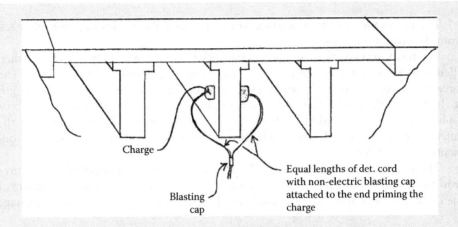

FIGURE 9.A6 Prestressed dock attack. (From CIA, *CIA Strategic Services Field Manual No. 3. The "Simple Sabotage Manual."* CIA, US Government, 2012 reproduction of the 1944 book. Available at https://www.cia.gov/news-information/featured-story-archive/2012-featured-story-archive/CleanedUOSSSimpleSabotage_sm.pdf, accessed August 30, 2015.)

THE OPEN CELL SHEET PILE SOLUTION

Open Cell sheet pile design and construction involve a special and patented application of sheet pile technology. On the front face of the dock, the interlocking sheets are driven in a rounded, scalloped pattern. Upon reaching the end of the scallop, a three-sided transition pile is driven (Figure 9.A7). One leg of the Y starts the next front face scallop.

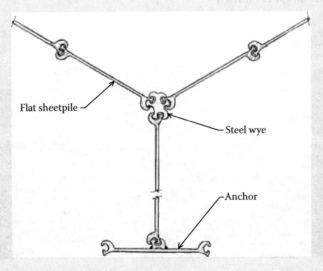

FIGURE 9.A7 Open Cell components. (Courtesy of John W. Pickering, PE, MBA, President, PND Engineers, Inc.)

The bottom leg of the Y starts a row of tie back sheet piles that extends back from the face of the dock.

The resulting cells that are open at the end (hence the name Open Cell) are then filled with soils that are compacted in layers during placement (Figure 9.A8). The force of the compacted soils on the tie back walls provides the horizontal strength at the face of the dock. The additional weight of crane rails and concrete slab or asphalt surfacing adds additional stability to the structure. This also provides the unusual characteristic of Open Cells being able to be used in weak soil environments (Figure 9.A9).

There are currently more than 150 installations of open sheet pile structures worldwide and not one has ever suffered a structural failure. The rounded nature of the dock face piles and the soil mass behind them provide protection from damage

FIGURE 9.A8 Open Cell elevation. (Courtesy of John W. Pickering, PE, MBA, President, PND Engineers, Inc.)

FIGURE 9.A9 Open Cell being backfilled. (Courtesy of John W. Pickering, PE, MBA, President, PND Engineers, Inc.)

to the dock from ramming by vessels. In fact, they are so strong that it is necessary to place a fendering system as part of the dock to provide a cushioned landing for berthing vessels. You can test this concept yourself by placing an egg lengthwise in your palm. No matter how hard you squeeze it, because of the rounded surfaces, you cannot break it (see Figures 9.A9 through 9.A11 to see actual deployments).

These Open Cell sheet pile structures have been used in the most extreme environments in the Alaska Arctic where they are subjected to incredible forces of ice driven by powerful ocean currents and regular gale force storms in the Aleutian Islands and Arctic. Open Cells have withstood severe impacts from ice and vessels without significant damage (Figure 9.A11).

FIGURE 9.A10   Open Cell bulkhead dock with fenders. (Courtesy of John W. Pickering, PE, MBA, President, PND Engineers, Inc.)

FIGURE 9.A11   Man standing on Open Cell dock overtopped with wind-driven sea ice, Nome, Alaska. (Courtesy of John W. Pickering, PE, MBA, President, PND Engineers, Inc.)

Vulnerabilities to Terrorist Attack

There are no vulnerabilities to terrorist attack with these structures. The integrated nature of the sheet piles, the rounded front face, and the sheer mass of the soil fill make them virtually indestructible. It would take something on the order of a huge concussion or atom bomb to destroy one of them. You could punch a hole in the face of the pile wall with a shaped charge, but it would not affect the structure and could be easily repaired with a welded patch.

In fact, one of the features of these structures is that they are virtually free of maintenance (with the exception of the cushioning fender system, which must be periodically replaced like any fendering system and cathodic protection), and they have a useful life of 75 to 100 years. To dismantle an Open Cell would require excavation of backfill and removal of pile sections one by one with a crane.

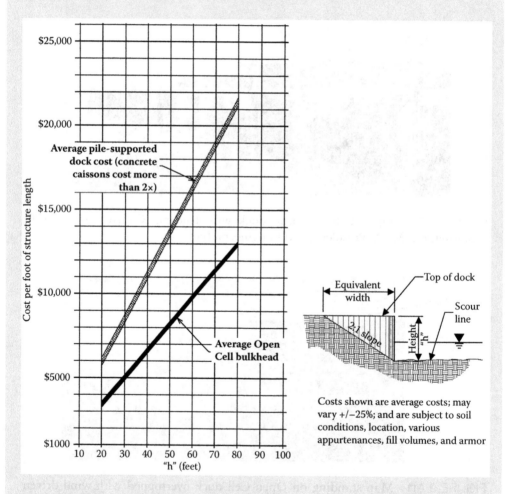

FIGURE 9.A12   Cost comparison of heavy duty. (Courtesy of John W. Pickering, PE, MBA, President, PND Engineers, Inc.)

The costs of Open Cell sheet pile structures are typically 60% the cost of pile-supported port structures (see Figure 9.A12).

For ports using Open Cell sheet pile installations, the threat profile of the port should be reduced to reflect the lowered risk of terrorist attack. This can potentially allow ports to reduce their security costs and premiums for insurance policies to insure against unintentional and intentional damage.

For more information, contact:
Paul Fuhs
329 E 10th Ave Anchorage, Alaska 99501
Phone 907.351.0407
paulfuhs@earthlink.net

For more information on Open Cell sheet pile structures contact:
PND Engineers, Inc.
1506 W. 36th Ave.
Anchorage, AK 99503
Phone 907.561.1011 Fax 907.563.4220
www.pndengineers.com

INTERVIEW AND CASE STUDY

Fuhs, Paul, Port Demolitions Expert and President of the Marine Exchange of Alaska, Case Study: Risk Assessment: Port Vulnerabilities and Engineering Countermeasures to Prevent Terrorism.

REFERENCES

Burns, M. 2012. "Effectiveness Evaluation of the Maritime Security Risk Analysis Model and the Dynamic Risk Management Model." Workshop Title: Risk Assessment and Decision Support Models and Tools. Transportation Research Board of the National Academies.

Burns, M. 2014a. *Port Management and Operations*. CRC Publishers, Taylor & Francis Group, Boca Raton, FL.

Burns, M. 2014b. Ensuring Optimum Resilience in Marine Transportation: Extended Applications of the Maritime Security Risk Analysis Model and the Dynamic Risk Management Model. Conference: Innovative Technologies for a Resilient Marine Transportation System. 3rd Biennial Research and Development Conference—June 24–26. The National Academy of Sciences Building, Washington, DC. Available at http://onlinepubs.trb.org/onlinepubs/conferences/2014/MTS2014/Burns.pdf. Accessed December 8, 2014.

DOD. 2006. *Risk Management Guide for DOD Acquisition*, Sixth Edition. US Department of Defense (Version 1.0). Available at http://www.acq.osd.mil/se/docs/2006-RM-Guide-4Aug06-final-version.pdf. Accessed December 1, 2014.

EPA. 2014. Risk Communication. Environmental Protection Agency. Available at http://www.epa.gov/superfund/community/pdfs/toolkit/risk_communication.pdf. Accessed December 12, 2014.

FEMA. 2013. Federal Emergency Management Agency. FEMA's National Planning Frameworks: 2nd edition, May. USA.

NASA. 2011. Risk Management Handbook. NASA/SP-2011-3422, Version 1.0, November 2011, NASA. National Aeronautics and Space Administration, NASA Headquarters, Washington, DC. Available at http://www.nasa.gov. Accessed December 8, 2014.

NRC. 1989–2015. Improving Risk Communication. The National Research Council (NRC). The National Academies, Washington, DC. Copyright © 2015 National Academy of Sciences.

READY.GOV. 2014. "The Ready Campaign" of US Government. Available at http://www.ready.gov. Accessed December 12, 2014.

Sponsoring Committee: Critical Transportation Infrastructure Protection ABE40. Co-Sponsoring Committees: Geographic Information Science and Applications Committee (ABJ60); Committee on Visualization in Transportation (ABJ95).

USCG-CREATE. 2010. Maritime Security Risk Analysis Model Overview for USCG-CREATE Maritime Risk Symposium. November 16.

CHAPTER 10

Combating Security Threats
The Human Factor

My center is giving way,
My right is retreating
Situation excellent,
I am attacking.

Ferdinand Foch (1851–1929)
Supreme Commander of Allied Forces, First World War

10.1 INTRODUCTION

The human factor represents a key aspect in global security. Without human participation or intervention, the security practices covered in this book (Chapter 7), the innovative technologies (Chapter 8), or even risk assessment techniques (Chapter 9) would not be attainable or successful. The reality in daily security practices is that it takes humans to operate technologies, comply with security regulations, and provide the primary input in sophisticated risk assessment software, algorithms, and metrics. In numerous cases of security incidents, it is the human factor that seems to determine the outcome of a threat, from the well-trained airline crew who manage to avert their plane from hijacking to the efficient cruise line seafarers who manage to evacuate a ship with thousands of pirates.

Personal security is defined as a state of preparedness and safety. It focuses on mitigating attempts to prevent, minimize, and forewarn prior to a security-related risk. It entails situational awareness and caution preceding the risk of a security attack and provides all methods, tools, and resources to obtain emergency help and be able to safeguard against the attack in a positive way. Individual security seeks to safeguard people from assault and any form of attack and intentional damage. *Bouvier's Law Dictionary* defines personal security as "the legal and uninterrupted enjoyment by a man of his life, his body, his health and his reputation" (Bouvier 1839).

The presence of security, or lack of security, has the power to influence a nation's or an industry's development, resilience, standards of living, and ethics. Nations, corporations, and societies around the world may be interested in promoting a security culture that will enable them to reach their full potential. However, the manner in which security is perceived is strongly influenced by their cultural approaches, priorities, and objectives.

The human factor has the potential to become either the security system's greatest strength or its greatest vulnerability. It is the unique intellectual and physical skills of security professionals—their distinguished personalities, abilities, and qualities that can strengthen or weaken national and commercial security. Be it logic, intuition, risk perception, or simply experience and training, the "human force" is the catalyst that impacts and determines any intention to harm a country's or company's security. Modern security systems have prioritized the development of "security-oriented cultures, conditions, and processes."

Understanding the human behavior enables security professionals to establish robust security platforms by recruiting the right people, designing optimum security training modules, and developing optimum rules and processes. The very same understanding can help security professionals to recognize suspicious human behavior and identify nonconformities, weaknesses, and vulnerabilities.

How people connect to technologies, and how judgments are made when it comes to security, is undoubtedly a rather intricate concern. Among the numerous aspects to be evaluated are a person's training, dispositions, and perceptions that affect the way persons comprehend and respond to security threats and suspicious behavior or environments. Examining human behavior can shed light on why people make particular judgments or why they follow certain patterns (Australian Government DOD, Parsons et al. 2010).

"Cognitive neuroscience" is the discipline that seeks to assess how human brain structure affects mental functions and how neural circuits facilitate situational awareness, observation, familiarization, and the building of muscle memory. Modern geneticists in pursuit of the "genius gene" have discovered genetic variants related to intelligence, perception, situational awareness, and other cognitive capabilities. Scientists have furthermore identified a connection among the CHRM2 gene and performance IQ, which determines a human's capacity to logical thinking, perception, and action. Genetic experiments over the past decade or so have shown that a person's mental ability is a holistic brain function, i.e., it is a combination of numerous genetic variants, such as educational, cultural, social, or even geospatial positioning, that may determine human behavior during life-threatening events (Burns-Kokkinaki 2006; Rietvelt et al. 2014).

This chapter shows that the human factor could be the strongest or weakest link in supply chain security.

10.2 STRESS VERSUS DISTRESS MODE: THE HUMAN BODY AND CRITICAL BODY FUNCTIONS

Now if you are going to win any battle, you have to do one thing. You have to make the mind run the body. Never let the body tell the mind what to do. The body will always give up. It is always tired in the morning, noon, and night. But the body is never tired if the mind is not tired.

George S. Patton
U.S. Army General, 1912 Olympian

10.2.1 Stressors

A stressor can be defined as an incitement or occurrence that triggers a stress reaction in an individual. Stressors are the perceived hazards or root causes of a human's situational anxiety. They are classified in terms of their intensity and exposure, i.e., as

- a. Acute (severe) and
- b. Chronic (long-term)

They are also classified in terms of their root cause, i.e., as

- a. External (caused by exterior factors) or
- b. Internal (caused by a person's perceived disadvantage, limited resources, and so on)

In case of security threats, stressors could be suspicious persons, activities, unattended luggage, or any out-of-place situation that resembles a familiar threat.

10.2.2 Perceived Threat, Stress, and Distress

The key word here is "perceived," because at the sight of a common stressor, different people may assess the threat differently and react differently.

The NR3C1 gene is a glucocorticoid receptor associated with adaptation to stress. When an individual perceives danger, this gene releases cortisol, a stress hormone, into the body cells. In view of a threat, the human brain observes and evaluates whether the obvious threat can be successfully handled. This evaluation may be objective, determined by realistic comparison, or subjective, driven by exhaustion, fear, lack of situational awareness, demotivation, a feeling of unpreparedness, and so on.

Regardless of the accuracy or objectivity of such an evaluation, the human brain will either prepare for fight or flight and according to this perception will generate specific hormones. Stress and distress are therefore psychological and biological states that occur in reaction to the perception of adequacy or inadequacy, in view of a possible hazard.

10.2.3 Stress and Preparedness

Stress is a mental reaction or alertness that happens when a person perceives that there are sufficient resources and physical levels to cope with the threat. In case of a security threat, this is a stage where security professionals feel that they have sufficient tools, training, knowledge, energy levels, and backup support. The cortisol level released into their cells is moderate, which provides them with elevated energy levels and alertness. At that point, the human body is in a state of stress.

10.2.4 Distress and Lack of Preparedness

On the other hand, when individuals fear that they are not adequately trained, equipped, protected, or prepared to encounter the threat, excessive cortisol levels lead to distress.

Distress is a condition of extreme and persisting stress levels that overwhelm the human body leading to reduced mental and physical abilities, poor focus, and irrational thinking. The difference between stress and distress lies in the human brain. When individuals are convinced that the threat they encounter is larger than they can handle, the human brain signals to request higher levels of cortisol in order to be able to cope with the threat. This cortisol "overdose" is an improper or unproductive method to handle threats, and therefore, individuals are exposed to the risk of temporary mental and physiological blocks.

10.2.5 The Impact of Distress or High Stress Levels

Extreme stress levels, as shown in Figure 10.1, affect the human body in any and all of the following ways:

a. High secretion levels of adrenaline hormone (epinephrine) lead to a "fight-or-flight" body condition led by the adrenal response.
b. Cardiovascular and nervous system: increased heart/pulse rate; high blood pressure; digestion.
c. Tunnel vision and pupil dilation.
d. Hearing loss.
e. Salivation.
f. Respiratory system: lungs dilated, increased breathing.
g. Endocrine system: adrenal glands; production of stress hormones.
h. Gastrointestinal system: stomach, esophagus, bowels.
i. Reproductive system: infertility.

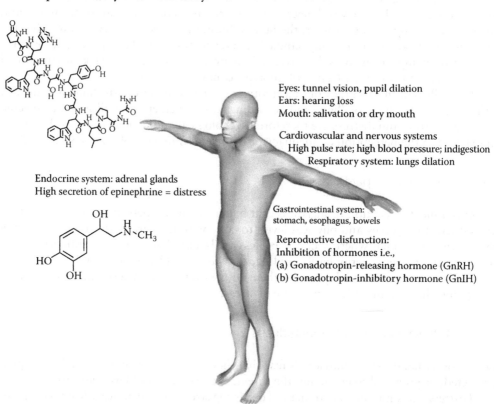

FIGURE 10.1 High stress levels.

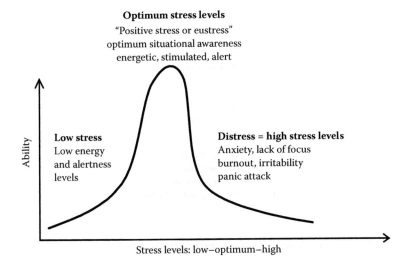

FIGURE 10.2 Stress response.

At this stage, it is important to observe that persons who have been exposed to real and significant security threats are likely to be methylated (or distressed) more easily and at greater levels compared to persons that have not encountered extreme physical threats throughout their lives. This shows an association between symptoms of post-traumatic stress disorder (PTSD) encountered in military veterans, law enforcement agents, and security professionals. Individuals can alleviate the distress symptoms once they are convinced that they can cope with potential stressors, such as security threats. Figure 10.2 demonstrates how the stress levels affect a person's energy, alertness, and situational awareness levels.

10.2.6 Distress and Permanent DNA Methylation

Recent genetic studies have associated highly stressful experiences with permanent modifications in DNA methylation, which may lead to major pathophysiologic alterations such as depression and/or PTSD (Klengel et al. 2014).

10.3 SECURITY, HUMAN MENTALITY, AND THE CULTURE FACTOR

> Living and conducting business in a Texas border county is tantamount to living in a war zone in which civil authorities, law enforcement agencies as well as citizens are under attack around the clock.
>
> **B. McCaffrey and R. Scales**
> *Texas Border Security: A Strategic Military Assessment, September 2011*

This section seeks to evaluate how the human factor can impact security through establishing a security culture. Security professionals share similar challenges despite the geographic locations and plethora of job specializations, i.e., working onboard ships and

FIGURE 10.3   Security Culture Pyramid. (From the author.)

antipiracy and being involved in land and air operations, border patrol, drones, cyber-security, money laundering, nuclear scanning, or counterterrorism. Low morale, limited training or funding for technologies and security tools, being understaffed and over-worked, or dealing with bureaucracy could be some of the many common experiences that public and private professionals may share.

The reasoning behind this commonality is that it is much more challenging to defend a system than to attack it. The security offenders have endless opportunities to attack a weak link within a supply chain, and all they need is to succeed once. On the other hand, law enforcement agencies, the military, and security professionals need to monitor and control the entire system all of the time, with limited resources and zero tolerance toward error.

For security professionals to successfully safeguard the integrity of the system, there is a compelling need to focus on a security culture that encompasses three significant areas, as depicted in Figure 10.3:

1. Establishing a *security culture* that unites and strengthens our people.
2. *Motivating our people* with a set of rewards and incorporating these motivators into our culture.
3. Developing *quality training*, with measurable objectives, realistic security drills, and tabletop exercises, and a system that continuously assesses and rewards participants.

10.3.1 Classification of Security Culture

At a commercial level, a security culture may be focused on the processes, tools, and actions that need to be taken in order to protect a system's resiliency. Security cultures may be classified according to different elements and measures, such as

1. Time and preparedness: proactive vs. reactive cultures:
   a. Proactive cultures have established and implemented a risk assessment protocol that enables them to be prepared to identify and avert potential security threats.
   b. Reactive cultures may not have the tools, resources, or know-how to be pro-active and may adopt a "wait-and-see" attitude focused mainly on emergency response once an event has occurred.

2. Security tolerance and prioritization:

Different geographical and industrial segments may be focused on different security threats and may have different levels of security tolerance or priorities.

As an example, maritime companies whose ships navigate near piracy-prone areas may be focused primarily on antipiracy measures. Meanwhile, supply chains that have been victims of cargo theft or illegitimate trade and transport may be focused on surveillance and antitheft technologies. Accordingly, areas or industry segments that are influenced by ideological or religious disputes may be more concerned about civil wars, terrorist threats, or social turmoil.

3. Security investment and resource allocation:

Regardless of a company's security culture and aspirations for preparedness, monetary and other resources' availability will determine to which extent security can be averted or mitigated. Economic recessions, limited funds, and commercial pressures may not allow companies or communities to develop a robust security framework.

4. Commercial continuity vs. security focus:

Ideally, corporations and industries seek to find the optimum balance between secure systems and commercial continuity. In the real corporate world, the scale may lean toward either side for multiple reasons, including

   a. Commercial or performance pressures may drive certain companies to focus on sustainable cargo flows.
   b. Actual security incidents and pertinent losses, including the loss of industry trust and market share, may urge other companies to focus on security.
   c. Situational unawareness, or lack of understanding of the actual benefits of a security culture, may deprive companies of the motivation to focus on security.

10.3.2 Motivating Security Employees

Modern global security challenges combined with excessive competition and economic pressures require employees to be proactive, flexible, and skilled. Most importantly, they need to think creatively in order to solve emerging security challenges. To meet these new demands, employee motivation is necessary.

Employees' morale refers to the mindset, job gratification, and overall attitude of personnel at a workplace setting. Section 10.2 of this book explained how our mindset affects our stress levels, situational awareness, professional confidence, and overall performance. Part of effective productivity is believed to be directly associated to the motivation and high morale of personnel.

Motivation and empowerment are therefore considered as vital tools for security employees. The increasingly complex security challenges urge public and private entities to improve their security culture. Human resources is a powerful weapon enabling organizations and federal agencies to meet this target.

10.3.3 Maslow's Hierarchy of Needs

An area of logistics security often overlooked is the topic of "human developmental psychology." Human developmental psychology theories can be associated with security and safety with human survival, deficiency, economic growth, and productivity.

In 1943, Abraham Maslow, an American psychologist, suggested his "hierarchy of needs" theory in his academic paper "A Theory of Human Motivation," published by the *Psychological Review*." In 1954, he verified the strong correlation between human needs and motivation, as published in his paper "Motivation and Personality" (Maslow 1943, 1954). Maslow differentiated from the researchers of his time, who mostly focused on biology or personality traits to explain individual motivation. Maslow, instead, presented a pyramid of human needs that consist of two levels: security/survival and growth/actualization.

Maslow's hierarchy of needs was further categorized by Clayton Paul Alderfer, an American psychologist who researched existence, relatedness, and growth (ERG). In 1969, Alderfer published his ERG "theory of motivation" in a paper named "An Empirical Test of a New Theory of Human Need" (Alderfer 1969, 1972). Figure 10.4 illustrates how Maslow's pyramid of human needs correspond with Alderfer's motivation categories.

The graph in Figure 10.4 illustrates the following human needs vs. motivation relationships:

Level 1: Lower level: Existence sector
>   The pyramid's foundation or primary human needs are built on resource deficiencies and the human desire to feel safe, secure, and have one's survival needs being met.

Level 2: Middle level: Relatedness sector
>   Once the basic needs of nations, societies, and individuals are met, it is necessary to use communication, transportation, and information exchange in order to not only ensure survival but also grow into the upper level of achievements and growth.

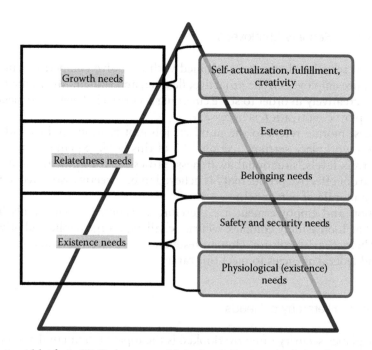

FIGURE 10.4   Alderfer's ERG theory and Maslow's Pyramid of Needs.

Level 3: Upper level: Growth needs

Once the basic needs of nations, societies, and individuals are met, they strive to meet the needs of the pyramid's upper level by being increasingly engaged in growth and accomplishments.

10.3.4 Improved Security through Corporate Quality

Todays' security professionals require rapid response and adaptation to ever-changing and unpredictable circumstances. Leaders are continually dealing with the issue of how to restructure their corporate culture to ensure that they safeguard our security while remaining competitive. Innovation and transformation are an integral part of this process.

Global security professionals and public/private entities should

- Keep abreast of the global security trends
- Adopt a proactive stance to solve emerging challenges
- Understand the association between national (homeland) security and commercial security
- Observe key forces and trends impacting the global security

Increased demands on the production (just-in-time delivery) of lean and agile organizations require increased motivation and the toolset to intervene during a security threat. Due to the time restrictions between identifying a security threat and calling for action, security employees should be well trained and prepared to perform their security duties, and ensuring that the overall performance, the standards aimed at, and the quality of the final product have been met. This involves establishing a security culture empowering employees through ongoing training, realistic security drills, and motivation.

10.4 PREPAREDNESS: THE UTILITY OF TRAINING, DRILLS, SIMULATIONS, AND SCENARIOS

10.4.1 Large-Scale Training: Time and Resource Management

After the September 11 terrorist attacks, 50,000 transportation security officers were employed and assumed their security duties involving handling state-of-the-art technologies, security screening, identification, and recognition equipment for both passengers and cargoes.

In the private sector, large cruise ships recruit over a thousand employees per vessel in order to handle multiple thousands of passengers. In case of a safety or security incident, it is possible that a large-scale evacuation needs to take place. Alarm systems and sirens indicate the time, place, and method in which the evacuation needs to take place, i.e., passengers need to wear their life jackets and gather at a designated muster station.

The Italian cruise ship Costa Concordia carried 3200 passengers and around 1000 crewmembers. The Costa Concordia grounded while navigating in the Mediterranean Sea in the ports of Civitavecchia, Palermo, Cagliari, Palma de Mallorca, Barcelona, Marseille, and Savona. While the reason for this incident was human error (safety incident), similar incidents could be caused by intentional security threats, i.e., terrorist attacks.

In the case of Costa Concordia, the half-billion-dollar ship had a gross tonnage (i.e., the ship's overall internal volume) of 114,147 metric tons. The role of training and muscle memory is apparent when considering that an average emergency evacuation needs to take place within about 30 min. In the case of the Costa Concordia ship grounding, 1000 crew members had to assist 3200 passengers (three passengers per crew member), including elderly or injured persons, infants, pregnant women, people in shock and distress (high stress levels), and so on.

Such a large scale of operations, both at times of "business as usual" and during an emergency, impose significant strains on employees and their confidence in the ability to perform effectively.

Effective training, motivation, and appraisal/reward systems are needed to be in place in order for the human brain to avoid the two dangerous extremes: distress and complacency.

10.4.2 Building Muscle Memory through Training and Drills

The global trade and transportation industry tends to learn from past threats and incidents, and the benefits of promoting a security culture are both measurable and noticeable. For a security culture to be efficient, it should be practiced throughout all levels of command in a holistic and consistent manner. The benefits of training, tabletop exercises, and simulations serve in the building of muscle memory; the time and performance is measurable, which offers the opportunity of continuous improvement.

The building of muscle memory or "brain training" through security drills helps professionals to become more confident and be able to control their stress levels in case of an actual incident. Muscle memory pertains to memory saved in a person's brain and muscles through repetition. This type of repeated, step-by-step memory ensures that individual performance improves through repetition, and this can be measured in terms of time and training objectives attained. If or when an incident occurs, the individual does not need to improvise or experiment during, e.g., a sabotage, a fire, or an evacuation procedure: the brain and body's memory will dictate the movements and actions to be taken based on the stored memory.

The value of repetition serves when professionals need to assume their emergency duties and take designated roles within an emergency response team. Periodic training, i.e., quarterly or monthly, may offer the type of muscle memory exercise that professionals require in order to become familiar, aware, and confident when a security incident occurs.

It is during an emergency that the benefits of training become apparent, as they can make the distinction between life and death or between rapid systemic recovery and total loss. Stressors, as mentioned in Section 10.2 of this chapter, may strike simultaneously. If individuals are totally unprepared, it will take precious time to improvise an emergency plan, such as a search-and-rescue or emergency response operations. On the other hand, a well-trained, well-familiar individual or team of professionals can assume their roles with limited need for reflection or even communication, as their brain and body will recall similar role-playing scenarios.

10.4.3 Complacency: Atrophy of Mental and Muscle Memory

For a number of years, it was commonly believed that the benefits of training, tabletop exercises, and familiarization with a security controlled area was reversible, and even when individuals would cease training for a long time, muscle memory would enable the mental and physical state of preparedness and alertness. This belief has been questioned as numerous security incidents uncover the fact that "refresher training" or "repeated training" that is conventional and not challenging enough leads to complacency. It has therefore been established that complacency or "muscle and skill atrophy" is equally harmful to a state of distress or overstress.

Figure 10.5 shows how conventional, repeated, and predictable training and security drills lead security professionals to a false state of preparedness and alertness. This leads to complacency and overconfidence, which are demonstrated through low stress levels, apathy, and atrophic muscle memory. During a security incident, such professionals may be surprised to see that the perceived skills, awareness, and familiarization obtained during drills and training are just not in place.

Complacency and a false sense of knowledge and situational awareness are the antipode of distress levels caused by poor training and lack of preparedness.

A well-trained security professional can make a difference in the lives of many. Building muscle memory is an effective technique for all security, transportation, and law enforcement professionals who wish to function properly before, during, and after a security incident. Muscle memory is a core competence for situational awareness and

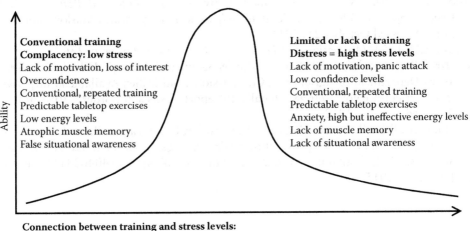

FIGURE 10.5 Connection between training and stress levels. (From the author.)

defensive preparedness. Regrettably, the hazards of incorrect and/or inconsistent muscle memory are frequently overlooked.

It is therefore the role of the security trainer to offer a high quality of training through realistic drills, simulations, and scenarios.

REFERENCES

Alderfer, C.P. 1969. An empirical test of a new theory of human needs. *Organizational Behavior and Human Performance*, Volume 4, Issue 2, pp. 142–175, May.

Alderfer, C.P. 1972. *Existence, Relatedness, and Growth: Human Needs in Organizational Settings*. New York: Free Press.

Australian Government DOD, Parsons, K., McCormac, A., Butavicius, M., and Ferguson, L. 2010. *Human Factors and Information Security: Individual, Culture and Security Environment*. Australian Government Department of Defense. Command, Control, Communications and Intelligence Division DSTO Defense Science and Technology Organization. Australia. Available at http://www.dtic.mil/dtic/tr/fulltext/u2/a535944 .pdf. Accessed December 12, 2014.

Bouvier, J. 1839. *Law Dictionary Adapted to the Constitution and Laws of the United States of America and of the Several States of the American Union, with References to the Civil and Other Systems of Foreign Law*, Volume I. T & J.W. Johnson, Law Booksellers. Philadelphia.

Burns-Kokkinaki, M. 2006. Cerebral evolution: The making of a genius and the theory of intellectual motivators. *International Journal of Anthropology*, Vol. 21, Issue 1–4, pp. 207–214. Available at http://www.pontecorboli.com/ejournals/ija/2006-AIJA14 .pdf. Accessed January 1, 2015.

Klengel, T., Pape, J., Binder, E., and Mehta, D. 2014. The role of DNA methylation in stress-related psychiatric disorders. *Neuropharmacology Journal*, Volume 80, pp. 115–132, May.

Maslow, A.H. 1943. A theory of human motivation. *Psychological Review*, Vol. 50, Issue 4, pp. 370–396. Available at http://psychclassics.yorku.ca/Maslow/motivation .htm. Accessed October 21, 2014.

Maslow, A.H. 1954. *Motivation and Personality*. New York: Harper. p. 236.

McCaffrey, B. and Scales, R. 2011. *Texas Border Security: A Strategic Military Assessment*. Texas Department of Agriculture. Commissioner Sid Miller. Available at http://www .texasagriculture.gov/.../46982_Final%20Report-Texas%20Border%20Security.pdf. Accessed October 2012.

Rietveld, C.A., Esko, T., Davies, G., Pers, T.H., Turley, P., Benyamin, B., and Chabris, C.F. et al. 2014. Smart genes prove elusive. *Proceedings of the National Academies of Sciences, USA*. Available at http://dx.doi.org/10.1073/pnas.1404623111. Accessed January 1, 2015.

CHAPTER 11

Strategic, Tactical, and Operating Process

Strategy is to war what the plot is to the play.
Tactics is represented by the role of the players;
Logistics furnishes the stage management, accessories, and maintenance.
The audience, thrilled by the action of the play and the art of the performers,
overlooks all of the cleverly hidden details of stage management.

Lt. Col. George C. Thorpe (1917)
Pure Logistics

11.1 CRISIS MANAGEMENT

11.1.1 Crisis Management Definition

Crisis management can be defined as the method of determining a possible threat, risk, or crisis and responding with internal or external and public or private resources. The practice of crisis management is typically implemented together with other techniques, for example, risk management and business continuity management. The successful management of crises ensures that the damage is controlled, and the nation, society, and industry are protected or rapidly recovering.

According to NATO (2014), "a crisis is a change, which may be sudden or which may take some time to evolve, that results in an urgent problem with a high level of uncertainty that must be addressed immediately." A crisis may occur in several areas, including but not limited to security, safety, environment, quality, economic, stakeholders, commercial, etc. Sometimes, crises may affect more than one area, i.e., a natural disaster may lead to economic disasters. Most important, a safety-related disaster, such as extreme weather, may not only endanger a ship's navigation but also reveal systemic vulnerabilities that could attract a security attack, such as piracy.

11.1.2 Classifying Crisis

- *Crises and the element of time*: Crises may be (a) acute, i.e., of short duration, or (b) chronic, i.e., last for a longer period of time and require continuous efforts toward response, mitigation, and recovery.
- *Crises and the element of surprise*: Crises may be (a) anticipated, i.e., expected to occur due to certain indicators, or (b) unexpected, i.e., characterized by the element of surprise.
- *Crises and the element of mitigation*: Depending on the conditions of a crisis, the early warnings, expectations, and resources, crisis managers of the public and private sectors may be able to intervene before, during, and after a crisis.
- *Proactiveness vs. reactiveness*: Proactiveness through the use of risk management techniques is regarded as the optimum method for avoiding a crisis to occur. In contrast, adopting a reactive stance suggests that the risk management methodology was unsuccessful, and the system lacks preparedness. Consequently, the element of surprise generates more damages and in case of intentional threat may imply that the attackers have identified the vulnerabilities and planned their attack based upon them.
- *Preparedness and contingency planning*: Crisis managers will ideally create a contingency plan and implement a strategy that forecasts, mitigates, and responds to potential crises. Building a proactive and prepared system leads to establishing a resilient, sustainable system. Training and drills build the foundations of preparedness, resource management, and crisis management. When crisis managers create training, drills, and tabletop exercises based on multiple different yet realistic scenarios, they create a robust system of proactiveness and preparedness. Such techniques help professionals build muscle memory, reveal vulnerabilities, and enhance the crisis managers' possibility of developing an efficient emergency response system. It is important to remember that preparedness should combine the building of muscle memory and creative thinking. Participants should be able to use different drills and scenarios yet be able to improvise during an actual crisis, as each incident occurs based on different factors, causes, and impacts.

Finally, *crisis recovery* entails building resilient systems that can quickly recover from an incident.

11.1.3 Crisis Management Timeline Model

Many models of crisis management exist in both the public and private sectors. The stages of crisis management, as described in Figure 11.1, illustrates the crisis management timeline model, which includes the following phases:

1. The "preparation phase," where the crisis management process is established with a set of risk management and contingency planning tools.
   a. *Leadership and teamwork*: Crisis management should base their system on both leadership and teamwork throughout the chain of command.
   b. An efficient *incident command system* has been confirmed to be especially beneficial where crises demand a response from a system of enterprises and in cases where misunderstandings and ambiguous messages are given.

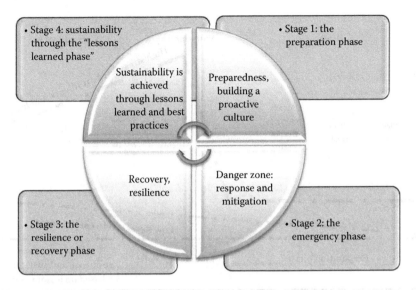

FIGURE 11.1   Crisis management timeline model. (From the author.)

    c. The *preparation process* helps cope with issues such as risk management, contingencies, and resource distribution and usage; control and command; and information management. It includes the following stages:

       i. Risk assessment

      ii. Contingency plan

     iii. Resource management

     iv. Building muscle memory through training and drills

2. The "emergency phase and danger zone" stage, i.e., the area where the incident actually occurs. This stage focuses on threat identification and prepares for the next phase of resilience by promoting situational awareness and by putting in place a set of rules based on the contingency plan. Once an incident occurs, the emergency response protocols also include hazard communication and media management.

3. The "resilience or recovery phase," where the system utilizes its resources, contingencies, and other capabilities in order to return to "business as usual." This stage includes threat identification and mitigation and should ideally encompass any and all types of threats related to the government or corporate entity in question, i.e., from cargo theft to illegitimate trade and travel, cybersecurity, or even terrorism. Ideally, potential forecasts and scenarios on security threats should be well-combined with safety threats, i.e., unintentional actions that could potentially create systemic vulnerabilities or damages.

    Such safety threats could be related to both (i) human error, negligence, and fatigue and (ii) natural disasters, such as hurricanes, extreme temperatures, and so on.

4. The "sustainability through lessons learned phase," which is a parallel stage occurring from the emergency to the recovery phase, where an actual incident unfolds and provides insight about the system's vulnerabilities, the attacker's strategies, the validity and efficiency of the current contingency, and emergency response plans. Sustainability is a level of maturity gained through experiences and sometimes losses incurred.

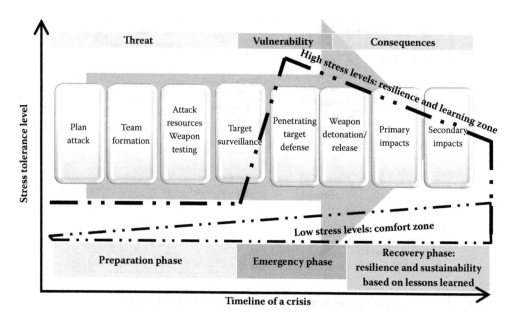

FIGURE 11.2   Crisis timeline stress model: comfort zone vs. resilience and learning zone. (From the author, based on Burns, M., Supply Chain Security: A Strategy to Resilience through Policies, Partnerships, and Technologies, Department of Homeland Security [DHS] Supply Chain Security Workshop, Houston—April 23, 2014; Burns, M., Ensuring Optimum Resilience in Marine Transportation: Extended Applications of the Maritime Security Risk Analysis Model [MSRAM] and the Dynamic Risk Management Model [DRMM]. Innovative Technologies for a Resilient Marine Transportation System, 3rd Biennial Research & Development Conference, Washington, DC, June 24–26, 2013.)

In accordance with the crisis management model, each system contains different strengths and vulnerabilities throughout the different phases of preparation, emergency response, resilience, and sustainability. As demonstrated in Figure 11.2, when a company or federal entity operates within low stress levels, their comfort zone does not expose them to new learning experiences. On the contrary, as the stress levels increase, vulnerabilities and strengths are exposed yet, during this critical period, could serve as a learning process that leads an entity toward resilience and sustainability. As discussed in numerous instances in this book, a crisis or a near miss can serve as a new awareness plateau that reveals the strengths and weaknesses of an attacker and the entity under attack.

11.2 THE THREE LEVELS OF WAR:
STRATEGIES, OPERATIONS, AND TACTICS

Matters of defense and homeland security share many common principles and standards with actual warfare, and hence, there are many lessons to be learned from military theories that can be applied in commercial security. Military strategy is actually the art and

Download the UH GO App to:

▶ **Enroll/Register** for Classes

▶ **Pay for Classes**

▶ Check **Grades**

▶ Access **Shuttle Routes**

▶ Get **Parking info**

▶ Manage **Tuition/ Financial Aid**

▶ ... and more stuff that will **make your life easier!**

science of military coordination and the methodology of incorporating and employing military forces to take control of a specific target.

The war theory divides the structure of war into three wide-ranging sectors of action in planning, organizing, and executing warfare, i.e., the strategic, operational, and tactical level. An in-depth understanding of the nature, usefulness, and interconnection of these three levels can significantly assist both military and commercial security professionals. While these three levels have well-defined borders, in real-life warfare and commercial security incidents, such borders may overlap differently in each incident and therefore may not concur to specific sectors of command and control. The common elements between military and commercial applications are shown in Figure 11.3.

Based on the above, this section examines the management and planning levels of strategy, operations, and tactics.

   a. Strategic management, planning, and resource management
      i. *Strategic management* can be defined as a degree of managerial strategy and decision making that determines tactics and operations. It offers a general path to the venture. The strategic level focuses on the big picture, i.e., concentrates on determining the target, the desired consequences, and the regulatory compliance issues.
     ii. *Strategic planning.* Strategy is the first and primary level of planning where specific objectives are designed to meet specific objectives. Strategy includes the long-term perspective of the organization, whereas tactics require the

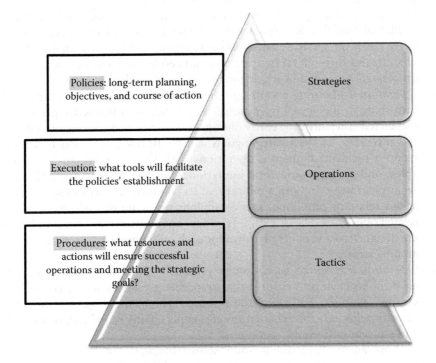

FIGURE 11.3 The three levels of war, with military and commercial applications. (From the author.)

measurable and precise actions required to reach that strategy. This is a corporate administration process that is employed to prioritize and establish strategies, assets, and procedures. It ascertains that the strategic decision makers operate in the direction of prevalent targets, set up an understanding of the possible consequences and effects, and evaluate and modify the company's path in reply to changing surroundings. It is a regimented attempt that creates elementary conclusions and methods that form and lead the purpose, aims, and future goals of the private or public entity. The success of strategic planning communicates the path of an entity and the potential strengths and vulnerabilities toward a potential risk.

The architecture of strategy calls for evaluating the current status and readiness of the company and subsequently figure out ways to get there. The evaluation of a strategic plan entails conducting a scenario examination and internal and external assessment. Within a contingency plan, goals and objectives should be established over a timeline of a foreseeable future.

iii. *Strategic resource management.* Strategic resource management concentrates on gathering, allocating, and controlling resources in the long term. It pertains to both the selection of resources needed to attain specific strategies and the potential effect of such resource utilization. Any and all security initiatives, methods, and protocols are needed to corporate positioning. The successful outcome of strategic planning depends on corporate alignment as a means of executing these plans.

b. Operation management, planning, and resource management

i. *Operational management* transforms the strategy to tactics by the architecture of models and helps attain the optimum use of resources and effectively reach the goals. Operational management enables the materialization of strategies through tactics. It is the end result pertinent to daily activities, processes, and expenditures through the use of quality systems.

ii. *Operational planning* entails specific resources, actions, and energies that contribute to the actual operations. When such operations are planned and conducted efficiently, the entity obtains superiority or a competitive edge over the adversary, as the strategic goals can be attained more easily. In a real security incident, numerous operations with specific prerequisites, deliverables, and resource and time limitations are employed to serve the larger security strategy. In both a military and a commercial security setting, operations relate to economic, social-, diplomatic-, commercial-, and resource-related objectives (USAF 1997). For these operations to be successful, tactics are designed as a support platform for each individual platform and the overarching strategy.

iii. *Operational resource management* primarily undertakes the project management segment and ensures that resources are effectively used in a time-sensitive manner. Following the resource management agenda in order of priority helps data interchange among supply chains or public/private entities and efficient options and actions.

c. Tactical management, planning, and resource management

i. *Tactical management.* Once a strategy is established for a specific goal, a tactic is used in order to materialize this particular strategy. Tactics are therefore designed to obtain a particular goal within a specific strategic plan. They entail a set of controls and maneuvering and are therefore closely related to situational awareness and any modifications in the conditions and surroundings related to the area that must be secured. The path for corporate management originates from the goals and strategic planning of the enterprise.

ii. *Tactical planning.* While strategic planning sets the framework for the course of action to be followed, tactical planning pertains to the actual set of actions that need to be taken in order for the strategy to succeed. Tactical planning examines the strategic goals and ensures that they are achieved within the specific environment, timeframe, resources, and intelligence information available. This is the stage where corporate strengths are used to cover the corporate vulnerabilities, and transform all resources into actions, to make the strategy succeed.

iii. *Tactical resource management.* Tactical resource management refers to bridging strategies and operations and proposing ways of materializing the tactics. Utilizing resources to function on the best suited project at the proper timing is essential to obtaining assignments from development to materialization. It is necessary to plan proactively with all the resources and limited disruptions.

11.3 SITUATIONAL AWARENESS: SURVIVAL TACTICS AND TECHNIQUES

To know your Enemy, you must "become" your Enemy.

Sun Tzu (孫子)
Chinese Military General (544–496 BC), The Art of War

Situational awareness (SA), as defined by the US Coast Guard, is "the ability to identify, process, and comprehend the critical elements of information about what is happening to the team with regards to the mission." It is the understanding of one's surroundings, both friendly and enemy powers (USCG 2014).

SA is a powerful, cognizant situational expression. It is the awareness of a person's surroundings related to data, occurrences, activities, and operations that have the potential to change the previously anticipated environment. SA can be influenced by significant data hints related to the opponent and the environment; hints of the opponents' conduct; and relevance of reactions.

Depending on the nature of the threat, there are numerous focal areas of situational awareness, as depicted in Figure 11.4. These include

a. *Homeland SA,* which focuses on a nationwide threat, such as a terrorist attack. This threat encompasses all of the following security threats.

b. *People-centric SA,* which pertains to the human factor as a threat or as a vulnerability.

c. *Critical infrastructure SA,* which refers to the 16 critical infrastructure sectors as per the US DHS, and encompasses prevention, mitigation, and resilience.

d. *Geographical SA,* which entails geospatial conditions, such as longitude, latitude, and altitude.

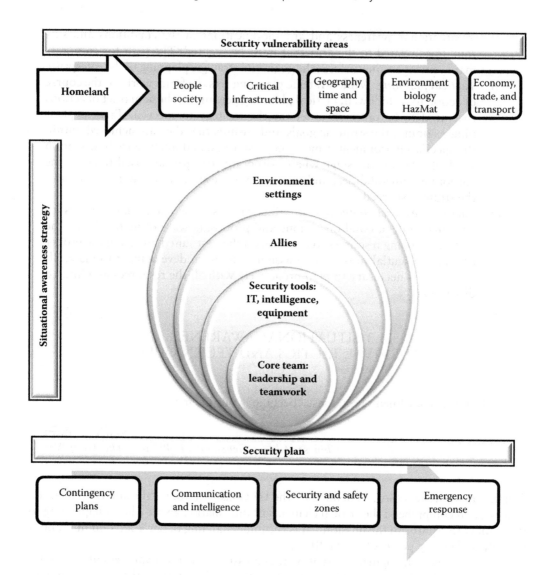

FIGURE 11.4 Situational awareness, vulnerabilities, and security plan. (From the author.)

   e. *Spatial/temporal SA*, which pertains to the elements of time and space.
   f. *Environmental SA*, which relates to information about ecological situations, hazardous materials, pollution, or biological hazards in the entire supply chain.
   g. *Economy, trade, and transport SA*, which encompasses the national economy, as well as the logistics and supply chain network.

An effective safeguard strategy is required to concentrate on these principal components:

   i. Real-time recognition of potential threats.
  ii. Comprehending the particular information, purpose, and task objectives of the security professionals and the potential threats.

iii. Adaptability and readiness to operate from prevention to response and defense. The ability to safeguard a specific area, i.e., of critical infrastructure, vehicle, etc., or the ability to eliminate and/or control the attacker's resources.

iv. Real-time threat communication, collaboration between allies or partners, and synchronization of efforts. The use of this data is to protect the system and defend it against the attackers.

Having a shared mental model is necessary to achieve situational awareness. In circumstances where this is lost or minimized, human error is more likely to occur. Successful communication among leaders and teams, together with designated roles within a team, strengthens the situational awareness and helps the team to:

- Foresee the system's weaknesses and requirements to support specific supply chain members
- Identify areas where changes in strategy, operations, and tactics are made; and
- Effectively implement these changes

According to Bedny and Meister (1999), situational awareness offers dynamic situational positioning, the possibility to reveal a situation over a time span, as well as the likely situational components. The situational awareness process relates to realistic, creative, cognizant, and spontaneous elements that make it possible to proactively formulate tactics of attaining external challenges.

11.3.1 Survival Techniques and Inaccurate Situational Awareness

Within a security context, emergency preparedness at a national or commercial level pertains to the actions taken by security professionals in order to mitigate any systemic disruptions or threats. This can be called commercial or social *"survivalism,"* and its concept is to enhance the situational awareness while proactively ensuring the sufficiency or resources should an incident occur. At a commercial level, this pertains to mitigating disruptions and bottleneck threats that may be derived due to intentional systemic attack and may affect the raw materials, production, distribution, and final markets.

Inaccurate situational awareness occurs when the input of a security risk assessment is inaccurate. In other words, when the security forecasts developed by humans and verified by technologies and metrics are not accurate, systemic vulnerabilities may occur.

When new or unknown forces affect the security environment, either impacting the side of the attackers or the supply chain, disruptions and vulnerabilities seem to appear. If security professionals fail to identify such threats at an early stage after their occurrence, such issues can magnify the vulnerabilities and enhance both the impact and the possibility of a security attack.

Woods (1988) conducted a meticulous research on efficient and accurate situational awareness and the necessity to break down the threat factors into smaller components, which seem to define the actual threat like pieces of a puzzle. Identifying the true segments that contribute to a security threat can be depicted as a set of steps where the security professionals are asked to operate. Figure 11.5 depicts and compares an accurate versus an inaccurate situational awareness and thus verifies the potential losses occurred due to this misjudgment.

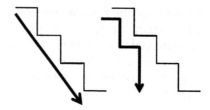

FIGURE 11.5   Accurate vs. inaccurate situational awareness. (After Woods, D., Coping with complexity: The psychology of human behavior in complex systems, in Goodstein, L.P., Andersen, H.B., and Olsen, S.E. [eds.], *Tasks, Errors and Mental Models*, Taylor & Francis, London, 1988.)

Chapter 12 will deal with the lessons learned about logistics and transportation security and will offer recommendations that will hopefully promote a proactive culture, enhanced situational awareness, more accurate risk assessment methodologies, and less security incidents.

CASE STUDY: UNIVERSAL WEATHER AND AVIATION

Interview: Bobby D. Butler, Jr.

Senior Vice President, Global Partnership Management and Enterprise Safety for Universal Weather and Aviation, Inc., USA

Crisis management, situational awareness, and mitigating risk factors are significant components in all transportation modes but especially in aviation. In an industry segment where millions of passengers are moved around the globe, commercial airlines are facing security and safety threats. Universal Weather and Aviation, Inc.® (Universal) is a corporation dedicated to providing complete trip logistics for operators and owners of business aircrafts. They have one goal: the success of their clients' trips. Whether it is a business opportunity, a humanitarian relief effort, or a medical emergency, their employees are committed to sharing their clients' sense of urgency and exhausting their global resources to get the job done. By helping their clients achieve successful missions, they move organizations and people who then move the world.

    For over 55 years, Universal has continued to grow and evolve, adding new services, solutions, and locations worldwide to meet the changing and ever-growing needs of those who utilize business aviation. As of 2015, they are represented in 47 locations in 20 countries, with over 1700 employees worldwide, and have facilitated more than 3 million trip legs. With the increasing complexity of business aviation, their clients rely on them to help them manage the expectations of their stakeholders, stay ahead of the ever-changing regulatory environment, and mobilize their global community on their behalf when an unforeseen event occurs. No matter what the security or safety challenges or other unexpected changes, Universal clients depend on a business partner who is ready to support them with a sense of urgency 24/7 anywhere in the world. By leveraging the full knowledge and expertise of their employees, vetted suppliers, and key contacts around the world, they problem solve and deliver solutions so their clients can keep the guarantees they make to their organizations.

The company does this through several primary business units, including

- Dedicated 24/7 trip support service teams who provide customized weather, flight plans, permits, global regulatory services, transportation and security arrangements, and more
- Ground support at more than 40 locations around the world, which is known for its adherence to standards for consistent, professional, and personalized services
- A contract fuel program, which includes a fueling card accepted worldwide at over 5000 locations and the volume-buying power of over 19,500 cardholders
- Inflight catering with 20 owned-and-operated kitchens and hundreds of associate catering partners on six continents

COPING WITH SAFETY AND SECURITY DISRUPTIONS

Universal manages to meet clients' expectations during different types of disruptions, such as extreme weather, aircraft mechanical issues, ground handling, or security issues.

In aviation, especially business aviation, disruptions of various types frequently occur. These disruptions or unforeseen events include, but are not limited to, sudden severe weather, aircraft mishaps, aircraft mechanical issues, and issues with service providers (e.g., ground handlers, caterers, transportation) and other service providers. Universal is fully committed to their clients' missions by reducing their operating risks while maximizing their efficiency gains on the ground and in the air. Universal works to be one step ahead of unforeseen events.

For example, in October 2013, hurricane force winds and weather hit the United Kingdom. Universal's ground-handling operations at Stansted (near London) took proactive preparations to minimize the potential damage to its clients' aircrafts. In this situation, Universal ground staff moved some aircraft into nearby hangars, but additional measures were taken to secure the aircraft parked on the ramp. After the storm had passed, the Universal ground-handling operations team was able to quickly assess the damage to the airport grounds and ramp. As a result of the properly trained ground staff as well as the safety and security plans in place to manage natural disaster events, no injury to personnel or damage to aircraft was identified.

For situations where the disruptions are unforeseen, Universal employees jump to action using their vast experience and worldwide resources. For example, a captain, who was a client of Universal, contacted Universal with issues that needed to be addressed immediately. His aircraft was experiencing transponder issues, his reduced vertical separation minimum certificate was delayed in being received from the US Federal Aviation Administration, and his copilot had quit three days prior. These issues created high stress for the captain. Through the company's vast global resources, Universal was able to address the three issues within 12 h from the time of being contacted, and the captain was able to complete his flights on schedule.

COPING WITH TRADE DISRUPTIONS

As a US-based company, Universal encounters trade disruptions through economic trade sanctions imposed by the US government on another country or specific individuals. Universal must assess what options are available in order to meet their clients' needs in real time. For these types of disruptions, Universal employs trade sanctions experts as well as engages outside legal counsel to provide guidance with respect to its options. Additionally, Universal has a compliance and internal audit department (in addition to its legal department) to oversee the process of addressing trade disruptions and to monitor its efforts of complying with US and international laws and regulations. These efforts not only benefit Universal; they also benefit its clients by navigating these complex regulations in an ever-changing legal and regulatory environment.

Moreover, Universal works in compliance with the US Office of Foreign Assets Control to understand how it can provide aviation service support to our clients flying to, from, or over a sanctioned country. These understandings are documented in company policies and made available to Universal employees.

Besides complying with economic sanctions, Universal is committed to complying fully with all laws that apply to the company's business, both in the United States and in foreign countries in which the company does business. Universal is fully committed to conducting business at the highest level of integrity and according to the highest level of ethical standards. One law that specifically comes to mind is The Foreign Corrupt Practices Act of 1977 or FCPA. The FCPA, a law of the United States, makes it illegal for US citizens and companies, their officers, directors, employees and agents, and any stockholder acting on their behalf to offer, give, or authorize giving anything of value to or for the benefit of a foreign (non-US) official, directly or indirectly, to obtain or retain business or gain a commercial advantage. Failure to comply with local anticorruption laws, for example, the UK Bribery Act of 2010, could have equally serious consequences.

CONTINGENCY PLANS FOR SAFETY AND SECURITY IN THE AVIATION INDUSTRY

The safety and security for both Universal's employees and clients are very important. Universal attempts to take a proactive approach in managing these unforeseen events to drive down risks for both employees and its clients. For their operations at Universal headquarters, both business continuity and disaster recovery plans are documented and communicated. Their business and operational units routinely update their business continuity plans and hold regularly scheduled business resumption and disaster recovery exercises to ensure that these plans are tested and ready should a need arise. Universal's international ground-handling operations are equipped with emergency procedures to provide instruction to local staff on the actions to be taken under adverse or disastrous conditions. Associated training is also provided to all applicable staff. For example, if lightning is observed within 5 mi of the airport, aircraft-fueling operations as well as other ground-handling activities must be stopped. Universal helps to protect its clients and employees by reducing the risk of injury or damage if lightning does strike an aircraft, a piece of equipment, or something else that is highly conductive. The safety and security for Universal's employees and clients are very important.

Sources of security for Universal's clients can come in several different forms. These range from security briefings about a destination country or city before the client's aircraft takes off to secure transportation and physical security for the passengers, crew, or aircraft. When unforeseen situations happen, Universal communicates with the client to determine the appropriate response and then uses its resources to provide the client with a greater safety solution, which reduces their exposure to various risks. For example, when missiles were being launched from the Gaza Strip into Israel, Universal conferred with its clients and helped them to safely reposition their aircrafts to safer airports.

While a security guard Universal arranged was posted at a client's aircraft, he observed that another aircraft being towed was about to hit the client's aircraft. He took immediate action to protect the client's aircraft by communicating the situation to the towing team. This response prevented the client's aircraft from being damaged and creating disruption in the client's travel plan.

CASE STUDY: RIGHTSHIP INC.

Interview: Captain Anuj Chopra
Vice President at RightShip Americas LLC

Captain Anuj Chopra.

Rightship CEO Warwick Norman on the left and the Australian Prime Minister Tony Abbot on the right. The Award is Australian Prime Minister's 2013 Exporter of the Year.

From the left: Kris Fumberger RightShip's Sustainability Lead, Jason Scherr Manager Environmental Sustainability, Prince Rupert Port Authority, and self (taken 29th May 2015 at Greentech in Seattle).

RAISING SAFETY AND AN EVIRONMENTAL STANDARDS IN SHIPPING

The ship-vetting specialist, RightShip, is focused on helping the maritime industry avoid preventable incidents while reducing the carbon dioxide emissions emitted by the world marine fleet. This is achieved by condensing information, providing rapid and consistent analysis and advice, monitoring and complying with international standards, and bringing expert support and advice within the reach of even the smallest business. Since its inception in 2001, RightShip has helped to improve global marine safety standards by identifying and eliminating substandard vessels from supply chains. RightShip provides vetting services to all types of ships including Oil Companies International Marine Forum Ship Inspection Report Program (OCIMF SIRE) inspections to the petroleum, chemical, and gas sector.

With a comprehensive Ship Vetting Information System (SVIS™) coupled with the maritime expertise of their vetting team, they help their customers to manage marine risk by identifying and eliminating substandard ships from their supply chain.

RightShip was formed to improve dry bulk safety and quality standards and draw on the significant ship-vetting expertise of global commodity companies, BHP Billiton and Rio Tinto. As major charterers and shippers, the founding businesses had developed vetting systems to manage their own marine risk. RightShip combined their expertise and resources to develop a SVIS as a comprehensive risk management tool. In 2006, international food, agriculture, and risk management company Cargill joined as an equal equity partner.

Risk Rating System

RightShip's SVIS is a comprehensive risk management tool. SVIS contains information on all commercial vessels over 500 tonnes that operate worldwide and draws data from reliable sources including IHS Fairplay, Port State Control (PSC), yards, and shipowners directly.

When a customer logs onto the system to vet a vessel, SVIS uses a sophisticated computer-based algorithm to evaluate over 50 risk factors with proven links to casualties and detentions, covering vessel building and maintenance, ownership and management, crewing, flag, class, PSC, inspections, and many other aspects of history and performance.

These risk factors go toward a "score," which combines with other factors including PSC performance to determine the overall star rating. Customers are provided with a risk rating for the vessel at that particular date and time ranging from one star (highest risk) to five stars (lowest risk).

The most common reason that RightShip downgrades a vessel is after an adverse PSC inspection. When a vessel is being vetted, and the vessel has an adverse PSC history, their vetting superintendents contact the shipowner to close out or finalize the PSC observations/detention. To speed up this process, a shipowner can contact us with the details and evidence clarifying any PSC performance or casualties and incidents including any investigative report, details of corrective action undertaken, and preventative action taken to prevent reoccurrence.

Owners can help ensure satisfactory performance against RightShip's risk factors by ensuring that their safety management system has adequate procedures for the effective management, supervision, and inspection of the vessel. This ensures that everyone involved with the vessel complies with regulatory requirements.

Due to the dynamic nature of the risk rating system, the risk rating is only valid for the particular customer requesting the vet on that day at that time. RightShip does not "approve" a ship but will recommend it as an acceptable risk.

RightShip supports the International Labor Organization's Maritime Labor Convention (MLC) to help protect the well-being of seafarers. Any vessel from a flag state that has not ratified the MLC now requires a manual vetting by RightShip when nominated for vetting.

While RightShip's primary tool is SVIS, customers are provided with 24/7 advice by vetting superintendents located in Melbourne, Houston, and London who have extensive maritime expertise and experience.

Customers

RightShip's SVIS is used by over 3000 users in more than 250 organizations worldwide including charterers and shippers, shipowners, ship managers, port authorities, flag states, port state control regimes, classification societies, terminals, agents, insurers, and maritime finance organizations. Around 70% of RightShip's business comes from the dry bulk sector. Customers screen vessels using standard or customized criteria, review risk-related data, and track vessel or fleet performance. In 2014, RightShip processed over 35,000 decisions across 3.07 billion tonnes of commodity and removed 950 vessels from customer supply chains.

Charterers

Fluctuating fuel costs, oversupply of capacity, turbulent freight rates, and pressure on the availability of skilled staff can result in vessel maintenance standards slipping as shipowners cut costs to remain competitive and profitable. With 20% of the fleet responsible for over 50% of casualties, a reliable vetting system, combined with advice and support from maritime professionals, is essential for charterers seeking to reduce the risk of casualties, cargo damage, costly delays, and detentions.

Shipowners

Shipowners with access to SVIS can track events such as casualties, incidents, and rating changes to their fleet and receive automated advice about any change to their vessels. This enables them to proactively address any deficiencies or incidents by providing information to close out the incident. Shipowners can also view the risk rating of their vessels and benchmark their company performance against both best practice and the RightShip global average.

Terminals

Terminal operators utilize SVIS to prevent substandard vessels from entering their facility while providing a full audit trail to substantiate decision making.

Once a vessel has loaded at a terminal that subscribes to RightShip, feedback from the terminal staff is recorded against the vessel for future reference ensuring that noncommercial performance critical information is readily available to all RightShip clients. Terminals can also benchmark their risk profile, quality assurance criteria, and environmental performance against other RightShip clients.

Some terminals also use a terminal questionnaire as part of their ship scheduling and nomination process to improve safety and ensure transparency. Every ship scheduled to enter their port is required to submit an online terminal questionnaire containing specific vessel information around mooring configuration, loading, and deballasting rates and helicopter suitability prior to berthing.

Banks and Insurance

Banks, insurers, and Protection and Indemnity (P&I) Association clubs utilize SVIS to supplement their internal risk processes and meet Basel III requirements. Many insurance brokers also use RightShip data to deliver premium relief across multiple lines of cover to their customers in recognition of the superior nature of the vessels they engage.

Ship Inspections

RightShip recognizes that there are a high number of ship inspections by class and PSC, which is why a RightShip inspection is only necessary when a dry bulk vessel is considered high risk or is over 18 years of age. The volume of inspections is also reduced as information is shared across 250+ customers.

Occasionally, an inspection may be required before RightShip can recommend it to a customer as an acceptable risk, for example,

- A poor PSC record with repetitive observations
- A detention has been recorded resulting (or likely to result) in prosecution subsequent to MARPOL or SOLAS infringement
- Repetitive submissions of inadequate root cause and corrective and preventive actions indicating weakness in the safety management system
- Major repairs or modifications have been undertaken; or
- At the request of a customer

RightShip has a global team of inspectors who are certified and trained to look at the overall safe working condition of a vessel and whether or not it adheres to industry best practices. Inspectors obtain firsthand validation of a vessel's condition and operational capability and address areas within and outside the scope of PSC, International Safety Management, and class assessments. Regulatory compliance and necessary certification are reviewed as well as the implementation of the management systems.

In consultation with the Union of Greek Shipowners and International Association of Classification Societies, RightShip has recently reviewed the inspection close out process to increase transparency and harmonize standards. Deficiencies that are considered to be of a serious nature and a safety or environmental risk will be reported to the relevant classification society or flag by the shipowner for review. When a class or flag is satisfied with the action taken by the shipowner to close the deficiency, evidence will be provided to RightShip.

Wherever possible, an inspection is undertaken in a discharge port to minimize the disruption to the ship and usually takes around one to two working days.

Improving the Efficiency of the Existing Fleet

In recent years, RightShip developed the Existing Vessel Design Index (EVDI™) to provide customers with a systematic and transparent framework for measuring the energy efficiency of the existing fleet. The EVDI provides a theoretical estimate of the amount of carbon dioxide emitted by any nominated ship, per tonne nautical mile travelled, based on the engine and vessel design characteristics when the ship is built. It is based on the same principles as the International Maritime Organization's Marine Environment Protection Committee's Energy Efficiency Design Index and positions the vessel compared to similar ships on an A–G scale with "A" being the most efficient and "G" being the least efficient.

RightShip also works closely with shipowners to validate the data used across their fleet lists, and the data can be accessed free of charge via http://www.shippingefficiency.org.

The benefits of the efficiency rating include

- Informed selection for reducing emissions
- Opportunity for charters to reduce their bunker bills
- Rewarding and recognizing sustainable operators through greater acceptance of their ships and port discounts, and
- Fast and easy access to data that has previously been dispersed and costly to gather

RightShip's elite customers transport over 1.8 billion tonnes of cargo per annum and currently factor the environmental rating into their vessel selection process. This represents around 23% of global noncontainerized trade. Feedback from the early adopters suggests that this framework has not only helped to reduce shipping costs but also has gone a long way to publicly demonstrate their commitment toward corporate social responsibility.

The Future

In 2015, RightShip is looking forward to launch "Qi," the new cloud-based holistic vetting platform with predictive analytics and real-time reporting, enabling customers to instantly access a wealth of information and undertake accurate forecasting. RightShip will be able to harness the Big Data within the system and better target substandard performance to further reduce customer risks. "Qi" is designed and optimized for smartphones and tablets and the system interface refreshed to improve the user experience.

INTERVIEWS AND CASE STUDIES

Butler, Bobby D. Jr., Senior Vice President, Global Partnership Management, and Enterprise Safety for Universal Weather and Aviation, Inc., USA.
Chopra, Anuj, Vice President at RightShip Americas LLC.

REFERENCES

Bedny, G. and Meister, D. 1999. Theory of activity and situation awareness. *International Journal of Cognitive Ergonomics,* Vol. 3, Issue 1, pp. 63–72.
Burns, M. 2013. Ensuring Optimum Resilience in Marine Transportation: Extended Applications of the Maritime Security Risk Analysis Model (MSRAM) and the Dynamic Risk Management Model (DRMM). Innovative Technologies for a Resilient Marine Transportation System, 3rd Biennial Research & Development Conference, Washington, DC, June 24–26.
Burns, M. 2014. Supply Chain Security: A Strategy to Resilience through Policies, Partnerships, and Technologies. Department of Homeland Security (DHS). Supply Chain Security Workshop. Houston—April 23.
NATO. 2014. Maritime Situational Awareness. Available at http://www.cmre.nato.int /research/maritime-situational-awareness. Accessed November 3, 2014.

USAF. 1997. Three levels of war. USAF College of Aerospace Doctrine, Research and Education (CADRE). In *Air and Space Power Mentoring Guide*, Vol. 1. Maxwell AFB, AL: Air University Press, USA.

USCG. 2014. Situational Awareness. Available at http://www.uscg.mil/auxiliary/training. Accessed November 3, 2014.

Woods, D. 1988. Coping with complexity: The psychology of human behavior in complex systems. In Goodstein, L.P., Andersen, H.B., and Olsen, S.E. (eds.). *Tasks, Errors and Mental Models*. Taylor & Francis: London.

The Future of Global Transportation and Supply Chain Networks

They've got us surrounded again, the poor bastards.

Creighton Williams Abrams, Jr. (1914–1974)
US Army General

12.1 INTRODUCTION

The concluding chapter of this security book aims to forecast the future security patterns by examining the global trade markets, especially the rapidly growing economies. Other chapters have duly covered the future trends of terrorism, piracy, cyber security, illegitimate trade and transport, human trafficking, and so on. This chapter will aim to reveal the security threats by examining the global economic and trade patterns. In particular, a focus on the rapidly developing economies will reveal the potential security threats associated with a change of trade patterns, new trade agreements, and any economic or military consortiums that may change the current trade and transportation routes.

12.1.1 Forecasting the Global Economy and Trade Patterns

According to the World Trade Organization (2015), the foreseeable future will likely experience a trade growth of about 4.7% for 2015, which is still beneath the 20-year average of 5.3% (1983–2013). World merchandise trade grew 2.1% in 2013 in volume terms, very close to the 2.3% increase from the previous year. Despite the slow growth of developed economies, nations like the United States, Canada, Australia, South Africa, Japan, and Northwestern Europe have encountered a moderate yet sustainable recovery.

12.1.1.1 The BRICS Countries: Brazil, Russia, India, China, and South Africa

This growth will likely be instigated by the rapidly developing economies, i.e., the BRICS countries (Brazil, Russia, India, China, and South Africa), whose high population (41.60% of the world population as of 2015), combined with low labor and production cost, will continue to be outsourcing havens. Another strong point is those nations' inner demographics, especially the positive ratio among the "fit for employment" versus under-age or retired population segments.

According to Goldman Sachs, by 2050, China and India will lead in terms of manu-factured goods, whereas Brazil and Russia will be the prevailing suppliers of raw materi-als (GS 2004–2014).

BRICS have launched their own bank as a major initiative to resist the influence of dollar-pegged trade and institutions such as the International Monetary Fund and the World Bank. The BRICS countries have created a $100-billion Development Bank and a reserve currency consortium exceeding another $100 billion. The BRICS banking sys-tem is anticipated to fund infrastructure and growth projects within BRICS nations (VI BRICS Summit 2015). The BRICS countries may need to overcome certain challenges at an internal and external level, such as

1. Wealth and productivity distribution among member states and internally in each state
2. Eventual dominance among these powerful nations
3. External pressures to pursue a globally recognized currency policy
4. Diverse socioeconomic and geopolitical characteristics, which they need to smoothen out in order to establish more homogenized relations

- Brazil is a major oil (energy), iron ore (construction), and coffee producer. The country also enjoys a vibrant industrial activity, which over the past few years seems to surpass the economists' expectations.

  As an antipode, Brazil has high crime rates, related to personal and cargo theft, as well as violent protests and strikes.
- Russia is a nation rich in valuable natural resources such as oil and gas and pre-cious metals, which constitute a large percentage of Russia's exports. Russia is also a manufacturer of military equipment, giving the nation military as well as economic advantages. After the dissolution of the Soviet Union in 1991, Russia's wealth of commodities was geographically restricted as the new country's coastal lines were only covering its northern part, yet there was limited maritime outlet in its southern territory. The Ukraine crisis was triggered by Russia's invasion of the Crimean Peninsula, an area of strategic geopolitical significance for Russia, which has intensively been looking for sea outlets to facilitate its trade with the Mediterranean Sea and Central/West Asia. This goal was achieved in 2015; Russia initiated an agreement with Cyprus, a European Union (EU) state-island by the Mediterranean Sea, to host Russia's aviation and naval bases. This is the first EU state to sign such an agreement.
- India's economy is based on a plethora of activities, including manufacturing, construction, education, tourism, trade and transport services, banking and invest-ment, entertainment, and much more.

  India is among the world's top producer of electricity and oil products and a major importer of coal and crude oil. India faces some security challenges due to a number of terrorist attacks from radical religious groups. As examined in Chapter 2 of this book, the nation has managed to develop a robust resilient sys-tem due to the ongoing hostilities with certain foreign radical groups. An inter-esting development pertains to China's recent agreement to outsource many of its manufacturing activities. This initiative is anticipated to promote growth and collaboration among the two nations. Complications may arise in the long term, as this intimate collaboration may involve sensitive areas of national security, cyber security, and matters of intelligence.

- The so-called miracle of China occurred in 1999, when the nation entered the US stock exchange and assumed a more extrovert economic strategy. The country's overpopulation, combined with favorable socioeconomic and demographic traits (such as high working population levels and low labor costs) have contributed to the country's rapid growth and continuous expansion. Over the past few years, the nation has been facing both external and internal security threats related to cyber security and the rapid spread of radical ideologies among younger groups affected by social media.

- South Africa's economy is the second largest in Africa, following Nigeria. The pillars of national growth include mining of diamonds, precious metals (platinum, gold), semiprecious metals (chromium), and other metals. The country's manufacturing, maritime, and touristic activities are also profitable. The nation's security challenges mainly pertain to social imbalances. The 1980s were characterized by social turmoil driven by apartheid (racial segregation and social injustice). Nelson Mandela was the country's legendary president from 1994 to 1999. His antiapartheid political agenda aimed to dissolve racism, social injustice, and poverty. The country's high unemployment rate (over 25%) is one of the serious challenges that need to be overcome. In the long run, scarcity of water is anticipated to become the nation's main challenge by 2070. To tackle this challenge, the government has initiated a water infrastructure strategy.

12.1.1.2 The MINT Countries: Mexico, Indonesia, Nigeria, and Turkey

According to many economists, the rapid growth of the BRICS countries may be followed by the growth of other nations, among which the MINT countries are the most prominent. Just like the BRICS countries, the MINT nations enjoy economic efficiency in their factors of production, especially labor and land, making them attractive trade and outsourcing partners. While this economic consortium enjoys a booming trade, and is likely to define the new major trade routes, internal challenges need to be overcome for each nation to grow to its fullest potential:

- Mexico's pillars of economic prosperity include manufacturing of electrical appliances, car manufacturing (among which many US companies are outsourcing), IT, and so on. This vibrant economic and industrial prosperity is overshadowed by internal unrest due to illegitimate activities associated with the drug cartels, human trafficking, illegal trade, and corruption.

- Indonesia, the second-fastest global economy after China, is rich in petroleum and natural gas. However, the national security challenges over the past 10 years have grown as much as the nation's economy: terrorism; piracy; drug trafficking; cyber security; and persistent civil, religious, and labor unrest make the nation's economy vulnerable.

- Nigeria's robust oil production is enhanced by sustainable growth in the sectors of agriculture, IT, services, and entertainment. Since 1990, the country has enjoyed a 90% increase, and the economic and production outlooks seem promising. Some of the security threats the nation faces include piracy, which is expanded in the Gulf of Guinea, Western Africa and is related with the oil-rich region and pertinent sea routes from Nigeria to the global markets. The nation also faces security threats in the northeastern regions and the Niger Delta.

- Turkey is considered by the International Monetary Fund as an emerging market, and as a newly industrialized state, with heavy construction, shipbuilding, manufacturing of motor vehicles and electronics, textiles, and much more. The country's main security threats pertain to terrorist groups of religious, ideological, and political nature (the country's borders are by Syria, Iran, and Iraq, and the regional unrest seems to have spread to the wider region).

The above examples demonstrated that an examination of the national economy can reveal security vulnerabilities. Therefore, what a conventional forecasting methodology cannot foresee is the developments based on new strategic alliances, trade agreements, and diplomatic relations. In fact, the future of the national and global economy is dependent upon formal and informal political and commercial alliances that may have the power to change the global security and economic trends. The price of oil is a characteristic example of this, and it will be discussed in Section 12.1.1.3.

12.1.1.3 The Energy Crisis and Transportation Challenges and Opportunities

According to the International Monetary Fund, international economic growth will be strengthened due to lower oil prices, which mirror an increase in supply (IMF 2015). This supply may reflect intensive raw materials, manufacturing, and distribution patterns. Nevertheless, this increase is anticipated to be balanced out by unfavorable trends, such as sluggish investment activities, due to low to moderate anticipations of market recovery.

This energy crisis has been caused by an artificial oversupply on behalf of Organization of Petroleum-Exporting Countries (OPEC) member states in a struggle to retain their existing market share and prevent the United States, Canada, Mexico, and other non-OPEC members to enter the global markets. OPEC's decision to produce more oil and gas than what is needed drives the fuel prices down.

This is great news for energy consumers but shattering news for the energy majors. Energy consumers will enjoy cheaper gasoline for their cars. Manufacturers and retailers will produce cheaper commodities, as their energy costs will drive production costs down. The energy majors will be able to withstand the crisis, yet smaller energy supplier companies may collapse. The energy economic miracle as experienced in the United States, Canada, Australia, Northern Europe, and the Mediterranean Sea has been experienced based on costly oil and gas exploration, i.e., deep sea drilling, directional drilling, shale fracking, etc. This means that energy in most non-OPEC nations costs more than the OPEC producers that can literally drill oil and gas in their backyard.

The United States is a key global energy player, as it is both a major producer and consumer: As a producer, it is not only among the top three shale oil and gas technically recoverable reserves but also the fifth-largest nation in terms of natural gas reserves and the tenth-largest nation in oil reserves.

The United States is also a major energy consumer: 28% of our energy is used for the transportation of passengers and cargoes. From this amount, over 60% is used for private vehicles, 3% for public transport (buses and trains), and 9% for aviation. The remaining 27% is used in sea transport and trucks. According to the International Maritime Organization, ships carry over 80% of global cargoes, and yet they only consume a quarter of global energy. Another interesting fact according to the US Transportation research board is that although the United States has less than 5% of the global population, we own over one-third of the private vehicles globally.

The transportation industry (sea, air, land) is closely related to the oil and gas industry in three ways:

1. Oil and gas are needed for fuel consumption in all transportation modes, e.g.,
   Cars, trucks: gas and LNG
   Rail: diesel oil and LNG
   Ships: IFO, diesel, and LNG
   Airplanes: jet fuel
   Spaceships: liquid hydrogen
2. As direct commodities: Oil and gas cargoes are carried by sea, land, and pipelines
3. As indirect commodities: Oil and gas exploration, shale fracking, etc., require the transportation of expensive "project cargoes" such as drilling equipment, chemicals, pipelines, spare parts, etc.

What does the collapse of oil and gas prices mean for the transportation industry?

- *Private vehicles*: In 2015, each US household may save around $500–1200 in gasoline money. When oil and gas are cheap, people tend to buy larger, fuel-inefficient cars, whereas when the market recovers, people trade their larger cars for smaller, fuel-efficient cars.
- *Airlines*: Shareholders are major winners in the oil and gas price collapse, as high earnings for 2014 and 2015 are combined with lower operational costs. Jet fuel represents about 30% of operating costs, and this amount is now almost sliced in half. As an example, Delta Airlines anticipate a $1.7-billion revenue in 2015. Energy brokers would not be happy though, as their commissions and overall earnings are severely affected by lower fuel prices.
- *Commercial trucks*: The cost of fuel represents around 40% of the operating costs. As an average truck consumes 20,500 gal of fuel, which cost around $70,000 each year, the price of fuel significantly impacts a company's cash flow.

The oil-and-gas boom over the past years has generated a high demand for trucks to carry drilling materials, chemicals, pipelines, spare parts, sand, and water, from the suppliers to numerous drilling sites, mostly in remote locations. Most importantly, trucks are flexible enough to secure employment among the manufacturing, construction, retailing, distribution, and many other components within a supply chain.

12.2 PROACTIVE SECURITY MEASURES IN A COST- AND TIME-SAVING FRAMEWORK

A supply chain's efficiency is mirrored in the quality and reliability of its infrastructure network, from production to the final consumer distribution. Efficiency signifies optimum performance, high service quality, minimum delays in production and transportation, and compliance with the principles of lean and agile and just in time (JIT). The carrier's speed should combine a timely delivery with affordable bunkers' cost. Also, regulatory compliance and compliance to the contracts of carriage should entail minimum nonconformities or observations. Efficiency entails service quality, customer satisfaction, and commercial viability. On the other hand, security focuses on a preventive strategy that solidifies and protects the supply chain from external malicious acts of terror or sea piracy (Burns 2014).

Interdependency characterizes the relation between efficiency and security: in order for a supply chain to be efficient, security is a prerequisite. For a supply chain to be secure, efficiency is also required.

For a security professional to be effective and efficient, it is fundamental to establish a proactive culture where risks are assessed and evaluated, and contingency plans are designed accordingly. A successful security strategy will identify vulnerabilities, strengthen the system's defenses, and hopefully avert security threats. The paradox here is that successful security systems alleviate threats, and since many of these threats never occur, their success cannot always be measured or valued. On the contrary, what is consistently and accurately measured entails to the resources allocated to protect a specific security system, including all of the factors of production, i.e., human resources (entrepreneurship and labor), land/technologies, and capital/budget allocation.

In a typical commercial setting, the success of an investment depends on the return on investment (ROI), i.e.,

$$\text{ROI} = \frac{\text{Gain} - \text{Cost}}{\text{Cost}} \times 100 \qquad (12.1)$$

However, in the case of security investment, it is not easy to estimate the gains acquired, as the actual benefits of the investment are often unseen, i.e., in the form of unmaterialized losses or adverted attacks that may not even be identified. Therefore, in the aforementioned ROI equation, only the cost can be calculated but not the gain. In a modern, capital-intensive industry where revenue and ROIs are significant motivators, security managers may be tempted to take shortcuts in security investments, some of the most common shortcuts being

a. Eliminating the security resources, such as investment in people, time, and resources
b. Compromising on the frequency and quality of security training, tabletop exercises, and familiarization protocols
c. Becoming complacent with the existing security measures and protective mechanisms

Due to this systemic incongruity, companies attribute to skills and preparedness the unmaterialized security losses, even in cases where it is a matter of pure luck. Accordingly, security professionals may stop being proactive, as identifying and rectifying multiple vulnerabilities is costly, and focus mainly on emergency response and resilience, as these budgets are focused on specific events in real time. Ironically, such investments are considered as measurable in accounting terms and efficient ROIs in business terms—yet from a security perspective, these are threats that could have been avoided and their consequences eliminated. Figure 12.1 reflects the low/optimal cost involved in reactive security culture vs. the higher costs entailed in emergency response and proactive security.

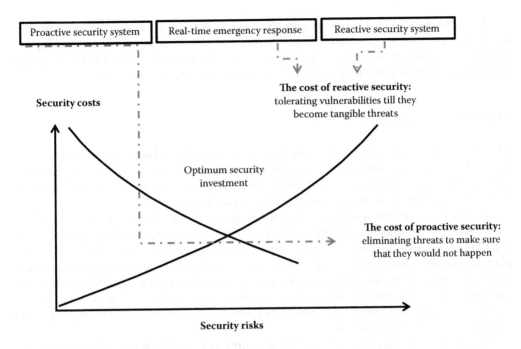

FIGURE 12.1   Reactive vs. proactive security costs. (From the author.)

12.3 THE BENEFITS OF PROACTIVE SECURITY MANAGEMENT

This section aims to help define and measure the benefits of proactive security systems through the adoption of a "cost- and time-saving framework."

12.3.1 The Element of Time

As far as time is concerned, proactive supply chain networks with ample time for preparedness are characterized by increased quality, optimum investment strategies, and efficient security systems. On the other hand, reactive companies or networks may be associated with higher or unidentified risks, compromised quality, possible bottlenecks, delays, and the tendency to take shortcuts in order to recover time lost. Such systems are not quality-standardized as their services, products, and/or security systems cannot be sustainable. Quality nonconformities can lead not only to security incidents but also to nonconformities, commercial penalties, and so on.

Limited time is also associated with limited availability or economic, commercial, and/or geographical restrictions: time restrictions dramatically reduce business options, be they an asset sale and purchase, commercial operations, repair works, assembly lines, or spare parts availability and smooth logistics.

The time element and its security implications cannot be accurately measurable. For a reactive operational approach, the losses involved are often justified by the company as a fair consequence of complex market dynamics. In other instances, the losses can be concealed or attributed to human error, fatigue, incompetence, and so on.

12.3.2 The Element of Cost

The cost factor, on the other hand, can be easily measured, and hence proactive vs. reactive actions can be compared in a straightforward manner. There are certain processes and cost-reduction methods applied by top-tier companies. All these effective methods are directly related to (a) proactiveness and (b) time management.

Security proactiveness suggests that the company achieved optimum gains as it had ample time for contingency planning based on a risk assessment methodology. Security reactiveness involves increased costs and last-minute decisions, orders, lack of time for planning, limited training and preparedness, and poor security checks. From a commercial stance, time delays imply high transportation costs; bottlenecks; and limited time for preventive measures, familiarization, and training. Increased costs due to this reactive stance may eventually impact the critical infrastructure protection, safety, security, and overall compliance to regulations.

On the other hand, proactive security measures increase the chances of optimum performance, standardization, and preparedness by high-standard professionals who will add value to the company and its asset(s) and will contribute to the company's success.

A proactive security methodology is not limited to technical, commercial, or operational effectiveness. Monitoring and measuring costs and profits are equally significant. The ultimate challenge of a security decision maker is to implement efficient security systems while retaining low costs. At the same time, an increase in proactiveness signals cost reduction, and consequently, an increase in cost savings is reflected in the increase of profit margins.

Productivity growth is measured as the growth rate in output minus a weighted average growth rate in inputs. Traditionally, cost measurement is associated with productivity and profitability ratios.

All methods of security monitoring and measurement are intermingled among the three fundamental elements—cost, productivity/preventability, and profitability—and are applied in the following manner:

a. Internally within the company
b. In different segments of the company, i.e., different segments of the supply chain, company branches, departments, and so on, compared with previous years' ratios
c. Compared with competitors' performance and the attackers' strategy (competitive security intelligence)
d. All the above must be analyzed within the given market conditions through different time periods

Among the advantages of monitoring and analyzing costs, to name a few, are cost-effectiveness, gaining the trust of stakeholders, organizing budget and cash flow arrangements, and so on.

12.4 BEHAVIORAL ASPECTS OF PROACTIVE MANAGEMENT

Section 12.3 confirmed the importance of adopting a proactive security culture applied in matters of skilled crew, investment, technologies, planned maintenance, logistical support, and so on. It has demonstrated how proactiveness or preplanning enables companies and executives to assess many different commercial or operational alternatives.

This section admittedly raises specific challenges on the desirable traits for the implementation of proactive security management. In the following list, it becomes evident that although traits are cultivated by top and middle management, different functions within the company require high levels of coherency and consistency in terms of timing and achieving desirable results. The list reveals the behavioral aspects of proactive security measures.

Behavioral aspects of proactive security management:

1. Planning (goals, standards, policies)
   Flexible, participative
   Timely planning
   Interactive communication
   Considering different strategic scenarios, contingency plans, and security standards
2. Organizing
   Proactive attitude
   Optimum delegation of authority and responsibilities
   Sustainable performance improvement
3. Staffing
   Encouraging security innovation and alternative solutions
   Flexible processes
   Motivating proactiveness/offering incentives
   Allowing time for preparedness, training, building muscle memory, and mitigating threats
   Creating motivated security professionals
4. Leadership
   Encouraging security proactiveness and proper time management
5. Controlling security systems and performance evaluation
   Setting goals and performance standards related to time and results
   Measuring performance
   Reporting and appraising performance
   Corrective action
   Rewards and accountability framework
   Follow-up activities, constant improvement of security systems
   Evaluation based on controllable performance and time management

Furthermore, as reflected in Table 12.1 and as Figure 12.2 demonstrates, a proactive stance assists governments and companies alike in the ongoing battle against security offenders.

While this section uses a theoretical approach of the modern "proactive organization," Section 12.5 describes how modern companies can promote a proactive culture.

TABLE 12.1   National Security Objectives vs. Terrorists and Security Offenders' Objectives

National Security and/or Supply Chain Security Objectives (Federal and Commercial Interests)	Terrorists/Security Offenders' Objectives
Protecting critical infrastructure and all possible targets	Identifying the strategic/critical infrastructure targets Terrorists and security offenders are focused on the outcome, i.e., the extent of the damage caused, and spotting the weakest link or target is not a priority, e.g., a difficult target may be chosen if their political, financial, religious, or other gains are greater
Optimum resource allocation	Optimum resource allocation
Proactive action • Architecture • Strategy • Ability to withstand the element of surprise • Ability to deter threats	Proactive action • Architecture • Strategy • The element of surprise
Reactive action • Consequences (political, legal, physical, etc.)	Reactive action • Consequences (political, legal, physical, etc.)
Optimum balance between security and supply chain efficiencies	Disruption of supply chain efficiencies
Advanced technology • One step ahead from terrorists/security criminals	Advanced technology • One step ahead from targets
Social consequences and public opinion • National Pride (for Department of Homeland Security [DHS]) • Industrial pride (for supply chain) • Promoting social stability and a sense of safety within the community	Social consequences and public opinion • Achieving commercial, financial, religious, or political goals • Creating social turmoil and a sense of insecurity within the target's territory

Source: Burns, M., *Effectiveness Evaluation of the Maritime Security Risk Analysis Model and the Dynamic Risk Management Model*, Washington, DC: TRB, Transportation Research Board of National Academies, Security Committee, January 14–16, 2013.

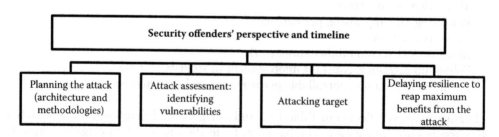

FIGURE 12.2   A security offenders' perspective and timeline.

12.5 CASE STUDIES ON PROACTIVE CORPORATE CULTURES

spliethoff

CASE STUDY: THE SPLIETHOFF GROUP

Interview: Thomas Damsgaard
Vice President of Spliethoff Americas

COMPANY PROFILE

The Amsterdam-based Spliethoff Group is one of the largest ship management companies in the Netherlands. The group consists of Spliethoff and her subsidiaries: BigLift Shipping (heavy lift), Sevenstar Yacht Transport (yacht transport), Wijnne Barends (short sea), and Transfennica (liner service).

Since the establishment in 1921, we built a reputation within the industry as a reliable, resourceful, and dedicated shipping partner with a wealth of experience. The Spliethoff Group plays a leading role worldwide in the transport market for forest products, projects, super heavy-lift, general cargo, and yachts.

The Spliethoff Group manages a large and modern fleet of well over 100 multi-purpose, heavy-lift and ro-ro vessels ranging in size from 2100 to 23,000 t. The Spliethoff Group-managed vessels have 1A Ice Class and even several 1A SUPER. They all sail under the Dutch flag.

To ensure that its customers have access to the latest technology in shipping, the fleet is constantly being renewed. Recently, four F-type vessels and six M-type vessels were added to the fleet.

The Spliethoff Group endeavors to minimize its vessels' environmental impact by limiting their emissions of SOx, NOx, soot (fine particles), and CO_2 by cleaning waste and ballast water, by doing the utmost to prevent oil spills, and by following

M/V Merwedegracht. (Courtesy of The Spliethoff Group, Spliethoff Americas.)

a strict waste management plan. The Spliethoff Group has high standards for the design, maintenance, and operation of the vessels and the training of the crew, which guarantees a minimal environmental impact.

The highly trained personnel in the company's global network offices, onboard their ships and in ports all over the world, are dedicated to maintaining our high standards. Their expertise enables them to offer their clients quality services ranging from optimum stowage plans to on-the-spot supervision of complex cargo operations.

MEETING CLIENTS' COMMERCIAL EXPECTATIONS

The primary objective of vessel operations' activities is to ensure that all services comply with customer requirements, and the voyages are carried out in a safe, cost-effective, and responsible manner. Whereas safety and security are the top priorities, all decisions start with the cargo and the customer's specific needs, and throughout the voyage, this is always the objective that the company is working to meet while hopefully being profitable—achieve the safest passage with the shortest time and maximum fuel savings considering cargo sensitivity.

> Safety is good business and good business is safety.

As a shipowner and operator, the company is exposed to a slew of risks, which they have to manage through and around:

1. Perils of the sea, including safety threats (weather, fog, navigation in narrow straits, etc.) and security threats (piracy, cargo theft, etc.)
2. Fluctuation in global markets such as commodities
3. Different regulations around the world—the shipowner rarely has any leverage on how vessels and crew are treated in the various nations, ports where they call
4. Cost structures vary in each port we call, and we rarely have any leverage in controlling or negotiating cost
5. Maritime lien rights against owners and their vessels are very liberal
6. Local regulations including for labor, security, etc., are as varied and unpredictable as can be
7. The challenge to manage remote assets such as a crew and a vessel sitting in the middle of the Atlantic Ocean

Some of these risks directly interface with the commercial expectations of their customers and thus will have to be managed by the shipowner's operation department with commercial concerns and needs in mind.

The most common obstructions are weather related, which may have an adverse impact on

1. Date-sensitive customer needs
2. Cargo operation in port
3. Safety of cargo at sea and the consequential unpleasant exposure to cargo damages

As it probably has become obvious by now, the unpredictability of our industry, e.g., due to extreme weather or bottlenecks, can often wreak havoc on a contractual commitment to be in a certain port or place at a certain time.

Supply chains may be disrupted, and transport may suffer delays, deviations, or other obstructions for factors that may be beyond the industry's control, i.e., delay at sea or at port due to extreme weather, port bottlenecks, and so on. Sometimes, the entire supply chain may suffer when deadlines are not met, irrespective if it is in the shipowner's control or not. A number of companies depend on the cargo, whether it is an aluminum plant needing petcoke to avoid smelter shutdown or a power plant with engineers and transportation equipment standing by to accept a big reactor.

This is why contingency planning and risk assessment methodologies are important in ensuring that the contractual deadlines and commercial obligations are being met throughout the supply chain.

Spliethoff, as a major carrier, employs all tools possible to ensure that the vessel is expedited with due dispatch. As shipowners, they try to make operational decisions *proactively*—this also goes for managing weather-related risks:

1. During negotiations of the contract of carriage, they clearly define customer expectations of cargo-readiness dates (laycan) in relation to the intended vessel's load readiness. Any specific date requirements for delivery of cargo in the discharge port are identified, and contract terms are agreed to meet these requirements—contract terms such as "last in first out," "sole cargo," etc.

   Attempts are being made by the owner to allocate the proper vessel on the required dates to meet contract commitments.

2. Also, during preloading preparations, lashing and securing plans are developed, prioritizing the safe and secure carriage of cargo. Procurement of adequate and proper lashing materials is done as well.

M/V Merwedegracht. (Courtesy of The Spliethoff Group, Spliethoff Americas.)

3. In direct preparation for the voyage, the ship's master will obtain updated weather-routing advice, which is being updated every 4 h *en route* to the destination.

4. Prior to and during the voyage, it is of critical importance to keep their customers closely advised of the vessel's schedule and estimated time of arrival (ETA) in the discharge port. This timely communication is one of the most important tools allowing for customers to plan cargo receipt and mitigate in case of delays.

   Communication may either be done by the operational staff directly, since they usually have the overall view of a vessel's schedule, and any *interim*-planned port calls and/or bunker calls, which have an impact on the ETA in the ultimate port of discharge.

   However, the master may also advise the customer directly of ETA if there are no *interim* ports, which facilitates a more expedient update that can be beneficial for customers across time zones and during weekends.

   Updates and vessel positions can be achieved via a vessel-routing company, such as Aerospace & Marine International (http://www.amiwx.com), while at sea and via the AIS while the vessel is in port or navigating in coastal areas.

5. During the voyage, it is important to recognize that weather factors may have an adverse impact on the vessel's navigation route—such as wind, current, waves and fog.

   However, during port calls, vessels are also exposed to weather such as

   a. Wind preventing vessels from doing safe cargo operations with cranes
   b. Fog preventing entry into or departure from port
   c. Rain preventing cargo operation for weather-sensitive cargoes
   d. Even day or night has an impact where certain cargoes can only be handled during daylight hours for safety or security reasons

Risks are inherent in business—managing it wisely is what makes companies successful both in respect of financial returns but more importantly in building lasting relationships with customers. It is Spliethoff's belief that by having open and timely communication with customers, especially during adverse situations, is a critical success factor.

Coping with Security Threats

Stowaways are every ship operator's nightmare. Not only do they pose a threat to the safety of the vessel, crew, and cargo, but also, they cause serious legal and financial problems for shipowners and port authorities, including delays, fines, repatriating cost to send stowaways back, etc. Most importantly, the safety and security of the stowaways themselves are being seriously jeopardized by their own high-risk actions, as the transportation professionals who discover stowaways onboard a ship may not know the stowaways' intentions and criminal disposition, e.g., if they impose security threats, such as terrorism, illegitimate trade, human trafficking, piracy, and so on. In recent years, the industry has seen an increase in the levels of violence encountered by the vessel's crew dealing with the problem.

Proactiveness, preparedness, and avoidance of the incident is the only viable solution to this great problem. Experience gained while trading, especially on Colombia, Brazil, and West Africa trade lanes, have yielded some valuable insights into how stowaways operate and therefore how we may proactively avoid this problem.

When a ship is at port, information about her next port of call or future itinerary will become common knowledge in the cause of the ship's crew carrying out regular business, which includes talking to stevedores, port workers, port agents, etc. This uncontrolled information of future ports of call is highly relevant to stowaways who are seeking a better life in a first-world country. Therefore, if a vessel is going to US ports, and this information gets to the potential stowaways, they will be attracted to the vessel as bees on honey.

One of the evasive tactics developed from this insight has been to not inform the vessel's crew and even the master what the next port of call will be but simply tell the captain to "proceed for orders," and as soon as the vessel has cleared port limits and dropped the pilot outbound, we will send a message with correct orders.

On the other hand, the company's operations department may send temporary orders to the master for a less desirable port such as Africa, which will work as a deterrent for stowaways who do not want to go to West Africa but only focused on first-world country destinations.

Spliethoff employs several security measures to prevent stowaways getting onboard and staying onboard the vessel, which includes having dogs search the vessel prior to departure of port, security for boarding vessel including only one access point and tracking of people, which falls in under the ISPS protocol (the International Ship and Port Facility Security Code).

Safety, security, and environmental protection are the major priorities in marine transportation, and while compliance is a starting point, we aspire to create a mindset and an active safety culture that goes beyond compliance. Every small action is part of a cumulative process that results in a safe, secure, and efficient operation.

CASE STUDY: HANSA HEAVY LIFT GmbH

Interview: Steven Neuendorff
Head of Hansa Americas

Hansa Heavy Lift GmbH specializes in the transport of heavy-lift, project, and break-bulk cargoes across all oceans of the world. They are dedicated in offering their clients the highest degree of safety, security, and reliability. Their young fleet of company-owned special heavy-lift vessels and their highly qualified crews, aboard as well as ashore, guarantees the secure and punctual transport of freight to all harbors worldwide—even, and particularly, in the niche market beyond the traditional routes.

From the very beginning, they take you "aboard" and guide you and your cargo throughout all phases of the voyage. Their clients enjoy a customized transport solution, which is planned and implemented by their expert team, working together with their clients.

The utmost care coupled with a high degree of flexibility and dedication—that is the quality for which they stand at Hansa Heavy Lift, in their offices in Singapore, Houston—and naturally in their headquarters in Germany.

At Hansa Heavy Lift, safety and environmental protection are integral to their mission of providing high-quality marine transportation services. They are committed to protecting the health and safety of their employees, clients, and other stakeholders and to preserving the environment in which we live and work. Their dedication to operating a modern and technologically advanced fleet in all of the core regions provides a strong foundation for this goal. They have built on

M/V Hansa Valparaiso. (Courtesy of Hansa Heavy Lift.)

M/V Hansa Valparaiso. (Courtesy of Hansa Heavy Lift.)

M/V HHL Tokyo. (Courtesy of Hansa Heavy Lift.)

M/V HHL Fremantle. (Courtesy of Hansa Heavy Lift.)

M/V Richards Bay. (Courtesy of Hansa Heavy Lift.)

this foundation with a robust safety management system that complies with the International Code for the Safe Management of Ships and Prevention of Pollution. Region-specific initiatives and enhanced certifications ensure that they meet or exceed our customers' increasing demands for best-practice solutions and consolidate their position as an industry first call operator.

At Hansa Heavy Lift, with rigorous application of company and industry guidelines, adoption of best practices, and a resolute commitment to excellence, they continue to strive for "an accident-free and injury-free workplace and a better environment for tomorrow."

Broussard
Logistics / BUYING POWER

CASE STUDY: BROUSSARD LOGISTICS

Interview: Paul Broussard
CEO of Broussard Logistics

Broussard Logistics manages $1 billion in transportation expense for 1000+ client companies in a customized way that provides unmatched transparency, strategic insight, and market intelligence.

Their business strategy revolves around the concept of "whole company, integrated solution" built on this framework:

1. Reveal cost visibility
2. Present options
3. Centralize resources
4. Create efficiency
5. Measure effectiveness
6. Manage continuously
7. Accelerate into the future

Manufacturing companies are frequently concerned with both inbound and outbound freight costs. Inbound costs are often very difficult to measure. In addition, many manufacturers have multiple departments (warehousing, purchasing, sales) that are decentralized, making cost analysis of transportation costs hard to determine. Broussard helps manage inbound and outbound costs by leveraging expertise, providing visibility of costs for all decision makers, using technology and introducing best-practices reporting. Sometimes, the only obstacle to enter new markets is transportation costs. With their buying leverage, Broussard can help open new markets for their client companies.

Retail companies deal with inbound transportation and freight costs that fluctuate. With significant inbound truckload, less than truckload, as well as parcel quantities shipped into a distribution center for fulfillment to stores, management of this process can be frantic. Matching actual data on shipment documentation to an internal receipt system, as well as handling charge backs and compliance issues, can pose an administrative burden. The Broussard Inbound Freight Management Solution provides an outsourced inbound freight call center to efficiently optimize time, cost, and service of carriers or transportation providers with cutting-edge technology and decades of expertise. At the purchase order level, Broussard can allocate cost to efficiently match retailer's enterprise resource planning information with the freight vendor's information and supplier compliance requirements to effectively manage this process and streamline a critical function for our retail clients.

Distribution companies employ a wide range of models for managing their freight strategy, which is unique to the company situation. All distribution companies share this common reality: customer satisfaction is absolutely critical because their entire business model is built around the supply chain. The Broussard comprehensive logistics management program, including electronic shipment notification, electronic bill-of-lading creation, and best-practices communication and management reporting, helps their distributor clients optimize their supply chain efficiency, which means happier, more satisfied customers. In addition, they have found that transportation costs can be a primary obstacle to entering new markets. With Broussard buying leverage, they help distributors become more competitive and expand their business.

For service firms, freight is a pure expense. Any reduction in freight and parcel costs goes directly to the bottom line. Transportation management decisions rarely affect the firm's end-user clients. Broussard buying leverage and experience, specifically in the areas of compliance and auditing, can help companies' compliance while reducing line-item expenses and increasing the firm's profit margin.

Paul Broussard. (Courtesy of Broussard Logistics.)

12.6 CONCLUSIONS

In the aftermath of the 9/11 terrorist attacks in the United States, compulsory transportation and logistics security measures have been implemented at a global and national level. On top of the terrorist threats, supply chains also encounter security threats related to illegitimate trade and transport. As the logistics and transport industries are critical components of the global economy and production, their capabilities and significance make them vulnerable targets of security threats. In a world increasingly exposed to terrorism, cyber security, piracy, and the trafficking of humans and narcotics, it is imperative to ensure an efficient global flow of goods and passengers without compromising security. Arguably, globalization has created more powerful and yet more complex alliances among global partners, which seem to blend global diplomacy, economy, and industrial production.

Modern supply chains can be controlled and managed by a single corporation whose segments are represented and headquartered in numerous countries. Similarly, political power is distributed among state governments that are both independent subnational components, yet the central government is given greater powers of influence and decision. Security threats may be targeting supply chains, or governments, yet in the aftermath of an attack, both entities are equally affected. Intergovernment and interindustry decisions have the power to transform the global balance. Both governments and industries seek for international partnerships in order to achieve sustainable growth and increased productivity for all. At the same time, their desire to grow and expand makes them vulnerable to security-related threats. The severe consequences of the 2008 global economic meltdown have severely affected both political systems and trade networks and have brought about a new perception on global security threats that urges nations and industries to partner against the "common enemy." Governments have become more introvert and cautious with global partners, whereas corporations seek to create more lean supply chains with fewer yet trusted vendors.

This is how global security concerns arise and the necessity for an all-encompassing security book was generated.

The book's primary purpose was to serve as a practical strategic, tactical, and operational manual of practical and tangible usefulness for security within the logistics and transportation security sectors. The subjects covered aimed to address the latest trends and notions of security risk mitigation from a technological, regulatory, and risk assessment stance. Since the modern supply chains are highly integrated, they are hereby addressed in a holistic manner as opposed to a segmented approach. Based on this observation, the book includes suggestions for standardized processes and harmonized regulatory frameworks. Another critical element that was addressed was the role of the public and private sectors in security investment and availability of resources. The book examined the benefits of such synergies and used a number of case studies to illustrate the increasing collaboration and benefits that result from this synergy.

Since security is a complex and wide subject, with infinite areas for analysis, the book's primary purpose was to focus on the following elements:

1. Focusing on the priorities of the US DHS, i.e., in "strengthening the security and resilience of critical infrastructures"
2. Promoting connectedness within the logistics- and transportation-related industries
3. Bridging the public–private sector for optimum mitigation of threat and optimum utilization of resources
4. Comparing diverse industrial security components, i.e., sea, land, air, warehousing, pipelines, offshore platforms, etc.

This powerful sourcebook aimed to offer readers the incentive to think out of the box and enhance their strategic thinking skills while offering empirical insight on global security practices. Its primary aim and purpose was to reveal the multidimensional aspects of the global transport and supply chain security, as an ongoing battle among governments and industries on one hand and security offenders on the other hand. It demonstrated how the public or private security entities are engaged in an ongoing effort to be ahead of the game and successfully combat security threats by employing capital-intensive, technology- and training-driven tools and protocols. Moreover, it explored the state-of-the-art partnerships, technologies, and methodologies to combat the different faces of security threats, i.e., terrorism; piracy; and illegitimate trade, transport, and travel.

INTERVIEWS AND CASE STUDIES

Broussard, Paul, CEO of Broussard Logistics, Case Study: Broussard Logistics, available at http://www.broussardlogistics.com/distribution/.
Damsgaard, Thomas, Vice President of Spliethoff Americas, Case Study: The Spliethoff Group.
Neuendorff, Steven, Head of Hansa Americas, Case Study: Hansa Heavy Lift GmbH, available at http://www.hansaheavylift.com/qhse.html, accessed January 1, 2015.

REFERENCES

Burns, M. 2013. *Effectiveness Evaluation of the Maritime Security Risk Analysis Model and the Dynamic Risk Management Model*. Washington, DC: TRB, Transportation Research Board of National Academies, Security Committee, January 14–16.
GS. 2004–2014. Goldman Sachs Annual Reports 2004–2014. Available at http://www.goldmansachs.com. Accessed January 1, 2015.
Hansa Heavy Lift. 2015. Available at http://www.hansaheavylift.com/qhse.html. Accessed January 1, 2015.
IMF. 2015. International Monetary Fund. World Economic Outlook. Cross Currents, 2015. Available at http://www.imf.org. Accessed January 15, 2015.
VI BRICS Summit. 2015. Available at http://brics6.itamaraty.gov.br. Accessed January 1, 2015.

Index

A

Advanced imaging technology (AIT), 266
Advance Passenger Information System (APIS), 108
AEO programs, *see* Authorized Economic Operator programs
Agile transportation, 31
Agroterrorism, CBP collaboration with US Food and Drug Administration to prevent, 116–121
    case study, 120–121
    Comprehensive Environmental Response, Compensation, and Liability Act, 118
    Department of Defense Total Asset Visibility initiative, 119
    emergency notification, 118
    Emergency Planning and Community Right-to-Know Act, 117
    extremely hazardous substances, 117
    ISO/PAS 28000, 118
    National Terrorism Advisory System, 117
    private sector initiatives, 118–119
    Smart and Secure Trade Lanes system, 118, 119
    Transported Asset Protection Association, 118
    US emergency response systems, 117–118
Air security threats, 74–76
Air waybill (AWB), 141
AIS, *see* Automatic Identification System
AIT, *see* Advanced imaging technology
Alpha radiation particles, 179
AMS plan, *see* Area Maritime Security plan
API, *see* Application Programming Interface
APIS, *see* Advance Passenger Information System
Apollo Soyuz Test Project (ASTP) mission, 224
Application Programming Interface (API), 109
Area Maritime Security (AMS) plan, 105
ASTP missions, *see* Apollo Soyuz Test Project mission

Authorized Economic Operator (AEO) programs, 100
Automatic Identification System (AIS), 73, 231, 244–248
    benefits, 247
    Electronic Chart Display and Information System, 245
    investigation and root cause analysis, 245
    maritime rules, 246
    regulations, 248
    Satellite-Automatic Identification System, 245
    vessel traffic services, 244
    VHF transceiver, 245
    voyage data recorder, 246
Aviation security technologies, 264–267
    advanced imaging technology, 266
    bottled liquid scanners, 266
    credential authentication technology, 264–266
    ETD, 267
    explosive-detection system, 266–267
    paperless boarding pass, 267
    security training software, 267
AWB, *see* Air waybill

B

Bacillus anthracis, 181
Backscatter X-rays, 263
Baltimore and Ohio Railroad, 37
Bareboat charter party (BB C/P), 141
BB C/P, *see* Bareboat charter party
BC/DR, *see* Business continuity/disaster recovery
Beta radiation particles, 179
Bill of lading (B/L), 141, 142
Biometric Optical Surveillance System, 253
Biometrics facial recognition and biometrics technologies, 251–255
    Biometric Optical Surveillance System, 253
    case study, 254
    closed-circuit television cameras, 253

crowdsourcing and facial recognition, 254
facial recognition and biometrics
        technologies, 251, 252–253
Handheld Interagency Identity Detection
        System, 254
iris and retinal scanning (ocular-based
        recognition), 251–252
Office of Biometric Identity Management,
        253
perfect iris match, 251
Bioterrorism, CBP collaboration with US Food
        and Drug Administration to prevent,
        116–121
    case study, 120–121
    Comprehensive Environmental Response,
        Compensation, and Liability Act, 118
    Department of Defense Total Asset
        Visibility initiative, 119
    emergency notification, 118
    Emergency Planning and Community
        Right-to-Know Act, 117
    extremely hazardous substances, 117
    ISO/PAS 28000, 118
    National Terrorism Advisory System, 117
    private sector initiatives, 118–119
    Smart and Secure Trade Lanes system, 118,
        119
    Transported Asset Protection Association,
        118
    US emergency response systems, 117–118
Bioterrorism, food security and, 84–86
    alternative food supplies, 86
    chemical risks, 85
    deliberate deprivation of food at times of
        peace, 85
    famine, 85
    food damage, 85
    intentional contamination, restricted food
        access due to, 86
    natural disasters, restricted food access due
        to, 85
    primary hazard risks, 85
    quality control, 85
    restoration of food supply chains, 86
    Ukraine's holocaust (Great Hunger), 86
    war, restricted food access due to, 86
Biothreat (health and environmental security),
        80–84
    case study, 84
    dispersal of chemical hazards into
        environment, 80
    environmental security, 83
    Global Health Security Agenda, 82
    HazMat equipment, 80

health security, 82–83
impact to human health, 83–84
infectious diseases, 82
public health, bioterrorism and, 83
zoonotic diseases, 82
B/L, see Bill of lading
Blister agents, 171, 177
Blood gases, 161
Boston Marathon bombings, 19, 64, 209, 234
Bottled liquid scanners, 266
Brain training, 314
BRICS countries (Brazil, Russia, India, China
        and South Africa), 337–339
Business continuity/disaster recovery (BC/DR),
        144, 146–148
    business continuity plan, 146
    business as usual, 147
    disaster recovery plan, 147
    DRP stages, 147
    incidents, 146
    reasons for neglect of disaster recovery, 147

C
Carcinogens, 158
Cargo-tracking and -monitoring systems (sea,
        land, air), 255–260
CAT, see Credential authentication technology
CBP, see US Customs and Border Protection
CBRN materials, see Chemical, biological,
        radiological, and nuclear materials
CCP, see Container Control Program
CCTB cameras, see Closed-circuit television
        cameras
Cell-All concept, 249
Central Intelligence Agency (CIA), 104
Charter party (C/P), 141
Chemical, biological, radiological, and nuclear
        (CBRN) materials, 180
Chinese BeiDou Navigation Satellite System,
        244
CIA, see Central Intelligence Agency
CIKR, see Critical infrastructure and key
        resources
CI security, see Critical infrastructure security
Clean Marina Day, 215
Closed-circuit television (CCTV) cameras, 253
Cloud-computing technology, 144, 248–249
Cognitive neuroscience, 306
Collective intelligence, 217
Columbus, Christopher, 33–34
Combating security threats (human factor),
        305–316
    cognitive neuroscience, 306
    genetic experiments, 306

personal security, 305
preparedness, 313–316
  brain training, 314
  building muscle memory through training and drills, 314
  complacency, 315
  large-scale training, 313–314
security, human mentality, and culture factor, 309–313
  classification of security culture, 310–311
  commercial continuity vs. security focus, 311
  commonality, 310
  improved security through corporate quality, 313
  Maslow's hierarchy of needs, 311–313
  motivating security employees, 311
  security tolerance and prioritization, 311
stress versus distress mode, 306–309
  cortisol "overdose," 308
  distress and lack of preparedness, 307–308
  distress and permanent DNA methylation, 309
  extreme stress levels, 308
  fight or flight, 307
  impact of distress or high stress levels, 308–309
  perceived threat, stress, and distress, 307
  post-traumatic stress disorder, 309
  stress and preparedness, 307
  stress response, 309
Commercial survivalism, 325
Common-strategy tactic (aircraft hijacking), 75
Comprehensive Environmental Response, Compensation, and Liability Act, 118
Consumer price index (CPI), 17
Container Control Program (CCP), 100
Container Security Devices (CSD), 257
Container Security Initiative (CSI), 105, 112, 114
Contract of affreightment, 141
Contract of carriage, 141
Copyright infringement, 189
Corporate asset management, 25
Cortisol "overdose," 308
Costa Concordia, 313
Counter-Terrorism Implementation Task Force (CTITF), 98–99
Coyotes, 77
C/P, *see* Charter party
CPI, *see* Consumer price index

Credential authentication technology (CAT), 264–266
Crime-brainwashed levels, 23
Crime opportunity theory, 47–48
Crisis management, 317–320
  classifying crisis, 318
  crisis recovery, 318
  danger zone, 319
  definition, 317
  elements, 318
  emergency phase, 319
  incident command system, 318
  leadership and teamwork, 318
  preparation phase, 318
  preparedness and contingency planning, 318
  proactiveness vs. reactiveness, 318
  resilience or recovery phase, 319
  strengths and vulnerabilities, 320
  sustainability through lessons learned, 319
  timeline model, 318–320
Critical infrastructure and key resources (CIKR), 127, 286
  chemical sector, 131
  commercial facilities sector, 131
  communications sector, 131
  critical manufacturing, 131
  dams, 133
  defense industrial bases, 133
  emergency services sector, 133
  energy sector, 133
  financial services, 133
  food and agriculture, 133
  government facilities, 134
  healthcare and public health, 134
  IT, 134
  nuclear reactors, materials, and waste, 134
  transportation systems security, 134
  water and wastewater systems, 135
Critical infrastructure (CI) security, 127–149
  business continuity/disaster recovery, 146–148
    business continuity plan, 146
    business as usual, 147
    disaster recovery plan, 147
    DRP stages, 147
    incidents, 146
    reasons for neglect of disaster recovery, 147
  critical infrastructure and key resources, 127
  cyber security, 144–146
    cloud-based technologies, 144
    criminal niche, 146

cybercrime types distinguished, 145
expansion, 144
hacking activities, 144
motivations behind attacks, 144
mutual responsibility, 146
need for new ways of policing, 146
new possibilities for criminals, 145
observations, 145
technology-as-instrument, 145
technology-as-target, 145
top 15 countries where cyber attacks
    originated, 145
virtual databases, 144
e-commerce transforming transportation,
    142–144
business continuity/disaster recovery,
    144
cyber security, 144
IT framework, 142
legal framework, 142
practical framework, 142
nation's CIKR, 130–137
chemical sector, 131
CI connectivity matrix, 132
commercial facilities sector, 131
communications sector, 131
critical manufacturing, 131
dams, 133
defense industrial bases, 133
emergency services sector, 133
energy sector, 133
existence sector, 135
financial services, 133
food and agriculture, 133
government facilities, 134
growth needs, 135
healthcare and public health, 134
IT, 134
nation's power status, 135
nuclear reactors, materials, and waste,
    134
relatedness sector, 135
sectors interconnected with society's
    needs, 137
supply chain CI matrix, 136
transportation systems security, 134
water and wastewater systems, 135
physical assets and key asset protection,
    137–139
physical assets' evaluation, 139
vulnerability of physical assets,
    138–139
Presidential Policy Directive 21, 127
sector-specific agency, 130

six nations, critical infrastructure sectors
    in, 128–129
trade and transport documentation,
    140–142
air waybill, 141
bareboat charter party, 141
bill of lading, 141, 142
charter party, 141
concerns addressed, 141
contract of affreightment, 141
contract of carriage, 141
electronic bill of lading, 142
electronic (paperless) trade, 140–141
reimbursement, 141
security threats, 140
time charter party, 141
voyage charter party, 141
United States, CI sectors and SSAs of, 130
Crowdsourcing, facial recognition and, 254
CSD, see Container Security Devices
CSI, see Container Security Initiative
CTITF, see Counter-Terrorism Implementation
    Task Force
C-TPAT initiative (DHS), 110–111
Cyber espionage, 27
Cyber security, 144–146
cloud-based technologies, 144
criminal niche, 146
cybercrime types distinguished, 145
expansion, 144
hacking activities, 144
motivations behind attacks, 144
mutual responsibility, 146
need for new ways of policing, 146
new possibilities for criminals, 145
observations, 146
technology-as-instrument, 145
technology-as-target, 145
threats, 80, 81–82
top 15 countries where cyber attacks
    originated, 145
virtual databases, 144

D

Dangerous Goods List (DGL), 168, 169,
    see also Hazardous materials
    (dangerous goods) categories,
    classifying security threats through
Data relay satellite, 222
Department of Defense (DoD), 133
global sector, 133
Total Asset Visibility initiative, 119
Department of State (DoS), 108
Dewitt Clinton Railroad, 37

DGL, *see* Dangerous Goods List
DHS, *see* US Department of Homeland
　　Security
Dirty bombs, 181
Disaster recovery (DR), 144, 146–148
Disaster recovery plan (DRP), 147
DMAIC, 204
DNA methylation, 309
Documentation (trade and transport),
　　140–142
　bills of lading, 142
　contract of carriage, 141
　　air waybill, 141
　　bill of lading, 141
　　concerns addressed, 141
　electronic bill of lading, 142
　electronic (paperless) trade, 140–141
　　bareboat charter party, 141
　　charter party, 141
　　contract of affreightment, 141
　　reimbursement, 141
　　security threats, 140
　　time charter party, 141
　　voyage charter party, 141
DoD, *see* Department of Defense
Domino effect, 18
Domino theory, 190
DoS, *see* Department of State
DOT, *see* US Department of Transportation
DR, *see* Disaster recovery
Drones, 236–240
　classification, 237
　commercial surveillance, 239
　control, 236
　drug cartels, 239
　extension of commercial use, 238
　federal law enforcement, 238
　government civilian law enforcement, 238
　industry and manufacturing applications,
　　238
　purpose, 236
　terrorist groups, 239
　unmanned aerial vehicles, 237
　US Air Force drone, 237
DRP, *see* Disaster recovery plan
Drug smuggling, 101
Drug trafficking (socioeconomic impacts),
　　78–79

E
eB/L, *see* Electronic bill of lading
EBM, *see* Economic base model
ECDIS, *see* Electronic Chart Display and
　　Information System

E-commerce transforming transportation,
　　142–144
Economic base model (EBM), 18
EDI system, *see* Electronic data interchange
　　system
EELVs, *see* Evolved Expendable Launch
　　Vehicles
EHS, *see* Extremely hazardous substances
Electronic bill of lading (eB/L), 142, 144
Electronic Chart Display and Information
　　System (ECDIS), 245
Electronic data interchange (EDI) system, 108
Electronic (paperless) trade, 140–141
Emergency Planning and Community Right-
　　to-Know Act, 117
Emergency services sector (ESS), 133
Employee empowerment (supply chain), 28
Energy networks (case study), 198–199
Energy sector (ES), 133
Environmental security threats (case study),
　　213–214
EPA, *see* US Environmental Protection Agency
ES, *see* Energy sector
Escherichia coli, 181
Espionage networks, 32
ESS, *see* Emergency services sector
Ethical justification of attack, 21
European Union Galileo Satellite Positioning
　　System, 244
Evolved Expendable Launch Vehicles (EELVs),
　　219
Extremely hazardous substances (EHS), 117

F
Facial recognition (2D and 3D biometric
　　technologies), 252–253
Fake retreat, 33
Falling domino principle, 190
FAST program, *see* Free and Secure Trade
　　program
Federal Emergency Management Agency
　　(FEMA), 107–108
Federal Immigration and Nationality Act,
　　76–77
FEMA, *see* Federal Emergency Management
　　Agency
Fight or flight, 307
Flash Point (FP), 162
FM principle, *see* Force multiplier principle
Food security (bioterrorism), 84–86
　alternative food supplies, 86
　chemical risks, 85
　deliberate deprivation of food at times of
　　peace, 86

famine, 85
food damage, 85
intentional contamination, restricted food
    access due to, 85
natural disasters, restricted food access due
    to, 85
primary hazard risks, 85
quality control, 85
restoration of food supply chains, 86
Ukraine's holocaust (Great Hunger), 86
war, restricted food access due to, 86
Force multiplier (FM) principle, 234
FP, see Flash Point
Free-ride effect (immigration), 77
Free and Secure Trade (FAST) program, 115–116
Freight pilferage, 27
Future of global transportation and supply
    chain networks, 337–357
  behavioral aspects of proactive
      management, 345–346
    controlling security systems and
        performance evaluation, 345
    leadership, 345
    organizing, 345
    planning, 345
    staffing, 345
  benefits of proactive security management,
      343–344
    element of cost, 344
    element of time, 343–344
    productivity growth, measurement of, 344
  case studies on proactive corporate
      cultures, 347–355
  forecasting the global economy and trade
      patterns, 337–341
    airlines, 341
    BRICS countries (Brazil, Russia, India,
        China and South Africa), 337–339
    collapse of oil and gas prices, 341
    commercial trucks, 341
    energy crisis and transportation
        challenges and opportunities, 340–341
    MINT countries (Mexico, Indonesia,
        Nigeria, and Turkey), 339–341
    miracle of China, 229
    Organization of Petroleum-Exporting
        Countries member states, 340
    private vehicles, 341
    United States, 340
  proactive security measures in a cost- and
      time-saving framework, 341–343
    efficiency, 341
    interdependency, 342
    just in time, 341

motivators, 342
reactive vs. proactive security costs, 343
return on investment, 342

G
Gamma radiation particles, 179, 262
Gaseous chemicals and fumigants, 182
GDP, see Gross domestic product
Genghis Khan, 31
GICNT, see Global Initiative to Combat
    Nuclear Terrorism
Global Health Security Agenda, 82
Global Initiative to Combat Nuclear Terrorism
    (GICNT), 102–103
Global Navigation Satellite System (GNSS), 242
Global Positioning System (GPS), 73, 189, 231,
    243–244
  Chinese BeiDou Navigation Satellite
      System, 244
  data pullers, 243
  European Union Galileo Satellite
      Positioning System, 244
  logger, 243
  NAVSTAR GPS satellites, 244
  Russian GLONASS, 244
  technologies, pioneer of, 244
  -tracking unit, 243
  transponders, 243
Global security and regulatory framework,
    91–125
  global security regulations, 95–103
    AEO program by WCO framework of
        standards, 101–102
    Authorized Economic Operator
        programs, 100
    bioterrorism, 101
    Container Control Program, 100
    drug smuggling, 101
    global CCP by UNODC and WCO,
        100–101
    Global Initiative to Combat Nuclear
        Terrorism, 102–103
    illegitimate cargoes, smuggling of, 101
    infectious diseases, 101
    International Maritime Organization,
        98
    League of Nations (1920–1946), 96
    major threats, 100–101
    maritime security (International Ship
        and Port Facility Security Code), 98
    national initiatives, 102
    North Atlantic Treaty Organization, 99
    radiological dispersion devices, terrorism
        and, 101

Securing and Facilitating Global Trade, 100
terrorism and explosives, 100
UN Counter-Terrorism Implementation Task Force, 98–99
United Nations Office on Drugs and Crime, 97
United Nations Security Council, 96–97
World Customs Organization, 99–100
historic overview of security regulations, 92–95
League of Nations (1920–1946), 96
diplomatic viewpoint, 96
ineffectiveness of, 96
international governmental organization, 96
Nazi Germany, 96
Rome–Berlin Axis, 96
structural weaknesses of, 96
United States, maritime security regulations in, 114–121
case study, 120–121
CBP collaboration with US Food and Drug Administration to prevent bioterrorism and agroterrorism, 116–121
Comprehensive Environmental Response, Compensation, and Liability Act, 118
Department of Defense Total Asset Visibility initiative, 119
emergency notification, 118
Emergency Planning and Community Right-to-Know Act, 117
extremely hazardous substances, 117
Free and Secure Trade program, 115–116
ISO/PAS 28000, 118
Megaports Initiative, 116
National Terrorism Advisory System, 117
private sector initiatives, 118–119
Secure Freight Initiative, 115
Smart and Secure Trade Lanes system, 118, 119
Transported Asset Protection Association, 118
US emergency response systems, 117–118
United States, security in, 103–114
Advanced Manifest Rule/Advance Cargo Information, 112
Advance Passenger Information System, 108
Application Programming Interface, 109
Area Maritime Security plan, 105
cargo security initiatives, 110–114
CBP initiatives, 108
CBP Office of Field Operations, 108
certification, 110
Container Security Initiative, 105, 112, 114
C-TPAT initiative, 110–111
electronic data interchange system, 108
family of plans, 104
Federal Emergency Management Agency, 107–108
federal programs and initiatives, 108–114
front-of-line examinations, 110
Immigration and Customs Enforcement, 108, 109
Importer Security Filing, 111–112
inbound travelers' security initiatives, 108–110
joint terrorism task forces, 108
Maritime Transportation Security Act of 2002, 104–105
Mutual Recognition Agreement (C-TPAT), 111
National Military Establishment, 104
National Security Act of 1947, 103–104
NEXUS Inspection Program, 110
non-intrusive inspection, 113
Office of Biometric Identity Management, 108, 109
radio frequency identification proximity prox-card, 110
Secure Electronic Network for Travelers Rapid Inspection, 109–110
Security and Accountability for Every Port Act of 2006 by DHS, 105
Student and Exchange Visitor Program, 108, 109
transportation security acts, 103–105
Transportation Security Administration, 106–107
Trusted Traveler Program, 110
US Coast Guard, 104
US Customs and Border Protection, 107
US Department of Homeland Security and its agencies, 105–114
US Immigration and Naturalization Service, 108
Western Hemisphere Travel Initiative, 110
GNSS, see Global Navigation Satellite System
GPS, see Global Positioning System
"Great arsenal of democracy," 38
Great Mongol Empire, 31
Gross domestic product (GDP), 17

H

Hacking activities, 144
Handheld Interagency Identity Detection
     System, 254
Hazard Communication Standard (HCS), 157
Hazardous materials (HazMat) (dangerous
     goods) categories, classifying security
     threats through, 151–185
  classes of HazMat, 160–166
     agricultural operations, 164
     consumer commodities, 164
     corrosives, 164
     explosives, 161, 164, 165
     flammable or combustible substances, 162
     gaseous products, 161–162
     materials of trade, 164
     miscellaneous hazardous materials
          (dangerous goods), 164
     other flammable substances, 162
     oxidizing substances and organic
          peroxides, 163
     radioactive (nuclear) materials, 173
     toxic (poisonous) and infectious
          substances, 163
     US DOT HazMat placards, 164–166
  HazMat classifications, 156–176
     air transport, 156
     bulk container code, 173
     carcinogens, 158
     class, 172
     Dangerous Goods List, 168, 169
     EmS, 173
     federal agencies, 157
     global HazMat regulations, 156
     global and national regulatory
          framework, 156–157
     Hazard Communication Standard, 157
     hazardous materials warning labels, 159
     HazMat Identification System, 174
     HazMat in the maritime industry,
          175–176
     HazMat table in the United States,
          170–171
     health risk, 158
     IBC packing instructions, 173
     identifying HazMat leakage, 175
     IMDG code, 168
     IMO tank instructions, 173
     limited quantities, 172
     list of DG code (IMDG code), 168–174
     nine classes of HazMat, 160–166
     North American identification numbers
          or DOT numbers, 167
     Orange Book, 167
     OSHA's hazard communication
          standard, 157–158
     packing instructions, 172
     Pipeline and Hazardous Materials Safety
          Administration, 157
     Proper Shipping Name, 172
     properties and observations, 173–174
     rail transport, 156
     Right-to-Know Law, 157
     sea transport, 156
     shipping documentation, 174
     special packing provisions, 172–173
     special provisions, 172
     stowage and segregation, 173
     subsidiary risk, 172
     tank special provisions, 173
     UN Committee of Experts on Transport
          of Dangerous Goods, 158–160
     UN identification numbers, 167
     UN markings of containers, 167–168
     UN number, 168, 174
     UN packing groups, 160, 172
     UN tank and bulk package guidelines, 173
     US HazMat-related departments,
          agencies, and regulations, 156–157
  overview, 152–156
     classification (physical, health, and
          environmental threats), 154–155
     criminal but nonterrorist incidents, 155
     incidents, 155–156
     intentional occurrences, 155
     mens rea (criminal act or incident), 156
     noncompliance, 155
     root cause analysis, 154
     statistics, 153–154
     terrorist attacks, 155
     unintentional occurrences, 155
     USA Patriot Act, 155
  security and health impact, 176–183
     acute versus chronic radiation exposure,
          179
     alpha, beta, and gamma radiation
          particles, 179
     assessment of health impact, 182
     Bacillus anthracis, 181
     biological hazards, 181
     blister agents, 171, 177
     blood gases, 161
     chemical, biological, radiological, or
          nuclear release, 180–181
     dirty bombs, 181
     electromagnetic radiation, 178
     Escherichia coli, 181
     exposures, 178

gaseous chemicals and fumigants, 182
harmful effects, 182
HazMat chemicals and health hazards,
    176–178
health mitigation, 183
health perils, 179
ionizing radiation, 178
legal and regulatory framework, 183
medical use and inhibiting agents, 182
military weapons, 182
nerve agents, 177
postdisaster HazMat contingency plans,
    183
predisaster HazMat plans, 183
proactive and reactive action, 183
radiation and health hazards, 178–180
radiological dispersal devices, 181–182
respiratory gases, 161
respiratory, pulmonary, or choking
    agents, 177
safeguarding from radiation, 179
technological mitigation, 183
toxic industrial chemicals, 182–183
tritium, 180
unintended consequences of, 182
HazMat, see Hazardous materials (dangerous
    goods) categories, classifying security
    threats through
HCS, see Hazard Communication Standard
Health and environmental security, see
    Biothreat
Homeland security, description of, 6
Human trafficking and illegitimate traveling/
    immigration, 76–78
containerized cargoes, 77
contraband, 77
coyotes, 77
definition of human smuggling, 76
drug cartels, 77
Federal Immigration and Nationality Act,
    76–77
free-ride effect, 77
illegal immigrants, classifications of, 76
organized immigration crime, 77
snakeheads, 77
Hurricane Ike, 29

I

IATA, see International Air Transport
    Association
ICAO, see International Civil Aviation
    Organization
ICE, see Immigration and Customs
    Enforcement

Ideological terrorism, 68
IGO, see International governmental
    organization
Illegal immigrants, classifications of, 76
Illegitimate cargoes, smuggling of, 101
ILO, see International Labor Organization
IMB, see International Maritime Bureau
IMDG Code, see International Maritime
    Dangerous Goods Code
Immigration (illegitimate), 76–78
containerized cargoes, 77
contraband, 77
coyotes, 77
definition of human smuggling, 76
drug cartels, 77
Federal Immigration and Nationality Act,
    76–77
free-ride effect, 77
illegal immigrants, classifications of, 76
organized immigration crime, 77
snakeheads, 77
Immigration and Customs Enforcement (ICE),
    108, 109
IMO, see International Maritime Organization
Importer Security Filing (ISF), 111–112
Incident command system, 318
Industrial Revolution, 36
Infectious diseases, 82, 101
Information management, 25
Information sharing and analysis centers
    (ISACs), 195
Information technology risk assessment, 281
Innovation, see Security technology and
    innovation
INS, see US Immigration and Naturalization
    Service
Interconnectivity in security economics, 18
Intergovernmental Organization for
    International Carriage, 156
International Air Transport Association
    (IATA), 142, 156
International Civil Aviation Organization
    (ICAO), 75, 156
International Convention for the Safety of Life
    at Sea (SOLAS), 98
International governmental organization
    (IGO), 96
International Labor Organization (ILO), 158
International Maritime Bureau (IMB), 73
International Maritime Dangerous Goods
    (IMDG) Code, 156, 168–174
bulk container code, 173
class, 172
columns, 168–174

EmS, 173
IBC packing instructions, 173
IBC special provisions, 173
IMO tank instructions, 173
limited quantities, 172
packing instructions, 172
Proper Shipping Name, 172
properties and observations, 173–174
special packing provisions, 172–173
special provisions, 172
stowage and segregation, 173
subsidiary risk, 172
tank special provisions, 173
UN number, 168, 174
UN packing group, 172
UN tank and bulk package guidelines, 173
International Maritime Organization (IMO),
      98, 156
International Organization for Standardization
      (ISO), 118, 285
International Ship and Port Facility Security
      (ISPS) Code, 98, 258
Ionizing radiation, 178
Iris and retinal scanning (ocular-based
      recognition), 251–252
Iris-scanning technologies, 232
ISACs, see Information sharing and analysis
      centers
ISF, see Importer Security Filing
ISO, see International Organization for
      Standardization
ISPS Code, see International Ship and Port
      Facility Security Code

J
Jamestown (early settlers to the New World),
      34–35
Jason Project, 215
JIT, see Just in time
Just in time (JIT), 25, 341

K
Kaizen, 201
Kanban, 202

L
Latin American drug cartels, 239
League of Nations (1920–1946), 96
Lean manufacturing method, 200
LEO, see Low earth orbit
Liberty ships (World War II), 38–41
   construction, 39
   "great arsenal of democracy," 38
   mass-produced design, 39

support package, 40
US contribution in WWII, 41
Young Women's Christian Association, 40
Logistics and transportation security,
      introduction to, 1–44
book contents, 2–5
formulas for risk assessment, risk
      mitigation, and incident investigation,
      14–25
   categorical trinity, 19
   consumer price index, 17
   crime-brainwashed levels, 23
   criminal profiling of security offenders,
         21–22
   domino effect, 18
   econometrics of risk tolerance, 22–23
   economic base model, 18
   economic cost, 23
   emotional cost, 23
   ethical justification of attack, 21
   expendable criminal members, 22
   exposure intensity factor, 16
   factors of production, 22
   formula 1 (security risk assessment), 14
   formula 2 (security risk assessment with
         risk indicates), 14
   formula 3 (single loss expectancy
         formula), 14–15
   formula 4 (total loss expectancy
         formula), 15
   formula 5 (risk assessment formula for
         structural integrity of assets), 15–16
   formula 6 (assessment of security-related
         expenditures), 16
   formula 7 (security threat probability
         model while target is in motion), 16–17
   formula 8 (commodity demand), 17
   formulas 9 and 10 (value at risk), 17–18
   formula 11 (attack types and scenario
         parameters), 18–19
   formula 12 (spatial autocorrelation
         (Moran's I works), 19–20
   formula 13 (security threat indicator
         of spatial correlation model for risk
         assessment and incident mitigation),
         20
   formula 14 (structural resilience), 21
   formula 15 (distance, time, and
         resilience), 21–23
   formulas 16, 17, and 18 (levels of risk
         tolerance), 23–25
   gross domestic product, 17
   incident investigation and spatial
         autocorrelation models, 19

interconnectivity in security economics, 18
management element, 22
martyr, 24
physical cost, 23
physical premises of outlaws, 22
proof resilience, 21
pseudo-achiever, 24
quality-sensitive commodities, 17
risk tolerance, 23
security offenders' means, 22
security offenders' motive, 21
survivor, 24
value at risk, 17
history of logistics and transportation security, 25–26
corporate asset management, 25
information management, 25
just-in-time schedule, 25
resource management, 25
supply chain, optimum performance of, 25
value-for-money principle, 26
relationship between transportation and logistics, 1–2
security economics (econometric modeling and analysis), 8–13
behavioral economics of security, 13
public–private sector coalition, 13
security economics, 12
security macroeconomics, 12
timeline for security economics, 12
security vs. safety (definitions and Maslow's pyramid of needs), 6–8
cabinet department, 6
defining security, 6–8
homeland security, 6
intention deceptive acts, 8
intention, potential targets, and vulnerabilities, 9–12
Pax Romana, 6
personal gain, 8
premeditated damage, 8
ranges of damages, 7
safety vs. security, 7
supply chain security (overview), 26–41
agile transportation, 31
ambushing, 33
Baltimore and Ohio Railroad, 37
case study, 30, 31
Christopher Columbus's voyages (logistics achievement), 33–34
common goal, 26
cyber espionage, 27

deliberate damage, 27
Dewitt Clinton Railroad, 37
East Coast traders, 36
employee empowerment, 28
espionage networks, 32
fake retreat, 33
freight pilferage, 27
geospatial criteria, 28
"great arsenal of democracy," 38
history of logistics, 28–29
hit and run, 33
Industrial Revolution, 36
Jamestown (early settlers to the New World), 34–35
Liberty ships in World War II, 38–41
logistics through the millennia, 29
mass-produced design, 39
medieval explorers, the first settlers, and the origins of modern America, 33
military logistics, 29
Mohawk & Hudson rail, 37
National DHS strategy, 27
natural disasters, mass migration to avoid, 28
procurement logistics, 29
railroads, 35–36
railroads in America, 36–37
real-time monitoring and response, 28
Silk Road, 31
standard actions, 26
supply chain disruptions, 27–28
survival logistics, 28
synchronized attacks, 33
trade disruption, 27
Transcontinental Railroad, 37
Yam postal system for military and political news, 33
Young Women's Christian Association, 40
Lone-wolf terrorism, 64
Long-Range Acoustic Device (LRAD), 271
Low earth orbit (LEO), 219
LRAD, see Long-Range Acoustic Device

M
Maritime Domain Awareness (MDA), 73
Maritime industry, HazMat in, 175–176
Maritime security, piracy and, 70–73
acts, 72–73
armed robbery and piracy, 72–73
defining piracy, 70–72
open seas, piracy amidst, 73
organized syndicates, 73
piracy at pot, 73

state-of-the-art technologies, 73
US DHS Maritime Domain Awareness, 73
Maritime security regulations (United States), 114–121
case study, 120–121
CBP collaboration with US Food and Drug Administration to prevent bioterrorism and agroterrorism, 116–121
Comprehensive Environmental Response, Compensation, and Liability Act, 118
Department of Defense Total Asset Visibility initiative, 119
emergency notification, 118
Emergency Planning and Community Right-to-Know Act, 117
extremely hazardous substances, 117
Free and Secure Trade program, 115–116
ISO/PAS 28000, 118
Megaports Initiative, 116
National Terrorism Advisory System, 117
private sector initiatives, 118–119
Secure Freight Initiative, 115
Smart and Secure Trade Lanes system, 118, 119
Transported Asset Protection Association, 118
US emergency response systems, 117–118
Maritime technologies, 267–271
Active Denial System (nonlethal), 269
armed security guards, 269
boat trap (nonlethal), 271
Long-Range Acoustic Device (nonlethal), 271
optical laser distractor (nonlethal), 270–271
technologies in ships' panic rooms (citadels or safe rooms), 268–269
Vehicle-Mounted Active Denial System, 269
Maritime Transportation Security Act (MTSA), 104
Maslow's hierarchy of needs, 311–313
Maslow's pyramid of needs, 6–8
MDA, see Maritime Domain Awareness
Megaports Initiative, 116
Mens rea (criminal act or incident), 156
Military logistics, 29
MINT countries (Mexico, Indonesia, Nigeria, and Turkey), 339–341
Mohawk & Hudson rail, 37
Moran's I measures, 19
MTSA, see Maritime Transportation Security Act
Muon tomography, 262
Muscle memory, 314

N
National Terrorism Advisory System (NTAS), 117, 240–241
NATO, see North Atlantic Treaty Organization
Natural disasters
mass migration to avoid, 28
restricted food access due to, 85
Nazi Germany, 96
Nerve agents, 177
Neutron radiation detectors, 261
NII, see Non-intrusive inspection
Non-intrusive inspection (NII), 113, 260–264
biosurveillance, 263
cargo scanning or non-intrusive inspection, 260
gamma and neutron radiation detectors, 262
in-motion scanning technologies, 260
muon tomography, 262
neutron radiation detectors, 261–262
non-intrusive scanning technologies, 260
radiation portal monitors, 262
special nuclear material detection, 260
targeting protocols, 260
thermal imaging, 263–264
visual inspections, 260
X-ray radiography (backscatter X-rays), 263
Nonpolitical terrorism, 68
North Atlantic Treaty Organization (NATO), 99, 317
NTAS, see National Terrorism Advisory System
Nuclear terrorism, 102, 103

O
OBIM, see Office of Biometric Identity Management
OECD, see Organization for Economic Cooperation and Development
Office of Biometric Identity Management (OBIM), 108, 109, 253
OPEC member states, see Organization of Petroleum-Exporting Countries member states
Open seas, piracy amidst, 75
Operational risk assessment, 281
Optical laser distractor (nonlethal), 270–271
Orange Book, 167
Orbital replacement units (ORUs), 254
Organization for Economic Cooperation and Development (OECD), 158
Organization of Petroleum-Exporting Countries (OPEC) member states, 340

ORUs, *see* Orbital replacement units
OSHA, *see* US Occupational Safety and
 Health Administration
OSHA hazard communication standard,
 157–158

P

Paperless boarding pass (PBP), 267
Pareto principle, 191
Pax Mongolica, 31
Pax Romana, 6
PBP, *see* Paperless boarding pass
Performance-oriented packaging (POP), 167
PHMSA, *see* Pipeline and Hazardous
 Materials Safety Administration
Pipeline and Hazardous Materials Safety
 Administration (PHMSA), 157
Piracy, maritime security and, 70–73
 acts, 72–73
 armed robbery and piracy, 72–73
 defining piracy, 70–72
 open seas, piracy amidst, 73
 organized syndicates, 73
 piracy at pot, 73
 state-of-the-art technologies, 73
 US DHS Maritime Domain Awareness, 73
Political terrorism, 68
POP, *see* Performance-oriented packaging
Port vulnerabilities (case study), 293–303
 interview, 293
 Open Cell sheet pile solution, 299–303
 vectors of attack, 294–299
Post-traumatic stress disorder (PTSD), 54,
 309
PPD-21, *see* Presidential Policy Directive 21
PRA, *see* Probabilistic risk assessment
Presidential Policy Directive 21 (PPD-21),
 127
Probabilistic risk assessment (PRA), 286
Procurement logistics, 29
Product risk assessment, 281
Project management risk assessment, 281
Proof resilience, 21
Proper Shipping Name (PSN), 172
Pseudo-achiever, 24
PSN, *see* Proper Shipping Name
PTSD, *see* Post-traumatic stress disorder
Public health, bioterrorism and, 83
Public and private partnerships, 207–230
 bombing events, 207
 interaction, 208
 interviews and case studies, 229
 key areas, 209
 models, 209

security vulnerabilities, 216–228
 case studies 218–228
 collective intelligence, 217
 harmonized risk management,
  crisis management, and resource
  management, 218
 legal, regulatory, and chain-of-command
  harmonization, 218
 security vulnerabilities, 217–218
 subcontracting, 217–218
 supply chain disruptions, 218
 supply chain visibility, 217
significance, 207
think tanks, 208
threat prevention, mitigation, and response,
 210–216
 benefits arising from partnerships, 211
 case studies, 211–216
 model architectures, 210

Q

QTL, *see* Qualified technology list
Qualified technology list (QTL), 250
Quality management, Deming's 14 points on,
 203–204
Quality-sensitive commodities, 17
Quasi-terrorism, 69

R

Radiation and health hazards, 178–180
 acute versus chronic radiation exposure,
  179
 alpha, beta, and gamma radiation particles,
  179
 electromagnetic radiation, 178
 exposures, 178
 health perils, 179
 ionizing radiation, 178
 safeguarding from radiation, 179
 tritium, 180
Radiation portal monitors, 262
Radio-frequency identification (RFID), 189,
 242
 acceleration sensors, 256
 biosensors, 257
 cargo pressure sensors, 256
 chemosensors, 257
 door intrusion and tampering sensors, 256
 inclination sensors/tilt sensors, 257
 prox-card, 110
 radioactive sensors, 257
 real-time cargo monitoring, 256
 real-time transportation monitoring, 256
 shock and vibration sensors, 256

temperature, light, and humidity sensors, 256
tire-pressure sensors, 256
Radiological dispersal devices (RDDs),
181–182
assessment of health impact, 182
dirty bombs, 181
harmful effects, 182
terrorism and, 101
unintended consequences of, 182
Railroads in America, 36–37
Baltimore and Ohio Railroad, 37
Dewitt Clinton Railroad, 37
East Coast traders, 36
Mohawk & Hudson rail, 37
Transcontinental Railroad, 37
RDDs, *see* Radiological dispersal devices
Real-time locating systems (RTLSs), 258
Red October cyber attack, 81
Resource management, 25
Respiratory gases, 161
Return on investment (ROI), 342
Reverse engineering (back engineering), 240
RFID, *see* Radio-frequency identification
Right-to-Know Law, 157
Risk, *see* Security risk analysis
ROI, *see* Return on investment
Rome–Berlin Axis, 96
Royal Canadian Mounted Police, cybercrime
types distinguished by, 145
RTLSs, *see* Real-time locating systems
Russian GLONASS, 244

S
SA, *see* Situational awareness
SAFE, *see* Securing and Facilitating Global
Trade
Satellite-based technologies, 232
Sector-specific agency (SSA), 130
Secure Electronic Network for Travelers Rapid
Inspection (SENTRI), 109–110
Secure Freight Initiative (SFI), 115
Securing and Facilitating Global Trade (SAFE),
100
Security, many faces of, 45–89
air security threats, 74–76
common-strategy tactic, 75
timeline of aircraft hijacking incidents,
75
weapons of mass destruction,
commercial planes used as, 75
backbone of economy, 46
bioterrorism (food security), 84–86
alternative food supplies, 86
chemical risks, 85

deliberate deprivation of food at times of
peace, 86
famine, 85
food damage, 85
intentional contamination, restricted
food access due to, 85
natural disasters, restricted food access
due to, 85
primary hazard risks, 85
quality control, 85
restoration of food supply chains, 86
Ukraine's holocaust (Great Hunger),
86
war, restricted food access due to, 86
biothreat (health and environmental
security), 80–84
case study, 84
dispersal of chemical hazards into
environment, 80
environmental security, 83
Global Health Security Agenda, 82
HazMat equipment, 80
health security, 82–83
impact to human health, 83–84
infectious diseases, 82
public health, bioterrorism and, 83
zoonotic diseases, 82
cyber security threats, 80, 81–82
drug trafficking (socioeconomic impacts),
78–79
globalization process, 45
human trafficking and illegitimate
traveling/immigration, 76–78
containerized cargoes, 77
contraband, 77
coyotes, 77
definition of human smuggling, 76
drug cartels, 77
Federal Immigration and Nationality
Act, 76–77
free-ride effect, 77
illegal immigrants, classifications of,
76
organized immigration crime, 77
snakeheads, 77
many faces of security, 47
original supply chain security theorem,
47–55
awareness space, 49
crime attractors, 49
crime generator, 49
crime opportunity theory, 47–48
crime pattern theory, 48–52
critical activity area, 49

Department of Homeland Security, 48
external logistics, 51
interconnectivity between national
    security and commercial security,
    52–55
lifestyle exposure or victimization
    theory, 48
likelihood of crime, 47
node, 49
personal gain, purpose of obtaining,
    40
personal pathway, 49
vulnerabilities, 48
piracy financing terrorism (growing
    threats), 74
piracy and maritime security, 70–73
    acts, 72–73
    armed robbery and piracy, 72–73
    defining piracy, 70–72
    open seas, piracy amidst, 73
    organized syndicates, 73
    piracy at pot, 73
    state-of-the-art technologies, 73
    US DHS Maritime Domain Awareness,
        73
terrorism (networks and affiliations),
    55–70
    case study (9/11 terrorist attack), 63
    categories of terrorism, 64–69
    civil unrest and riots, 68
    connectivity, 64
    defining terrorism, 55
    ideological terrorism, 68
    individual acts of terrorism, 64, 65–67
    logistics security threats and terrorism,
        69
    lone-wolf terrorism, 64
    motive, 66
    nonpolitical terrorism, 68
    organized terrorist group attacks, 56–62
    piracy versus terrorism, 55
    political terrorism, 68
    quasi-terrorism, 69
    semi-autonomous groups, 64
    small-scale political terrorism, 69
    socioeconomic consequences of 9/11
        attack, 54–55
    state sponsors of terrorism and
        disruption of commerce, 69–70
    state terrorism, 69
    terrorism, global trade, and transport,
        63
Security and Accountability for Every Port Act
    of 2006, 105

Security risk analysis, 275–304
    case study (port vulnerabilities), 293–303
        interview, 293
        Open Cell sheet pile solution, 299–303
        vectors of attack, 294–299
    identifying security vulnerabilities,
        275–286
        Composite Risk Index, 281
        information technology risk assessment,
            281
        intangible vulnerabilities, 277
        ISO 31000:2009 for risk management,
            285–286
        operational risk assessment, 281
        product risk assessment, 281
        project management risk assessment, 281
        resource management, 278
        risk analysis (challenges and
            opportunities), 283–284
        risk assessment, 279–282
        risk communication, 282
        risk management, 277–279
        risk matrices, 285
        security in "high-risk, high-reward"
            industry, 275–276
        security impact analysis, 276
        security risk analysis and its
            components, 276–282
        security risk assessment, 281
        standard operating procedures, 281
        strategic risk assessment, 281
        supply chain risk assessment, 281
        tangible vulnerabilities, 277
    incident reporting and risk management
        software, 286–303
        Critical Infrastructure and Key
            Resources, 286
        DRMM, 290
        MSRAM, 286–290
        probabilistic risk assessment, 286
        timeline of MSRAM, 288–290
Security risk assessment (SRA), 14, 281
Security technology and innovation,
    231–274
    AIS, 244–248
        benefits, 247
        Electronic Chart Display and
            Information System, 245
        investigation and root cause analysis,
            245
        maritime rules, 246
        regulations, 248
        Satellite-Automatic Identification
            System, 245

vessel traffic services, 244
VHF transceiver, 245
voyage data recorder, 246
aviation security technologies, 264–267
 advanced imaging technology, 266
 bottled liquid scanners, 266
 credential authentication technology,
  264–266
 ETD, 267
 explosive-detection system, 266–267
 paperless boarding pass, 267
 security training software, 267
biometrics facial recognition and biometrics
  technologies, 251–255
 Biometric Optical Surveillance System,
  253
 case study, 254
 closed-circuit television cameras, 253
 crowdsourcing and facial recognition,
  254
 facial recognition (2D and 3D biometric
  technologies), 252–253
 Handheld Interagency Identity Detection
  System, 254
 iris and retinal scanning (ocular-based
  recognition), 251–252
 Office of Biometric Identity
  Management, 253
 perfect iris match, 251
cargo-tracking and -monitoring systems
  (sea, land, air), 255–260
 electronic seals, 258
 mechanical seals, 257
 radio-frequency identification, 255–257
 real-time locating systems technologies,
  258
 smart container technologies (United
  States), 258–260
cloud-computing technology, 248–249
 CAPEX system, 248
 corrective action, 249
 deterrent action, 249
 OPEX system, 248
 preventive action, 249
 threat identification, 249
drones as commercial and law enforcement
  tools for security, 236–240
 classification, 237
 commercial surveillance, 239
 control, 236
 drug cartels, 239
 extension of commercial use, 238
 federal law enforcement, 238
 government civilian law enforcement, 238

industry and manufacturing
  applications, 238
 purpose, 236
 terrorist groups, 239
 unmanned aerial vehicles, 237
 US Air Force drone, 237
GPS, 243–244
 Chinese BeiDou Navigation Satellite
  System, 244
 data pullers, 243
 European Union Galileo Satellite
  Positioning System, 244
 logger, 243
 NAVSTAR GPS satellites, 244
 Russian GLONASS, 244
 technologies, pioneer of, 244
 -tracking unit, 243
 transponders, 243
innovative technology and accessibility,
  two-edged sword of, 231–234
 Automatic Identification System, 231
 classification of transportation security
  technologies, 232–234
 fast-speed boats, 231
 Global Positioning System, 231
 iris-scanning technologies, 232
 satellite-based technologies, 232
 security technologies as "force
  multipliers," 234
logistics and supply chain industries,
  242– 271
 AIS, 244–248
 aviation security technologies,
  264–267
 biometrics facial recognition and
  biometrics technologies, 251–255
 cargo-tracking and -monitoring systems
  (sea, land, air), 255–260
 Cell-All concept, 249
 cloud-computing technology, 248–249
 Global Navigation Satellite System and
  satellite navigation technologies,
  242–243
 GPS, 243–244
 intelligence technologies (satellite and
  communication systems), 242–251
 maritime technologies, 267–271
 non-intrusive inspections, 260–264
 radio-frequency identification, 242
 smartphones with HazMat detectors,
  249–250
 Transportation Worker Identification
  Credential card and readers by TSA,
  250–251

maritime technologies, 267–271
  Active Denial System (nonlethal), 269
  armed security guards, 269
  boat trap (nonlethal), 271
  Long-Range Acoustic Device (nonlethal), 271
  optical laser distractor (nonlethal), 270–271
  technologies in ships' panic rooms (citadels or safe rooms), 268–269
  Vehicle-Mounted Active Denial System, 269
non-intrusive inspections, 260–264
  biosurveillance, 263
  cargo scanning or non-intrusive inspection, 260
  gamma and neutron radiation detectors, 262
  in-motion scanning technologies, 260
  muon tomography, 262
  neutron radiation detectors, 261–262
  non-intrusive scanning technologies, 260
  radiation portal monitors, 262
  special nuclear material detection, 260
  targeting protocols, 260
  thermal imaging, 263–264
  visual inspections, 260
  X-ray radiography (backscatter X-rays), 263
terrorism, 234–241
  case study, 236
  drones as commercial and law enforcement tools for security, 236–240
  elevated threat alert, 240
  how technology makes us vulnerable, 234–235
  imminent threat alert, 240
  National Terrorism Advisory System, 240–241
  reverse engineering (back engineering), 240
  terrorist threats ("anti-access area-denial" threats), 241
  weapons of mass destruction, 241
Security threat indicator of spatial correlation (STISC) model, 20
Security threats, see Combating security threats (the human factor)
SENTRI, see Secure Electronic Network for Travelers Rapid Inspection
September 11, 2001 terrorist attacks (9/11)
  attack type, 56
  case study, 63
  public–private partnerships and, 207–208
  socioeconomic consequences of, 55
  systemic vulnerabilities revealed by, 138
  terrorists as pilots, 75
  two-edge sword of technology and, 234
  types of loss, 54, 63
SEVP, see Student and Exchange Visitor Program
SFI, see Secure Freight Initiative
Silk Road, 31
Situational awareness (SA), 323–334
  case studies, 326–334
  critical infrastructure SA, 323
  economy, trade, and transport SA, 324
  environmental SA, 324
  focal areas, 323–324
  geographical SA, 323
  homeland SA, 323
  people-centric SA, 323
  real-time threat communication, 325
  safeguard strategy, 324
  spatial/temporal SA, 324
  survival techniques and inaccurate situational awareness, 325–326
  threat factors, 325
Six Sigma, 202
Small-scale political terrorism, 69
Smartphones with HazMat detectors, 249–250
Smart and Secure Trade Lanes (SSTL) system, 118, 119
Snakeheads, 77
SNM, see Special nuclear material
Social survivalism, 325
SOLAS, see International Convention for the Safety of Life at Sea
SOPs, see Standard operating procedures
Space Shuttle (case study), 219–228
  crew time, 225
  data, 225–226
  data relay satellite, 222
  downmass, 225
  elements of space transportation supply chain, 220–224
  Evolved Expendable Launch Vehicles, 219
  ground segment, 220
  international partners, 227–228
  launch element, 221
  low earth orbit, 219
  obsolescence, 228
  orbiting element, 222
  replenishment, 226
  return element, 223
  security, 226

services of space transportation supply
    chain, 224–227
upmass, 224–225
Space transportation supply chain security
    (case study), 218–219
Spatial autocorrelation models, 19
Special nuclear material (SNM), 260
SRA, *see* Security risk assessment
SSA, *see* Sector-specific agency
SSTL system, *see* Smart and Secure Trade
    Lanes system
Standard operating procedures (SOPs), 281
State terrorism, 69
STISC model, *see* Security threat indicator of
    spatial correlation model
Strategic risk assessment, 281
Strategic, tactical, and operating process,
    317–335
    crisis management, 317–320
        classifying crisis, 318
        crisis management definition, 317
        crisis management timeline model,
            318–320
        crisis recovery, 318
        danger zone, 319
        element of mitigation, 318
        element of surprise, 318
        element of time, 318
        emergency phase, 319
        incident command system, 318
        leadership and teamwork, 318
        preparation phase, 318
        preparation process, 319
        preparedness and contingency planning,
            318
        proactiveness vs. reactiveness, 318
        resilience or recovery phase, 319
        strengths and vulnerabilities, 320
        sustainability through lessons learned, 319
    levels of war (strategies, operations, and
        tactics), 320–323
        operational management, 322
        operational planning, 322
        operational resource management, 322
        strategic management, 321
        strategic planning, 321
        strategic resource management, 322
        tactical management, 322
        tactical planning, 323
        tactical resource management, 323
        war theory, 321
    situational awareness, 323–334
        case studies, 326–334
        critical infrastructure SA, 323

        economy, trade, and transport SA, 324
        environmental SA, 324
        focal areas, 323–324
        geographical SA, 323
        homeland SA, 323
        people-centric SA, 323
        real-time threat communication, 325
        safeguard strategy, 324
        spatial/temporal SA, 324
        survival techniques and inaccurate
            situational awareness, 325–326
        threat factors, 325
Stress versus distress mode, 306–309
    cortisol "overdose," 308
    distress and lack of preparedness,
        307–308
    distress and permanent DNA methylation,
        309
    extreme stress levels, 308
    fight or flight, 307
    impact of distress or high stress levels,
        308–309
    perceived threat, stress, and distress, 307
    post-traumatic stress disorder, 309
    stress and preparedness, 307
    stress response, 309
Student and Exchange Visitor Program
    (SEVP), 108, 109
Supply chain
    CI matrix, 136
    disruptions, 27–28
    employee empowerment, 28
    food, restoration of, 86
    global, security of, 45
    optimum performance of, 25
    risk assessment, 281
    security
        management, ISO specification for, 118
        space transportation (case study),
            218–219
        threats, 69
    terrorism, 27
Supply chains, cyber security threats in,
    192–199
    activity types, 195
    cyber security resources, 196–197
    dependence on information, 192
    example, 193–195
    growing cyber threats, 193
    implementing cyber security programs, 196
    information sharing and analysis centers,
        195
    mitigating supply chain cyber security risks,
        195–196

organizations in the supply chain, 195
potential vulnerabilities and risks, 193
security programs, 195
Supply chain security, overview of, 26–41
case study, 30, 31
   agile transportation, 31
   ambushing, 33
   espionage networks, 32
   fake retreat, 33
   hit and run, 33
   Silk Road, 31
   synchronized attacks, 33
   Yam postal system for military and
      political news, 33
Christopher Columbus's voyages (logistics
   achievement), 33–34
common goal, 26
history of logistics, 28–29
   military logistics, 29
   natural disasters, mass migration to
      avoid, 28
   procurement logistics, 29
   survival logistics, 28
Industrial Revolution, 36
Jamestown (early settlers to the New
   World), 34–35
Liberty ships in World War II, 38–41
   construction, 39
   "great arsenal of democracy," 38
   mass-produced design, 39
   support package, 40
   US contribution in WWII, 41
   Young Women's Christian Association,
      40
logistics through the millennia, 29
medieval explorers, the first settlers, and
   the origins of modern America, 33
National DHS strategy, 27
railroads, 35–36
railroads in America, 36–37
   Baltimore and Ohio Railroad, 37
   Dewitt Clinton Railroad, 37
   East Coast traders, 36
   Mohawk & Hudson rail, 37
   Transcontinental Railroad, 37
standard actions, 26
supply chain disruptions, 27–28
   cyber espionage, 27
   deliberate damage, 27
   employee empowerment, 28
   freight pilferage, 27
   geospatial criteria, 28
   real-time monitoring and response, 28
   trade disruption, 27

Supply chain security, systemic gaps in,
   187–205
case studies, 192–199
   logistics networks (strengthening of supply
      chains), 192–199
quality implementation, setting of security
   standards through, 199–205
   bridging the security gaps, 199–200
   Deming's 14 points on quality
      management, 203–204
   DMAIC, 204
   5s, 200–201
   4D methodology, 205
   Kaizen, 201
   Kanban, 202
   lean and agile, 202
   lean manufacturing method, 200
   Six Sigma, 202
   TQM, 202–203
trade flow, trade routes, and the economy,
   187–191
   account payables, 189
   account receivables, 189
   categories, 188–189
   copyright infringement, 189
   falling domino principle, 190
   forecasting risks, 188
   inventory or stock, 188
   Pareto principle, 191
   production capability, 188
   purchasing and procurement, 189
   sale and purchase, procurement, 188
   security threat domino effect, 190
   supply chain disruptions and potential
      security gaps, 187–189
   supply chain visibility and integration,
      188–189
   Swiss cheese model (incident causation),
      189
   technologies, 188
   time delays, 188
   Trojan horse, 190
Survivalism, 325
Survival logistics, 28
Swiss cheese model (incident causation),
   189
Synchronized attacks, 33
Systemic gaps, see Supply chain security,
   systemic gaps in

T
TAPA, see Transported Asset Protection
   Association
TC/P, see Time charter party

Technology, *see* Security technology and
      innovation
Terrorism, technology and, 234–241
   case study, 236
   drones as commercial and law enforcement
         tools for security, 236–240
   elevated threat alert, 240
   how technology makes us vulnerable,
         234–235
   imminent threat alert, 240
   National Terrorism Advisory System,
         240–241
   reverse engineering (back engineering), 240
   terrorist threats ("anti-access area-denial"
         threats), 241
   weapons of mass destruction, 241
Terrorism networks and affiliations, 55–70
   categories of terrorism, 64–69
      civil unrest and riots, 68
      connectivity, 64
      ideological terrorism, 68
      individual acts of terrorism, 64, 65–67
      lone-wolf terrorism, 64
      motive, 66
      nonpolitical terrorism, 68
      political terrorism, 68
      quasi-terrorism, 69
      semi-autonomous groups, 64
      small-scale political terrorism, 69
      state terrorism, 69
   defining terrorism, 55
   logistics security threats and terrorism, 69
   piracy versus terrorism, 55
   state sponsors of terrorism and disruption
         of commerce, 69–70
   terrorism, global trade, and transport, 63
   case study (9/11 terrorist attack), 63
   organized terrorist group attacks, 56–62
   socioeconomic consequences of 9/11
         attack, 54–55
Threat image projection (TIP), 232
Threats, *see* Combating security threats (the
      human factor)
Time charter party (TC/P), 141
TIP, *see* Threat image projection
Total Asset Visibility initiative (Department of
      Defense), 119
Toxic industrial chemicals, 182–183
   chemical weapons, 182
   gaseous chemicals and fumigants, 182
   health mitigation, 183
   legal and regulatory framework, 183
   medical use and inhibiting agents, 182
   military weapons, 182

postdisaster HazMat contingency plans,
      183
predisaster HazMat plans, 183
proactive and reactive action, 183
technological mitigation, 183
TQM, 202
Transcontinental Railroad, 37
Transportation Security Administration (TSA),
      106–107, 108, 232
Transportation security incidents (TSIs), 104
Transportation Workers Identification
      Credential (TWIC), 211, 250–251
Transported Asset Protection Association
      (TAPA), 118
TSA, *see* Transportation Security
      Administration
TSIs, *see* Transportation security incidents
Turnover ratio, 189
TWIC, *see* Transportation Workers
      Identification Credential

U
UAV, *see* Unmanned aerial vehicles
Ukraine's holocaust (Great Hunger), 86
UN, *see* United Nations
UNCLOS, *see* United Nations Convention on
      the Law of the Sea
United Nations (UN)
   Committee of Experts on Transport of
         Dangerous Goods, 158–160
   Convention on the Law of the Sea
         (UNCLOS), 72
   Counter-Terrorism Implementation Task
         Force, 98–99
   identification numbers, 167
   Office on Drugs and Crime (UNODC), 97
   Security Council (UNSC), 96–97
United States, maritime security regulations
      in, 114–121
   case study, 120–121
   CBP collaboration with US Food and
         Drug Administration to prevent
         bioterrorism and agroterrorism,
         116–121
   Comprehensive Environmental Response,
         Compensation, and Liability Act, 118
   Department of Defense Total Asset
         Visibility initiative, 119
   emergency notification, 118
   Emergency Planning and Community
         Right-to-Know Act, 117
   extremely hazardous substances, 117
   Free and Secure Trade program, 115–116
   ISO/PAS 28000, 118

Megaports Initiative, 116
National Terrorism Advisory System, 117
private sector initiatives, 118–119
Secure Freight Initiative, 115
Smart and Secure Trade Lanes system, 118, 119
Transported Asset Protection Association, 118
US emergency response systems, 117–118
United States, security in, 103–114
    cargo security initiatives, 110–114
        Advanced Manifest Rule/Advance Cargo Information, 112
        certification, 110
        Container Security Initiative, 112, 114
        C-TPAT initiative, 110–111
        front-of-line examinations, 110
        Importer Security Filing, 111–112
        Mutual Recognition Agreement (C-TPAT), 111
        non-intrusive inspection, 113
    federal programs and initiatives, 108–114
    inbound travelers' security initiatives, 108–110
        Advance Passenger Information System, 108
        Application Programming Interface, 109
        CBP initiatives, 108
        CBP Office of Field Operations, 108
        electronic data interchange system, 108
        Immigration and Customs Enforcement, 108, 109
        joint terrorism task forces, 108
        NEXUS Inspection Program, 110
        Office of Biometric Identity Management, 108, 109
        radio frequency identification proximity prox-card, 110
        Secure Electronic Network for Travelers Rapid Inspection, 109–110
        Student and Exchange Visitor Program, 108, 109
        Trusted Traveler Program, 110
        US Immigration and Naturalization Service, 108
        Western Hemisphere Travel Initiative, 110
    transportation security acts, 103–105
        Area Maritime Security plan, 105
        Container Security Initiative, 105
        family of plans, 104
        Maritime Transportation Security Act of 2002, 104–105

National Military Establishment, 104
National Security Act of 1947, 103–104
Security and Accountability for Every Port Act of 2006 by DHS, 105
transportation security incidents, 104
US Coast Guard, 104
US Department of Homeland Security and its agencies, 105–114
    Federal Emergency Management Agency, 107–108
    mandates, 107
    persisting impediments, 106
    Transportation Security Administration, 106–107
    US Customs and Border Protection, 107
    US Department of Homeland Security, 105–106
UNIX system, vulnerabilities in, 81
Unmanned aerial vehicles (UAV), 237
UNODC, see United Nations Office on Drugs and Crime
UNSC, see United Nations Security Council
US Air Force drone, 237
USA Patriot Act, 155
USCG, see US Coast Guard
US Coast Guard (USCG), 104, 215
US Customs and Border Protection (CBP), 107
    Advanced Manifest Rule/Advance Cargo Information, 112
    Advance Passenger Information System, 108
    Container Security Initiative, 112
    C-TPAT initiative, 110
    Free and Secure Trade program, 115–116
    Importer Security Filing, 111
    inbound travelers' security initiatives, 108
    joint terrorism task forces, 108
    NEXUS Inspection Program, 110
    Office of Field Operations, 108
    Secure Electronic Network for Travelers Rapid Inspection, 109–110
US Department of Homeland Security (DHS), 3, 48, 105–114
    Cell-All concept tested by, 249
    C-TPAT initiative, 110
    Federal Emergency Management Agency, 107–108
    lifestyle exposure or victimization theory, 48
    mandates, 107
    Maritime Domain Awareness, 73
    National Terrorism Advisory System, 240–241

Office of Biometric Identity Management, 108, 109
persisting impediments, 106
Secure Freight Initiative, 115
Transportation Security Administration, 106–107
US Customs and Border Protection, 107
US Department of Transportation (DOT), 50, 152
US Environmental Protection Agency (EPA), 152
US Food and Drug Administration,
  collaboration with CBP to prevent bioterrorism and agroterrorism, 116–121
  case study, 120–121
  Comprehensive Environmental Response, Compensation, and Liability Act, 118
  Department of Defense Total Asset Visibility initiative, 119
  emergency notification, 118
  Emergency Planning and Community Right-to-Know Act, 117
  extremely hazardous substances, 117
  ISO/PAS 28000, 118
  National Terrorism Advisory System, 117
  private sector initiatives, 118–119
  Smart and Secure Trade Lanes system, 118, 119
  Transported Asset Protection Association, 118
  US emergency response systems, 117–118
US Immigration and Naturalization Service (INS), 108
US Occupational Safety and Health Administration (OSHA), 152

V
Value-for-money principle, 26

Value at risk (VaR), 17
VaR, see Value at risk
VDR, see Voyage data recorder
Vehicle-Mounted Active Denial System, 269
Vessel traffic services (VTSs), 244
Victimization theory, 48
Virgin Galactic Spaceship 2, 225
Virginia Company of London, 34
Virtual databases, 144
Voyage charter party (Voy C/P), 141
Voyage data recorder (VDR), 246
Voy C/P, see Voyage charter party
VTSs, see Vessel traffic services

W
War, 86, 321
WCO, see World Customs Organization
Weapons of mass destruction (WMDs), 75, 241
Western Hemisphere Travel Initiative (WHTI), 110
WHTI, see Western Hemisphere Travel Initiative
WMDs, see Weapons of mass destruction
World Customs Organization (WCO), 99–100

X
X-ray radiography (backscatter X-rays), 263

Y
Yam postal system for military and political news, 33
Young Women's Christian Association, 40

Z
Zoonotic diseases, 82
Z score, 20